T0271130

The Business of Waste

Great Britain and Germany, 1945 to the Present

The advent of consumer societies in the United Kingdom and West Germany after 1945 led to the mass production of garbage. This book compares the social, cultural, and economic fallout of the growing volume and changing composition of waste in the two countries from 1945 to the present through sustained attention to changes in the business of handling household waste. Although the UK and Germany are similar in population density, degrees of urbanization, and standardization, the two countries took profoundly different paths, from low waste to throwaway societies, and more recently toward the goal of zero waste. The authors explore evolving balances between public and private provision in waste services; the transformation of public cleansing into waste management; the role of government legislation and regulation; emerging conceptualizations of recycling and resource recovery; and the gradual shift of the industry's regulatory and business context from local to national and then to international.

Raymond G. Stokes is professor of business history at the University of Glasgow and director of the Centre for Business History in Scotland.

Roman Köster is senior lecturer in economic and social history at Bundeswehr University in Munich.

Stephen C. Sambrook is research associate at the Centre for Business History in Scotland at the University of Glasgow.

The Business of Waste

Great Britain and Germany, 1945 to the Present

RAYMOND G. STOKES

University of Glasgow

ROMAN KÖSTER

Bundeswehr University, Munich

STEPHEN C. SAMBROOK

University of Glasgow

CAMBRIDGE
UNIVERSITY PRESS

CAMBRIDGE
UNIVERSITY PRESS

Shaftesbury Road, Cambridge CB2 8EA, United Kingdom

One Liberty Plaza, 20th Floor, New York, NY 10006, USA

477 Williamstown Road, Port Melbourne, VIC 3207, Australia

314–321, 3rd Floor, Plot 3, Splendor Forum, Jasola District Centre, New Delhi – 110025, India

103 Penang Road, #05–06/07, Visioncrest Commercial, Singapore 238467

Cambridge University Press is part of Cambridge University Press & Assessment, a department of the University of Cambridge.

We share the University's mission to contribute to society through the pursuit of education, learning and research at the highest international levels of excellence.

www.cambridge.org
Information on this title: www.cambridge.org/9781107027213

© Raymond G. Stokes, Roman Köster, and Stephen C. Sambrook 2013

First published 2013

A catalogue record for this publication is available from the British Library

Library of Congress Cataloging-in-Publication data
Stokes, Raymond G.
The business of waste : Great Britain and Germany, 1945 to the present / Raymond G. Stokes, University of Glasgow, Roman Köster, Bundeswehr University, Munich, Stephen C. Sambrook, University of Glasgow.
pages cm
Includes bibliographical references and index.
ISBN 978-1-107-02721-3 (hardback)
1. Refuse and refuse disposal – Great Britain – History. 2. Refuse and refuse disposal – Germany – History. 3. Recycling (Waste, etc.) – Great Britain – History. 4. Recycling (Waste, etc.) – Germany – History. I. Köster, Roman, 1975– II. Sambrook, Stephen C. III. Title.
HD4485.G7S76 2014
363.72´80941–dc23   2013012157

ISBN 978-1-107-02721-3 Hardback

Contents

Preface and Acknowledgments

This book had its origins in the mid-1990s in the personal experience of one of the coauthors, Ray Stokes. Having lived to that point for a number of years in the United States and Germany, I was struck upon taking up residence in Scotland in 1995 by what seemed to be a completely different attitude toward rubbish than I had encountered elsewhere. My initial impressions about this were later confirmed: for instance, recycling rates in Glasgow at that time were about 4 percent in the mid-1990s, while those in Germany – and even upstate New York, where I last lived in the United States – were at the same time vastly higher. What could account for such differences, given that all three countries were advanced industrial/consumer societies with more or less active environmental movements, and where environmental consciousness had increased dramatically in light of growing evidence of the harmful effects of pollution and climate change?

For various reasons, it took some time to get started on a concrete research project. The Aggregate Foundation (now the William Lind Foundation) provided seedcorn funding for it in 2006, when I became director of the Centre for Business History in Scotland. This allowed me to secure the services of Dr. Stephen Sambrook as a postdoctoral research associate to develop a proposal for funding. In early summer 2007, the application was successful in attracting major financial support from the Economic and Social Research Council (ESRC) (Project Reference RES-062-23-0580), and we started work on the project in earnest in September 2007. Stephen continued under the grant as a postdoctoral researcher and in that capacity carried out most of the UK-based archival research for the project. He is also a coauthor, of course. Our other coauthor, Roman

Köster, joined the team as a postdoctoral researcher funded by the ESRC grant, and he was responsible for most of the German-based archival research for the book.

The research and writing involved all three of us moving out of our comfort zones in two key ways. First, although we approached the history of public cleansing and waste management in Britain and West Germany since 1945 as economic and business historians, this project involved going beyond our usual sources and methods to consider the overlay of business/economic history on the one hand, and social, political, and environmental history on the other. Although this has been difficult at times, we believe that it has made the analysis more compelling in various ways. We also hope that the result will enrich all of these disparate fields in some ways.

The second, more important way in which this project pushed us out of our comfort zones revolved around the writing process. I have previously been involved in coauthoring four books. In each of these cases, however, coauthors undertook research and writing of discrete sections, and each coauthor worked for the most part completely independently on that. In this book we opted for a different arrangement, which proved extremely challenging, although it has also been extraordinarily fruitful. Following intensive discussion among the three of us about each chapter, I drafted an overview of it indicating the overall structure and its main themes and arguments. Stephen and Roman then provided details based on their archival and other research in the UK and Germany, respectively. I subsequently combined what all three of us had written into a single narrative, which we then discussed, corrected, and refined as a team. The writing process therefore took a long time, but it was worth it. We strongly believe, therefore, that to a greater degree than usual, writing has been as crucial to the research for this book as the archival and other investigations that have provided its empirical detail.

Our teamwork on research and writing depended, of course, on a number of organizations and individuals, and we are very pleased now to be able to thank them here formally. Generous financial support came from the William Lind Foundation and from the UK Economic and Social Research Council, while the finances (and many other things related to the project) were administered effectively and cheerfully between 2006 and early 2013 by Christine Leslie, the administrator of the Centre for Business History in Scotland. Christine's support has been essential to the smooth running and ultimate success of the project.

Without archival and other primary data, historians cannot do their job, and we are therefore very grateful indeed to the archivists and librarians who provided assistance in identifying and consulting primary sources. The archives we used are listed in the bibliography. In addition, we would like to like to thank the Chartered Institute of Wastes Management (CIWM) in Northampton for allowing us access to their library early in the project. Other practitioners have also helped us in various ways in the course of research and writing, including the editor of the *CIWM Journal*, Ben Wood; Lewis Herbert; Stan Dagg; and Karl Pulver. A number of practitioners (including representatives of the Scottish Government, local authorities, the private sector, and the third sector) also took part in a workshop we organized in June 2010 on "The Business of Waste." Held at the Centre for Business History at the University of Glasgow, the workshop featured presentations not only from practitioners but also from a range of scholars of varied disciplines who hailed from several different countries (including the United States, Hungary, and Germany, as well as the UK). This and subsequent interactions between scholars and practitioners have proven extremely fruitful, and some of the insights obtained through this process have found their way into the book.

We have also benefited from feedback that followed presentations of our ideas and findings at seminars and conferences in the UK, the Netherlands, Italy, Denmark, France, Germany, and Canada. We are grateful to all participants for their critical engagement with our work and in particular to the audiences present at three separate presentations: the Copenhagen Business School, Bocconi University in Milan, and the Erasmus University in Rotterdam. The three seminars took place at a critical phase in the writing in May and June 2012, and the comments and questions from the floor were both challenging and encouraging, especially from several participants from other disciplines. We have thought of them carefully as we prepared the final manuscript. And we are particularly grateful to the two formal discussants in Milan, Professors Andrea Giuntini and Antonio Massarutto. Both provided some excellent comments, as well as copies of some of their publications.

Last but not least, we would also like to thank the following individuals: Frank Smith, Eric Crahan, and Debbie Gershenowitz, our editors at Cambridge University Press (CUP), who have been very supportive of this project and who, one after the other, shepherded it from the proposal stage to the finished product; Abby Zorbaugh, the senior editorial assistant at CUP, who has patiently worked with us in the final preparation of the manuscript for production; Alison Daltroy (CUP), Anuj Antony (Aptara Inc.), and Lee Motteler (PETT Fox, Inc.), who led us skillfully through the production process; the referees for CUP, whose comments were extremely useful; Sean Johnston, who provided incisive and extensive comments on early drafts of our research proposals; Heike Weber, who has been very generous in sharing some of the results of her own research and thinking on the history of waste management with us; Dirk Wiegand from the SASE Institute, who not only shared his research with us but also helped us identify pictures for the book; and Anne Stokes, who carefully read through the penultimate draft of the manuscript for the book, making numerous suggestions that have both improved the style of the writing and helped us avoid some mistakes. All remaining stylistic infelicities and errors, of course, are our responsibility.

List of Abbreviations

AbfG	Abfallgesetz (waste law)
AkA	Arbeitskreis für kommunale Abfallwirtschaft (Working Group for the Municipal Public Cleansing Industry)
BA	Bundesarchiv (Federal Archives)
BBC	British Broadcasting Corporation
BDE	Bundesverband der deutschen Entsorgungswirtschaft (Federal Trade Association of the Waste Management Industry)
BMI	Bundesinnenministerium (Federal Ministry of the Interior)
BRD	Bundesrepublik Deutschland (Federal Republic of Germany)
BS	British Standard
BSI	British Standards Institution
BUND	Bund für Umwelt und Naturschutz Deutschland (German Federation for Environment and Nature Conservation)
CDU	Christlich Demokratische Union (Christian Democratic Union)
CIPFA	Chartered Institute of Public Finance and Accountancy
COPA74	Control of Pollution Act 1974
CSU	Christlich Soziale Union (Christian Social Union)
DDR	Deutsche Demokratische Republik (German Democratic Republic)
DDT	dichlorodiphenyltrichloroethane (insecticide)
DEFRA	Department for the Environment, Food and Rural Affairs
DGB	Deutscher Gewerkschaftsbund (German Trade Union Federation)
DIN	Deutsche Industrie-Norm (German industry standard)

List of Abbreviations

DM	Deutsche Mark
DOE	Department of the Environment
DPWA72	Deposit of Poisonous Wastes Act 1972
DSD	Duales System Deutschland (Grüner Punkt or Green-Dot System)
EEC	European Economic Community
EPA	Environmental Protection Act
EsEm	Schmidt & Melmer
ETH	Eidgenössische Technische Hochschule (Swiss Federal Institute of Technology)
EU	European Union
FoE	Friends of the Earth
GDP	gross domestic product
GDR	German Democratic Republic
GmbH	Gesellschaft mit beschränkter Haftung (limited liability company)
GMC	Greater Manchester County Council
HStA	Hauptstaatsarchiv (Central State Archive)
IPC	Institute of Public Cleansing
IWM	Institute of Wastes Management
KPD	Kommunistische Partei Deutschlands (Communist Party of Germany)
KUKA	Keller und Knappich Company
LA	Landesarchiv (State Archives)
LAGA	Länder-Arbeitsgemeinschaft Abfall (Working Party of the States for Waste)
LGA	Local Government Act
MGB	Müllgroßraumbehälter (large capacity garbage container)
MLG	Mitchell Library, Glasgow
OED	Oxford English Dictionary
ÖTV	Gewerkschaft Öffentliche Dienste Transport und Verkehr (public-sector employees' trade union)
PPP	public-private partnership
RIC	resin identification code of the American Society for the Plastics Industry (1988)
SCT	Society of County Treasurers
SEPA	Scottish Environmental Protection Agency
SERO	Sekundärrohstoffsystem (secondary raw materials system)
SPD	Sozialdemokratische Partei Deutschlands (Social Democratic Party of Germany)

StA	Stadtarchiv (City Archive)
StJB	*Statistisches Jahrbuch für die Bundesrepublik Deutschland* (*Statistical Yearbook for the Federal Republic of Germany*)
TA	Technische Anleitung (technical specification)
TA Luft	Technische Anleitung zur Reinhaltung der Luft (technical specification for controlling air pollution)
TNA	The National Archives of the United Kingdom (TNA)
TU	Technische Universität (technical university)
UBA	Umweltbundesamt
UK	United Kingdom
VKF	Verband kommunaler Fuhrparksbetriebe (Association of Municipal Public Cleansing Departments)
VPS	Verband Privater Städtereinigungsbetriebe (Association of Private Municipal Cleansing Companies)
WCA	Waste Collection Authority
WDA	Waste Disposal Authority
WRA	Waste Regulation Authority
WSL	Warren Spring Laboratory
ZfA	Zentralstelle für Abfallbeseitigung (Central Office for Waste Disposal)

Introduction

When World War II ended in 1945, two of Europe's largest economies, the United Kingdom and what would eventually become West Germany, struggled to provide even the most basic necessities to the bulk of their populations. But, devastating as the war and its consequences were, they were not the sole factors responsible for this situation. After all, although Britain, unlike Germany, had long been one of the richest countries per capita,[1] most citizens in both countries had little surplus income. The two could thus be characterized as societies of need rather than of plenty. Through 1945, moreover, neither managed to implement techniques of mass production broadly across industries, despite extensive attempts to emulate the pioneer in this area, the United States.[2] In the decades that followed the end of the war, however, both the United Kingdom and West Germany developed the capability to produce large amounts of goods for their own citizens and, for the Germans in particular, to export around the world, although their paths toward mass production regimes differed considerably from that of the United States and also from one another.[3]

---

[1] Adam Tooze makes this important and often overlooked point in *The Wages of Destruction: The Making and Breaking of the Nazi Economy* (London: Penguin Books, 2007).

[2] See, for example, David A. Hounsell, *From the American System to Mass Production: The Development of Manufacturing Technology in the United States* (Baltimore, MD: Johns Hopkins University Press, 1984); Steven Tolliday, *The Rise and Fall of Mass Production* (Cheltenham, UK: E. Elgar, 1998).

[3] See, for example, Charles Sabel and Jonathan Zeitlin, "Historical Alternatives to Mass Production: Politics, Markets, and Technology in Nineteenth-Century Industrialization," *Past and Present* 108 (1985): 133–176; Charles Sabel and Michael Piore, *The Second Industrial Divide: Possibilities for Future Prosperity* (New York: Basic Books, 1984); Charles Sabel and Jonathan Zeitlin, eds., *World of Possibilities: Flexibility and Mass*

Mass production formed an important prerequisite for mass consumption. For this reason, key characteristics of the consumer society – substantial disposable income across broad swaths of society, widespread car ownership, broad dispersion across the population of consumer durables such as radios, washing machines, and refrigerators – were already emerging in the United States before the 1930s. And even though the full flowering of this trend was interrupted by the Great Depression and wartime rationing, by the 1950s, America was well on its way in this direction. Not long afterward, by the 1960s, most citizens in both the United Kingdom and West Germany were also moving steadily toward experiencing the transition from need to plenty, if still to a far lesser degree than the United States and with some lag. This signaled not only a massive economic change but also an extremely important social and cultural one.

Mass production enables – indeed, to some degree requires – mass consumption. But the third element of the sequence is an inevitable if often overlooked concomitant of the advent of the consumer society, following along immediately in its wake: substantial increases and significant qualitative changes in streams of waste. As scholarly studies of the United States – the first consumer society and thus also the first to have to deal with consumerism's detritus – demonstrate, the flip side of consumption also involved important changes in social and cultural attitudes, and such changes also came, with some delay, to European and then other followers.[4] Larger and different waste streams also entailed important economic changes, as more and more resources related to all of the factors of production – land, labor, capital, entrepreneurship, and technology – were brought to bear on the collection and disposal of waste. And this in turn entailed development over time of new technologies, new management methods, and altered ownership arrangements and industry structures.

This book explores the social, cultural, and economic fallout of the emergence of the consumer society through sustained attention to changes in the waste handling business over time. It focuses not on the United States, the pioneer about which much has already been written. Because of its sheer scale, relatively low population density, and other factors,

Production in Western Civilization (Cambridge and New York: Cambridge University Press, 1997).

[4] Susan Strasser, Waste and Want: A Social History of Trash (New York: Henty Holt and Company, 1999).

the United States was very different from most other countries in its path of development.[5] Instead, our focus is on the British and West German cases. Consumer society emerged at about the same time in both of these countries in the decades immediately after the end of World War II, the starting point for the study. The two were also similar in terms of population density, degrees of urbanization, eventual Europeanization, and other factors relevant to the production, collection, and disposal of waste. And there is yet another compelling reason to choose the two for comparison: in the period after the end of World War II, they sometimes drew inspiration from one another, rather than from the United States, about how best to manage and reform waste collection and disposal systems. Despite these commonalities, however, a comparison of the two will also highlight profound differences, among other things in technology, industry structures and practices, and legislation. Explaining similarities as well as differences is one of the key tasks in the chapters that follow. Before we get to an overview of the structure of the book, though, we need to further contextualize the topic and to define some key concepts.

The problems of production and disposal of solid and other waste resulting from human consumption and subsequent disposal of that waste have been a constant feature of all human societies, but they were kept in check for a long time by a number of factors, including poverty, which severely constrained consumption of goods and thus also production of waste; generally low levels of urbanization and population density; limited use of packaging, especially nonbiodegradable packaging; and limited scientific understanding of the public health implications of poor waste disposal practice. Consequently, until relatively recently it was typical worldwide for collection and disposal of waste to be devolved to the individual and/or the private sector, with the latter engaged in particular in what was then termed the "salvage" of any waste that could be

---

[5] Strasser, *Waste and Want*; Joel A. Tarr, *The Search for the Ultimate Sink: Urban Pollution in Historical Perspective* (Akron, OH: University of Akron Press, 1996). The issue of scale is a crucial one: already in the 1930s, the United States was a major exporter of scrap metal, a key component of steel production. Indeed, this was one of the export items denied to Japan in 1940, which was one important factor leading eventually to the attack on Pearl Harbor. See, for instance, Michael A. Barnhart, *Japan Prepares for Total War: The Search for Economic Security, 1919–1941* (Ithaca, NY: Cornell University Press, 1987), pp. 168, 186–188, 190, 193–194, 201. The United States continues to provide the world with huge amounts of metal scrap, wastepaper, and other "waste" materials. Indeed, the United States is "known in the trash world as 'the Saudi Arabia of scrap.'" See Evan Osnos, "Wastepaper Queen," the *New Yorker* (March 30, 2009), p. 49.

reused. It was only in the mid-nineteenth century, in the wake of industrialization and ever-higher levels of urbanization, especially in Western European countries, that things changed. At that time, legislation and growing municipal activism led to the establishment of cleansing departments within local authorities in Britain, the German states (a unified German nation came about only in 1871), and other industrialized or industrializing areas in Europe. Their remit was regular removal of waste, primarily to protect public health, and this public health dimension has remained an essential desideratum of publicly funded municipal waste collection authorities to the present day.

In spite of this focus on public health by local authorities, however, there have always been important economic and business dimensions to household waste, too. Financing collection and disposal has been one perennial issue, as have the related goals of efficiency and value for money in carrying out these activities. Professionalization of the engineers and managers responsible for city waste collection was also an important factor, leading eventually to the establishment of a recognizable practice of "waste management" (although that particular phrase is of relatively recent vintage). And collection of municipal household waste has also always involved a large workforce, with associated issues of management and industrial relations.

There are other key economic and business dimensions as well. For one thing, in spite of the municipalization of waste collection in much of the industrialized and urbanized world in the latter part of the nineteenth century, there has always been a role for the private sector. It certainly predates the 1980s, when, led by Margaret Thatcher and Ronald Reagan, widely held perceptions about the respective roles of government and private industry changed dramatically across the capitalist world in favor of the latter.[6] As we shall see, there were often times when private contractors were – for a fee – permitted to pick through municipal rubbish heaps for salvage to sell off, and "rag and bone men" from the private sector collected a range of items directly from households.[7] What is more, even though the collection of municipal household refuse in most European cities had become a public function during the period from the 1850s until the 1980s, its disposal was often not. For example, until the advent of British legislation in the 1970s, which placed significant

---

[6] Robert Millward, *Private and Public Enterprise in Europe: Energy, Telecommunication and Transport, 1830–1990* (Cambridge: Cambridge University Press, 2005).

[7] For an excellent overview of scrap collectors in the United States, see Carl A. Zimring, *Cash for Your Trash: Scrap Recycling in America* (New Brunswick, NJ, and London: Rutgers University Press, 2005).

restrictions on the operation of landfills for the first time, dumps were often not only privately owned and operated (as they were even after the legislation), but also virtually unregulated. City governments, in other words, paid the private sector to dispose of the trash they collected but paid little heed to where it might eventually end up. Thus, eventually, in many municipalities the private sector became much more involved in the whole range of what became known as "waste management" practice by taking over some of the traditional municipal functions, by forming partnerships with the public sector, and by other means. As time has gone on, the nature of the private sector of the waste handling industry has changed dramatically. Largely family firms with low capitalization to begin with, many of the private companies have become very large indeed, with some becoming joint-stock companies and a number even developing into multinationals. We want to examine this process of evolution in the private sector in a range of contexts.

One of the themes of this book, then, is the evolving relationship between the public and the private sectors through time in the two countries, with simultaneous investigation of the associated balance that had to be struck between the public health desideratum of waste handling on the one hand and its business and economics on the other. The former has been a consistent feature of municipal household waste collection since the mid-nineteenth century and is embodied in the designation "public cleansing." The business and economics of waste played a crucial role in public cleansing from the beginning as well, as we show throughout this book. But they have become more explicitly recognized only relatively recently, something captured in the modern designation of the field as "waste management." This suggests a number of questions. How can the most efficient and cost-effective system of waste collection and disposal be set up if the public health remit – which often cannot be made "to pay for itself" – stands at the center of waste handling practice? What were the incentives for the private sector to enter the industry, and what were the barriers to entry? How have incentives and barriers changed through time? Why and how has the private sector become more prominent over time, not only in areas in which it had a long tradition, such as salvage collection and reprocessing (related but not identical to what we now term recycling) and landfill ownership, but also in others, such as household waste collection? We explore all of these questions at length, both historically and comparatively, in this book.

But before we go any further, let us pause to consider this: What *is* "waste"? Once we start trying to unpack this deceptively simple word, we find that it is far from straightforward. Therefore, we will also have to consider these related questions: Which aspects of waste are dealt with in this book, which are not, and why?

"Waste" might be defined simply as anything that human beings discard. In other words, it can range from wastewater from baths and showers and waste from the human body delivered through sewage systems to rubble from torn-down buildings, the cardboard box in which a shop owner received a shipment of merchandise and is now surplus to requirements, the television that broke down and is discarded by its owner, or the sweet wrapper tossed onto the street as litter. Broadly speaking, then, we can discern two categories of waste: liquid and solid. We do not deal with the former here at all. For one thing, liquid waste is examined much more extensively in the secondary literature than is solid waste.[8] Second, it involves different technologies, infrastructure, and players than does solid waste. And finally, to a large degree, growth in output and processing of sewage is arguably not so much a function of the emergence of consumer society as of growth in population and urbanization.[9] Thus, liquid waste would have been far less suited than solid waste for a thorough examination of one of the key relationships at the heart of this study: the relationship between emergent consumerism on the one hand and quantitative and qualitative changes in the waste stream on the other.

We are not able to deal with the whole of the solid waste stream either, however. As outlined already, there are several different categories here. Construction waste is typically the largest part of this stream, whether measured by weight or by volume, followed by industrial and trade waste.[10] Construction waste is by and large inert – that is, there are few organic components in it. Consequently, while it may contain substances such as asbestos or other toxins, it is often considered to be "clean fill" and can go straight into the ground without much concern about

---

[8] See, for example, James Benidickson, *The Culture of Flushing: A Social and Legal History of Sewage* (Vancouver: University of British Columbia Press, 2007); Martin Melosi, *The Sanitary city: Urban Infrastructure in America from Colonial Times to the Present* (Baltimore, MD: Johns Hopkins University Press, 2000); H. H. Stanbridge, *History of Sewage Treatment in Britain* (Maidstone: Institute of Water Pollution Control, 1976).

[9] No doubt there have been some effects from consumerism (e.g., more showers and baths are taken per capita per day in consumer societies than was the case earlier).

[10] According to the *Financial Times*, in 2004 for the EU 27, construction waste accounted for 45.2 percent of the total waste stream by weight, followed by 38.8 percent for industrial/trade waste. Household waste accounted for 11.9 percent, with 4.1 percent being composed of toxic waste. See Ross Tieman, "A Problem That Comes in Heaps," in *Financial Times, Water & Waste Management Special Report* (December 16, 2008), p. 4.

effects on groundwater or public health. Trade and industrial waste, on the other hand, may be more complex than construction waste in composition, but it is also often heavily composed of clean and frequently inert elements as well. Not coincidentally, then, both construction and trade and commercial waste collection and disposal are often dominated by the private sector owing to the relative simplicity of dealing with them, even in the context of present-day regulations.

Household waste, which constitutes one of the smallest parts of the solid waste stream, is also the most visible, and it is also important in a number of other ways. Coming to terms with household waste for the purpose of preserving public health was the central impetus behind initial legislation empowering municipalities to collect it and supervise its disposal. If household waste is not collected, whether because of inefficiency, lack of funding, or industrial action, public health concerns are quick to follow, often with substantial political fallout. And even if it is collected efficiently and on time, other concerns have emerged. This has been especially true since the 1970s, as a broader conception of "environmental health" gradually displaced the older public health dimension, again with social, cultural, and political impacts. Finally, household waste is composed not only of substantial organic waste, primarily from food, but also of other materials that have increased in quantity and complexity with the growth of consumerism and that – depending on markets and technologies – may be capable of being salvaged and/or recycled.

Examination of household waste therefore brings into focus the complex interactions among the public/environmental health dimension of waste, the impact of the consumer society on the waste stream, the effects of changing political and cultural perceptions of what should be done about waste, and the economic and business dimensions of the waste industry. To be sure, the interaction of all of these elements sometimes taxes the public sector's commitment to efficiency and financial prudence, but because it also provides a business opportunity, it often attracts the attention of the private sector. Focusing on household waste allows careful investigation of these complexities, although, as we shall see shortly, defining and quantifying "household waste" is not a simple task.

Two tensions, therefore, stand at the heart of this book. The first involves a tension among three potential objectives: preserving public health (or more broadly, environmental health) at practically any cost; delivering waste handling services at the lowest possible price; and efficient delivery of waste services. The second key tension is between the private and public sectors. These tensions and changes in the balance struck between them since 1945 in the United Kingdom and West Germany form major themes of this book. In addition to these, there are four others that we would like to explore as well. All four are interconnected to some extent with the first two but also with one another in various ways.

The first has to do with the perennial issue of the possibility of gaining value from waste, of getting "cash for your trash,"[11] such as through salvage (reconceptualized as "recycling" since the 1970s), recovery of methane gas from landfill, or from incineration of waste to generate electricity. This pursuit has exercised professionals in the cleansing industry certainly since 1945, and it has become a more pressing concern more recently, especially since the 1970s. Yet, it is vexed in many ways. For one thing, it gives rise to the sometimes difficult legal issue of who owns the waste, which is something we address from time to time throughout the book. What is more, there is also a definitional issue: in the strictest sense, once something has been retrieved (or diverted) from the waste stream and sold – as scrap iron for use in steel manufacture or a first edition of a Charles Dickens novel fished from the dump and auctioned to the highest bidder – it has ceased to be waste at all and thus might be seen as outside the purview of this study.

At the same time, this process of salvaging value is a vital component of waste handling as a business (or businesslike) activity, something emphasized to a greater or lesser degree in both public and private sector practice. Salvaging value, however, is far from straightforward: markets for "waste" food, paper, glass, metals, and other products fluctuate considerably depending on supply and demand. It is often expensive to recycle particular things, such as certain plastics, which, given legislation, political will, or social pressure may in any case be mandated. To what extent and how are such risks and uncertainties integrated into budget processes for city- or state-owned enterprises in the industry or into business strategies for private sector firms? Similarly vexing questions arise in relation to the incineration of waste, where the need for fuel to power incineration plants has resulted in market demand for waste that sometimes exceeds local output. Waste therefore must be brought in from further afield for incineration, sometimes even from abroad. What can be counterintuitive in this case, however, is the fact that the power

---

[11] The phrase comes, of course, from Zimring's history of salvage in the United States, *Cash for Your Trash.*

plant requiring the waste for fuel is often *paid* to take the waste from those who produce it in another town or another country, frequently owing to shortage of landfill and/or legislative mandate. The bottom line is that generating electricity from trash through incineration may solve some problems such as shortage of landfill, but it generally does so at the expense of undermining other goals such as waste reduction or limiting airborne emissions. Clearly, then, even if the salvaging value from waste makes it not waste at all, it is still a major issue for public cleansing and waste management. It also highlights the tradeoffs and tensions between political and social goals on the one hand and market forces on the other in the management of waste, and it thus forms a natural – indeed necessary – theme to consider carefully throughout this book.

A second additional theme, related in part to salvage/recycling, is technological change. For salvage/recycling, the issue of technology is perhaps a self-evident one: except for relatively easily recycled items such as paper, glass, aluminum, and ferrous metal, technological breakthroughs were required to enable recycling to take place at all.[12] For particular plastics, but also for composite materials, these have often proven particularly difficult to develop. But technological change has been important in the industry's development in other ways as well. Rationalization of garbage can design and of collection has been extremely important, as have developments in the design and construction of landfills, which have changed dramatically from mere dumps into sophisticated technological systems. Automation and new vehicles have also led to substantial changes, not least in the number of workers required per unit of trash collected. Optical and mechanical separation technologies have often obviated the need for human intervention as well, such as in relation to initial separation of "recoverables" from items to be disposed of in more traditional ways through landfill or incineration. Incineration technology has also changed markedly through time, often allowing greater throughput, more efficient combustion, less pollution, and more output of electricity. What is more, these technologies have often been interrelated in various ways, interrelationships that have shaped the relative economic viability and attractiveness of landfill and incineration, as well as salvage or recycling. And all of these developments and more have been underpinned by a more general process of "scientification" of waste

---

[12] Jeffrey L. Meikle, *American Plastic: A Cultural History* (New Brunswick, NJ: Rutgers University Press, 1995).

handling involving extensive research and development work and incremental innovation.[13] Technology is thus clearly a central aspect of the development of the industry and is addressed in the chapters that follow, with particular attention devoted to this theme in Chapter 2.

The third additional theme is closely related to the first two: regulation. Government regulation of and legislation regarding this industry have certainly formed key drivers in its development. Government action has led to major rethinking of the fundamental tasks the industry seeks to carry out. It has significantly affected the costs of carrying out legally mandated waste collection and disposal activities; the extent of and conditions set on salvage/recycling; limits placed on emissions of incinerators and/or on groundwater contamination through landfills (thus forming a key determinant of the economic viability of each of them); and therefore, at least to a certain degree, the extent to which the public sector or the private sector takes primary responsibility in a particular time or place for carrying out waste-handling related activities.

Finally, technological change and evolving regulations form a large part of the basis for our exploration of the theme of potential convergence over time of policy and schemes of practice in relation to waste handling in the United Kingdom and Germany. On the technological side, one plausible explanation for any convergence might be the process of scientification already noted; another is the fact that industry professionals and policy makers were more or less aware of best practice in the other country and more or less willing to try to emulate it. On the regulatory side, we can identify a cascading series of processes of regionalization, nationalization, and eventually Europeanization. Waste management (or more accurately "public cleansing" from about the mid-nineteenth to the late twentieth century) was historically speaking a local concern, something that remained true long after 1945. Certainly, national legislation imposed some standard expectations on local practice, but it was only in the early 1970s that effective national legislation

---

[13] For the "scientification" concept as applied to the development of economic policy in Germany after World War II, see, for instance, Tim Schanetzky, *Die große Ernüchterung: Wirtschaftspolitik, Expertise und Gesellschaft in der Bundesrepublik 1966 bis 1982* (Berlin: Akademie-Verlag, 2007); as applied to the discipline of political science in the United States, see Jon R. Bond, "The Scientification of the Study of Politics," *Journal of Politics* 69 (2007): 897–907; and more generally, see Peter Weingart, "The Moment of Truth for Science: The Consequences of the 'Knowledge Society' for Society and Science," *EMBO reports* 3 (2002): 703–706, available at http://www.outreach.psu.edu/programs/rsa/files/Reading_Weingart_Peter_The_Moment_of_Truth_for_Science_EMBO_reports_3_8_2002.pdf (accessed July 14, 2009).

in both countries began to address the many local and regional peculiarities. Both the UK and West Germany strengthened national legislation in the 1980s, but by then this was overlaid with European legislation and regulation, with effects on both countries after 1973 (when the UK joined the European Economic Community and the EEC almost simultaneously began to interest itself in such matters). Such European intervention has become more pronounced since the 1980s. We would therefore expect to see a gradual process of convergence between 1945 and the present day, first toward nationwide deployment of nationally mandated standards in each country and then toward European ones in both. But can we demonstrate such convergence? This is a question we investigate closely in what follows.

To investigate and integrate these varied themes and questions, we have made a number of methodological and other decisions. One thing we have tried to do is to develop a number of time series of quantitative data to underpin what is predominantly a qualitative analysis. After all, to assess decision making and implementation of decisions by policy makers and practitioners, it is necessary to know as much as possible about the scale of what faced them. Thus, we focus on trying to compile data for each country and/or local authority we are examining: changes over time in the weight, volume, and material composition of waste streams; the development over time of costs of (and income from) collection and disposal of household waste; changes in the scale and composition of the workforce involved in waste handling activities; and the evolution of markets for salvaged or reclaimed waste.

Those readers whose eyes are beginning to glaze over at this point should take heart in the knowledge that we present such quantitative data *selectively* in this book, leaving more thorough presentation to separate, specialized publications. What is undoubtedly important to point out now, however, is that compiling the data has been easier said than done. Although there are a very few exceptions for which there are rich, consistent, and long-term data – such as the evolution of the market for wastepaper in the United Kingdom – most statistics we have managed to collect are substantially less than perfect in one way or another. Labor data, for example, are often aggregated in local authority statistics; in other words, waste collection staff are combined with street cleaners and sometimes even vehicle maintenance engineers in the reported figures. The same is true of data on costs and income, which sometimes apply to the whole cleansing department of a local authority rather than just to household waste collection.

Still, one would think that getting at least some ballpark figures for the output of waste – and perhaps for the waste stream's composition – would be possible for the entire period. This, however, is not the case. It was, after all, not really until the 1990s, as a result of legislative requirements and growing public awareness, that reporting of household waste collection and disposal took on any sort of standardized form across – and even sometimes within – countries. Before then, reporting was often piecemeal and voluntary, with predictable consequences for data consistency and reliability, especially over time. Moreover, even if data on quantities of waste collected are available for a particular local authority over a particular time period, they are not necessarily internally consistent. To name just one example with concrete implications for our analysis, statistics reported for waste collection sometimes changed over time from measures of weight to those of volume (and sometimes back again). The two types of measurement are, of course, incompatible because it is impossible to "norm" the statistics from one to the other. The fact that the reporting often changed would therefore seem to confirm a hypothesis that waste streams from the early post–World War II period – when reporting by weight was the norm – were heavier than those of later years. The former contained a lot of ash and cinders from coal fires, while the latter had little of either (owing to widespread adoption of gas and electric central heating) and featured increasing amounts of plastic artifacts and packaging low in weight but high in volume. The volume of what was collected eventually became extremely important in managing landfill, probably accounting for the change in reporting. But it would have been ideal to have a consistent measure of either weight or volume – or even better, both – to confirm this hypothesis fully.

Taken together, all of these considerations help explain why, even with the best will in the world, a quantitative picture of the waste stream is difficult to pin down. There is one further explanation: it is far simpler to distinguish between household and other waste in theory than in practice. An example from the experience of one of the coauthors, who had a new central heating boiler installed in his apartment in 2008 during the research for this book, might help exemplify this. One way of disposing of the old boiler would have been for him to take it directly to the dump, in which case it would have been classified as household waste and (under Glasgow's landfill rules for city residents current at the time) accepted without charge. If, on the other hand, the plumber who installed it had taken it to the same dump, the very same boiler would have been classified as trade waste, and there would have been a fee for disposing of it. As it happened, there was no chance to make a final decision between these two options: the boiler sat for no more than two hours in an alleyway behind the apartment building while the plumber was putting the final touches on his installation before it disappeared, collected no doubt for its scrap value by some entrepreneur from the "private sector." The boiler might have entered the Glasgow waste statistics for 2008 as either household or trade waste; in the end, it did not figure in waste statistics at all. No wonder, then, that it is so difficult to determine changes over time in the quantity and quality of household waste collection and disposal over time! The incident is illustrative for another reason: it brings into focus an idea that we have already identified as an important issue addressed in this book. What is at stake, after all, is not just who pays for the disposal of waste and how it is categorized but also, given that it can have value, who owns it.

Thus, although quantitative data are essential for setting questions for further investigation and for establishing the contours of our story, they remain in the background in much of what follows. Qualitative investigation and analysis play a much more important role in the construction of the narrative within individual chapters, and it is therefore worthwhile to briefly outline how we have designed the research to maximize the relevance of our results while at the same time keeping the project within reasonable, doable bounds.

Here too, we started by gathering some basic data, which remain by and large in the background in the chapters that follow. One priority has been to establish the development through time of national (and eventually European) legislative frameworks for the collection, handling, and disposal of waste in the United Kingdom and Germany between 1945 and the present, because these have had obvious implications for defining the parameters within which practitioners in the industry have operated. Similarly, we have tried through a variety of means and sources to gain an overview of the evolving national and international structures of the industry, including trade and professional associations, ownership patterns, and changes in the division of labor between the public and the private sectors. For the entire period we investigate, the nation-state is an essential unit of analysis. By virtue of national-level legislation, reporting requirements, governmental agencies that intervened in the industry from time to time, professional associations, and other means, waste collection and disposal policy and practice *within* each of the two countries we are studying shared a number of key characteristics that simultaneously differentiated the industry in one country from that in the other. There are, in other words, identifiable national styles and systems of waste handling, which one scholar has called "waste regimes."[14] We examine these closely, without going into too much detail on the bureaucratic side and at the same time keeping in mind the increasingly important European dimension.

There is, however, no getting around the fact that generation, collection, and disposal of waste have historically been profoundly local or, at most, regional activities. This remains the case to the present day, despite harmonization of practice through national and international legislation, increasing size and multinationalization of some waste management companies to take advantage of economies of scale, and growth in national and international trade in waste products. Investigating developments at the local level is thus essential here, although clearly not every locality can be considered in any detail; therefore a case-study approach is required.

We decided that three local authority case studies for each of the countries would be optimal. One or two such case studies for each would be too limited because this would prohibit thorough examination of local and regional variations within national practice. Four case studies for each country, on the other hand, would have been unwieldy in terms of carrying out research within a reasonable amount of time and in terms of integration into the analysis and narrative. Four would also probably lead to a lot of redundancy of information. Three case studies per country thus seemed ideal.

In choosing local authority case studies, we focus on large cities. Already by the mid-nineteenth century, cities confronted the public health effects of large concentrations of human population on the air, water, and land – including those related to household waste – and quickly developed organizations to deal with these issues. By 1945, local cleansing departments were well established in all major cities in the UK and in what would become West Germany, and they had also established procedures (if sometimes dubious ones) for disposing of the waste they collected. Large cities also arguably felt the effects of consumerism on waste streams earlier and more intensively than did smaller ones or rural areas.

But which cities would be most appropriate to include? We quickly ruled out the largest city in each country: London and Berlin. London's population is so large that it is not really comparable to any other city in

---

[14] Zsuzsa Gille, *From the Cult of Waste to the Trash Heap of History: The Politics of Waste in Socialist and Postsocialist Hungary* (Bloomington, IN: Indiana University Press, 2007).

the UK. Moreover, largely owing to the British capital city's size, responsibility for collection and disposal of waste has traditionally been borne by a number of district or other authorities, not by a unitary authority. Overwhelming size, on the other hand, was not the problem with choosing Berlin as a case study, although it was the largest city in Germany throughout the postwar period. More importantly, Berlin is not readily comparable with other West German cities for other reasons. Here, we note its unique status between 1945 and 1990 as a city occupied by the four victorious Allied powers in the Second World War, a city that was divided politically into two, half of which was an island outpost of capitalism and liberal democracy in the middle of a socialist country, while the other half of the city served as the capital of that socialist country. Furthermore, a scholarly study of the development of public cleansing in West Berlin appeared not long ago.[15] So, while we have occasion from time to time in the course of the book to look at the Berlin case – and in particular at the role of the East German Democratic Republic (GDR) in the evolution of waste handling policy and practice in West Berlin and West Germany – the city will not be included in any sustained way as a case study.

Having thus excluded London and Berlin, we deployed three criteria for choosing the cases presented in detail throughout this book. First, the cities had to be large and densely populated. Second, they had to reflect as much variation as possible, not only in terms of the region within which they are located (involving topography and other factors) but also in terms of type (e.g., industrial, commercial, etc.). Finally, there had to be sufficient primary sources to allow for in-depth historical research. A number of candidates for the in-depth cases were considered, and sometimes research began only to be curtailed owing to limitations of sources. In the end, we decided on six varied and rich local case studies: Birmingham, Glasgow, and Manchester in the United Kingdom and Dortmund, Mannheim, and Frankfurt in West Germany. Although they are not presented separately as case studies, they each inform the general narrative.

The book explores the themes, cases, comparisons, and methodologies just outlined in a unified chronological narrative that at the same time explores specific topics in depth. It is divided into three parts for the former purpose, while it comprises eight substantive chapters to

---

[15] Jinhee Park, "Von der Müllkippe zur Abfallwirtschaft: Die Entwicklung der Hausmüllentsorgung in Berlin (West) von 1945 bis 1990" (PhD dissertation: TU Berlin, 2004).

enable the latter. Part one focuses on the reconstruction of the cleansing industry in the two countries between 1945 and the 1960s. The period started for both countries in a context of continued relative deprivation for most of the populace in the wake of the Great Depression and World War II, and economic disruption (including rationing and foreign exchange controls) lasted well into the 1950s. By the late 1950s, however, people in both countries were experiencing unparalleled wealth, enabling mass consumption, which – combined with a number of other developments such as new materials and widespread adoption of oil- and gas-fired central heating systems – led to vast increases in the waste stream.

Chapter 1 presents some prewar background on the organization and practice of cleansing in the two countries and in selected local authorities within them to explore the extent to which there was continuity or change from the pre– to post–World War II period. One concern here is with the evolving role of the private sector, in particular in Britain in the area of waste disposal. We also address changes in the waste stream and other pressures for restructuring and rationalizing the industry. The actual process of rationalization, meanwhile, forms the subject of Chapter 2, where issues connected to organizational and technological innovation during the first two decades following the end of the Second World War are explored in particular depth. Measures aimed at achieving rationalization included moves to "professionalize" practice and organize the service, attempts at standardization of household waste containers, and efforts to introduce new machinery. Moreover, the process of rationalization frequently involved interaction between the public and the private sector. Chapter 3 then turns to the issue of "salvage" (akin to but not identical to what we would now term "recycling") and how it fit into the operation of the business conceptually, financially, and in terms of labor allocation.

Part two considers the period between the 1960s and about 1980. Although it is extremely difficult to place an exact date on the emergence of the "consumer society" in any country, it is clear that both the UK and West Germany were by the late 1960s well on the way to becoming societies of plenty rather than societies of want, with pronounced effects on waste collection and disposal. By the early 1970s, both countries were consequently faced with challenges owing to dramatically increased volumes and an unprecedented composition of the waste stream. Also – because of these very challenges – they were faced with a variety of other issues, such as pressure on landfill capacity, the political impact of the nascent environmental movement, and increasing reluctance of many to work in the industry given other more attractive job opportunities. Chapter 4 therefore takes up the story of the evolution of the waste stream in each country again, while Chapter 5 examines the political response in the form of national and regional legislation and growing political activism. Chapter 6 then deals with the ways in which the industry itself reacted to physical, legal, and political challenges in the context of economic turmoil (in the form of inflation and/or the oil crises). And it also considers the ways in which "salvage" was reconceptualized as "recycling" and the ramifications of that change.

Part three addresses the period from 1980 to the present, during which, we argue, there were additional conceptual changes, first of all in relation to defining "waste" and what could be done about it, and second in relation to elaborating the concept of "waste management" as a replacement for that of "public cleansing." Chapter 7 takes up the thread of our ongoing story about the development of the waste stream in both countries again, examining the subject not only in terms of quantitative and qualitative changes but also the attempts by practitioners to grapple with the cumulative effects of decades of such change through better record keeping, statistics, and other measures. It also assesses the factors behind and the implications of apparent conceptual divergence between West Germany and Britain in relation to waste. The West German Waste Management Law (Abfallwirtschaftsgesetz) in 1986 was based on the premise that waste had considerable potential for added value and that this potential had to be exploited organizationally and technologically, while Britain appeared to lag behind in older conceptualizations of the industry. At the same time, there were instances of apparent convergence, as both countries were affected (although to differing degrees and at different times) by moves to privatize public services and by the impact of European legislation and regulation. We conclude Chapter 7 by looking at the ways in which industry organization and practice in the two countries evolved in the 1980s in light of all of these developments.

Chapter 8 considers the themes developed in the previous chapters for the United Kingdom and Germany during the period from 1990 to the present. Increasing levels of power and activism by the European Commission during this period, as well as growing public awareness and environmental concern, moves toward privatization, and multinationalization of the waste management industry, *should*, all other things being equal, have resulted in increasing convergence of the waste management systems in the two countries. We explore the extent to which this has in fact been the case and offer some explanations for recent developments. Finally, we round off with a conclusion, summarizing the arguments and findings of our research and reflecting on their implications both for historical scholarship and for present-day policy.

PART I

CLEANSING SERVICES, 1945 TO THE 1960s

From Societies of Want to Societies of Plenty

Establishing (and Reestablishing) an Industry

Waste Services in the United Kingdom and Germany from the Late Nineteenth Century to the 1950s

Introduction

Aerial bombardment and the ravages of combat during the Second World War caused widespread human suffering and extensive physical damage in the United Kingdom and still more in Germany. Even those spared the worst horrors of the fighting keenly felt the effects of the war economy. Producing for the war effort, after all, required that civilians curb their consumption severely. And when the fighting finally ended, rationing and supply shortages remained bleak features of daily life in both countries. In sum, given the scale of death, damage, disruption, and want, this hardly seemed a situation in which collection and disposal of household waste would rank high on the agenda of things to do.

Yet, even the most impoverished produce some household waste, and there was therefore an urgent need to undertake action to preserve public health, in part by organizing waste services quickly and efficiently. Obviously, because of both the urgency of the situation and the pressures of competing priorities for allocation of scarce human and financial resources, the easiest way to do this was simply to reconstruct waste handling systems that had existed prior to 1945. Before we look at the process and effects of postwar reconstruction in the two countries, it is therefore necessary to examine what exactly it was that practitioners and policy makers were seeking to reconstruct. The best way to do that is to start at the beginning to establish the challenges that led to the creation of "modern" waste services in the UK and Germany, as well as the organizational, financial, legal, and technological responses to those challenges. Whereas the challenges were similar in each country, the responses to them differed, sometimes considerably. Moreover, there were different responses to the issues even *within* the two countries.

Organizing Waste Services: From the Late Nineteenth Century to 1945

Picture a cityscape in the 1870s in a large metropolis such as Glasgow (population ca. 500,000) or Berlin (population slightly fewer than one million in 1875). In many ways, both cities already had some recognizably "modern" elements: paved streets with prominent and numerous streetlights teemed with people walking past buildings that in many cases (especially in Glasgow, but also in Berlin) are still part of the streetscape today. In other ways – lots of horses and carts, no cars, chimneys belching smoke – things could not be more different.

Arguably, however, there is a great class of things that are largely invisible in photographic images of these two cities in the 1870s, in that the biggest difference between then and now is that the infrastructure we now take for granted frequently did not exist. And if it did, ownership and organizational structures differed from those prevalent today, sometimes dramatically. Both cities had a centralized drinking water supply, a product of large-scale mid-nineteenth-century engineering projects.[1] Electric power and lighting systems, however, did not yet exist, and the telephone system was likewise to make its first appearance in cities later in the century, but there were also still no centralized systems for sewage removal, gas lighting, and trams. The same held true for waste collection and disposal systems.

There had, of course, long been demand for many of these services, not least because the human being "is a wasting animal."[2] Finding ways of dealing with human waste and clearing up household waste – chiefly

---

[1] Glasgow's centralized water supply from Loch Katrine was completed in 1859 and began operation in 1860 following a three-and-a-half-year major engineering project. See Andrew Aird, *Glimpses of old Glasgow* (1894), pp. 136–141, especially p. 140, available at http://gdl.cdlr.strath.ac.uk/airgli/airglio114.htm (accessed December 1, 2009). See also Robert Crawford, "Glasgow's Experience with Municipal Ownership and Operation: Water, Gas, Electricity, and Street Railways," *American Academy of Political and Social Science* 27 (1906): 1–19, especially pp. 8–9. Meanwhile, L. Pawlowski, "Historical Overview on Water Management in Berlin," n.d. [ca. 2003], p. 2, dates the centralized water supply in Berlin as starting in 1856, while sewage services did not start until 1878. http://www.iwc-berlin.de/medienpool/iwc_m77_61000000012/iwc_20071011135914_1_840856.pdf (accessed December 1, 2009).

[2] J. C. Wylie, *The Wastes of Civilisation* (London, Faber and Faber Ltd., 1959), p. 9.

food scraps, ashes and cinders from fireplaces, and discarded personal possessions – were in fact perennial problems, and they were exacerbated by rapid population growth and urbanization in the eighteenth and nineteenth centuries. Although legislation seeking to address such problems existed as early as the seventeenth century in Britain,[3] organized activity to tackle them remained piecemeal and halting. Well into the nineteenth century, the preferred solutions in both Britain and the German area were basically the same ones that had been deployed for centuries: generally a combination of benign neglect, muddling through, and/or leaving it to the private sector. Leaving it to the private sector was indeed the most common way to organize a variety of urban infrastructure systems through the first half of the nineteenth century. Just as private firms and contractors generally built and operated municipal water and city gas supply systems and trams, they also provided solid waste collection and disposal services to cities. For household waste services, the private sector was attracted by the possibility of profit from the sale of what they collected or from fees charged to those whose premises they served.[4]

Centralization and "municipalization" of infrastructure and services started with water supply in the mid-nineteenth century. By the latter part of the century, however, most of the others had also been centralized, turned into monopolies, and brought under city ownership or control. (See Figure 1.1.) The largest British cities, such as Birmingham, Glasgow, and Manchester, for instance, had by the end of the nineteenth century set up large specialist departments that not only organized the collection of household refuse but also frequently sorted it to enable "salvage" of some components and more efficient disposal.[5] In Germany, too, things began to change dramatically in the last quarter of the nineteenth century. Frankfurt, which had employed private contractors, mostly local peasants, to cart away household waste from the inner city from the 1860s, introduced a regular waste collection service in 1873. Mannheim

---

[3] A Scottish act of Parliament in 1686 required Edinburgh's magistrates to provide effective measures to cleanse the city's streets. *Public Cleansing and Salvage*, October 1945, "Report of Annual Conference of the Institute of Public Cleansing," p. 88.

[4] P. D. Fairlie, *A Review of Public Cleansing in Glasgow: From 1868 to 1968* (Glasgow, Corporation of the City of Glasgow, 1968), p. 2.

[5] See, for instance, Corporation of the City of Glasgow, *Municipal Glasgow: Its Evolution and Enterprises* (Glasgow: Robert Gibson & Sons Ltd, 1914), pp. 155–159, and C. A. Vince, *History of the Corporation of Birmingham*, vol. 4 (Birmingham: Corporation of Birmingham, 1923), pp. 177–179 and 472–473.

FIGURE I.I. A municipal dump in Glasgow, ca. 1914. Photograph courtesy of the City of Glasgow, © Glasgow City Council 1968.

followed in 1880 and Dortmund in 1889. In most cases, however, the service in German municipalities was confined to the inner city, where it was regular and city owned and operated.

Economic theories were, of course, eventually developed to justify this process (e.g., "natural monopoly,"[6] or the economics of network industries[7]), and there were also, in the late nineteenth and beginning of the twentieth century, ideological/programmatic justifications for it (e.g., "municipal socialism"[8]). But by far the most important impetus for centralizing and municipalizing infrastructure industries such as waste collection beginning in the late nineteenth century was neither economic/ theoretical nor ideological but rather medical: growing awareness of the origins and spread of disease in the course of the nineteenth century led

---

[6] See, for instance, Manela Mosca, "On the Origins of the Concept of Natural Monopoly: Economies of Scale and Competition," *European Journal of the History of Economic Thought* 15 (2008): 317–353. Mosca points out that the term was used already in the early nineteenth century by Thomas Malthus, but that the modern usage of the term referring to networked, capital-intensive industries, often involving public utilities, first came into use in the last two decades of the century. See especially pp. 322–324.

[7] See, for instance, Nicholas Economides, "The Economics of Networks," *International Journal of Industrial Organization* 14 (1996): 673–699.

[8] J. R. Kellett, "Municipal Socialism, Enterprise, and Trading in the Victorian City," *Urban History* 5 (1978): 36–45.

to a concern with ensuring regular and reliable service, which could not be left to the private sector.[9]

This point cannot be emphasized strongly enough: the primary desideratum for the establishment of municipal waste services beginning in the late nineteenth century was to keep the city hygienic to preserve public health, and this remained by far the most important rationale behind municipal waste handling until at least the 1970s. It is thus no accident that the organizations established in the waning decades of the nineteenth century to carry out these services were called departments of "cleansing" in Britain and "*Stadtreinigung*" (city cleansing) in Germany. The overall aims were to keep streets and pavements clean to avoid accumulations of waste and dirt in areas inside the city and to find hygienic ways of getting rid of the by-products of urban civilization.

To establish this service, two things had to happen. First, there had to be governmental authorization (or ordering) of local authorities to carry out cleansing functions through legislation. And second, some means had to be devised to pay for the service. Let us now look at each of them in turn.

In Britain, nineteenth- and early-twentieth-century legislation on waste handling took place at the national level. The Public Health Act of 1848 is generally recognized as an early driver in the eventual creation of the country's public health system, of which waste services formed one element.[10] The law provided for a comprehensive municipal system for collection and disposal of domestic refuse that would shape organization and practice more than a century. It was, however, in typical nineteenth-century British fashion, voluntary. Local authorities were empowered – but not obliged – to establish waste collection and disposal systems, and the act also explicitly granted ownership of the refuse to the local authority, allowing them to sell the salvage if they wished and to credit

---

[9] See, for instance, Martin Melosi, *The Sanitary City: Environmental Services in Urban America from Colonial Times to the Present* (Baltimore, MD: Johns Hopkins University Press, 2000); Martin Melosi, *Garbage in the Cities. Refuse, Reform, and the Environment* (Pittsburgh: University of Pittsburgh Press, 2004); Peter Münch, *Stadthygiene im 19. und 20. Jahrhundert: Die Wasserversorgung, Abwasser- und Abfallbeseitigung unter besonderer Berücksichtigung Münchens* (Göttingen: Vandenhoeck & Ruprecht, 1993), esp. p. 227ff.

[10] Great Britain, *Public Health Act, 1848, 11 & 12 Vict., cap. 63* (London: HMSO, 1848). Section 55 enabled local health boards to make bylaws regulating the removal of waste matter from premises and the prevention of "nuisance" to the public, and Section 87 required them to raise a "general district rate" to pay for the handling of waste where such services were provided.

any resulting revenue specifically to the cleansing account. The subsequent Public Health Act of 1875 then elaborated on the first one by empowering local authorities to remove waste regularly and to make local regulations for storage of domestic waste.[11] In direct contrast to Britain, however, late-nineteenth-century legislation in Germany on waste handling took place at the state (Land) rather than national level, and it varied in detail from state to state. Still, by the end of the century, all German states had laws in place empowering (and sometimes requiring) cities to collect and dispose of waste, or else to arrange for someone in the private sector to do so.

The solution to the second issue – that is, how to pay for cleansing – represented another area of difference between Britain and Germany. According to Section 207 of the Public Health Act of 1875, British local authorities were not permitted to charge directly for cleansing services.[12] Instead, payment was indirect through local taxation as part of the "rate demand" levied on householders. The rates, moreover, were based on the value of the property being serviced rather than the amount of rubbish collected. Proceeds from the sale of salvage could supplement this, but, of course, money raised in this way could never pay for the full cost of the service. For their part, German cities initially did not have a sustainable method of funding their cleansing operations, but this soon changed. In Prussia, the largest German state by far, for instance, a *Gebührenordnung* (fee regulation) was enacted in 1893, enabling cities to charge fees for their services.[13] And here, in contrast to the British case, charges were explicitly and directly linked to the service provided.

Regular waste collection by local authorities in the United Kingdom and Germany funded by taxpayers or users had thus begun in the late nineteenth century, although provision of a service comparable to one we would recognize today did not emerge until the interwar period. One key factor driving the development of such a service was the ongoing professionalization of practitioners. The Association of Cleansing Superintendants of Great Britain, the forerunner of today's Chartered Institution of Wastes Management, held its first meeting in 1898. Led in its initial years

---

[11] Great Britain, *Public Health Act 1875, 38 & 39 Vict., cap. 55* (London: HMSO, 1875), Sections 42 and 44.
[12] Great Britain, *Public Health Act 1875*: Section 207 required all such expenses to be met from public funds.
[13] Hermann Bausch et al., "Es herrscht Reinlichkeit und Ordnung hier auf den Straßen," in *Aus 400 Jahren Geschichte der Stadtreinigung und Abfallentsorgung in Dortmund: 111 Jahre kommunale Abfallwirtschaft, 10 Jahre EDG* (Dortmund: EDG, 2001), p. 33.

by northern English and Scottish professionals, the association's purpose was to facilitate transfer of best practice among authorities. Among other things, it organized correspondence courses for training, and in 1910 it also established a professional journal, the *Cleansing Superintendent*.[14] A parallel German organization was not established until somewhat later. The Verband kommunaler Fuhrparksbetriebe (Association of Municipal Public Cleansing Departments, or VKF) was founded in 1912, and the new professional organization and its journal *Die Städtereinigung*, started by the organization's main scientific activist Heinrich Erhard, were instrumental in spreading information on innovations in waste handling from the interwar period onward.[15]

To sum up, then, both professional organizations had the explicit remit of diffusing best practice, but they did so in differing contexts and with different effects. For this reason, we need to look briefly and separately at developments in each country during the interwar period.

Great Britain's Public Cleansing System on the Eve of the Second World War

By 1939, Britain's comprehensive system of public cleansing, already firmly established in many cities by 1914, had been extended to provide virtually universal coverage for urban households. Collection, removal, and disposal of everyday household waste, along with sweeping and clearing of streets and sidewalks, were regulated by the 1936 Public Health Act, which gathered together an assortment of nineteenth- and early-twentieth-century legislation. Notionally overseen by the Ministry of Health, in practice there was never any more than occasional very general advice from the central government. Instead, British local authorities were left almost entirely to their own devices in the organization and provision of services. The 1936 act empowered but (maintaining the

---

[14] Lewis Herbert, *The History of The Institute of Wastes Management, 1898–1998: Celebrating 100 Years of Progress* (Northampton: IWM Business Services Ltd, 1998), p. 12.

[15] Heinrich Erhard, *Aus der Geschichte der Städtereinigung* (Stuttgart: Kohlhammer, 1954). Erhard gathered a huge amount of material on the history of waste collection and disposal and outlined it in this book, one of the first to appear on the history of German waste handling. The "Erhard Collection" (Sammlung Erhard), which can be found in the Umweltbundesamt (Federal Environmental Office) in Dessau, is one of the most important sources of waste handling history even today. Erhard was on the payroll of Schmidt & Melmer, a company that had a strong interest in the widespread adoption of its proprietary waste handling system, and his collection of materials was no doubt aimed at promoting that system.

established tradition of nineteenth-century legislation) did not require local government bodies to run waste-handling operations, which actually left them free to contract the whole or part of the work out to private operators – or indeed to opt out altogether if they wished and instead to require individual householders to make their own arrangements. In practice, however, no authorities withdrew from their notionally voluntary responsibilities, and only a very small number of rural councils subcontracted the whole of the service, usually on economic grounds.[16]

Overall, then, private enterprise played only a relatively small part, usually connected with disposal rather than collection. While local authorities sometimes rented vehicles from the private sector to supplement their own fleets at times of unusual demand or to clear backlogs after bad weather, they more often entered into contracts with private haulers to transport the refuse they collected to its final disposal site. Such dumps were also frequently in the private sector, not least because capacity was sometimes inadequate, although many local authorities owned their own sites. (See Figure 1.2.) With these relatively minor exceptions, however, private commercial waste operators did not and could not compete with municipal authorities in the handling of domestic refuse, and this would remain the case until well after the end of the Second World War.

However, although it appears that both those served by public cleansing operations and those who ran them had no major complaints, the extent and standards of provision tended to be inconsistent from place to place,[17] not least because policy making within local authorities was determined by elected politicians through cleansing committees.[18] Thus, not all local authorities were able, or willing, to provide first-class waste handling for their residents,[19] although even the worst of them provided

[16] Great Britain, Ministry of Health, *Public Cleansing (Refuse Collection and Disposal; Street Cleansing) Costing Returns for the Year ended 31st March, 1938* (London: HMSO, 1939). Tables 1 to 9 provide data on the scale and costs of operations for individual authorities.

[17] For analyses of expenditure and relative efficiency of local authorities, see Great Britain, Ministry of Health, *Local Government Financial Statistics, England and Wales, 1936–37* (London: HMSO, 1939), Tables 1 and 3, and also Great Britain, Ministry of Health, *Public Cleansing*, Tables 1 to 9. This also applies only to England and Wales.

[18] See, for instance, G. C. McArthur, address to Annual Conference of the Institute of Public Cleansing, 1945, in *Public Cleansing and Salvage* (October 1945), pp. 71ff, and J. C. Dawes, "Presidential Address," in ibid., pp. 83ff. Both provide retrospective summaries of practitioner aspirations.

[19] For instance, see M. Marshall, on problems of collection, "Report of North East England Branch of Institute of Public Cleansing," in *Public Cleansing and Salvage* (September 1945), p. 24. See also McArthur and Dawes in the previous note.

FIGURE 1.2. A recently landscaped area of formerly waste ground at Cranhill, Glasgow, which was reclaimed by tipping residue from incinerated municipal refuse to fill and level the site. Ca. 1959. Photograph courtesy of the City of Glasgow, © Glasgow City Council 1968.

regular and nearly universal refuse collection. At their best, moreover, services were both comprehensive and efficient. Cities like Birmingham and Glasgow, for instance, took a good deal of civic pride not just in providing frequent collection rounds, but also in recovering materials of commercial value and processing wastes to generate electricity, to produce building materials, and to provide animal feed, among other things.[20] (See Figure 1.3.)

The cleansing departments of these large cities represented what was regarded at the time as "best practice" by the practitioner organization, which by 1928 had been renamed the Institute of Public Cleansing (IPC).[21] The IPC had a national structure of branch offices that by

---

[20] For Birmingham, see H. J. Black, *History of the Corporation of Birmingham*, vol. 6: *1936–1950* (Birmingham: Birmingham Corporation, 1950), passim. For Glasgow, see Fairlie, *Review of Public Cleansing in Glasgow.*

[21] Herbert, *History of the Institutes of Waste Management*, chapter 4, details its evolution through the 1920s and 1930s and, unless otherwise indicated, provides the source for the rest of this section.

FIGURE 1.3. Electrically powered refuse collection vehicle, Glasgow, 1950s. Its lead-acid batteries were recharged using power generated by the incineration of the city's refuse. Photograph courtesy of the City of Glasgow, © Glasgow City Council 1968.

the late 1930s regularly held meetings to promote regional and national exchanges of experience and opinion. It also organized annual conferences that combined practitioner discussion with comments from guest speakers outside the profession and featured a trade exhibition at which suppliers could display specialized public cleansing equipment from hand brushes to collection vehicles.

Nevertheless, incremental rather than radical innovation characterized UK refuse collection and disposal practice before 1939. This was typified by the emergence of a British Standard "dustbin" design in 1938,[22] which was essentially no more than a codification of a pattern already in wide use. What is more, adoption of the "standard" remained entirely voluntary. A further example of the glacial pace of technological change involved the slow introduction of specialized bodies for collection vehicles that were intended to reduce rather than eliminate spillage and dust creation (such as ash from the remnants of coal fires) known as "dustless loading." In Britain, moreover, these were not used universally, and even in those cases where they were deployed, they amounted to little more

[22] British Standard BS 792.

than modified versions of vehicles already widely used and could easily be used alongside existing types of trash cans.[23]

The lack of radical revision to equipment or working practices was, however, not so much from inherent conservatism as from the conviction – which was supported by evidence – that municipal waste collection and disposal in Britain worked satisfactorily. By 1939, domestic waste handling had become a substantial local government business activity, driven by an ethos of public health practice and municipal *amour propre* and governed primarily by political rather than commercial considerations.

Germany's Public Cleansing System on the Eve of the Second World War

In Germany, in contrast to Britain, the 1920s were particularly significant in the development of public cleansing, primarily because of the work of practitioners and industry in promoting rationalization. Several technical innovations improved service substantially. First, the decade witnessed the rise of what was then called *System-Müllabfuhr* (the waste collection system), which meant that German urban householders generally no longer had to provide an individual bin or garbage can; this in most cases had until that time amounted to no more than a box of some sort. Instead, such containers were henceforth provided to householders by the local authority and were of a uniform design.[24] Just as in the United Kingdom, the changeover was justified by the goal of making waste collection "dust free," because older systems allowed dust and debris to escape when they were discharged into the vehicle. The dust-free system enabled the cleansing departments to avoid this by virtue of the fact that the standardized cans locked onto a fitting on the vehicle, sealing the two together while the can's contents were emptied into the collection truck. The most important innovation in this context was a system devised by Schmidt & Melmer from Weidenau (in Westphalia), which applied for a patent on it in 1925. The patent did not apply to the can per se but rather to the connection between it and the collection vehicle. Any German city claiming to operate an advanced waste collection system during the 1920s and 1930s most likely had adopted the Schmidt & Melmer

---

[23] Barrie C. Woods, *Municipal Refuse Collection Vehicles* (Appleby in Westmoreland: Trans Pennine Publishing, 1999), p. 12.

[24] Ralf Breer et al., *Asche, Kehricht, Saubermänner. Stadtentwicklung, Stadthygiene und Städtereinigung in Deutschland bis 1945* (Selm: SASE, 2010), pp. 135–136.

FIGURE 1.4. German refuse cans from various dustless loading systems of the 1920s. The large and small cans on the far right-hand side with two hooks at the front of each can and the hole fitting on top are from the Schmidt & Melmer (EsEm) system, the most popular dustless loading system in Germany from then into the postwar period. These EsEm cans were used in tandem with dedicated collection vehicles that mechanically lifted the cans and tipped them into specialized garbage trucks. Photograph courtesy of Erhard Sammlung, Umweltbibliothek, Umweltbundesamt.

system. (See Figure 1.4.) The company's success was supported by the "lobbying" of the VKF, especially by Heinrich Erhard, who was also on the firm's payroll.

But not all German cities adopted the Schmidt & Melmer system. In 1911, for example, the city of Dortmund installed a so-called *Tonnen-wechselsystem* (container-changing system). Here the garbage can was not emptied but instead replaced by an empty one carried on the vehicle. Full containers were brought to a transfer point (*Umladestelle*) where they were discharged into a large railway car for transfer to the waste's final destination. Then the cans were cleaned and used in the next collection cycle to replace full ones once again. However, although this was a hygienic system, its great disadvantage was that twice as many containers were required. This was one of the main reasons why it was eventually abandoned in the mid-1950s.[25]

Another important innovation of the 1920s was the development of new vehicles for waste collection. Krupp, on the one hand, and the Kuka

[25] Bausch, "Es herrscht Ordnung und Reinlichkeit hier auf den Straßen," pp. 58–59, 87–88.

(short for "Keller und Knappich") Company from Augsburg on the other each invented new vehicle systems that featured a waste compression apparatus. Relatively quickly, however, the companies decided to cooperate rather than compete: Krupp manufactured the chassis and Kuka the top of the vehicle and the waste compression system. Kuka, along with Daimler-Benz and MAN, went on to dominate the market for waste collection vehicles in Germany during the 1920s. But there were exceptions in the case of the vehicles, too. Once again, Dortmund came up with an idiosyncratic solution in the form of electric collection trucks that could be recharged at the depot.

Germany, then, like Britain, had established a well-functioning service by the 1920s and improved upon it further during the 1930s, but in contrast to the United Kingdom, this was achieved mainly by deploying new technologies. Still another major difference remained: German cleansing departments normally restricted their activities exclusively to the city center. In the city's outer districts, no service was offered, or it was provided by private contractors. Hence, in contrast to Britain, there were opportunities in Germany for the private sector to operate in urban waste collection, with local legislation limited to areas where regular service was offered by public authorities. This indeed would not change until the 1950s, when a drastic rationalization of service provision eventually took place. In the short term, however, the Second World War had a significant impact on waste collection and disposal organization and practice in both countries, presenting major challenges to public cleansing systems in the medium to longer term, especially in severely damaged German cities.

The Impact of the War

When the Second World War broke out in Europe in September 1939, the Third Reich was already experiencing severe labor shortages. Government spending programs in general – and, especially after 1936, on armaments – meant that there was virtually full employment by 1938. By then, importation of labor from abroad had begun, something that would intensify during the course of the war.[26] Misallocation of labor resources made the situation even worse – especially through Hitler's pet projects such as the construction of the Westwall (often referred to as

---

[26] Mark Spoerer, *Zwangsarbeit unter dem Hakenkreuz: Ausländische Zivilarbeiter, Kriegsgefangene und Häftlinge im Deutschen Reich und im besetzten Europa 1939–1945* (Stuttgart: DVA, 2001).

the "Siegfried Line") beginning in 1938, on which half a million workers were deployed to build a fortification that would have no impact whatsoever on the conflict.[27] Inevitably, of course, the labor shortages had an impact on public cleansing services, something that was exacerbated when many of those who worked in refuse collection – that is, relatively fit males under forty years old who could handle the heavy lifting that was required for long periods of time – were called into military service. And skilled vehicle mechanics as well as experienced maintenance workers in waste processing plants also vanished quickly.

Britain, on the other hand, entered the conflict in 1939 having only recently committed itself to heavy spending on armaments and with quite a large number of workers still out of work from the severe economic downturn that started earlier in the decade. Still, unemployment rates dropped sharply here, too, and very swiftly. And again, conscription had a severe negative impact on staffing of waste collection services: within eighteen months of the start of the war, very few young males remained to do the heavy lifting required, and skilled personnel either entered military service or were deployed in other areas.

Labor was, of course, not the only thing in short supply as each nation's economic and industrial commitment to the fighting grew. Other priorities, too, meant that replacements for worn-out garbage cans and collection and disposal vehicles became difficult to come by, while spare parts for everything were in chronic short supply. Managing all of these difficulties, furthermore, would have been hard enough in the context of prewar patterns of work, but the workload for cleansing services actually increased during the war. In both Britain and Germany, compulsory collection of "salvage materials," which included metals, paper, textiles, and waste food, was mandated by the government. Once gathered, the materials then had to be sorted and ultimately disposed of or reused. Contemporary reports in both countries expressed the frustrations caused by this diversification and intensification of work on the one hand and, on the other, by the apparent unwillingness of the government to make available either manpower or material needed to carry this out.[28]

In such a situation, there were basically two options available to those operating public cleansing departments: service frequency could

---

[27] John Heyl, "The Construction of the *Westwall*, 1938: An Exemplar for National Socialist Policymaking," *Central European History* 14 (1981): 63–78, especially p. 69.

[28] BCA, BCC/BP, Reports and Agendas, labour report, March 1946; Kriegstagebuch Stadtreinigung Paul Schroeder. StA Frankfurt, Tiefbauamt, 133.

be stretched out, especially for collection of refuse; and/or alternative sources of labor could be found. The first option was used by many local authorities in both countries. Delays of collection were eventually measured in weeks in some places, although public health was not really endangered in Britain throughout the conflict. The same was true even in Germany until fairly late in the war. We shall return to Germany's divergent experience of the latter stages of the conflict shortly. In the meantime, it is worth noting that the surprisingly limited public health impact of severely reduced and restricted collections resulted in large part from the nature of the refuse being generated. Wartime rationing of both food and consumer products, combined with the requirement to segreg-ate "salvage materials," generally tended to reduce the level of household waste, particularly of the putrescent matter that becomes most offensive when uncollected in summer. Garbage cans were far from overflowing at the end of a week in either country, although they would have been very full in Birmingham, where collections were sometimes more than a full calendar month behind. Even in Birmingham, however, much of the contents between early autumn and late spring would have been inert ash and clinker from open fires and thus relatively innocuous as a public health hazard.

Both countries also sought alternative sources of labor, although the options available and the strategies pursued differed. In Britain, labor problems caused by the war were probably more qualitative than quanti-tative. Thus, although overall workforce reductions owing to conscrip-tion to the armed forces appear to have been relatively small, conscrip-tion removed the fittest younger workers from cleansing departments.[29] In addition, it took them from the general labor pool that cities relied on for the regular supply of replacements for the very high turnover rates experienced by all refuse departments.[30] Faced with having to fill these gaps, municipalities could look to three possible sources: those too young for conscription, those such as women who were ineligible for the

---

[29] By the end of the war, for example, Manchester's cleansing department employed 1,278 workers compared to 1,481 in 1939, a reduction of about 14 percent.

[30] Birmingham, Manchester, and Glasgow all noted similar problems. See: BCA, BCC/BP, Salvage and Stables Committee, Reports and Agendas, *Labour Report*, March 1946; Mitchell Library Glasgow, Records of the City of Glasgow (subsequently MLG), Cleans-ing Department, DTC 7/3/1 (5), *Cleansing Department, Annual Report, 1945–1946*; and Manchester City Archives (subsequently MCA), records of the Cleansing Committee, collection reference M595/2/2/59, *Annual Report, 1948/49*, p. 19, chart showing histo-rical survey of labor.

draft, and those too old to serve in the armed forces. Youths between fifteen and eighteen, however, were not generally considered physically mature enough for handling full trash cans and were thus employed only as salvage sorters. Women, who made up by far the greatest part of the population not liable to military conscription, carried out physically arduous factory and agricultural work during the war, yet few seem to have been recruited for public cleansing work by any of the British cities whose records we have examined. Nor was serious consideration given to using prisoners of war. Even when Birmingham was experiencing a massive backlog of collection in 1944 and early 1945, for instance, the idea of employing them was rejected almost peremptorily.[31] Thus, instead of seeking to make up shortfalls through very young or female or conscript labor, cities continued to rely on a substantial core element of aging but experienced workers who were too old to join the armed forces, many of whom continued to work well past the normal retirement age of sixty-five. They were, however, supplemented by a substantial though transitory and marginally efficient workforce who, following patterns not much different from those in peacetime, drifted into refuse collection and disposal work through necessity of employment rather than through choice. As a result, labor shortages were a persistent problem throughout the war, but never so severe that services were threatened with total collapse.

In Germany, too, alternative sources of labor were sought, and as in Britain, solutions adopted in the public cleansing service to deal with labor shortage conformed to more general patterns of the German war economy. Here, the wartime diary of the director of Frankfurt's cleansing department, Paul Schröder, is an instructive source. As early as 1939, the department had to struggle to find workers because so many had to join the Wehrmacht or were employed to build the Westwall. Moreover, the shortages increased over time, and from 1941 on numerous forced laborers and prisoners of war carried out the work of the department. Up until 1942, many Jews were also forced into the waste collection service before the Gestapo separated them from other workers and subsequently began to deport them to the east.[32] Consequently, at the end of the war, in nearly all city departments in Germany including cleansing, most staff members were old and/or disabled people, war prisoners, or forced laborers, all of whom were required to do very exhausting work.

---

[31] BCC/BP, *Labour Report*, March 1946.
[32] Kriegstagebuch Stadtreinigung Paul Schröder. StA Frankfurt, Tiefbauamt, 133.

There were in sum long-standing differences between the two countries in their responses to labor shortages brought about by war, but these differences became especially pronounced as the conflict approached its end, mainly because of the growing level of destruction of German cities through aerial bombardment. In Germany, therefore, frequency of collection sometimes suffered to such a degree that it was essentially abandoned, and as a result German cities faced far more serious public health problems than did British ones. In the aftermath of a massive air raid in June 1944, for example, the city of Mannheim had to stop service for several weeks, and as a result inhabitants started to dispose of the waste in ruins, backyards, and gardens. A local newspaper described the problems graphically (and scathingly):

The flies and mosquitoes are delighted with their wonderful breeding conditions. When the lid of the garbage can was raised, they flew out into the open air in thick swarms, much to the delight of those in the neighborhood.... Indeed, even this method [of disposing of household waste] was preferable to the more primitive one of "solving" the problem by leaving the detritus in the destruction caused by air raids on Mannheim. People dumped ashes onto the rubble, tossing withered bouquets, empty tin cans, cheese rinds, and herring tails tossed into the mixture. These are all idylls that might grace the alleys of a port city in the Far East, but they're not very popular in this country. Thank God there were no fish rations available during the past four weeks – except, of course, for the salted herring.[33]

The *Kreisleiter* (district leader) of the Mannheim National Socialist Party, in contrast, wrote a sternly worded letter of warning to the city's mayor indicating that suspension of waste collection had had an extremely bad "emotional and political" effect on the people.[34] The unsavory state of affairs lasted a month before service could be resumed.[35]

Air raids also caused direct damage to physical plants and equipment used in provision of cleansing services, just as they did more generally. Frankfurt's main depot, the Luisenhof, for example, was damaged by two direct hits in March 1944, which handicapped waste collection considerably. And in the case of Dortmund, bombing actually had an even more pronounced effect. The city, situated in the northeast of the Ruhr district, featured important armaments factories (e.g., Hoesch, Union Steelworks,

---

[33] *Mannheimer Bote*, "Ende der Orientidyllen in Mannheim," July 10, 1944, StA Mannheim, Hauptregistratur, Zugang 1955/1964, 1581.

[34] Letter from Kreisleiter NSDAP to Renninger (June 26, 1944). StA Mannheim, Hauptregistratur, Zugang 1955/1964, 1581.

[35] Bekanntmachung Müllabfuhr (July 7, 1944). StA Mannheim, Hauptregistratur, Zugang 1955/1964, 1581.

and others) and was also relatively close to Britain. As a result, Dortmund was struck by eight major Allied air offensives and eventually counted among the most heavily damaged of German towns.[36] In autumn 1944, in one of these raids, the cleansing department's main depot was struck by a direct hit, which led to the destruction of many vehicles and – even more importantly – of the recharging station for the city's electric collection vehicles. The postwar director of the city's cleansing department, Anton Kalt, reported that, in total, 70 percent of depots and 80 percent of vehicles in Dortmund were destroyed in the bombing raid.[37] The result was the emergence of widespread illegal dumping in makeshift and unofficial sites, which in turn led to the spread of rats, vermin, and disease.

In both countries, then, public cleansing was severely affected by the war. In the case of Germany, however, the latter stages of the conflict entailed not just a severe strain on the service but led in some cases to its total breakdown. Authorities in Britain and (even more so) in Germany thus faced enormous challenges in first resuming and then reconstructing and reforming waste collection and disposal systems in the aftermath of the war.

Resuming Service in the Immediate Postwar Period

While resumption of waste collection and disposal services posed significant difficulties for both Britain and Germany, the starting conditions differed so substantially between the two that it makes sense once again to consider their experiences separately.

Resuming Public Cleansing Service in Postwar Britain

No matter how well British municipal cleansing departments had coped under the stresses of war, their overall condition in the autumn of 1945 could hardly be viewed as healthy. Although the organizational structures remained essentially unchanged from what they had been in 1939, departments found themselves faced with smaller and weakened workforces, worn-out equipment, and chronic shortages of garbage cans. Serious as those problems were, however, many cleansing department managers saw this as an opportunity to build on past accomplishments and to

---

36 The degree of destruction in Dortmund's inner city was estimated at 97 percent.

37 Anton Kalt, "Haltet die Straßen sauber! Wiederaufbau der Stadtreinigung und des Fuhrparkes," in *Von der toten zur lebendigen Stadt: Fünf Jahre Wiederaufbau in Dortmund* (Dortmund: Mayer, 1951), pp. 235–237, especially p. 235.

rectify any shortcomings that had existed by changing philosophy and practice.

In September 1945, the practitioners' professional association, the Institute of Public Cleansing, called a conference to allow its most active members to discuss these issues. According to its president, J. C. Dawes, in the preceding twenty years "the quality and efficiency" of public cleansing had generally kept up not only with what the "man in the street" wanted, but also with the "economic requirements" of most municipalities. Dawes pointed out shortcomings that stemmed from inadequate legislation, highlighting that there was no legally mandated minimum standard of service. Councils could decide arbitrarily on whatever level of "civic sanitation" they thought fit. And, although some were progressive in their outlook, others took advantage of the legal laxity to "skimp" on refuse handling to save money because other services were considered more important. In some areas, the public had to tolerate "annoyance and nuisance" because of this stinginess, something that could be dealt with only by changes in law accompanied by "a measure of financial assistance" from central government. Dawes consequently wanted public cleansing to "be improved and developed on scientific lines," and he urged councils to adopt "better . . . and more economical" equipment to increase efficiency, although in 1945 there was almost certainly none to be had.[38]

These observations were echoed and extended by other speakers at the conference. It was recognized, for instance, that the state now had an increasingly "intimate" relationship with public services and furthermore that "paternalism in government" was going to continue whatever practitioners might think about it. One consequence of the war was namely that waste had come to be viewed by government as "harmful and antisocial," while the public was seen as having "ingrained habits of extravagance" that added to the generation of domestic refuse. What is more, government policy on reclaiming salvage from waste had the potential for substantial impacts on municipal waste handling and its economics. All in all, therefore, it was highly important for practitioners to be well informed on ministerial thinking.[39]

There were also calls for changes within the profession itself, not just for more technologically advanced and economically efficient plant and

---

[38] *Public Cleansing and Salvage* (October 1945) provides a summary of the proceedings of the conference; for quotations, see "Presidential Address," pp. 83–84.

[39] Ibid., "Opening Address," pp. 60, 62.

equipment but also for increased levels of professionalism. Glasgow's
director of cleansing, G. C. McArthur, for example, wanted better departmental accountancy with altogether higher standards of costing and
record keeping. He also wanted "more fully trained officers" to direct
the service better, along with the provision of training courses for "all
ranks" of workers. While the institute already ran correspondence courses
leading to a distinctive qualification, McArthur called for government-
sponsored classes to which local authorities "would be invited, if not
compelled" to send employees. He also wanted the state to take "a much
keener interest in public cleansing" but emphasized that both the profession and its local authorities had much to do on their own account,
warning that "obsolete conceptions of what had been good enough" had
to be abandoned, especially for the labor force. In the future, he argued, it
would be essential to provide workers with "decent conditions" to avoid
recruitment problems.[40]

The profession's mood at the end of the war, then, was a mixture of
idealism and pragmatism. The desire to provide a more efficient service
with enhanced status was tempered by recognition that progress would
be shaped by national and local political factors and, for the short term
at least, would be retarded by economic difficulties caused by the war.
Over the next fifteen years, in fact, idealism increasingly had to take a
back seat to the practicalities of restoring, maintaining, and developing a
refuse service.

Indeed, during the five years following the end of the war, problems
of reconstructing a war-damaged service in the face of continuing problems in obtaining equipment, plants, and labor dominated the attention
of practitioners. Britain's generally weak economic state was reflected
in the government's continued emphasis on maximizing exports while
simultaneously minimizing imports. And public cleansing operations were
naturally affected adversely by such policies, experiencing chronic shortages of vehicles and trash cans, along with delays in approving new
waste handling plant projects.[41] Continuing governmental demands for
refuse operations to be involved in salvage collection and waste processing

---

[40] Ibid., conference paper by G. C. McArthur, p. 72.
[41] The National Archives, Kew, London (subsequently TNA), HLG 51/808, Ministry of
Health [transferred to Ministry of Housing and Local Government], "Public Cleansing, Supply of Dustbins [trash cans] to Local Authorities, 1946–1948"; HLG 51/814,
Ministry of Housing and Local Government, "Supply of Public Cleansing Vehicles,
1947–1948." See also MLG, DTC 7/3/1 (5), City Cleansing Department, *Annual
Reports,* 1946–1947 to 1950–1951, for delays in plant projects.

projects only added to these problems because they diverted a persistently inadequate labor force into areas that many cleansing managers would have happily avoided.[42]

Another problem was that garbage cans (referred to as dustbins in Britain), were in short supply during the war, and difficulties continued for some time after it ended. Chronic shortages of sheet steel persisted, and local authorities complained regularly that it was difficult or even impossible to obtain containers in sufficient numbers.[43] Households with no trash cans kept waste in improvised containers that were frequently difficult to handle and slowed down the collection process, while damaged or corroded cans leaked their contents, causing further operational problems. Matters were made even worse by the Ministry of Supply's periodic insistence that only inferior grades of metal be used in the manufacture of trash cans. And at times, particularly in 1947, deliveries were significantly worse than during the war.[44]

The situation with vehicles was at least as bad. Steel shortages affected the vehicle manufacturing industry as well, but because refuse collection trucks were considerably more complex than cans, production lagged even further behind demand.[45] Although there were over twenty manufacturers of collection vehicles in Britain, many of them did no more than fit bodies to chassis and drive trains that they bought from other commercial vehicle makers.[46] Furthermore, the small number of firms that did make complete refuse-handling vehicles, such as the Dennis firm and Shelvoke & Drewry, manufactured other lines as well.[47] Vehicle manufacturers thus prioritized production where there was greatest

---

[42] See TNA, HLG 51/812, Ministry of Housing and Local Government, "Salvage Collection by Local Authorities, 1946–1949," and MLG DTC 7/3/1/ (5), *Annual Reports*, 1946 to 1951.

[43] See, for instance, TNA, HLG 51/808, Institute of Public Cleansing to Ministry of Health, January 19, 1948. Local authorities also lobbied the Board of Trade: see NAK HLG 51/808, Board of Trade memo to Minister of Health, October 26, 1945, on complaints already received.

[44] The best that could be said was that supplies in early 1948 were "more nearly meeting demand" than previously. See TNA, HLG 51/808, Board of Trade memo to Minister of Health, February 24, 1948.

[45] See TNA, HLG 51/814. An unsigned memo of February 17, 1948, referring to a draft cabinet paper notes that "We have not been very successful in getting statistics [on deliveries], but I am not sure it is entirely a bad thing: the fewer figures we have the fewer arguments there can be about them."

[46] Woods, *Municipal Refuse Collection Vehicles*, pp. 26ff, describes these relationships in some detail.

[47] Ibid., p. 43.

demand – such as trucks for general haulage – with the result that specialized vehicle body builders consistently found it difficult to obtain chassis,
engines, and/or transmission units.

   Shortages of equipment were exacerbated by the problem of maintaining an adequate workforce, particularly in view of the nature of the job.
Undoubtedly, few British males saw it as their life's ambition to be a "bin
man." The work was physically demanding, generally unpleasant, and to
add insult to injury, by no means well paid. It was widely regarded as
a job "fit only for the scrapings of the industrial man-power barrel."[48]
In times of substantial unemployment, it was of course relatively easy
to hire labor, but with the postwar British economy retaining much of
its wartime momentum, competition for labor was fierce, and retaining workers proved even harder than it was before the war.[49] Constant
high turnover led inevitably to endemic workforce inexperience, which,
combined with poor motivation, inhibited efficiency. The low status of
the work was particularly difficult to overcome: dustmen were perceived
as socially inferior, even among the working class. Added to this, local
authorities tended to place refuse services at the bottom of civic hierarch-
ies and priorities, in spite of the fact that cleansing operations featured
some of the highest budgets and employed some of the largest workforces
in municipal governments.[50]

Resuming Public Cleansing Service in Postwar (Western) Germany
After the war, cleansing departments in Germany tried to restart a
functioning cleansing service. The problems, however, were much more
severe than in Britain. After all, in Germany, scarcity of workers was
compounded by substantial rates of destruction to physical assets, including vehicles, depots, and, not least, garbage containers. In Mannheim,
for instance, of the approximately 27,000 garbage cans that formed the

---

[48] *Public Cleansing and Salvage* (October 1945), M. Marshall, Sunderland Cleansing
Department, p. 72.
[49] For instance, MLG, DTC 7/3/1 (5), *Annual Report* 1946, "Shortage of Fit Workers,"
p. 3; *Annual Report* 1949–1950, "Better Conditions Needed to Retain Workers," p. 3.
Also MCA, Cleansing Department *Annual Report* 1952, "Factors in Recruiting and
Retaining Workers."
[50] *Public Cleansing and Salvage* (November 1950), Bailie [councilor] Mrs. J. Craig, Glasgow City Council, "On Social Acceptability of Dustmen to the Working Classes and
on the Prioritization of Attendance at Committee," p. 362. On budgets and manpower:
in Glasgow, for instance, only the education and public health departments had larger
budgets in this period, while employment levels are documented in Cleansing Department Annual Reports for Birmingham, Glasgow, and Manchester.

city's normal complement before the war, just 3,000 emerged unscathed from the conflict, and 7,000 were completely destroyed.[51] In Frankfurt, Dortmund, and Augsburg, the situation was perhaps even worse. In Dortmund, the cleansing department claimed in 1946 that during the war more than 90 percent of the city's refuse containers had been destroyed.[52] For all German cities, then, the first task after the war was simply to resume service at the most basic level, although the complexity of this task varied among the different cities. In Mannheim and Frankfurt, waste collection resumed already in summer 1945. In Dortmund, on the other hand, employees of the cleansing department first had to clean up the extensive wreckage caused by the bombing of the main depot. In addition, staff members were involved in cleaning up and removing the omnipresent detritus of the heavily damaged city. Furthermore, vehicles and garbage cans had to be repaired, something generally carried out through cannibalization, essentially making one good piece of equipment out of three that were more or less damaged. It was therefore not until the end of 1945 that a rudimentary collection service could be started in Dortmund, and even then it operated at levels far below what had been common before Word War II.[53]

In the initial period after the end of the war, there was certainly no free play in the German system to allow space, time, or resources to begin to think about any reform of techniques and organization of waste collection. Instead, improvisation was the watchword as service was gradually restored. It was initially impossible, or at least extremely difficult, to purchase new trash cans and vehicles. The Schmidt & Melmer plant had been partly destroyed during the war, but the company suffered even more from shortages of raw materials and restrictions set by the allies.[54] In any case, public authorities had other more important priorities, at least as long as the removal of wreckage and detritus remained the first order of the day. Once that was done, reconstructing reasonably functioning infrastructure for water, sewage, electricity, gas, and public transport networks then constituted the highest priority. Consequently, replenishing the capital stock of the cleansing departments ranked well down the list of most pressing tasks for German cities for some time. And for those

---

[51] Questionnaire Müllabfuhr, n.d. (ca. end of 1945), StA Mannheim, Tiefbauamt, Zugang 54/1969, 145.

[52] StA Dortmund, Bestand 199, 8. Unterlagen Verwaltungsbericht 1945–1946.

[53] Stadtreinigungsamt, Berichtsjahr 1945–1946. StA Dortmund, Bestand 199, 8.

[54] Letter from Schmidt & Melmer to Städtisches Tiefbauamt Mannheim (December 8,1947). StA Mannheim Tiefbauamt, Zugang 3/1968, 953.

cities that used the Schmidt & Melmer system (such as Frankfurt and Mannheim), this situation proved particularly problematic because they had no access to spare parts for the specialized garbage cans used in the system. Moreover, they could not simply order these items somewhere else because of patent protection. To be sure, Schmidt & Melmer, anxious to protect both the company's market and intellectual property positions insofar as possible, made great efforts to assure city departments that it would be only a matter of time before its plant would be in a position to supply parts and other items once again.[55] Production returned to normal, however, only when the West German "economic miracle" began in earnest in the early 1950s.

Immediately after the end of the war, of course, public standards and expectations concerning waste collection were very low. For most people, there were much more pressing problems than illegal and unhygienic landfills and irregular waste collection services. Rubbish lying around had become simply a part of heavily damaged townscapes and so did not attract much attention or complaint. But it did not take long for these issues to move back up on the political agenda, appearing in the context of campaigns against vermin such as rats and other contamination responsible for the spread of disease. At the beginning of 1947, for example, public authorities in Mannheim urgently advised people not to dispose of their household waste by depositing it in the ruins of houses and civic buildings: "Otherwise you people pollute the air and thus endanger health. Rubbish in the rubble attracts vermin back again and provides nourishment to it, something against which such an expensive campaign is being waged at the moment. Use only garbage cans [for disposing of your waste]. These are emptied regularly by the cleansing department."[56]

Patchwork improvisation after 1945 in Germany also appears to have strengthened the conviction that rationalization and modernization of

---

[55] Ibid. In 1949, a lawsuit revolved around the question of whether the acquisition of spare parts and cans from another company was a violation of Schmidt & Melmer's rights. The court's decision was negative: "Gutachten erstattet im Auftrage des Verbandes Städtischer Fuhrparksbetriebe Frankfurt/M. über die Frage: 'Stellt die Verwendung von Müllgefäßen, die nicht von der Patentinhaberin bezogen wurden, für Mülleimerschüttvorrichtungen nach dem DRP 486 177 einen unzulässigen Eingriff in das dem Patentinhaber zustehende Auschließungsrecht dar?'" (July 4, 1949). StA Mannheim Tiefbauamt, Zugang 3/1968, 953.

[56] Städtischer Informationsdienst (January 17, 1947), "Keine Abfälle in die Trümmer!" StA Mannheim, Hauptregistratur (Zugang 1955/1964), 1581.

waste-handling systems were necessary. Once the most severe problems of the immediate postwar period were addressed, it soon became obvious that technical standards of waste collection lagged well behind the state of the art. Most collection vehicles were in extraordinarily bad shape. It also became clear to many that the improvised waste collection system devised in the immediate aftermath of the war was in fact relatively costly. Hastily patched vehicles were in constant need of repair not only because of the repairs themselves, which were often done quickly and poorly, but also because of their age. Their running costs were also correspondingly high, especially because they consumed large amounts of fuel.[57] Improved types of vehicles were slowly becoming available, principally from Daimler and Krupp, but most cities could not afford to buy them at first or had other budgetary priorities. Reconstruction of existing residential properties and construction of new houses and flats caused ever-growing shortages of garbage cans. And by the late 1940s, all of these factors contributed to increasing pressure for investment.

This pressure was intensified by a simultaneous increase in the amount of domestic waste, which had been extremely low immediately after 1945 compared to the prewar period. By the early 1950s, however, prewar levels of domestic waste were again reached. Still, the return to normality was quite manageable until the mid-1950s because it was accompanied by the recovery of funding for public cleansing services as economic constraints eased and deliveries of new garbage cans and vehicles steadily improved. It is significant that the growing waste stream at this point was not perceived as changing fundamentally, nor was it seen as the forerunner of a consumer society; rather, it was regarded as a process of recovery and normalization that accompanied the return of peace and some measure of prosperity.[58]

All in all, then, waste collection during the decade following the end of the war followed lines of prewar practice in West Germany. Those cities that had used the Schmidt & Melmer system continued with it. Even in the mid-1950s, for instance, the city of Mannheim still judged the "EsEm" (Schmidt & Melmer) system as the best standard of systematic

---

[57] "Vortrag des Magistrats an die Stadtverordnetenversammlung betr. Beschaffung von 10 Großraummüllwagen" (August 1, 1952). StA Frankfurt, Stadtkämmerei Nr. 356.

[58] For instance, "Denkschrift über die Einführung einer neuen Müllabfuhreinrichtung in der Stadt Dortmund" (1951), StA Dortmund, Bestand 170, 221.

waste collection available on the market.[59] In Dortmund, on the other
hand, the cleansing department did not even contemplate abandoning
their tried and true *Tonnenwechselsystem* in the immediate aftermath
of the war, despite the fact that this system, which required twice the
number of garbage cans as in other systems, caused constant headaches
and aggravated postwar difficulties.

Conclusion

The presumption by some Germans that a return to prewar levels of
household waste by the early 1950s was simply a return to normality
was soon to be proved wrong. In West Germany, but also to a lesser
extent in Britain, the 1950s were years of substantial economic growth
and increased household income that were accompanied by growing consumer spending, lower levels of unemployment, increased use of new
materials and packaging, and therefore much larger household waste
streams. Both countries experienced all of this. In West Germany, however, the more pronounced need for reconstruction, especially of housing
stock, the pace of its economic growth, and some of the traditions of
rationalization and industry-practitioner cooperation that had developed
already in the 1920s combined to create very different pressures on
the existing system than those in Britain, and these conditions led to
a heightened sense of urgency that changes had to be made.

   One of the key drivers in the changing waste stream in both countries was the emergence, beginning in the mid-1950s, of the self-service
store. Prepackaged goods were the norm in these new stores, and the
rise in packaging that had to be discarded or destroyed thus proceeded
apace.[60] In the past, such packaging – provided it was made of paper
or cardboard – might have been dealt with by burning it in a wood or
coal fire. But such fires were becoming less common, especially in cities.
New fuels such as heating oil and, later, natural gas were being adopted for new central heating systems, while smoke abatement legislation
such as the UK's Clean Air Act of 1956 tended to discourage reliance on

---

[59] Letter from Tiefbauamt to Stadtverwaltung III (September 13, 1949). StA Mannheim
Tiefbauamt, Zugang 3/1968, 953.
[60] Jens Scholten, "Umbruch des genossenschaftlichen Förderauftrages durch Innovation
und Wachstum: Nachkriegsentwicklung und Einführung der Selbstbedienung bei der
REWE Dortmund," in Jan Otmar Hesse et al. (ed.), *Das Unternehmen als gesellschaftliches Reformprojekt* (Essen: Klartext 2004), pp. 167–200. Andrea Westermann, *Plastik
und politische Kultur in Westdeutschland* (Zürich: Chronos 2007).

the more traditional fuels.[61] That act's geographic coverage was by no means complete to begin with. Instead, it was first phased into densely populated urban areas and was extended nationally only gradually, over a number of years. The transition to newer heating systems was faster in West Germany than in Britain because of the need to rebuild housing stock – or more frequently to construct it anew – and owing to the effects of Allied bombing. Despite any differences, the impact of the growing adoption of new home heating systems led to a major change in the waste stream in both countries. The share of ashes (previously about 30 percent of the total household waste stream) slowly fell, while the share of paper and packaging, food waste, and other waste items such as cans, worn-out products, and so on, increased markedly. Household waste, in short, became relatively lighter but at the same much more voluminous.

If, however, West Germany's waste stream changed more quickly during the 1950s compared to that of Britain owing to the faster pace of modernization of home heating systems, another factor was even more important in the urgency with which West Germans came to view the issue of how best to deal with the changing waste stream. By the mid-1950s, the West German "economic miracle" was in full flowering, and one of the effects was virtually full employment. German cleansing departments thus faced a massive shortage of labor, not least because of the generally negative image of refuse collectors, relatively poor payment, and the hard and dirty work that refuse handling involved.

This negative image applied broadly in Britain as well, but there the problem was not so much in recruiting as in retaining workers. While cities such as Glasgow and Manchester maintained nominally adequate manning levels, annual turnover rates could exceed 100 percent and inexperience was a constant source of inefficiency.[62] In Germany, the situation was made more acute in 1958, when, after a massive campaign by the trade unions (*"Samstags gehört Vati mir,"* or "Daddy belongs to me on Saturdays"), Saturday no longer counted as a regular working day for public-sector workers. In Britain at about the same time, trade unions also negotiated reductions in working hours for their members, but there the "reduced" hours were frequently simply converted into overtime work. The impact on service delivery in Britain was thus more on budgets than man-hours available.

---

[61] Great Britain Ministry of Housing and Local Government, *Clean Air Act 1956*, 4 and 5, Elizabeth II, ch. 52 (London, HMSO, 1956).

[62] Figures are from each city's cleansing department annual reports.

During the 1950s, then, the pressure to rationalize and reform waste collection and disposal systems was more pressing in Germany, but it was also being felt in Britain. We now turn to the process of rationalization and the ways in which it was developed and implemented differently in the two countries.

2

Rationalization Measures

Introduction

Resumption of public cleansing in both the United Kingdom and West Germany immediately after World War II occurred on the basis of prewar legislation, practices, and personnel. Nevertheless, as we have seen, there were considerable impulses for reform of the public cleansing systems in both countries. A number of factors gave rise to this desire for change to existing practice, including changing waste streams; growing affluence; the development of new materials such as plastics (which would not only cause problems for practitioners, but would also offer potential solutions to some of them); growing awareness of environmental issues such as air and water pollution; and constrictions on the labor market.

The reforms took a number of organizational and physical forms, which we consider here under the general rubric of "rationalization." Rationalization, of course, is a difficult concept. Like democracy, it is something that few would oppose in principle. In practice, however, it has many meanings and manifestations, not all of which might be desirable to a particular social group. "Rationalizing" the workplace through replacing workers with machines, for instance, is rarely going to be popular with trade unions.[1] We use the term nonetheless. Or more accurately, we use it precisely *because* we want to highlight the contested nature of

---

[1] See, for instance, J. Ronald Shearer, "Talking about Efficiency: Politics and the Industrial Rationalization Movement in the Weimar Republic," *Central European History* 28 (1995): 483–506.

the developments we describe in this chapter. People and their interests constructed the organizations and artifacts that "rationalized" public cleansing in the 1950s and beyond.

We begin therefore with a consideration of the central actors in the piece, the groups of people and organizations that shaped the delivery of public cleansing services. We then turn to the ways in which these actors interacted during the 1950s and 1960s in Germany and the United Kingdom to bring about change in various techniques and artifacts, interactions that we explore in a series of case studies of key artifacts and techniques. The first involves the evolution of the household receptacle used to store waste: the garbage can. We then investigate collection technologies, concentrating on vehicles. Finally, we analyze developments in relation to disposal, in particular the widespread adoption of sanitary landfill and in some cases incineration. The interaction among institutions and interest groups shaped the artifacts and organizations that began to emerge by the early 1960s in West Germany, but such interactions also help explain the more gradual changes experienced in Great Britain during the same period.

The Organizational Framework for Public Cleansing in the 1950s and Early 1960s

In many important ways, as the previous chapter indicates, there was little new in the organization of public cleansing in the UK and West Germany in the course of the decade and a half following the end of the war. In both cases, service was reconstructed along the lines that had existed before the war and on the basis of prewar legislation. The municipality or local authority remained the primary provider of the service in both countries. And the interest groups involved in the delivery, usage, and regulation of the public cleansing service in both countries also continued with few changes from the prewar to the postwar period.

Essentially, there were five distinct interest groups involved in shaping public cleansing services, and each of them played a different role in postwar reform in municipal waste handling. Two of them played essentially passive roles, although both theoretically had a considerable interest in the governance of domestic refuse collection and disposal. Two were much more active in shaping reforms directly. The final one played a more indirect role in waste collection and disposal practice, but a direct and essential one in the development of technologies.

The first set of actors worked for the state, whose role was traditionally a restricted one, featuring minimal direct involvement in public cleansing. The "state" in Britain was at the national level, whereas in Germany it involved the individual provincial (federal state) governments primarily rather than the national government (at least until 1972, when the West German federal parliament, the Bundestag, changed the Basic Law and decided that it should be responsible for waste legislation).[2] Up to 1951 in Britain, the Ministry of Health was the key state organization associated with public cleansing, an institutional reminder of the original anchoring of municipal waste-handling systems in public health and sanitation that had been established in the late nineteenth century. Oversight then passed to the newly created Ministry of Housing and Local Government, which became responsible for local government functions that were not specifically viewed as health related. Under the new structure, refuse handling was in fact seen more as a service benefiting individual households than as ensuring the health of the community as a whole. In practice, however, neither ministry was intimately involved with the provision of services. The British state's role was thus largely confined to the issue of guidance on good practice in areas such as the location of disposal sites and collation of some statistical material relating to the costs of refuse collection and disposal across local authorities. The state's relationship to public cleansing, then, was essentially passive: as long as refuse services created neither threat to public health nor any political nuisance, there was no need for intervention. Normally, the ministries' presence was scarcely noticed in municipalities. This was also the case in Germany, although it is necessary to differentiate here clearly between waste collection and disposal: collection was the sole responsibility of municipalities, but problems with disposal that arose by the late 1950s forced the state authorities to intervene and organize ways to deal with these issues.[3]

The second major interest group was the general public – in effect, the customers of the service – those who both created the need for it and, consequently, also paid for it. In Britain, this payment was indirect, which had the effect of concealing actual costs and thus lessening

---

[2] Gottfried Hösel, *Unser Abfall aller Zeiten: Eine Kulturgeschichte der Städtereinigung,* 2nd expanded ed. (Munich: Kommunalschriften-Verlag J. Jehle, 1990), p. 196.

[3] It remained, however, very often unclear which ministry was actually responsible. E.g., Vermerk (Klosterkemper) betr. Bearbeitung von Müllfragen (June 21, 1961), LA Düsseldorf NW 354,1096.

the extent to which public cleansing became an overt political issue.[4] In Germany, in contrast, things were different because citizens paid a fee for waste disposal directly to the city, making the costs of waste collection a more overtly political question, although it must be stressed that these costs were relatively low compared to the general taxes people had to pay. For both countries, because members of the general public lacked any direct representation in the bureaucracy of municipal authorities, the pressures that people could bring to bear on reform of refuse handling were limited to deployment of one of two levers: direct representations to elected councilors or the bureaucracy through personal visits and/or letters sent through the mail; or public complaint through newspapers or other media. Whichever method was adopted, the dissatisfactions generally fell into one of four categories. Failure to have garbage cans emptied on time was the first of them. Shortage of space in waste containers was the second, while illegal disposal of waste in household garbage cans represented the third. Finally, problems caused by disposal sites constituted the fourth. Such objections – which amounted to indirect calls for reform through improved organization and practice – often had a galvanizing effect on those with political responsibility for the service, particularly when they were accompanied by newspaper publicity. With some exceptions, however, the general public represented a large and important – although generally unnoticed – interest group within the public cleansing system whose presence was felt only when problems arose.

The third interest group played a much more active and thus a much more prominent role: the local politicians who reacted to complaints from the general public. In Britain, these people were elected councilors who formed the management committees for the various city council departments, including public cleansing. In principle, this was also true in Germany, but in practice, most directors of cleansing departments held their jobs for a very long time and "survived" elections and changes of local governments owing to the fact that they were engineers and thus viewed as apolitical. Councilors were indirectly responsible to relevant government ministries and more directly to their local electorate for performance of services that were, after all, funded principally by local

---

[4] The costs were part of the annual "rate demand" sent to each householder, which gave no detailed breakdown of how the money payable was apportioned. Each local authority did make available full details of individual departments' budgets, but these were normally only available for inspection at municipal offices.

taxation. In the case of public cleansing, however, direct contact with government agencies was relatively rare, but the local electorate was an ever-present element that could not be disregarded even if the general public only rarely exercised its power. The desire to avoid public outcries about shortcomings in waste collection services frequently led municipal public cleansing committees to take a close interest in the micromanagement of refuse services.[5] This was sometimes because citizens wrote letters of complaint directly to the mayor rather than to the cleansing departments. Consequently, rationalization for local politicians often consisted of fairly generalized calls for greater efficiency in collection, such as for a more trouble-free and low-cost collection service. And these demands were inevitably made against a background of budget constraints and other competing demands on municipal funds.

The fourth interest group, those who used these funds and actually provided the service directly, were the practitioners themselves, and they clearly dominate the story of the evolution of municipal waste handling. The distinction between this group and the politicians was less pronounced in Germany than in Britain, for reasons that we have seen already. In both countries, however, the practitioners identified problems with existing practice and suggested solutions, which involved negotiation with elected officials on resources for investment, and their role in rationalization processes was thus pivotal. Practitioners alone among the interest groups considered here viewed themselves as having common interests, a view that expressed itself concretely through formal organizations in both countries. As mentioned in Chapter 1, public cleansing officers in Britain developed scientific knowledge and provided training on refuse management and best practice through their professional body, the Institute for Public Cleansing (IPC), which acted as a nationwide discussion forum for practitioners.[6] In the case of Germany, the Verband kommunaler Fuhrparkbetriebe (Association of Municipal Public Cleansing Departments, or VKF) was also extremely important in spreading the latest information about techniques and standards of waste collection among its membership.

---

[5] For instance, see Birmingham City Archives, "Records of the Salvage and Stables Committee," Collection reference BCC/CP (subsequently BCA BCC), April 13, 1949, "Report on Councillor's Enquiry about Use of Hired Haulage Contractors," and BCA BCC, January 14, 1953, "Report on Soliciting of Christmas Gratuities by Refuse Collectors."

[6] For background, see Lewis Herbert, *The History of the Institute of Wastes Management 1898–1998: Celebrating 100 Years of Progress* (Northampton: IWM Business Services Ltd, 1998).

Both organizations were consequently essential conduits through which notions of rationalization were debated and articulated in the context of formal meetings, conferences, and publications. For this reason, they also formed a mechanism through which rationalization measures could be transferred from person to person and place to place. Their effectiveness, however, varied between the two countries because of the differing constitutional structures of the IPC and the VKF. The IPC was composed of a membership of individual practitioners who, although they of course very often worked for city authorities, were members by virtue of their individual professional interests and not as official representatives of their city. This was in direct contrast to the VKF, whose members were official representatives of their municipalities. The ideas and techniques developed within the VKF were thus much more likely to have a direct impact on practice within cities than those developed within the IPC. Additionally, the effectiveness of the VKF was further enhanced by the fact that its director for more than thirty years, Hans Baumann, was at the same time head of the city of Frankfurt's cleansing department, which was generally recognized as one of the most innovative units in Germany, continually searching for further improvements in the collection and disposal of household waste.[7]

Another difference between the VKF and the IPC was that the German professional organization had much more sustained contact with the fifth and final interest group in the waste handling system – the providers of goods and services to the authorities. These suppliers were of course not directly involved in the provision, regulation, or "consumption" of waste collection and disposal services, but their role was crucial in enabling practitioners to realize their desires for rationalization. In particular, German manufacturers of garbage cans and of collection vehicles had far more frequent interaction with the VKF than was the case with the relationship between the IPC and British manufacturers. This was perhaps also a function of the officially sanctioned membership of the VKF in contrast to the IPC, which meant that members of the VKF were far more likely to have direct influence over the adoption and procurement of new equipment and technology within the service.

Finally, one other factor lending additional urgency to rationalization measures in Germany compared to Britain lay in the fact that practitioners and politicians in German cities in the postwar period felt compelled, on

---

[7] Stadtreinigungsamt Frankfurt (ed.), *100 Jahre Stadtreinigung in Frankfurt am Main 1872–1972* (Frankfurt: City of Frankfurt, 1972), pp. 20ff.

account of growing affluence and political pressure, to extend public cleansing services from the central core of the city, the traditional focus of such service, to all households within the city limits. British cities, on the other hand, had long featured nearly universal public cleansing services.

Regardless of these differences, however, the interactions of this mixture of relatively passive, relatively active, and peripheral (but at the same time crucial) players resulted in both countries in a dynamic and contested definition and redefinition of best practice within the prevailing "waste regime" through time.[8] The process can perhaps best be explored through consideration of deliberations about and attempted implementation of rationalization measures in relation to specific waste-handling artifacts and practices in the two countries. We begin with the lowly garbage can.

Containing Waste: The Evolution of the Garbage Can

Although produced in both Britain and Germany by a variety of manufacturers who made them in differing sizes, domestic garbage cans through the mid-twentieth century were generally designed with a number of considerations in mind.[9] First, they had to be light enough to be handled manually, even if they were sometimes part of a collection system called "dustless loading" (this involved linking the trash can directly to the collection vehicle using a mechanical device for lifting the container and emptying its contents, something that was still in its infancy in mid-twentieth century Britain but was more developed in Germany). Second, the trash cans had to be cheap enough to be provided to as many households as possible. Additionally, and perhaps most importantly, they were designed to contain disease and odor associated with household waste in as large a volume as possible until such time as it could be collected. And finally, they were also designed to minimize, insofar as possible, the

---

[8] For the concept of contested waste regimes, see Zsuzsa Gille, *From the Cult of Waste to the Trash Heap of History: The Politics of Waste in Socialist and Postsocialist Hungary* (Bloomington: Indiana University Press, 2007). See also Zsusza Gille, "Actor Networks, Modes of Production, and Waste Regimes: Reassembling the Macro-Social," *Environment and Planning A* 42 (2010): 1049–1064.

[9] This section summarizes our research and findings on this subject, which are available in greater detail in Roman Köster, Stephen Sambrook, and Ray Stokes, "Containing Garbage: The Design and Deployment of Household Waste Bins in Britain and West Germany, 1945–1975," unpublished manuscript.

TABLE 2.1. *Design Parameters for Household Waste Containers*

Design Parameter	Key Considerations
Size	– Length of collection cycle – Average household "production" of waste within that period – Need to preclude bulky or trade waste
Weight	– Number of persons available to lift into collection vehicle – Lifting by mechanical means
Durability	– Cycle of replacement – In shelter or not – Likely extent of harsh treatment
Shape	– Generally round or rectangular – Smooth or fluted
Fit with collection vehicle	– Central consideration in case of "dustless loading" – Standardization becomes essential
Fit with other aspects of urban environment	– Houses or flats as prevailing form of accommodation – Width of streets – Existence of lanes/alleyways for access
Safety	– Contains health risks of putrefying food – Safe from vermin – Noise associated with process of emptying – Fireproof
Cost per unit	– Complexity of manufacturing process – Expense of construction material(s) – Extent of standardization of design

danger of fire from hot ashes at a time when coal and sometimes wood fires were the main methods of domestic heating. These and other general design parameters are outlined in Table 2.1.

From the late nineteenth century until after the Second World War, optimizing these design parameters led virtually without exception to the choice of a single kind of material: steel alloy (usually, steel and zinc). Almost all garbage cans were cylindrical in shape and, owing to generally manual collection, were manufactured within a fairly narrow band – but not uniform or standard – in terms of size and weight, although British waste containers tended to be lighter and less long lasting on average than their German counterparts. The material from which the containers were made – steel alloy – and the way they were handled – manually and labor intensively – thus epitomized essential characteristics of the modern industrial world that had emerged by the first half of the twentieth century. And this was also true of a large proportion of their contents. When garbage cans were filled and ready for collection, the largest single item by weight was the remains of consumption of another classic industrial product, coal, which was the most typical means of heating in urban Britain and Germany at the time. Cinders and ash from coal fires varied according to season and type of house, but in winter a typical British trash can's contents averaged around 65 percent of its total weight in cinder and ash.[10]

The period between the end of the Second World War and the 1960s, however, provided a number of incentives and opportunities to change the archetypal steel garbage can. New materials, especially modern thermoplastics, offered the possibility of designing lighter trash cans that were also quieter to empty. They could also remain lighter while at the same time being somewhat larger than the usual steel trash can, which was important in accommodating the growth in volume (but not weight) of garbage in postwar Britain and Germany. Although plastic trash containers were not fireproof, this became a less important design consideration with increased adoption of gas- or oil-fired central heating systems and the consequent decline in cinder and ash as major components of the waste stream. Equally important here was the increased conviction among practitioners that dustless loading would be cleaner, more efficient, and less labor-intensive than conventional collection methods, and it in turn dictated more standardized designs and close integration of the design of the garbage can with that of the vehicle's mechanical lifting and emptying apparatus.

These pressures, incentives, and opportunities to change the design of the conventional steel garbage can existed in both countries during the quarter century following the end of the war. By the end of that period, however, the overwhelming majority of household waste containers in Britain remained cylindrical in shape, steel in construction, and nonstandard in weight and size. During the same time in Germany, on the other hand, garbage cans for households gradually became rectangular in shape, plastic in construction, and highly standardized in weight and size,

---

[10] In Manchester, the summer proportion of "fine dust" and clinker could be as low as 25 percent, but in winter it was typically 65 percent or more. Figures are from Manchester City Archives, Records of Manchester City Council (subsequently MCA), Cleansing Department, M595/2/2/61, Annual Report 1950–1951, tables detailing analysis of refuse from different classes of property. In Glasgow, the proportion of fine dust and clinker in households could exceed 70 percent. Mitchell Library Glasgow, Records of the City of Glasgow (subsequently MLG), Cleansing Department, DTC 7/3/1 (5), Annual Report 1946–1947, analysis of refuse collected.

a process that was completed by the early 1980s. So, what accounts for this wildly different response to virtually identical drivers for change? In the following sections, we examine the gradual evolution of practice and artifacts in each country and then move on to suggest some explanations for growing divergence between the two.

Britain's Household Waste Container: Continuity of Practice

Although public cleansing services in Britain's cities operated throughout the war and into the postwar period with little disruption, many household waste containers were worn out or damaged during the conflict because normal replacement cycles could not be maintained. Into the 1950s, then, the dominant preoccupation of practitioners was with acquiring new containers, something made particularly difficult by continued shortages of key materials in the postwar period, in part due to the continuation of wartime controls over their allocation and use. As late as 1951, for instance, an editorial in *Public Cleansing and Salvage*, the leading industry practitioner journal, complained about a government order banning production and sale of galvanized steel bins owing to "the shortage of spelter [zinc]."[11]

Such shortages of materials prompted some moves to rethink the design of household waste containers. As early as 1945, there were discussions about possibly using plastic as a substitute for steel, but the consensus then was that this would have to await the development of appropriate synthetic materials by the chemical industry.[12] In fact, the benefits of plastic as a suitable material for manufacture of waste bins continued to be debated into the 1960s.[13] Compared to the still controversial possibility of plastic bin construction, development of a new British standard for the traditional steel garbage can construction in 1947 (BS 792/1947) had perhaps far greater potential for bringing about change, although the "standard" had quite a few shortcomings. First, it specified not one but two types of "galvanised mild steel bins with plain sides," one with a capacity of 2.5 cubic feet and weighing 23 pounds (approximately 71 liters and 10.5 kilos), and the other with a capacity of 3.25 cubic feet and weighing 28 pounds (about 92 liters and 12.7 kilos).[14] (See Figure 2.1.)

---

[11] Anon. editorial article, *Public Cleansing and Salvage* (July 1951), p. 567.
[12] *Public Cleansing and Salvage*, "Public Cleansing and Public Relations" (September 1945), p. 30.
[13] UK Ministry of Housing and Local Government, Working Party on Refuse Storage and Collection, *Report 1967* (London, 1967), p. 18.
[14] Ibid.

FIGURE 2.1. Typical UK 2.5-cubic feet capacity metal domestic refuse cans, Manchester, ca. 1959. These were manually lifted and carried to a nearby collection vehicle, using the two handles, one of which is visible in the picture. Photograph courtesy of Manchester City Council.

Second, the motivation behind the standard was not rationalization but the shorter-term issue of economy in use of materials. Third and perhaps most importantly, the standard was not binding, and manufacturers continued to make containers in a broad range of types.

There was yet another factor at work in the postwar period that, all other things being equal, might have provided an impetus for fundamental changes in garbage can design as well. As problems of materials shortages dissipated in the course of the 1950s and levels of affluence rose, the waste stream began to change, tending toward being both lighter and more voluminous. Government legislation, in particular the 1956 Clean Air Act, played a key role in this process.[15] The act was intended progressively to reduce emissions from smoke-producing fuels, especially coal.

[15] Great Britain Parliament, *Clean Air Act 1956*, 4 & 5 Elizabeth II, Ch. 52. (London, HMSO, 1956. This covered England and Wales; parallel legislation provided for Scotland.

By simultaneously encouraging adoption of gas and oil as alternatives, in particular for central heating, the act had the dual effect of decreasing the amount of cinders and ash and increasing the amount of paper and other products in the waste stream, because the latter could no longer be burned in open fires.

This and other developments meant that there were clear incentives to think about changing existing practices, and this was indeed seriously considered by the Working Party on Refuse Storage and Collection in the mid-1960s. The Working Party heard complaints that steel garbage cans were nonhygienic and otherwise deficient, whereas plastic containers had certain clear advantages. It nevertheless recommended that steel containers, many of which were produced using the British industrial standard developed in 1947 as amended in 1965, should remain the most common type. This conservatism in design and practice in spite of changes in the waste stream and despite the shortcomings of the steel garbage can arose from two key criteria identified by the Working Party. First of all, there was the issue of longevity: "Experience has shown that they [traditional steel garbage cans] give long service." The other criterion identified by the Working Party was perhaps even more important. The main requirement of any container, members contended, was that "it should not give rise to nuisance while awaiting collection." Steel containers, of course, had a proven track record for containing "nuisance" in the form of decomposing waste food, which was still believed to be a serious threat to public health, while simultaneously holding back obnoxious smells. Furthermore, they also reduced the danger from accidental fires caused by hot ashes or the actions of those householders who would "deliberately fire the contents" of their garbage cans to purge them of putrefying matter.[16] Thus, plastic was, through the mid-1960s at least, manifestly not yet an option for the British. The situation in Germany, on the other hand, was quite different.

Germany's Household Waste Container: The Emergent Artifact

As mentioned in the previous chapter, during the Second World War, garbage cans in considerable numbers were damaged or destroyed in the fighting, in particular through air raids. Consequently, immediately after the war, cleansing departments had to repair them, partly because it was initially very complicated to get new ones owing to the scarcity of sheet metal and other materials, but also owing to restrictions set

---

[16] Working Party, *Report 1967*, p. 18.

by the Allies.[17] Then, when the situation started to relax in the early 1950s, most cities strived to revive their old systems of waste collection. Those cities that used the patented Schmidt & Melmer dustless loading system described in Chapter 1 (for instance, Mannheim and Frankfurt) went back to using it.[18] Dortmund, on the other hand, initially refused to abandon its *Tonnenwechselsystem* in the immediate aftermath of the war, even though there were constant problems with transfer of waste from the exchange station to the dump, as well as with regular shortages of garbage containers. These persistent difficulties did, however, led eventually to the ultimate abandonment of the system in the mid-1950s.[19]

Over time, the waste stream in West Germany grew extremely rapidly as the "economic miracle" brought about substantial increases in standard of living and widespread adoption of oil-fired central heating systems. There was also a push to extend public cleansing services to more households in cities, moving for the first time beyond the innermost core. These factors, combined with increasing scarcity of labor, naturally brought about discussions in cleansing departments regarding potential changes to the organization of waste collection and possible improvements in container design. And it became clear that traditional sheet-metal garbage cans designed for individual household or apartment building use posed a particular obstacle to effective rationalization of service.

The life expectancy of a traditional German household waste container was much longer than that of its British counterpart, with German garbage cans regularly having ten – but sometimes up to twenty – years of service. This very durability, however, also carried with it the distinct disadvantage of much higher weight. An empty German 110-liter sheet-metal garbage can weighed about 35 kilos (77 pounds), and a full one up to 85 kilos (187 pounds), far heavier than the British standard of 1947, which called for smaller containers of about 10.5 kilos (23 pounds) and larger ones around 12.8 kilos (28 pounds) when they were empty.

---

[17] Stadtreinigungsamt StA 94, Berichtsjahr 1945/46, StA Dortmund, Bestand 190, 8; Anton Kalt, "Haltet die Straßen sauber! Wiederaufbau der Stadtreinigung und des Fuhrparkes," in *Von der toten zur lebendigen Stadt: Fünf Jahre Wiederaufbau in Dortmund* (Dortmund: Dortmund City, 1951), pp. 235–237.

[18] Hösel, *Unser Abfall aller Zeiten*, p. 169.

[19] Stadt Dortmund, *Es herrscht Ordnung und Reinlichkeit auf den Straßen: Aus 400 Jahren Geschichte der Stadtreinigung und Abfallentsorgung in Dortmund* (Dortmund: Dortmund City, 2001), pp. 58–59; Vermerk Umstellung der Müllabfuhr, April 14, 1953, StA Dortmund, Bestand 170, 73.

Lifting and carrying the German containers from backyards and cellars thus made for extremely exhausting work for the garbage men.

Consequently, German public authorities were on the lookout for different solutions, one of which seemed to lie in the installation of large containers in areas outside the city center that would contain the waste of many households and be emptied mechanically. The city of Frankfurt's cleansing department, for instance, sounded an optimistic note when officials announced the "successful" introduction of containers in 1957 with a capacity of 4 cubic meters or more.[20] The containers did not solve the city's waste storage problem, however, for several reasons. Not only were many householders reluctant to share a container with other people instead of having their own individual garbage cans; large containers also had a way of rapidly attracting commercial and bulky waste. To make matters worse, they were sometimes set on fire, as well as fast becoming a focus for disorderly behavior by teenagers.[21] The drawbacks of the large containers for household waste thus ensured that their use quickly came to be limited to large institutions such as hospitals, where access was restricted.

Around 1960, however, the city of Wiesbaden developed a more promising solution: the MGB 1.1 (MGB stands for *Müllgroßraumbehälter*, or large capacity garbage container). The city collaborated with manufacturers to devise a metal dumpster with a hinged lid and lockable wheels. Combining ease of movement with safety, these early "wheelie bins" had a capacity of 1.1 cubic meters (almost 40 cubic feet) of waste.[22] The MGB 1.1 became a DIN (*Deutsche Industrie-Norm*) standard for larger containers. (See Figure 2.2.) Rapid adoption in many cities came about in part because it was promoted by the VKF, but more importantly perhaps because design of the MGB 1.1 neatly met typical needs for waste storage and collection in urban apartment developments. In other words, it was big enough to hold a week's refuse from a group of dwellings, yet small enough to deter dumping of bulky wastes. And at the same time it was robust, yet easily handled by a transfer vehicle with only a two-man crew. Large volumes of household waste could thus be stored safely and

---

[20] Letter from Stadtreinigungsamt Frankfurt to the Personalamt (November 1, 1961), StA Frankfurt, Magistrat 1898.

[21] "Große Pleite mit Sperrmüllbehältern," *Rhein-Neckar-Zeitung* (May 12, 1966); letter from Tiefbauamt to Referat VII (May 17, 1966); both in StA Mannheim, Hauptregistratur, Zugang 42/1975, 1084.

[22] *Mitteilungen des Verbandes kommunaler Fuhrparks- und Stadtreinigungsbetriebe* 2/1964, StA Dortmund, Bestand 170, 217.

FIGURE 2.2. An early example of a German 1.1-cubic meter metal Müllgroßraumbehälter (large capacity garbage container). Known as the MBG 1.1, it was intended for use at apartment blocks. This advertisement shows the dedicated collection vehicle associated with the MGB 1.1 and emphasizes that one of the new dumpsters replaced ten of the previous 110-liter type. Photograph courtesy of the Sammlung aus Städtereinigung und Entsorgungswirtschaft (SASE), Iserlohn.

collected cost effectively, the two most important considerations for both practitioners and politicians.

Besides widespread adoption of larger containers, there were also moves to address the issue of weight for the traditional steel 110-liter containers through experiments with new synthetic plastic materials. The Germans appear to have been behind the British in considering this: it was not until 1958 (rather than 1945) that German practitioners brought up the idea that in the future, plastic would be the preferred construction material for garbage cans.[23] As in Britain, however, there were a number of problems to be solved before this would be possible. It required the development of stable and heat-resistant plastics that would meet the normal operating requirements of a garbage can, together with plastics producers and manufacturers of the containers. Many German practitioners, like their British counterparts, also had doubts for some time that plastic would ever achieve the traditional sheet-metal container's durability and ability to withstand hot ashes.[24]

Nonetheless, the advantages of plastic were obvious: production costs were much lower, the containers were much lighter, and handling them was much quieter.[25] Use of plastic garbage containers was therefore piloted in the city of Freiburg starting in 1964.[26] Again, the experience was broadly discussed within the VKF, and although adoption of plastic garbage containers was slower than adoption of large, standardized metal ones, Freiburg's experiment soon came to be imitated more widely throughout West German cities.

Consequently, key innovations in design were made in Germany around 1960 involving the emergence of a dominant standard size and shape that would eventually be constructed of plastic for the most part. But German cities could not introduce new types of garbage cans in one fell swoop, mainly because of budgetary restrictions on annual spending for new ones. The pattern of adoption indicated in Chart 2.1 for Mannheim can indeed be taken as typical. In Mannheim, as in other German cities, it would be the 1970s before these innovations became widely diffused, with the traditional 110-liter container in particular rapidly and

[23] For instance, Walter Kaupert, "Moderne Städtereinigung, eine Ingenieursaufgabe," *Der Städtetag* (October 1958), pp. 487–489.

[24] Mitteilungen des Verbandes, StA Dortmund, Bestand 170, 217.

[25] Otto Tope, "Stand der Lärmbekämpfung in Stadtreinigung und Fuhrpark," *Der Städtetag* (March 1960), pp. 145–149, 146.

[26] "Freiburgs Mülleimer machen Schule," *Rhein-Neckar-Zeitung* (August 15, 1969), seen in StA Mannheim, Bauverwaltungsamt, Zugang 52/1979, 940.

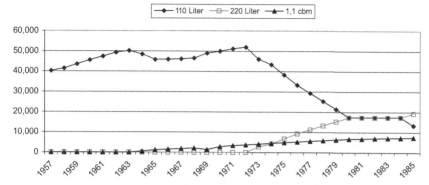

CHART 2.1. Mannheim's mix of household waste containers by capacity, 1958–1985. *Source:* based on statistics reported in Karl Pulver, *Von der Abfuhranstalt zum Eigentrieb: 125 Jahre Stadthygiene in Mannheim* (Mannheim: City of Mannheim, 2005), p. 118. Note that these figures are for the absolute numbers of containers of each type and are not normed for capacity.

largely replaced beginning in the early 1970s by 220/240-liter and MGB 1.1 containers. (See Figures 2.3 and 2.4.)

The introduction of garbage cans made of new materials also significantly affected the garbage can manufacturing business. In the early

FIGURE 2.3. The plastic 240-liter wheelie bin, which by 2012 had become the normal domestic refuse container for most local authorities in the UK. It was supplied in different colors for waste segregation in connection with recycling schemes. It is based on an original design for 220-liter bins from Germany in the 1960s. Photograph courtesy of Craemer UK Ltd.

FIGURE 2.4. A German-designed and manufactured Kliko™ wheelie bin in use in Scotland, 2013. Authors' photograph.

1960s, the formerly dominant Schmidt & Melmer Company went out of business, although it is unclear whether this was because they ran out of money or because they shied away from making the high investments necessary to meet changes in the market. The most important new entrants into this field were the SULO Company (Herford/Westphalia) and the OTTO Company (Kreuztal/Sauerland). Both companies were initially established to produce sheet-metal garbage cans, but they took advantage of the opportunities offered by the wholesale replacement of household waste containers in German cities in the late 1960s and early 1970s to move into plastic and standardized waste container manufacture. In particular, they cooperated closely with the VKF and later also with private waste handling companies. They thus established themselves as major players in this field. In addition, beginning in the 1970s, the two companies established a very successful export business, mainly in the Americas but also in the United Kingdom.

Accounting for Different Approaches to Containing Garbage

What accounts for the emergence of such profound divergence in garbage can design between the United Kingdom and West Germany during the decades after the end of the Second World War? One obvious answer would be to resort to cultural explanations based on vague notions of Teutonic efficiency versus Anglo-Saxon muddling through. The explanation, however, is far more concrete and also more complex than such stereotypes would suggest, although the design solutions preferred in each case were indeed firmly embedded in the two countries' respective economic, social, and political systems.

As noted already, both countries starting in the 1950s experienced greater affluence, higher standards of living, and widespread adoption of oil-fired (and later gas-fired) central heating systems, which led in turn to ever-increasing volumes of household waste for urban public cleansing practitioners to deal with. The rate of increase was far greater in Germany, however, which started out the postwar period far poorer than Britain per capita but by the late 1960s had become richer on average.[27] Also, because German city dwellers by and large lived in rented apartments rather than in the owner-occupied individual houses more typical in Britain, especially England, German urbanites tended to have more disposable income on average than their British counterparts, which resulted in a massive increase over a short time in household waste production. As mentioned already, too, the strain on German public cleansing was also exacerbated by simultaneous extension of service to an increasing proportion of urban households, and this translated in turn into a pressing need for new containers and – perhaps not surprisingly given the scale of demand – new ways of designing and deploying them.

[27] By 1969, Germany's per capita GDP exceeded that of Britain and remained higher until 1998, when British per capita GDP once again overtook Germany's. See figures in Matthew Shane, "Real Historical Gross Domestic Product (GDP) Per Capita and Growth Rates of GDP Per Capita for Baseline Countries/Regions, 1969–2010 (in real 2005 US$ per capita)," September 22, 2010, available at http://www.ers.usda.gov/Data/Macroeconomics/ (accessed October 20, 2010).

Part of the explanation for divergence, then, lies in increased affluence connected to the West German "economic miracle," which is conventionally dated as lasting until 1966.[28] But there was another effect of this extraordinary growth: unemployment in Germany became practically nonexistent by the early 1960s and remained that way well into the 1970s.[29] Consequently, finding people to work in the generally undesirable area of waste collection and disposal proved increasingly difficult, leading to a willingness among practitioners to consider more radical solutions to all aspects of the system, including improved waste containers. In contrast, Britain, which also enjoyed relatively low rates of unemployment on the whole during this period, had proportionately higher rates of employment in the larger cities. The problem in the United Kingdom was not recruiting workers but getting them to stay in this generally unpleasant, poorly paid, and physically demanding job. High turnover, in short, continued to be the main problem for British public cleansing departments, not absolute labor shortage.[30] This in turn translated into less pressure for change in practice.

Four other factors also appear to be especially important in explaining the increasing divergence between the two countries over time in the area of waste container design and deployment. First, the ideal of the "rational" city seems to have been more prevalent in Germany than in Britain in the postwar period, largely because German city planners keen on such notions were in a particularly advantageous position to implement them in the aftermath of the war, not least because of the unfortunate condition of many German cities when the fighting had ended. In contrast, British cities were far less damaged, and rational city planning had less scope for realization. Indeed, for some of these German planners, the garbage can played an explicit role in the emergent cityscape in reconstructed cities. Otto Tope, the head of the city of Hannover's cleansing department, for instance, complained in 1953 that the trash can was

---

[28] Herbert Giersch and others, *The Fading Miracle: Four Decades of Market Economy in Germany* (Cambridge: Cambridge University Press, 1992); Tim Schanetzky, *Die große Ernüchterung: Wirtschaftspolitik, Expertise und Gesellschaft in der Bundesrepublik 1966 bis 1982* (Berlin: Akademie-Verlag, 2007).

[29] Werner Abelshauser, *Deutsche Wirtschaftsgeschichte seit 1945* (Munich: Beck, 2004), p. 301.

[30] For a Glasgow example, see MLG, DTC 7/3/1 (5), Annual Report, 1968–1969. 3,017 workers had left during the year, or 102 percent of the department's establishment. Absenteeism averaged 12.5 percent. See also, for Manchester, MCA, M595/2/2/78, Annual Report 1967–1968, where 52 percent of those leaving had been employed for less than three months.

"an orphan of West German urban design." Waste containers, their design, and their location, he argued, needed to play a bigger role for planners.[31] This argument was taken increasingly on board by West German waste handling professionals over time.

A second additional factor lay in the respective constitutions of professional organizations in the two countries. The British IPC, remember, differed from the German VKF in that the former was composed of individual practitioners, while members of the latter were official representatives of their public cleansing departments. The VKF was therefore far more likely to exert direct influence over decision making than the IPC, whose members discussed issues along similar lines to their German counterparts but were far less effective in realizing change.

Third, there were differences in the structure of the garbage can manufacturing industry in each country, although it is difficult to discern whether this was an effect or a cause of the emergent design divergence. Britain, on the one hand, featured at least a dozen different manufacturers of sheet-metal garbage cans, all of whom produced them to different specifications and designs and none of whom specialized in production of waste containers. Germany, on the other hand, featured a much smaller number of manufacturers, with one or two dominant. As noted earlier, Schmidt & Melmer had a major presence from the mid-1920s until 1961 with the company's patented system of dustless loading, which required specific types of garbage cans. OTTO and SULO followed after Schmidt & Melmer went out of business, pioneering in the design and standardization of plastic wheelie bins. In all of these cases, there was heavy specialization and concentration on supply to the cleansing industry in particular. Close working relationships between the companies on the one hand and the VKF and cities on the other constituted both cause and effect of this specialization and concentration, and growing sales – not just within Germany but also abroad – were the result.

The final factor that must be mentioned may also have been more effect than cause: earlier and much more widespread adoption of dustless loading in Germany than in Britain required greater standardization of design of waste containers so that they would couple seamlessly with the waste collection vehicle. Standardization of design then promoted economies of scale for manufacturers and necessitated close cooperation among many of the key interest groups in the waste-handling system. It is not

---

[31] Otto Tope, *Die Mülltonne: Eine Stiefkind der westdeutschen Städtegestaltung* (Frankfurt: Schön & Wetzel, 1953).

surprising, therefore, that Germany's waste containers over time became
very different from those in Britain; nor is it unexpected that the development of vehicles and lifting apparatus would also diverge. Another aspect
of the development of collection vehicles that was common to both countries was compression/compaction technology, indicating clearly that
there were some shared notions of public cleansing as primarily a logistical operation. For this reason, we now turn from the garbage can to the
next link in the waste-handling chain: machinery and vehicles.

Mechanization and Automation

Collection of household waste by public cleansing departments, usually
on a weekly basis, had long been carried out in both Britain and Germany
using trucks powered by internal combustion engines (although there
were also often battery-powered electric vehicles in use in both places),
and this continued in the post–World War II period. But just as had been
the case with waste containers, there were divergences in development.
Collection vehicle fleets in German cities were far more drastically reduced
by the war – through bombing, heavy use, and loss when they were
commandeered by the Wehrmacht – than were British ones. Combined
with extension of cleansing services to more households as the 1950s
went on, there was therefore much greater pressure there than in the
United Kingdom to purchase new vehicles. The city of Dortmund, for
instance, estimated in the mid-1950s that the number of garbage cans
needed to supply its households was rising by about four thousand per
year, necessitating corresponding increases in vehicles to service them.[32]
Other German cities were in a similar situation.

As was the case with garbage cans, German cleansing departments had
only a handful of manufacturers to turn to for supply of vehicles. Krupp,
MAN, and Daimler-Benz were, of course, not specialist waste collection
vehicle manufacturers, but they worked with cleansing departments, the
VKF, and producers of garbage cans and lift systems to supply suitable
vehicles. By way of contrast, in Britain, there were at least six companies
providing chassis units and twice as many supplying complete vehicles to
public cleansing departments. There was also a degree of specialization
within the latter group, with some providing simpler and smaller units,
some larger and more complex types, but few if any making the whole

---

[32] Feststellung StA 70 (12.11.1956). Betr.: Beschaffung von Müllwagen im Haushaltsjahr
1957. StA Dortmund, Bestand 170, 83.

range of patterns. Nor was there any unifying industry body of refuse vehicle contractors. Competition and isolation rather than cooperation and interaction were thus the norm in Britain, with little sign of integrated research and development effort or of generalized collaboration with the practitioners' own professional body, although there were some cases where individual manufacturers had a more or less strong rapport with a particular city and its practitioners.

One reason for this differing industrial structure may have lain in the earlier and much more widespread adoption in Germany of dustless loading systems. Such systems, of course, required a high level of standardization of garbage cans so that they could be integrated into the system, which in turn necessitated cooperation among public cleansing professionals and manufacturers. In Britain, on the other hand, despite some interest in dustless loading even in the late 1920s, the adoption of such systems was only done experimentally on a small scale, often using continental European systems.[33] Although there were attempts to promote continental – mostly German – systems even before 1930 and again after the war,[34] the only major city to adopt dustless loading through the 1960s was Birmingham. There the director of cleansing had done a survey and report on European practice in 1957 and managed to persuade the city council of the potential benefits of such a scheme.[35] But even in Birmingham, adoption of dustless loading occurred only slowly. Beginning in 1959, the system was to be phased in over the next decade to spread out costs and to allow for adjustments as learning took place. Elsewhere in Britain, the high levels of investment needed to implement such a system, combined with a sense that traditional methods were by and large working, served to hinder widespread adoption until later in the twentieth century.

British professionals were, however, more successful in the design, development, and implementation of another set of technologies that involved modification of traditional collection vehicles: compaction. It was an enthusiasm that their German counterparts shared, not least

[33] Barrie C. Woods, *Municipal Refuse Collection Vehicles* (Appleby-in-Westmoreland, Cumbria: Trans-Pennine Publishing, 1999), p. 18. Sheffield City Council experimented in the early 1930s with the Dennis-Eagle dustless loader, "whose ideas were, if anything, a little too ambitious."

[34] For example, the "Shefflex" system using a typical contemporary garbage can with a special vehicle incorporating a cable-operated lift platform. See advertisement in *Public Cleansing and Salvage* (October 1950), p. 521.

[35] *Public Cleansing and Salvage* (March 1967), p. 131.

FIGURE 2.5. Manhandling a washing machine into a refuse compression vehicle, Germany, 1970s. Such vehicles were able to crush similar rigid, bulky household items. Photograph courtesy of the Sammlung aus Städtereinigung und Entsorgungswirtschaft (SASE), Iserlohn.

because they, too, were facing growing volumes of waste coupled with physical limits on the size of collection vehicles owing to the width of streets and alleyways. Several varieties of mechanisms for compacting refuse in the collection vehicle during the collection route were developed by specialist refuse collection vehicle manufacturers, including moving partitions and floors, hydraulic ram and screw types, and rotation of the entire storage section.[36] In Germany, however, there was again more specialization and cooperation. Daimler-Benz and KUKA, for instance, agreed already in the 1920s not to act as competitors on the market for waste vehicles but instead to cooperate. By the 1950s, KUKA was providing powerful compression systems for the loading space on Daimler-Benz vehicles that could easily crush a refrigerator or other household appliances. (See Figure 2.5.) Furthermore, the new vehicles were explosion-proof, not a small consideration given that methane-gas buildup during

---

[36] Woods, *Municipal Refuse Collection Vehicles*, p. 19. For examples of various types, see *Public Cleansing and Salvage* (October 1968), p. 539, "Refuse Collection Vehicles."

collection had killed a garbage man in Mannheim in 1956 and pushed the issue to the top of the agenda in West Germany.[37]

Systematic development and relatively rapid implementation and diffusion of new technologies were thus not unusual in Germany during the 1950s and 1960s, as we have seen. But compaction was a rare example of this happening in Britain because compaction collection vehicles comprised one of the few areas of rationalization that could be "sold" to the elected city councilors who paid the bills. Practitioners were able to show convincingly that the additional expense of these more complex vehicles was balanced by reductions in operating costs by virtue of longer collection rounds and reduced transit time to unloading sites, with the additional benefit that public cleansing departments could easily be shown to be more efficient to the public – that is, the clients who actually paid for the service.

The development and widespread diffusion of compaction technologies in the 1950s and 1960s that occurred in both countries points to another key point about the way waste professionals in both places viewed their job and the way it should be done. Faced with rising volumes of household waste during the 1950s and 1960s, professionals did not really consider how to slow or reverse this trend but instead focused on how to adapt systems to cope with these increases. Essentially, they regarded their task as a specialized form of logistics, taking away whatever trash households cast off as quickly and efficiently as possible. Where they took it is the issue we explore next, because this too was an area of rationalization, technological development, and design.

Thinking About Disposal: Landfill Limits and Incineration

From time immemorial, there have been only four ways to get rid of household waste: use it again for something else; bury it; burn it; or simply dump it on the ground. The first of these options is something we consider at length in the next chapter, which examines salvage. The last one was not very commonplace in the period we are considering, although there are still instances of "fly tipping," or illicit dumping, especially in Britain, even now. Here, the focus is on the two major ways in which

---

[37] Daimler-Benz AG: "Description of the New Waste Collection Vehicle" (1952), StA Frankfurt Stadtkämmerei, 358. On the death of the garbage man in Mannheim in 1956 as a result of an explosion, see Letter from Oberbaudirektor Mann to Mayor of the city of Mannheim (October 1, 1948), StA Mannheim Hauptregistratur, Zugang 1955/1964, 1581.

practitioners responded to an ever-increasing and fast-changing waste
stream during the two decades or so after the Second World War: burial
and incineration.

Landfill and Its Limits

The landfill – also known as a tip, garbage dump, or midden – is probably
the oldest form of organized waste disposal devised by human beings.
Not only is it an easy solution, it is also relatively cheap, which is why
it was the overwhelmingly preferred form of disposal for cities in Britain
and Germany through the 1950s, although practice in the operation of
landfills changed dramatically over time.

In its earliest and simplest form in Britain as well as in Germany,
landfill involved "crude tipping," in which the entire contents of waste
containers were taken to the site and left to natural processes of decay.[38]
Although a relatively low-cost operation, it was only feasible where suitable ground was available and frequently created what we would now call
"environmental problems," such as scattering of material by the wind,
offensive odors owing to decomposition, and the concomitant attraction
of scavenging wildlife, vermin, and insects. And these in turn naturally
brought complaints from those who had the misfortune to live nearby.[39]
Cleansing departments, for the most part, quite understandably preferred
tipping sites to be as close as possible to their collection routes, which
meant that dumps tended to be located near dwellings on the outskirts
of urban areas, not only in pits but also in some cases on flat or even
elevated ground.[40]

Dissatisfaction with the side effects of crude tipping, however, had
become widespread among public cleansing professionals in Britain even
before the the First World War. The principle of "controlled tipping"
was thus introduced in some large cities even prior to 1914, although,
as Timothy Cooper points out, widespread adoption of the practice took
place only over the course of a number of years as practitioners convinced
themselves and others that it was a sanitary and scientifically "proven"

---

[38] J. C. Dawes, "Presidential Address," *Public Cleansing and Salvage* (October 1945),
p. 84.
[39] Ibid., Letter from Gemeinderat Neuried to Verwaltung der Hausunratsabfuhr der Stadt
München (July 7, 1950), StA Munich, Bürgermeister und Rat, 2781.
[40] For instance, see illustration sections in Manchester's Annual Reports 1954–1955, MCA,
M595 2/2/65, and also 1957–1958, MCA, M595 2/2/78, showing proximity of tips to
dwellings.

process.[41] In Germany, too, by the 1950s and 1960s, widespread consensus emerged among practitioners about the efficacy of sanitary landfill as a viable solution. Indeed, it was a solution that they had learned from the British, but with some of the German applications and adaptations of the concept singled out in an international meeting of waste practitioners in 1969 as indicative of "what can be achieved by taking the broad view, by creating a large-scale organisation and by the use of technical expertise."[42]

Controlled tipping, also known as sanitary landfill, involved refuse being put down in shallow layers and then covered with earth, which was compacted before being again covered with more waste. The process was then repeated until eventually the site was filled. The prevailing conviction was that a process of "slow fermentation" would then take place, which would lead to decomposition but at the same time prevent foul odors and eliminate scavengers and the breeding of flies.[43] Originally, British professionals hailed it as a significantly healthier and more socially acceptable method of disposal. During the 1930s, indeed, the country's Ministry of Health was sufficiently convinced of this argument to recommend the practice strongly to local authorities in its *Suggested Tipping Precautions*, although it had no powers to make it compulsory.[44]

By 1939, controlled tipping was already commonplace, accounting for the largest proportion of the local authority domestic waste disposals reported to the Ministry of Health. Of the approximate total of ten million tons involved, controlled tipping accounted for 60 percent and crude tipping only 6 percent.[45] Incineration dealt with 31 percent of the disposal, while an assortment of other methods accounted for the remaining 3 percent. Public cleansing professionals could therefore present controlled landfill as a satisfactory alternative to mechanical methods

[41] J. C. Dawes, "A Timely Warning about Controlled Tipping," *Public Cleansing and Salvage* (October 1950), p. 519. Dawes argued that controlled tipping had "been held back for several years by the First World War." See also Timothy Cooper, "Burying the 'Refuse Revolution': The Rise of Controlled Tipping in Britain, 1920–1960," *Environment and Planning A* 42 (2010): 1033–1048.

[42] See R. E. Bevan, "Controlled Tipping of Solid Urban Refuse and Suitable Industrial Waste," *Aquatic Sciences: Research across Boundaries* 31 (1969): 378–379 (quotation from p. 378).

[43] J. C. Dawes, "A Timely Warning," p. 519.

[44] Ibid., p. 520.

[45] Ibid., p. 519. His figures were drawn from the 1937–1938 "Ministry of Health Annual Cleansing Cost Return," p. 517.

of separation and incineration, both of which required not only considerable capital investment in plant but also trained workforces to run them.[46] Additional costs of controlled versus crude tipping, furthermore, were relatively low, and even these could be offset by the greater amount of waste that could be put down in a given volume of tip space. Nevertheless, a key point to bear in mind here is that controlled landfill was never universally employed by British cities, partly because there was never any legal requirement for them to do so. But even so, it remained the most widely used means of disposal. In fact, by the late 1960s, 71 percent of Britain's domestic waste was going into sanitary landfill, plus 28 percent by "semi-controlled methods,"[47] despite the fact that it was never required by statute throughout this period. In Germany, on the other hand, it was legally mandated by the 1960s.

Although controlled landfill became the dominant means of disposal in Britain, there was growing criticism of it, even as early as the late 1940s. Individual as well as heavily organized group complaints about landfills were fairly commonplace, especially from those living nearby.[48] (See Figure 2.6.) Still, the prevailing conviction among senior practitioners in both countries was that sanitary landfill, even if it could provide "only a part of the overall solution," was nonetheless a highly satisfactory one in many ways. One of the key benefits lay in "reclamation or improvement of land," something that was not just the case in the United Kingdom but also in Germany.[49] And cities with exhausted mines and quarries within their city limits, such as Glasgow and Dortmund, considered themselves especially fortunate in this regard.

Manchester's director of public cleansing, A. E. Bevan, indicated to an international conference of practitioners in 1969 that perhaps, given projections about the growth in wastepaper streams, salvage should be seriously considered as a key alternative. He also ruminated at length, however, about the ways in which the changing and growing waste stream might make controlled tipping *more* rather than less viable. He made the point that, although "lighter, bulkier refuse takes up more tip space ... in

---

[46] For a summary of the evolution of controlled tipping in Britain, see Cooper, "Burying the 'Refuse Revolution.'"

[47] Department of the Environment, *Refuse Disposal: Report of the Working Party on Refuse Disposal* (London, HMSO, 1971), p. 8. The report does not identify the difference between the two methods.

[48] See, for instance, Cooper, "Burying the 'Refuse Revolution,'" pp. 1043–1046.

[49] Bevan, "Controlled Tipping...Opening Paper," p. 365, and Bevan, "Controlled Tipping...Conclusions," pp. 376, 378 (quotations from pp. 376 and 365).

FIGURE 2.6. "Controlled tipping" at Tweedle Hill, Manchester, 1955. The original caption for this official picture in an annual report emphasized how controlled tipping could be carried on in close proximity to houses "without causing offence." Photograph courtesy of Manchester City Council.

the short term, it does not seem reasonable to conclude that this factor is likely to add to the problem of finding tipping space." He went on,

It has been assumed that the present tendencies to[ward] low-density refuse will be that tipping space will be used up more quickly, and that the answer will be to treat the refuse in some way by pulverizing, composting or burning to reduce volume. This assumption ignores the natural phenomenon of decomposition – the reduction of complicated substances to simple elements and the reduction in volume achieved. The increase in vegetable and putrescible content to 40 per cent or so of the total refuse, now a fact in refuse from houses without open fires, and the increase in paper content for similar reasons, means that 80 per cent or so of the refuse will be in a form which will decompose to gases, water and humus ... reach[ing] a final irreducible residue at the moment of inertia of about 10 per cent of the original weight. It would seem therefore that by the time refuse with high organic content has become inert the reduction will be much greater than with present-day refuse from houses with open fires having an ash and cinder content of 50–60 percent.[50]

---

[50] Bevan, "Controlled Tipping ... Conclusions," p. 377; long quotation from Bevan, "Controlled Tipping ... Opening Paper," p. 368.

Bevan's comments did not take into account the impact on water tables of placing new forms of plastic, electronic, and other sometimes toxic household waste into landfills. This effect was, however, largely unknown and unsuspected at the time, although some suspicions were noted in Germany already in the early to mid-1960s.[51] It would not be until the 1970s that this scientific knowledge began to accumulate and to change prevailing thinking and practice, something we will come back to in Chapter 5 in particular. In the 1950s and 1960s, however, and in spite of Bevan's optimism about future space requirements, the most pressing issue in relation to landfills was that they were filling up quickly owing to the increasing volume of garbage collected by city cleansing departments.

In Britain, even during the late the 1940s, it was already becoming clear that suitable sites were a finite and diminishing resource, causing many progressive practitioners to voice concerns about the long-term dangers of running out of space to bury their cities' waste. To counter this, cleansing superintendents in larger authorities engaged in cooperative programs with their city surveyors and planning officers to identify and secure future sites, at times going so far as to earmark the ultimate use for the reclaimed land.[52] Glasgow, for instance, avoided the worst concerns over tipping space until the mid-1950s, largely because it separated and incinerated all its waste. But Glasgow also benefited from the fact that the city's parks department used most of the waste residues left after separation and incineration to recover ground by filling holes with them.[53] However, the weakness of the city's waste disposal practices was demonstrated when a catastrophic fire at the main incineration plant in mid-1955 meant that unburned waste had to be tipped into an "emergency site" close to a housing scheme, an unsatisfactory situation that lasted almost a year.[54] The long-delayed completion and commissioning of a new incineration plant in 1959, along with the acquisition of a very large quarry site on the northeastern outskirts of the city, eventually eased matters, and incineration substantially reduced the volume of refuse going into the

---

[51] Letter from Klosterkemper (MELF) to Innenminister des Landes NRW (February 1962), LA Düsseldorf, Bestand NW 354, 1096; Vermerk Köster, "Bearbeitung einer Planungskarte für die Lagerung von Abfallstoffen (Müll. u.a.) im Hinblick auf den Schutz des Grundwassers" (December 13, 1965), LA Düsseldorf, Bestand NW 354, 586.
[52] MLG, DTC 7/3/1 (5), Annual Report 1946–1947, p. 4.
[53] MLG, DTC 7/3/1 (5), Annual Report 1953–1954, p. 7.
[54] MLG, DTC 7/3/1 (5), Annual Report 1955–1956, p. 10.

city's own dumps throughout the 1960s, while the dumps themselves remained conveniently close for refuse vehicles.[55]

In Manchester, there was a somewhat different set of problems. Already by the end of the 1940s, the city faced difficulties owing to the short life and uncertain conditions prevailing in at least some of its tipping sites. Because it was unknown just how much capacity was actually available and how long it would take to exhaust it, practitioners decided to carry out a detailed survey so as to be in a position to estimate the sites' life expectancy.[56] On the basis of the report, a program of land acquisition was then started that kept pace with requirements until 1957, when subsidence at the city's largest disposal site threatened to flood "a large part of the [site's] potential volume."[57] The ensuing reexamination of the city's long-term disposal strategy did not change anything, however, and more sites were acquired for both immediate and future use. In 1960, for instance, a redundant sewage works was rented, and plans were also made to excavate peat from municipally owned farmland on the city's outskirts to provide still more capacity. Both sites were sufficiently isolated to avoid complaints but near enough to allow short transit times from city depots.[58]

Despite Manchester's continued and active program to enhance its tipping spaces, by 1966, it was accepted that it was "inevitable" that at some point there would be no further room within the city boundaries and that therefore "alternative methods [of waste disposal] must be faced sooner or later."[59] For the moment, the status quo prevailed, although further sites outside council ownership were identified and targeted, and by 1968, six of these were earmarked to be bought, if need be by "compulsory purchase orders" – an indication of their importance to the immediate future of the controlled tipping program.[60]

[55] MLG, DTC 7/3/1 (5), Annual Report 1966–1967, p. 10. A new quarry site with a life expectancy of ten years had just been acquired. An additional incineration plant was also to be built.
[56] MCA, M595/2/2/61, Annual Report 1950–1951, p. 4.
[57] MCA, M595/2/2/67 Annual Report 1956–1957, p. 3. The site at Clayton Vale was adjacent to the River Medlock whose course was to be diverted by building a culvert to prevent the likelihood of flooding, which would make the ground useless for tipping. Mining subsidence meant that a new culvert would itself be under threat, posing an unacceptable risk.
[58] MCA, M595/2/2/70, Annual Report 1959–1960, p. 4.
[59] MCA, M595/2/2/76, Annual Report 1965–1966, p. 4.
[60] MCA, M595/2/2 78, Annual Report 1967–1968, p. 4.

In Germany, shortage of landfill also became acute in some cities by the 1950s and 1960s. Augsburg, for instance, possessed no central landfill and had to deal with a constant shortage of dump space. It had a number of small tips, but most of these had to be shut down when capacity was exceeded in the early 1960s. The immediate solution to the problem – something of a Band-Aid, to be sure – was to rent landfill space outside the city limits in the small village of Gersthofen. But this proved to be quite a problematic solution, not only because it cost considerable amounts of money but also because it led to ongoing conflicts with villagers.[61]

Frankfurt also had problems with landfill space. The city set up a central landfill in the municipal forest in 1925 called "Monte Scherbelino" ("Mountain of Shards" in the vernacular, owing to the broken glass prevalent there), and this eventually became its official designation. But during the late 1950s, as the landfill reached its capacity limit, the city's cleansing department had to consider alternative solutions. Frankfurt's confined cityscape made the designation of new spaces for tips within city limits impossible, and the prospects for establishing new landfills outside city limits were also bleak owing to likely opposition. Finding a workable solution, furthermore, was made more urgent because Monte Scherbelino constantly caught on fire, polluting the city's air; even the fire-extinguishing facilities installed by the city at the dump during the 1950s offered no satisfactory solution. The dump, which had begun its existence in the 1920s as a hole in the ground and reached the limit of its capacity in the 1950s, nevertheless continued to be used, growing dramatically into a mountain by the mid-1960s. It eventually had to be closed in 1968.[62] But four years earlier, the city had already built an incineration plant that pioneered in waste-to-energy processes.

By the late 1960s, then, many cities in the United Kingdom and West Germany were in the throes of a crisis as landfill capacity was exhausted, while finding new sites became increasingly difficult. In Britain, the challenge was to locate sites suitably near the city center so as to minimize transportation times and costs. This prompted practitioners to embrace a number of short-term, emergency solutions such as going beyond capacity limits for existing landfills by building them up into hills or contracting outlying areas to provide landfill for city waste. There were also flirtations

[61] For instance, "Stellungnahme Stadtreinigungs- und Fuhramt Betr.: Beschwerde der Marktgemeinde Vershofen" (August 7, 1963), StA Augsburg, Bestand 49/1473.
[62] Stadt Frankfurt, *100 Jahre Stadtreinigung in Frankfurt*, p. 20.

with the private sector in some cases. Immediately after the war in 1945, for instance, Birmingham contracted a haulage company to take part of its refuse to that firm's own disused quarry to conserve the city's limited landfill capacity.[63] This practice in fact continued into the late 1960s, although it became less and less significant.[64] In German cities, on the other hand, nothing like this happened just yet, mainly because local authorities were rather hostile toward private firms, which they perceived as not very reliable. Waste collection and disposal were considered to be municipal tasks. In any case, in both countries one solution to the problem came to be seen as having the potential for long-term sustainability: burning trash.

Incineration

There are at least four potential drawbacks to trash incineration. First, it can be extremely expensive owing to high capital costs and costs of operation, and this is one reason why wags over the years have sometimes termed it "cash incineration." Second, incineration can also pose – at least, potentially – public health hazards. Awareness of the dangers of smoke resulted in smoke-abatement legislation in Britain and Germany already in the 1950s. Awareness of the invisible and potentially even more dangerous effects of burning came only later, in part because changes in the waste stream (and therefore of the "fuel" for incinerators) made this a more pressing problem, but this danger was of course there from the outset. Third, no matter how hot the burning process is, it will not consume everything, and hence there will always be something left over for disposal through landfill. And finally, an incinerator – a more or less technologically sophisticated technical system with high capital costs – requires, like most capital-intensive goods, a high utilization rate to make it pay, which in turn means that there must be a guaranteed stream of trash to burn.

Nevertheless, the idea of permanently eradicating waste by burning it proved attractive to some. Use of furnaces known as "destructors" to burn refuse began in the late nineteenth century in Britain.[65] In Germany,

---

[63] BCA, BCC Salvage Sub Committee, Special Report April 13, 1949, summarizing the established practice of contracting out transportation and eventual disposal. Use of hauliers had first started some thirty years previously.

[64] BCA, BCC Salvage Sub Committee, Annual estimates of the Salvage and Stables Committee and the Salvage Committee in committee papers indicate that less and less money was being allocated to pay for private haulage through 1968.

[65] Herbert, *History of the Institute of Wastes Management*, pp. 23 and 24.

FIGURE 2.7. Polmadie refuse disposal works, Glasgow. Originally planned in the early 1950s, the final design was for a separation-and-incineration plant that, unlike the earlier works at Govan, had no provision for electricity generation. Construction was delayed by site problems and financial stringency, and the plant's construction was only completed at the very end of 1958. It was fully operational by the beginning of the 1960s. Photograph courtesy of Glasgow City Council, © Glasgow City Council 1968.

Hamburg pioneered with an incinerator as early as 1894, and a second followed in 1912.[66] Cologne built one in the 1920s, although it was something of a disaster. The "business case" for it involved selling the residue of the incineration process as a construction material, but this did not work out. The plant was eventually shut down in 1939.[67]

British cities in general developed and adopted incineration technology far earlier than German ones, for three main reasons. (See Figures 2.7 and 2.8.) First, relatively greater population density in the British Isles compared to Germany meant that space was at a premium earlier. Second, the relative wealth of Britain meant that waste disposal using landfill became more problematic earlier. Finally, there was something else connected to this greater British wealth that is also perhaps less obvious at

---

[66] Hildegard Frilling and Olaf Mischer, *Pütt un Pann'n: Geschichte der Hamburger Hausmüllbeseitigung* (Hamburg: City of Hamburg, 1994), pp. 73ff.

[67] AWB, Köln (ed.), *111 Jahre Abfallwirtschaft in Köln* (Cologne: City of Cologne, 2001), pp. 55ff.

FIGURE 2.8. Exhortation to recycle, 1950 style. One of Manchester's electrically powered collection vehicles in 1951 encourages people to burn more of their house refuse in order minimize the amount of waste the city had to handle, thus reducing "rates" or local taxes. Photograph courtesy of Manchester City Council.

first glance. Britain's pioneering role in industrialization and economic growth had many explanations, but one of them had to do with its relatively large market, unimpeded by internal tariffs and with the vast majority of the population accessible first by water transport and then by rail. Not surprisingly, this resulted in greater uniformity in consumption patterns and, indeed, of goods consumed, which in turn led to more standardized waste streams throughout the country, making it more reliably flammable.

In contrast, through much of the 1950s in West Germany, regional "waste profiles" still persisted: Bavarian rubbish, for instance, was substantially different from what the people in Westphalia threw away. By the 1960s, however, these differences were disappearing, and from the 1980s on it would have been nearly impossible to determine on the basis of the contents of any given waste container alone where the waste had come from.[68] All in all, then, the waste stream's homogenization eventually made incineration in Germany much more predictable. And, combined

---

[68] "Selbst Abfall ist Geschichtsquelle: Schweizer Experte für Müllbeseitigung am Rhein," *Rheinische Post* (October 23, 1959), seen in LA Düsseldorf, Bestand NW 354, 1099.

with the common experience of severe strains on landfill capacity, this led eventually to more widespread adoption of incineration in Germany as a viable alternative.

In Britain, on the other hand, throughout the postwar period and into the 1960s, many practitioners continued to see "separation and incineration" as the most satisfactory way to dispose of refuse, although there were some undeniable problems associated with them. On the plus side, several aspects of incineration commended themselves to practitioners. First and most important was the large degree of volume reduction that took place, thus decreasing the costs of transportation and tip space. There was the additional advantage of elimination of putrescent material through incineration, which was otherwise a perennial cause of problems at tipping sites. And finally, there was the production of useful and (sometimes) saleable by-products. Heat generated by furnaces could be used to create steam, which was then utilized either to heat nearby premises or to generate electricity.[69] The latter was then either sold on to local power companies prior to the nationalization of electricity supply or used on-site to charge the storage batteries that powered the electrically propelled collection vehicles favored by some of the largest cities.[70] Besides allowing monetization of the heat generated in the process, the ash and clinker furnace residues from it could also be marketed for deployment in construction work.[71] Although income from all of this was relatively small within overall cleansing budgets, practitioners highlighted it in their reports to local authority supervisory committees, no doubt owing to its symbolic role in defraying overall costs.

Incineration, however, declined in popularity in Britain toward the end of the 1960s, encouraged by a variety of factors that were not always directly related. High capital costs were disadvantageous in a period when economic stringency was commonplace, as were the higher running expenses owing to changes in the waste stream. Previously, refuse (aside, of course, from ash and most clinker) had been easy to ignite and virtually self-sustaining in its combustion. It became increasingly difficult to light, as well as harder to keep burning without the addition of other fuel. Perhaps more important than this was the emerging political consensus that the entire structure of local government was due for radical

---

[69] Both of these were done at Birmingham: see Harold J. Black, *History of the City of Birmingham*, vol. 6, Part II (Birmingham: Corporation of the City of Birmingham, 1957).

[70] Glasgow in particular favored electric vehicles. See MLG DTC 7/3/1 (5), Annual Reports 1946–1947 and later.

[71] See MLG, DTC 7/3/1 (5), Annual Reports 1946–1947 to 1955–1956.

overhaul, including a major revision of how responsibility for collection and disposal of household waste should be divided.[72] In this combination of circumstances, local authorities understandably became unwilling to commit to long-term investment in a technology that was beginning to seem less than economically viable.

In Germany, on the other hand, for reasons already mentioned, developments proceeded more slowly at first. Into the mid-1950s, German waste had a reputation for simply not burning, at least not uniformly. In 1958, however, a modern incineration plant was established in Düsseldorf with the primary task of testing waste from various cities to see how well it would burn.[73] Soon other cities were utilizing the knowledge generated from this experiment as they adopted incineration technology. Not surprisingly, it was the cities that had the greatest difficulties with finding adequate landfill space that pioneered in moving toward incineration as an alternative. This was especially the case in the densely populated and highly industrialized Ruhr district, which already in the late 1950s had enormous problems with shortages of landfill capacity. Under the auspices of the Ruhrsiedlungsverband (Ruhr Settlement Association) in 1959, the Arbeitskreis Müll (Working Group on Refuse) was founded, the predecessor of the highly influential Zentralstelle Abfallwirtschaft, (Central Office for the Waste Industry), created in 1965.[74] Cities on the Rhine and Ruhr thus pioneered incineration after the Second World War, with the notable exception of Dortmund, which had plentiful landfill capacity located away from the main population. Dortmund in fact did not start moving toward incineration as a solution until the 1980s. In contrast, Düsseldorf, as already mentioned, and also Essen and Frankfurt, built incineration plants in the early 1960s. And cities such as Augsburg, Munich, Stuttgart, and many others followed later in the decade.

Conclusion

During the first two decades or so after the end of the Second World War, both Britain and Germany faced dramatic changes in both the volume and

---

[72] For refuse managers, deliberations about this had started in 1967 when the central government commissioned a working party to consider the methods and "the practical aspects of refuse disposal generally." Working Party, *Report 1967*, p. 1.

[73] "Die Schweiz-Fahrt des Mülls: Düsseldorfer studieren moderne Müllverbrennungs-anlage," *Rheinische Post* (March 3, 1959), seen in LA Düsseldorf, Bestand NW 354, 1099.

[74] "Vermerk über die mündliche Unterrichtung über die Einrichtung einer Zentralstelle für Müllbeseitigung" (March 1964), LA Düsseldorf, Bestand NW 354, 586.

the composition of their household waste streams. Practitioners resp-onded in a variety of ways, sometimes preserving existing practice and artifacts and sometimes adopting more or less radical changes to them. There is no question, however, that – with the exception of incinera-tion technology, which Britain pioneered in, and compaction technology, which the Germans also developed – British practitioners were less likely than their German counterparts to adopt solutions to emerging problems in public cleansing that involved standardization, systems integration, and substantial investment. As we have seen, the divergent response to simi-lar problems did not arise because the British were unaware of or even resistant to change. Instead, a variety of political, social, and economic factors interacted to shape Britain's relative lag in adopting more modern technologies of waste collection and disposal. And yet ironically, despite Britain's relatively poor reputation for recycling today (and Germany's comparatively good one), the United Kingdom seems to have been more advanced in the area of salvage, at least through the mid-1960s. We turn to this next.

3

Salvage and the Industry

Introduction

City cleansing managers in both Germany and the United Kingdom faced problems of reconstruction of collection and transport services in the immediate post–World War II period. By the second half of the 1950s, they also had to come to grips with changing household waste streams and tighter labor markets, with both of these trends related to noticeably rising prosperity among the general populace. As we have seen in Chapter 2, the response of the cleansing professionals was to reorganize and rationalize.

Throughout the period, these professionals carried out their duties within the context of clear economic constraints. City budgets were never adequate to do everything managers might have wanted, and they were often very constrained indeed. Capital investment, too, had to be carefully planned and amortized over a number of years, and changes in labor markets were a growing challenge as the postwar period progressed.

Still, these undeniable economic influences on decision making and practice did not equate to full exposure to market forces. In spite of professionalization of cleansing and the widespread adoption of businesslike practices for accounting and planning, managing equipment and personnel, and carrying out other duties, cleansing departments remained sheltered from the full impact of the market in crucial ways by virtue of the public health ethic that provided the foundations for their work. Cost was a consideration, but it was not the ultimate one. It was much more critical that cleansing professionals provide their service than for them to function as if they were running a traditional business. Municipal public cleansing units had no need, for instance, to turn an annual profit or even to generate additional income to cover costs, including investment. Indeed, most practitioners in both countries would no doubt have agreed with the sentiment animating an official in Mannheim in 1961 who pointed out that "Municipal waste collection is not a business, but rather a public institution, the expenditures of which... are to be covered from income from fees."[1] Although British funding was, as we have seen, more indirect (because direct fees could not be charged, with operations instead financed out of general local taxation), the point applies to the United Kingdom as well.

There was, however, one major exception to this general rule that public cleansing was shielded from the ravages of the market. Salvage, which was akin to but not quite the same as what we now term recycling,[2] formed an important component of the postwar waste-handling systems in both countries.[3] Although a number of nonmarket considerations shaped decisions on how to deal with some types of salvage, this was also the one area of public cleansing practice that was exposed to (sometimes very harsh) market forces, especially in relation to waste paper or metal, in large part because local authorities often did not possess the expertise to process salvage into useable products. Nor, on the other hand, did they have any motivation for acquiring such knowledge; it was, after all, not part of their core business.[4]

Thus, the private sector and the market played important roles, alongside and in tandem with the public sector. Indeed, salvage brought up an issue as much at the heart of capitalism as the market itself: ownership. The question of who owns household waste would not occur to most of us, and to the extent that it does it is clear that ownership of

---

[1] Stadtdirektor Borelly, "Die Mannheimer Müllabfuhr heute" (1961), StA Mannheim, Hauptregistratur Zugang 40/1972, 291.

[2] As discussed in Chapter 6, however, there are some important differences between salvage and recycling.

[3] For excellent overviews of salvage/recycling and their political context in twentieth-century Britain, see Timothy Cooper, "Challenging the 'Refuse Revolution': War, Waste and the Rediscovery of Recycling, 1900–1950," *Historical Research* 81, no. 214 (2008): 710–731; and Timothy Cooper, "War on Waste? The Politics of Waste and Recycling in Post-War Britain, 1950–1975," *Capitalism Nature Socialism* 20, no. 4 (2009): 53–72.

[4] There was an exception to this rule in the area of food waste "processing" where, for instance, Birmingham and Manchester had municipal operations already before the end of the Second World War. For Birmingham, see H. J. Black, *History of the Corporation of Birmingham*, vol. 6, 1936–1950 (Birmingham Corporation, 1950), pp. 477, 506. For Manchester, see Manchester City Archives, collection reference M595, records of the Cleansing Department (subsequently M595), Annual Report 1951–1952, p. 5 with reference to wartime Defence of the Realm regulations.

and responsibility for waste have usually been gratefully transferred – although sometimes illegally and/or in stealth – to the public sector, at least in cities. If, however, the waste has monetary value, ownership can be contested and debates over it can be fraught.

This chapter begins by considering the issue of ownership of waste and its implications. The next section explores some of the key factors that generally serve to shape value and practice in salvage markets. We then move on to analyze the evolution of some of those markets in the two and a half decades following the Second World War. There were certainly a number of commonalities between the two countries. In the postwar period, both continued practices that had been developed and deployed in response to wartime exigencies, and we will examine this in relation to the collection and processing of organic waste, mostly food for compost and for animal feedstuffs. On the other hand, there were important ways in which developments in the area of salvage during the twenty-five years or so that followed the end of the Second World War in Germany were very different from those in the United Kingdom, especially in the commercial sphere. British markets were far more highly developed, and British municipal authorities could therefore be far more active in recovery of metal, glass, and paper from the household waste stream than those in Germany, for reasons we will explore. It is important to note, however, that there were a few *global* markets for some types of reclaimed waste even in the nineteenth century.[5] Most, though, were local or national, and the amount of space devoted within this part of the chapter to each country's case is thus unequal, with the British experience in markets for waste dealt with at much greater length.

An essential point of this chapter is to establish three things: first, that there was a general replacement of salvage practices established in wartime and shaped primarily by nonmarket forces with more normal market-based salvage; second, that markets for different types of salvage varied considerably from one another; and third, that these markets were volatile, which at its extreme might result in utter collapse of the market. The latter two factors clearly had enormous consequences for policy makers and practitioners, playing in turn an important causal role in the more or less rapid abandonment of both wartime and long-standing

---

[5] Hermann Stern, "Die geschichtliche Entwicklung und die gegenwärtige Lage des Lumpen-handels in Deutschland" (PhD dissertation, Erlangen, 1914). Our thanks to Heike Weber for pointing out this source and for highlighting the existence of early globalized salvage markets.

commercial salvage practices in both countries. Finally, in the concluding
section we look at the implications for salvage's role in the handling of
waste as consumer society began to develop even more extensively in the
United Kingdom and West Germany in the 1960s and beyond.

Ownership of Household Waste and Its Implications

Until relatively recently, certainly until around the middle of the nineteenth century, refuse was seen as the property and – by implication at
least – the responsibility of the person who created it.[6] Personal property
is traditionally regarded as something that may be freely disposed of,
and because there has long been a market for at least some household
refuse, the practice of selling discarded possessions or materials became
a familiar one in most cities.[7] An individual householder could obtain
payment from the "rag and bone" men (the collective term for independent dealers in textiles, scrap metals, or wastepaper) for waste that could
subsequently be turned into something of value.[8] And such individual
cash transactions continued even after the advent of municipal cleansing
services in industrialized countries beginning in the 1870s.

The introduction of organized and regular collection of municipal
household waste in the late nineteenth century, however, changed things
somewhat. In Britain, for instance, the householder could still sell waste
to a private buyer, but only *before* it was placed outside the property
in a "suitable receptacle" for municipal collection. Once it entered that
container and was put out for collection, the waste belonged to the city,
something established in English law by the Public Health Act of 1875.[9]
Over time, it became increasingly common for cities to supply garbage
cans to householders, which only reinforced this notion of effective transfer of ownership. The city's claim to ownership of waste remained in
place during the period of storage in the garbage can prior to collection
by authorities.[10] Consequently, if any third party decided to sift through

---

[6] J. C. Wylie, *The Wastes of Civilisation* (London: Faber and Faber Ltd, 1959), p. 94.

[7] For the interaction of early urban refuse collectors with householders, see Brian Maid-
ment, *Dusty Bob: A Cultural History of Dustmen 1780–1870* (Manchester: Manchester
University Press, 2007).

[8] For an excellent study of scrap metal dealers in the United States, see Carl Zimring, *Cash
for Your Trash* (New Brunswick, NJ: Rutgers University Press, 2005).

[9] Great Britain, *Public Health Act 1875* (London, HMSO 1875), Part 3, Section 42.
Similar "mirror legislation" applied in Scotland.

[10] Great Britain, *Public Health Act 1936* (London: HMSO 1936). Part 2, Section 72(e)
permitted local authorities to prohibit the removal by third parties of "any matter which

the contents and take anything, whether for sale or for personal use, that person was liable to prosecution. The 1936 Public Health Act, which brought together much previous British public health legislation, in fact actually prohibited anyone not specifically employed by the municipal council for this purpose from sorting through or removing the contents of any garbage container awaiting collection.[11]

In Germany, too, state and local legislation on and attempts to define waste generally were based on the same notion – that when individuals discarded something, it ceased to be their property. In practice, however, the issue of ownership of waste was for some time of more minor importance, at least until the National Socialist seizure of power. Before that time, German cities (with the notable exception of Munich) were not usually involved in salvage collection and trade, with the business instead mainly in the hands of local traders. After 1936, however, as part of the operations of the National Socialist Four Year Plan, which sought to prepare Germany for war, authorities eagerly sought all sorts of salvageable waste, claiming it as property of the German people.[12] But with the collapse of the Nazi regime in 1945, the centralized salvage operations they introduced also disappeared, and the issue of ownership of waste then retreated again into insignificance in Germany.

British cities, on the other hand, seem to have been more consistent over a longer time period in their vigorous defense of their ownership of waste, a pattern that continued into the postwar period. Birmingham's cleansing department, for instance, took a firm hand with those who removed materials put out for collection. In April 1945, the city brought charges of theft against three boys for stealing books from salvage collection boxes outside council offices and also charged two adults with removing kitchen waste from household garbage cans.[13] In November of the same year, furthermore, with wartime regulations about gathering "salvage materials" still in force, the city prosecuted three of its own refuse collectors for removing – that is, in legal terms, stealing – not only scrap metals from the garbage containers but also the garbage cans

---

the authority have undertaken to remove" – that is, refuse put in whatever receptacle was emptied by the authority. Householders could, however, retrieve items from the bin as long as it remained on their premises.

[11] *Public Health Act 1936*, section 76(3).

[12] See Friedrich Huchting, "Abfallwirtschaft im Dritten Reich," *Technikgeschichte* 48 (1981): 252–273.

[13] Birmingham City Archives, collection reference BCC/BP, Salvage and Stables Committee records, 1919–1952 (subsequently BCC/BP), "Minutes and Agendas," May 9, 1945.

themselves. And to drive home the point about municipal property rights, they also prosecuted the "fence" who had subsequently handled the stolen materials. All four accused were found guilty and sentenced to terms of imprisonment, and the three city employees were summarily dismissed.[14] To be sure, this extreme interpretation of policy and the law may have been encouraged by wartime regulations, but it continued even after they had long since been relaxed. As late as May 1956, a driver and two refuse collectors were prosecuted and convicted for passing "scrap metals and rags" to a dealer who had formerly worked for Birmingham's salvage department.[15] Once again, the council employees were sacked, presumably under the motto *"pour encourager les autres."*

But these policies went beyond mere legalistic, formal, and perhaps petty assertions of the city's ownership rights over household waste. The issue had real economic importance because cities wished to extract value from at least some of the rubbish they collected. Indeed, from the time local authorities began to organize collection of domestic refuse in the nineteenth century, they recognized that selling at least some of the waste they "owned" would help offset the costs of cleansing.[16] We return to municipalities' own recovery operations and sales to salvagers in the private sector later in the chapter. It is important to note here that cities often made use of another option, especially in the two and a half decades after the end of the Second World War. In Britain, for instance, those local authorities that sent refuse direct to landfill without any prior sorting sometimes sold the rights to "picking" at tipping sites, usually to individuals and often for only nominal amounts.[17]

In this case, income generation appears to have been less important than regularizing the status of independent operators who would otherwise have been removing municipal property illegally. Clearly, then, this represented an alternative to the practice of prosecuting illegal picking adopted by some local authorities and thus highlights the sometimes

---

[14] BCC/BP, "Minutes and Agendas," November 21, 1945.

[15] Birmingham City Archives, collection reference BCC/BP, Salvage Committee records, 1952–1974 (subsequently BCC/BP), "Minutes and Agendas," May 1956.

[16] Mitchell Library, Glasgow, Records of the City of Glasgow (subsequently MLG), Cleansing Department Annual Reports, DTC 7/3/1, Annual Reports 1869–1888. The 1869 report notes that Birmingham, Glasgow, Leeds, Liverpool, and Manchester were all then engaged in such work.

[17] Greater Manchester County Record Office, Greater Manchester Council, records of the Refuse Disposal Committee (subsequently GMCRD), "Report of the County Engineer," January 7, 1982, provides source material for the rest of this paragraph unless otherwise stated.

extreme differences in practice within the United Kingdom. In any event, cleansing managers viewed these licensed "contract pickers" as a mixed blessing. Although they worked by hand and removed only what could easily be carried off-site, the pickers tended to disrupt the handling of refuse at the landfill, and their presence was often a cause of friction with council staff. Also, besides slowing down a site's workflow, there was a constant risk of injury because the pickers worked in close proximity to collection vehicles discharging their loads.

The same was true when similar licenses were issued at treatment plants to allow individuals to sort through refuse awaiting incineration. This practice was very much a carryover from the early years of the twentieth century, and although there seem to be no records documenting the scale of activity, independent operators must have formed only a small segment in the postwar salvage business. And obviously, as affluence grew, there were fewer and fewer who were interested in becoming pickers. Their ultimate demise in the United Kingdom was finally ensured through the introduction of stringent workplace health and safety legislation in the 1970s, which made local authorities responsible for any injuries suffered on-site by independent contractors.[18] Faced with such potential liabilities, councils terminated licenses, and legal picking became a thing of the past.

Until shortly after the end of the Second World War, contracting out rights for picking through refuse at dump sites to private operators was common in Germany, too. Again, the practice formed only a small part of the salvage business and indeed was also of minor importance for the municipality involved. Dortmund, for instance, sold picking rights at its landfills to private firms for just DM 1,200 in 1951, a drop in the ocean in terms of the cleansing department's overall budget.[19] Frankfurt, however, contracted a private firm to sort nonferrous metals and tin cans from its landfill site, and in 1960, 4,000 tons were recovered, a figure that seems to have been quite reasonable for the time.[20] Munich, on the other hand, worked via a different model. As early as 1898, the city signed a long-term contract with a private operator to collect the city's waste, and the contractor was in turn encouraged to recover as much salvage as possible

[18] Health and Safety at Work...Act 1974: Elizabeth II, 1974, Chapter 37 (London, HMSO, 1974).
[19] "Denkschrift über die Einführung einer neuen Müllabfuhreinrichtung in der Stadt Dortmund" (1951), StA Dortmund, Bestand 170, 221.
[20] Stadtreinigungsamt Frankfurt am Main, *15. Jahre Wiederaufbau*, Internationale Industrie-Bibliothek Bd. 149/54 (Basel: Internationale Industrie-Bibliothek, 1960), p. 18.

from it. The scheme was never profitable, however, which was the reason it had few imitators. Still, it lasted until after the end of the Second World War, largely because bureaucrats working for the city believed that it would be cheaper to guarantee prices to the contractor for materials that could be reused and to pay him for collection and landfill services than to establish a municipal service and related infrastructure to do the same thing.[21] After the end of the war and the total disruption of collection that accompanied it, however, Munich was no longer willing or able to purchase the company's services, and the contract finally ended.[22]

Elsewhere in West Germany, the practice of contracting private firms for picking in municipal dumps died out during the 1950s. The city of Augsburg used such contracts in the immediate postwar period with the aim of supporting war invalids.[23] In 1950, negotiations between the city of Dortmund and a wholesale trader of salvage materials failed when the company realized there was no way to make a profit from the business.[24] Beginning in the mid-1950s, too, the West German labor market became very tight, and picking jobs, dirty and exhausting, must have appeared extremely unattractive at a time when even the official public cleansing departments themselves had severe problems hiring workers. At the end of the day, until the sorting process was mechanized, something that came much later, it was extremely difficult to make picking cost-effective.

It is worth bearing in mind, however, that picking in rubbish heaps continues to be an important economic activity even in the twenty-first century in poorer countries. It continues to be motivated primarily by poverty and is carried out by those marginalized within the broader society, although some have argued that it has great potential for positive economic and environmental impacts if properly organized into cooperatives to maximize economic return and minimize exploitation.[25] These

---

[21] Peter Münch, *Stadthygiene im 19. und 20. Jahrhundert: Die Wasserversorgung, Abwasser- und Abfallbeseitigung unter besonderer Berücksichtigung Münchens* (Göttingen: Vandenhoeck & Ruprecht, 1993), pp. 243–244.

[22] Referat 13 to Stadtratsfraktionenen der SPD, BP, CSU, KPD, Betr.: Erhöhung der Hausunratsabfuhrgebühren, March 7, 1950, StA Munich, Bürgermeister Nr. 2781.

[23] "Beschluss des Allgemeinen Ausschusses der Stadt Augsburg" (January 28, 1953). Betr. "Vergabe der Verwertungsrechte an den drei Schuttplätzen der Stadt Augsburg an den Schuttbergungsunternehmer Karl Lenz," StA Augsburg, Bestand 49/1473, 1.

[24] "Denkschrift über die Einführung...," Bestand 170, 221.

[25] See, for instance, Martin Medina, "Waste Picker Cooperatives in Developing Countries," paper prepared for WIEGO/Cornell/SEWA on membership-based organizations of the poor, Ahmebabad, India, January 2005. Available at: http://wiego.org/sites/wiego.org/files/publications/files/Medina-wastepickers.pdf (accessed September 16, 2011).

practices are unlikely to return to Germany or the United Kingdom, of course, although recent legislation on deposits on all drink containers in 2002 in Germany (see Chapter 7) has had the effect of encouraging some to sift through public rubbish bins to collect them. In any case, it is striking how recently the practice of picking through dumps for salvage died out even in these highly developed, wealthy countries.

Shaping Commercial Value in Salvage Markets

The issue of ownership of waste was important, then, because at least some of it had commercial value.[26] Obviously, not all of it did, and markets for various types of salvage also changed over time. Indeed, this was so much the case that on occasion what was of value at one point in time often became a liability later. In Britain, during the late 1940s and early 1950s, for example, there was a market for both household and incinerator clinker and ashes for use as foundation in the expanding road construction industry. But demand fell away quickly: by the end of the 1950s, the only productive use for such waste was as "clean fill" for landscape reclamation.[27] In those municipalities that possessed no disused gravel pits or quarry workings that could absorb the large amounts of domestic coal fire residues ubiquitous in both Britain and Germany before the widespread adoption of central heating, the ash and cinder had instead to go into landfill sites. This highlights some of the complexities associated with the use and value of "waste." Cinders and ash not only gradually lost monetary value but also, for some cities at least, added significantly to what had to be buried in tipping spaces, which were in turn often limited and a scarce resource. On the other hand, they had an alternative use as part of the layering process of sanitary landfill, which avoided the effort and expense of having to bring in topsoil for the sandwiching process.[28] Refuse residues, in other words, could possess a double identity, functioning even at times simultaneously as asset and liability.

---

[26] In this section, we consider only the factors shaping *commercial* value of waste. Clearly, there were other noneconomic factors that played a role in price formation as well, including notions of thrift and/or patriotic responsibility. These are addressed in greater detail later in the chapter.

[27] MLG, DTC 7/3/1 (5) Annual Reports of the Cleansing Department: see 1950–1951, p. 8, 1951–1952, p. 7, and 1957–1958, p. 9.

[28] Sanitary landfill, or "controlled tipping" uses alternating layers of compacted refuse and earth, or other suitable material, to promote decomposition supposedly without odor or health hazards.

Significant parts of the waste stream, however, did have value in the marketplace even if that value varied massively depending upon material. Before the age of mass consumption of thermoplastics, which did not really begin until the late 1950s and 1960s, there were just a few main categories of household waste:[29]

- Cinders, dust, and ash, which we have already considered in terms of market value, and that formed the heaviest component of the household waste stream during the two and a half decades after the end of the Second World War;
- Paper and cardboard;
- Food scraps;
- Metals, whether ferrous or nonferrous;
- Glass (often broken, as the one-way disposable bottle or jar did not come into widespread use until the 1960s);
- Textiles, wood, and other assorted other materials (e.g., rubber, early plastics such as Bakelite, paint, etc.)

As already mentioned, there were few if any markets for the items in the first of these categories, and markets for the last category were variable and often quite small. Markets for wastepaper, food, metals, and glass did exist, however, at least at some times, and were often large and widespread.

These markets were shaped primarily by four factors (see Table 3.1). First, the ease with which the waste item could be turned into something useful was important and was affected in turn by technologies of transformation/processing of the waste material and by energy usage in the transformation process. Second, how clean, dry, and/or "pure" the waste product was when it entered the salvage process also affected its value. One key implication of this was that, for the most part, materials needed to be separated from one another either at the household level or (mechanically or manually) at a centralized site to be useful and valuable. Third, the level of concentration of the salvage material in a given place

---

[29] Even as late as the mid-1960s, these categories accounted for the vast majority of estimated average "output" of household waste. It was estimated that "fine matter" (i.e., cinders, dust, and ash) accounted for between 35 and 40 percent of the total, paper and cardboard for 25–30 percent, vegetable and putrescible waste 10–15 percent, metals and glass for 5–8 percent each, and other materials for the balance. These percentages were by weight. Ministry of Housing and Local Government, Working Party on Refuse Storage and Collection, *Report* (London: HMSO, 1967), p. 12.

TABLE 3.1. *Factors Shaping the Value of Salvage*

Factors	Key Dimensions/Considerations
1. Ease of transformation into something viewed as useful/ valuable by the market	Energy usage in transformation process Technological capabilities
2. "Purity" of material to be salvaged	Cleanliness Dryness Degree of separation from other materials
3. Level of concentration at point of collection	Weight Volume
4. Supply and demand	Competing "virgin" or other materials Local, regional, national, or international markets

affected its value. It could, for instance, make a difference to the economics of metal salvage whether a particular household was disposing of a broken boiler or water heater, which might contain a substantial amount of steel and other metals and might therefore be quite worthwhile for the salvager to collect, or a simple burned-out pot or a used tin can, which might be far less so. This factor also affected the cost of collection, of course. And finally, the fourth factor was the good old-fashioned law of supply and demand.

It is perhaps best to move from this somewhat abstract examination of the development of salvage markets to a more concrete one, because demand for scrap and salvage tended to be both highly variable depending on the type of material involved and highly localized. Moreover, a range of nonmarket forces was at work in some of the activities, which would also benefit from more detailed exploration.

Salvage Markets from 1945 to the Late 1960s

Salvage markets in Britain and West Germany developed differently from one another in the immediate postwar period, and there were also significant differences within each country depending on the material involved. In this section, we consider each country under two separate rubrics, first examining food and other organic waste that was processed for either compost or animal feed, a market heavily shaped by wartime experience, organization, and infrastructure. We then turn to an assessment of markets in which commercial and long-term factors were more significant.

The treatment of the two countries in relation to this latter aspect is decidedly unequal, with Britain receiving far more attention, for reasons that we explore below.

Salvage Markets in the Shadow of the War

Probably the most important factor shaping salvage markets in both West Germany and the United Kingdom in the decade and a half following the end of the Second World War was a noncommercial one: the long-term effect of the experience of the war itself, something that was more political and social than commercial. The reaction to that experience, however, differed markedly between the two countries, although both were influenced by increasing importance of commercial and market factors over time.

Composting of food and other organic waste in Germany had its origins in the war but also formed a key focus of public cleansing in Germany during much of the 1950s. This is mainly because it fit in well with the ethic of German public cleansing practitioners favoring reuse of materials insofar as possible that continued into the postwar period. For Heinrich Erhard, the elder statesman of German public cleansing, as well as for many others, composting was the best way of reusing waste because it could be used as fertilizer and thus would contribute to an improvement of the disastrous food supply situation in postwar Germany. In 1952, the Arbeitskreis für kommunale Abfallwirtschaft (Working Group for the Municipal Waste Industry, or AkA) was founded with a primary focus on development of composting projects and techniques.[30] Within this group, Franz Pöpel, a professor of sanitary environmental engineering (*Siedlungswasserwirtschaft*) at the University of Stuttgart, played a decisive role. It is worth noting, too, that he made vital contributions to the "scientification" of waste handling in West Germany. Many leading experts ended up studying with him, including, for example, Werner Schenkel, the first director of the waste section of the Umweltbundesamt, or Federal Environmental Agency, which was founded in 1974.

Initial attempts to organize large-scale composting plants started in 1942, when the Dano-Company, a Danish pioneer in waste composting, built a plant in Berlin. (It was probably their agricultural focus and prevailing agrarian conditions, including relatively poor soil and relatively

---

[30] Vermerk. Betr.: Mineralöl-Rohstoff-Handel GmbH, Mühlheim/Ruhr (March 26, 1965), LA Düsseldorf, Bestand NW 354, 589.

small farm size, that led countries such as Denmark or the Netherlands to do pioneering work in the field of composting.[31]) After the war, composting plants were built in Baden-Baden, Heidelberg, and a number of other places with promising results, and they were generally applauded in practitioner journals.[32] In the middle of the 1950s, in fact, composting appeared to many people, especially scientists, to be the best way to reuse waste, thus avoiding the squandering of resources.[33] The most obvious advantage of composting over incineration was that it appeared to be much cheaper: until the late 1950s, German public cleansing practitioners remained skeptical about incineration because of high projected costs and unproved technology. On the other hand, many practitioners expressed doubts about the efficacy of composting techniques, mainly because of metal scrap and (especially) shards of broken glass in household waste, which impaired the compost's quality.[34]

The composting euphoria of the early postwar years faded away very quickly by the late 1950s, however, owing to a number of difficulties. One grave problem was that most farmers were unwilling to accept fertilizer made of waste, even at prices that were so low as to be unprofitable for producers. This was partly because of poor quality, but more importantly, people were simply suspicious about using fertilizer made from household waste. A second problem was that composting did not work as a solution for densely populated industrial areas such as the Ruhr district, which faced the biggest problems with waste disposal. Composting plants there were never able to process the necessary amount of waste. What is more, they produced acceptable fertilizer only in combination with sewage water, which was in turn very often contaminated with heavy metals. Indeed, only one test plant using this process was built, in Duisburg-Huckingen, and it was from the outset dogged by protests from neighbors who complained in particular about the facility's strong smell. In winter of 1958, to try to allay objections, the authorities took

---

[31] Letter from Beigeordneter Dr. Ing W. Herrmann to Oberbaudirektor Köster (September 1, 1950), LA Düsseldorf, Bestand NW 354, 1097.

[32] Letter from Paul Otto to Staatssekretär Tillmann (January 16, 1965); Letter from Voith Müllex GmbH to Ministerium für Ernährung, Landwirtschaft und Forsten (July 20, 1965), both in LA Düsseldorf, Bestand NW 354, 590.

[33] Letter from Abteilung II to Abteilung V im Hause (8 August 1960) betr.: Beseitigung des im Ruhrgebiet anfallenden Mülls durch Kompostierung für landwirtschaftliche Zwecke, LA Düsseldorf, Bestand NW 354, 1096.

[34] "Denkschrift über die Einführung...," Bestand 170, 221.

the drastic step of deploying perfume in the plant, but this, of course, did not solve the long-term problem.[35]

In 1960, the AkA was in fact heavily criticized by the highly influential Verband kommunaler Fuhrparkbetriebe (Association of Municipal Public Cleansing Departments, or VKF) for concentrating research solely on composting and virtually ignoring alternative solutions, especially incineration, which would eventually turn out to be the most effective answer to the waste crisis already appearing on the horizon in West Germany in the late 1950s.[36] Composting, of course, still remained on the agenda, but only for small municipalities, despite the fact that it was big cities that had to struggle with the most important problems associated with waste disposal starting at that time.[37] But even for small cities, composting very often turned out to be an economic failure. The importance of composting in Germany thus declined inexorably until rediscovered by a generation fixated as much upon environmental and political goals as on economic ones. We return to this development in Chapters 5 and 7.

In Britain, as in Germany, there was a long holdover of wartime practice in relation to reuse of food and organic waste into the late 1950s, despite growing affluence. In the British case, however, the continuity appears to have been in spite of rather than because of the enthusiasm of practitioners.

The British market for waste food for use as animal feed was very much a creature of the war. When in 1940 shortages of feed in the United Kingdom threatened to cut the pig and poultry population by over 30 percent, alternative sources were urgently needed to avoid a failure in meat production, which was already scarcely adequate to satisfy the population, however minimally.[38] Emergency regulations were then introduced that eventually compelled virtually all urban local authorities to collect

---

[35] Hans Rossberg, "Kompostwerk Duisburg-Huckingen ein Jahr in Betrieb," *Der Städtetag* (April 1959), pp. 188–190; "Parfüm-Spritze für den Müllteufel: Städte an Rhein und Ruhr gehen die verschiedensten Wege, um ihren Müll loszuwerden," *Rheinische Post* (December 13, 1960), seen in LA Düsseldorf, Bestand NW 354, 1099.

[36] See Ralf Herbold et al., *Entsorgungsnetze: Kommunale Lösungen im Spannungsfeld von Technik, Regulation und Öffentlichkeit* (Baden-Baden: Nomos, 2002).

[37] "Der Müll wird gebändigt," *Energiewirtschaftliche Tagesfragen: Zeitschrift für die Elektrizitäts- und Gasversorgung* 17, 1–2 (1967): 13–14, seen in LA Düsseldorf, Bestand NW 354, 589.

[38] The National Archives, Kew London (subsequently TNA), records of the Ministry of Agriculture and Fisheries, MAF 35/1102, "Waste Food Salvage Scheme: An Account of Its Operation 1939–1954," p. 1. See also David Edgerton, *Britain's War Machine: Weapons, Resources, and Experts in the Second World War* (Oxford: Oxford University Press, 2011), for observations on food supply.

waste food with the goal of processing it into a sterilized, hygienic form in "concentrator plants" that were organized into regional zones.[39] By the end of the war, these plants had processed 2.29 million tons of waste food, with a further 2 million tons processed by private (though state-licensed) operators.[40] Waste-food processing, therefore, had become a substantial activity by 1945, although it was hardly something that most local authorities were happy to continue.

The reason for this lack of enthusiasm was simple: even when buoyant demand absorbed the entire output of local authorities, food collection and processing operations were uneconomic and were really justified only by regulatory demands. What is more, they could be sustained only by government subsidies.[41] The "processing authorities" – the local authorities that operated the plants – were not permitted to contract out collection (although the few private firms that were in the waste-food collection business before the war continued operating "under orders from the Agricultural Departments" but were restricted to servicing the premises from which they had been collecting before the wartime regulations came into force).[42] This added to existing logistical problems of manpower and vehicle shortages. What is more, maximum prices for both raw food waste and the concentrated sterilized feedstuff were fixed at levels favorable to livestock producers.[43] Authorities that supplied material to processing plants thus certainly operated at a loss. In fiscal year 1944–1945, they spent an estimated £1.97 per ton on average to collect waste food; in contrast, the selling price was fixed at £1.50 per ton, something later described with typical British understatement as "un-remunerative."[44]

Clearly, this was a resource recovery effort that, all other things being equal, could not survive in an open market, but in the short term the question was how to bridge the yawning gap between cost of collection and the price fetched by sale. The provisions of the 1936 Public Health Act were after all never meant to embrace a massive state-mandated resource

---

[39] TNA, records of the Ministry of Housing and Local Government HLG 51/812, Inter-departmental Committee on Salvage, Interim Report 1947, p. 10.

[40] Ibid., p. 8.

[41] TNA, MAF 35/1102, p. 5, and HLG 51/812, Interim Report 1947, p. 10.

[42] M595, Annual Report 1951–1952, p. 9.

[43] TNA HLG 51/812, Interim Report 1947, pp. 9 and 10: the sale of raw waste for feeding directly to pigs was allowed under controlled circumstances.

[44] Ibid., pp. 1, 10. The actual figures were 1 pound 19 shillings and 9 pence and 1 pound 10 shillings, respectively.

recovery program. In the absence of any guidance in the legislation, cities were understandably reluctant to pass the costs on to their "rate payers" (local taxpayers), but in the absence of any guidance in the legislation they looked to the government to defray the extra costs. During the war, both the Board of Trade and the Ministry of Agriculture and Fisheries were anxious to encourage waste-food recovery and successfully lobbied the Treasury to increase subsidies. After the war, the government's Interdepartmental Committee on Salvage Collection, set up in 1946 to consider long-term policy on salvage, was anxious to see such inducements increased still further or replaced by completely new arrangements that would be "not less favourable to Local Authorities."[45] Subsidies did indeed continue and were recognized by the relevant departments of state as a necessary component of waste-food recovery, until the eventual rescinding of wartime regulations in 1954.

No matter how patriotically motivated cleansing departments were, however, they saw things differently from government departments. From their perspective, dealing with waste food from the public not only imposed financial burdens, it also placed extra pressures on structures already suffering from shortages of manpower and equipment. Thus, even with government subsidies, local authorities considered the task uneconomic and an interference with their core duties of collecting and disposing of general domestic waste.[46] But no matter how keen cities may have been to close down their food collection activities, lingering economic doldrums in the postwar period entailed continuation of government mandates and the subsidies needed to maintain them. Indeed, the activities actually expanded during the late 1940s as the pig population began to grow again, although collections declined again rapidly during the course of the 1950s, as can be seen in Chart 3.1.

Despite regular government exhortations to increase the amount of waste food collected and the occasional glimmer of enthusiasm,[47] the general public also showed little appetite for continuing wartime practice. After all, a key issue was that food waste had to be segregated and collected separately from other domestic refuse. The usual way of

---

[45] For its goals, remit, and constitution, see TNA, HLG 51/812, Interim Report 1947, p. 1. The wartime regulations were scheduled to expire in 1950.

[46] TNA, MAF 35/1102, Report, "The Waste Food Salvage Scheme 1939–1954," pp. 8 and 9.

[47] See TNA, HLG 51/812, p. 11 for comments relevant to 1947, and MLG/DCT/7/3/1 (5), Cleansing Department, Annual Report 1951–1952, p. 10 regarding trial introduction of individual waste food containers at houses and flats.

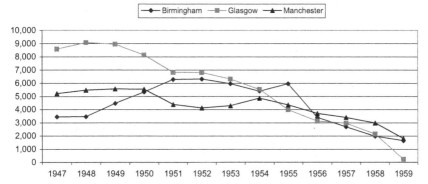

CHART 3.1. Waste food tonnages output: Birmingham, Glasgow, and Manchester, 1947–1959. *Source:* Extracted from annual and departmental reports for each city, 1947–1959.

organizing this involved use of large, communal containers. The "pig bins," however, posed a number of difficulties for both the general public and practitioners, two of which were particularly prominent.

For one thing, although waste food's controlled selling price in the early 1950s may have been inadequate for local authorities to deal profitably in it, for some in the private-sector, prices were high enough to offer opportunities for profitable trading, although only on the black market. To serve demand from small-scale urban pig-rearers, traders regularly engaged in theft from communal bins, which provoked legislation to combat it in 1950.[48] However, government officials – but not the police – had to shoulder the burden of monitoring reported offenses and prosecuting those stealing or dealing in it illegally.[49] Monitoring, enforcement, and in some cases prosecution took time and effort, however, and the penalties imposed by the courts apparently neither deterred theft from communal bins nor provided adequate compensation to the municipalities themselves.

A second major problem with the "pig bins" lay in the fact that, in summer in particular, they generated offensive odors and encouraged the breeding of flies unless emptied regularly and frequently, something not always possible, particularly in the late 1940s when vehicle shortages

---

[48] The Kitchen Waste Order, 1950 (S.I. 1950 no. 505, article 11) made it an offense to remove kitchen waste from any container provided for it by a local authority.

[49] BCA, BCC, Town Clerk to Salvage and Stables Committee, November 7, 1953, on problems of prosecuting offenders.

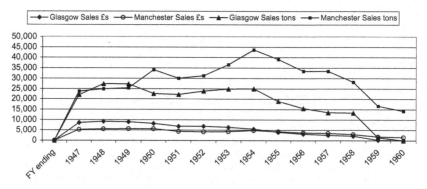

CHART 3.2. Waste food sales by weight, Glasgow and Manchester, 1947–1960. *Source:* Extracted from Annual Reports, Glasgow MLG DTC/7/3/1 (5), and Manchester MCA M595.

were chronic.[50] This in turn led to public outcry but also to conflicts between public cleansing and public health officials.

Public health officials regarded the communal bins, of which more than nine thousand remained in Birmingham alone in 1952, as "a possible source of danger" to public health and thus campaigned for their removal as a matter of urgency.[51] They lobbied their cleansing colleagues vigorously, pointing to the dangers of putrefying animal and vegetable matter left uncollected in communal bins. As long as wartime regulations remained in force, however, there was little that could be done apart from trying to empty the containers at frequent intervals and to ensure they were in good enough order to contain decaying matter effectively. Neither course of action could be guaranteed easily, however: shortages of vehicles, prioritization of emptying domestic garbage cans (many of which also contained decaying food residues), and even a shortage of steel to replace rusted "pig bins" all conspired to ensure the continuing presence of malodorous communal containers in the residential urban landscape.

Gross income from food waste, whether raw or processed, was modest compared to other more traditional salvaged materials such as metal and paper, averaging only around 20 percent of total gross income in Birmingham and 26 percent in Manchester between 1947 and 1959. *Profits,* moreover, were almost certainly minimal, if they existed at all (see Chart 3.2). Manchester's Annual Reports from 1949–1950 to

---

[50] TNA, MAF 35/1102, Appendix 2, p. v.
[51] BCA, BCC, Health Committee to Salvage and Stables Committee, "Report on the Collection and Treatment of Kitchen Waste," January 1954.

FIGURE 3.1. Collecting kitchen waste containers using a dedicated articulated vehicle, Manchester, 1960. Empty, sterilized bins were exchanged for the full ones at the time of collection. Photograph courtesy of Manchester City Council.

1951–1952 all refer to a lack of "economic stability" and to the need both to increase efficiency and to obtain higher prices. Cities such as Manchester that both collected waste and ran processing plants to treat it probably fared worse than those that simply collected and passed on the material for further treatment, despite the disparity in prices paid – which at times amounted to three times as much for processed as for raw material. (See Figures 3.1 and 3.2.) Glasgow, in contrast, was exclusively involved in collecting food waste. Income from sales of waste food was greater in Scotland's largest city than in Manchester up to 1955, while overheads were almost certainly lower because Glasgow did not have to operate a processing plant.

Not surprisingly, the combination of inconvenience, public health worries, and poor financial returns led to the rapid decline and eventual discontinuation of waste-food collection not long after wartime controls were removed early in 1954.[52] Happy as many professionals may have been to be rid of the task, however, they also recognized that its cessation

[52] TNA, MAF 35/1102, pp. 9 and 10.

FIGURE 3.2. Full kitchen waste containers about to be shipped off for processing at Manchester's waste food plant, 1960. The illustration shows what appears to be a school in the background. The food waste depicted here was the residue of the meals service then universally provided for schoolchildren in Britain. Photograph courtesy of Manchester City Council.

meant that substantial extra tonnages of refuse would now need to be dealt with by cleansing departments themselves. Not only would more material have to be incinerated or buried, but because food waste was "one of the most offensive components of house refuse," it would also tend to add further to pressures for more frequent collections.[53] Waste professionals were not slow to see the dangers inherent in finally gaining what they had so long desired.

Not everyone, however, rushed to abandon food waste completely. Although quick to eliminate communal containers, cities such as Birmingham and Manchester that had their own processing plants even before the war continued for some time to handle materials collected from other municipally owned departments such as markets and abattoirs, as well as kitchen waste from restaurants and canteens. But as the market for

---

[53] BCA, BCC, Health Committee to Salvage and Stables Committee, "Report on the Collection and Treatment of Kitchen Waste," January 1954, p. 5.

concentrated animal feedstuffs was freed from restrictions and demand began to decline precipitously, the output of the processing plants shifted toward fertilizer and composts.[54] By 1960, Birmingham had in fact completely abandoned processing waste food for feedstuff, and in 1961, Manchester followed suit, indeed going further and dismantling its plant, intending to concentrate instead exclusively on wastepaper and scrap metals, for which there had long been vibrant markets.

Municipal Authorities and Commercial Salvage Markets

In Germany, collection of scrap metal, wastepaper, textiles, and other *Altstoffe* (literally, "old materials," or salvage) played an important role before the 1930s. In this as in other areas relating to household waste in prewar Germany, however, little happened at the national level: just as contents of garbage cans differed substantially by region, there was no national salvage market; instead there were highly localized ones, dominated by small traders for the most part.

This changed to some degree after 1936, however, when National Socialist state authorities pushed forward the collection of such materials to contribute to the so-called Vierjahresplan (Four Year Plan) and other Nazi German autarky policies.[55] This involved the creation of a highly centralized bureaucratic salvage operation, seen previously in Germany only during World War I, which, besides featuring such highly symbolic acts as the melting down of church bells, entailed government-sponsored collection of all sorts of raw materials that could be used for war-related production, including metals, textiles, paper, and so on.[56]

The unprecedented centralization of salvage markets under the National Socialists was clearly motivated in large part by preparation for and the conduct of the war effort. But there was another motivation: many of the small traders involved in this trade before 1936 were Jews under the definitions set out in racial legislation enacted by the Nazis, and the combined effect of centralization, bureaucratization, and racism was to deprive most of them of their livelihood.[57]

---

[54] For Birmingham, see BCC, BCA, City of Birmingham, *Abstract of Statistics*, Number 1, Table 133; Number 2, Table 138; Number 3, Table 191; Number 3, Table 112; Number 4, Table 122; Number 5, Table 284. For Manchester, see MCA, M595, Annual Reports, Salvage reports, 1948 to 1961.

[55] Huchting, *Abfallwirtschaft im Dritten Reich*, pp. 252ff.

[56] For instance: Letter from Stadtreinigungsamt to Oberbürgermeister (November 19, 1936), StA Dortmund, Bestand 170, 35.

[57] Huchting, *Abfallwirtschaft im Dritten Reich*, pp. 252ff.

When the war was over, then, not only did the recently created centralized infrastructure disappear, there were also few small local salvage traders and only small local markets to take the place of regional let alone national ones. For this reason – although it seems that *industrial* reuse of metal scrap and wastepaper remained important and even grew in significance in Germany in the twenty-five years or so following the end of the war[58] – household waste salvage operations entered the postwar period in a severely distressed state. Consequently, sources on these small-scale local traders and markets are virtually impossible to come by.

Compounding the structural collapse of many traditional salvage dealers and markets was a widespread disaffection with collection of salvage on the part of the German people as a result of their wartime experience. Then, as the German economy subsequently experienced the "economic miracle," people stopped collecting salvage altogether, with the result that virtually all of the limited number of remaining small but stable local markets that had previously made the practice possible died out entirely. And many no doubt viewed the disappearance of salvage collection as no bad thing: it was, after all, a palpable sign of better times.

The most important explanation for this general abandonment of salvage in West Germany in the first twenty to twenty-five years after the end of the war, then, was that economic relations had changed. People could afford *not* to engage in salvage activities; owing to rising productivity and wages, most people were suddenly much wealthier. Rising productivity also meant falling prices for the manufacture of glass and paper, while on the other side of the equation the costs of waste collection remained the same or fell much more slowly than did prices. The economic necessity of collecting materials for the purpose of salvaging them, in other words, ceased to exist. This growing productivity gap between industrial production and the costs of waste collection was also in part a result of the "heavy" infrastructure of West German waste collection outlined in the previous chapter, which made waste collection more expensive and less flexible. (It is significant in this context that the "comeback" of salvage through recycling during the 1970s corresponded with the gradual introduction of plastic bins, as we shall see in a later chapter.[59]) This all fits well

---

[58] BMI (ed.), "Verwertung von Altpapier. Untersuchung über die Möglichkeit der Verwertung von Altpapier. Gegenwärtiger Stand und zukünftige Entwicklung. Bericht des Battelle-Instituts Frankfurt am Main" (Berlin 1973), p. 7.

[59] Cp. Dirk Wiegand, "Die Entwicklung der deutschen Städtereinigung, der NKT und die Normung des MGB 240 – eine Erfolgsgeschichte," conference paper, Bochum 2010, pp. 23ff.

with what historian Christian Pfister has called the "1950s syndrome": a transformation of the relationship between human beings and nature, which he argues arose in West Germany (and elsewhere) during the 1950s and involved among other things a massive growth in the consumption of energy, goods, and landscapes, as well as rising quantities of waste, mainly owing to falling prices for fuel and other energy sources.[60] Pfister perhaps overinterprets this development, however. For waste handling, the explanation probably lies in the generally uneven development of productivity between the manufacturing sector and the service sector.[61] In any case, it is clear that recovery of salvage from household waste lost economic sense and, for this reason, stopped for all practical purposes in West Germany by the 1960s.

The sole – although also important – exception to the general trend toward abandonment of salvage in postwar Germany was the widely used and long-standing glass bottle deposit system, but even that was under threat by the mid-1960s, providing both a clear and compelling example of the process of abandonment longstanding salvage practice, and of the limits to that process. The German deposit system for beer bottles and other alcoholic (and eventually nonalcoholic) beverages originated in the nineteenth century. People paid a small deposit when they bought beverages at a brewery's sales point, for example, which they could then redeem when the bottles were returned. In this way, a bottle could be reused about twenty times. This system, highly institutionalized, persisted in spite of the abandonment of most other reuse and salvage practices for household waste during the course of the 1950s and early 1960s. Eventually, however, even the bottle deposit system was endangered as part of the process of breaking with long-standing traditions as Germans moved toward discarding practically everything that the household had used and no longer needed. Indeed, in 1965, trading companies in the beverage business actually went so far as to announce the abandonment of the bottle deposit system. The announcement, however, did not go uncontested. In fact, it occasioned renewed discussions in Germany on salvage that culminated in gradual elaboration

---

[60] Christian Pfister, "Energiepreis und Umweltbelastung: Zum Stand der Diskussion über das 1950er Jahre-Syndrom," in Wolfram Siemann (ed.), *Umweltgeschichte, Themen und Perspektiven* (Munich: C. H. Beck, 2003), pp. 61–86.

[61] What Jean Fourastie has called the "great hope of the 20th century" could, in case of salvage, also lead to the decline of a service industry. Jean Fourastié, *Le grand espoir de XX siècle* (Paris: Gallimard, 1963).

of the idea of recycling. We deal with this development in Chapter 6 in particular.

Britain, unlike Germany, featured a much more highly developed national market in many things by the 1950s, and this included trade in some salvage materials. The two most important markets were for scrap metals and wastepaper, and commercial considerations played a key role in each case. For municipalities, the demand and market for wastepaper was by far the greater, but for some cities, at least, scrap metal was also seen as an important component in refuse management. Both markets involved the private sector as well, but the private firms involved were relatively small and therefore are difficult to get information on. We thus focus here on the ways in which municipal authorities participated in these markets.

Unlike the large-scale collection of waste food, organized recovery of other materials because of their potential as income generators was for many British local authorities hardly a novelty brought about by the war. Some cities, such as Glasgow, had begun to extract a variety of saleable commodities such as scrap metals and wastepaper materials from their collected household wastes by the turn of the twentieth century. Others, such as Birmingham and Manchester, began to organize large-scale salvage operations during the 1930s. These recovery operations were driven by economics rather than politics or concern for the environment and took into account local conditions and opportunities for sale. In Glasgow, from the outset, the sole aim was to separate "the saleable from the un-saleable."[62] Salvaged waste was seen as having the potential to produce "a considerable revenue" when "the most modern methods and equipment" were employed to manage it.[63] Although those principles were somewhat distorted by the exigencies of war, the underlying philosophy of revenue-driven resource reclamation remained firmly in place from 1945 through to the end of the 1970s, its logic being more rigorously applied as markets for recovered materials changed over time.

Still, there is no doubt that the war changed previously existing salvage markets profoundly by introducing controls, regulations, and subsidies to channel activity in service of the war effort. Many of these government regulations remained in force well into the postwar period. In contrast to the waste-food market, however, which disappeared not long after

---

[62] Corporation of the City of Glasgow, *Municipal Glasgow: Its Evolution and Enterprises* (Glasgow: Robert Gibson & Sons, Ltd, 1914), p. 155.
[63] Ibid., p. 156.

government controls were lifted, those for scrap paper and metal resumed, although each took a different course. Let us look first at the wastepaper market and the participation of municipal authorities in it during the first two and a half decades after the war ended.

The market for wastepaper and cardboard in Britain was a large sector of economic activity even before 1939. Estimates of total collections from immediately before the war vary from a low of 700,000 tons to a high of 868,000 tons,[64] with around 23 percent of the paper collected, some 203,000 tons, being exported. The balance was used domestically, accounting for nearly 20 percent of the country's paper and cardboard consumption of around 3.2 million tons.[65] The market was heavily dominated by the private sector, and local authorities played a relatively minor role in collecting paper-based materials, with their cleansing departments providing only around 60,000 tons per annum, although that role increased substantially during the war.[66]

Wartime restrictions, however, caused paper production to decline substantially. From approximately 3.2 million tons in 1938, it fell to about 1.82 million tons in 1940, and it reached its nadir in 1943 at only 1.16 million tons.[67] Imports of timber for pulping also declined drastically during the war, so that even at these greatly reduced levels of output, collection of wastepaper for input into the production process became vital. Emergency regulations thus required local authorities "to ensure a regular and efficient collection of waste paper," eventually drawing 1,277 local authorities of all sizes into the wastepaper business.[68]

As was the case with food waste, however, any hopes local authorities may have entertained of being quickly rid of the responsibility when the war ended were immediately dashed. The nation's dire economic straits meant that emergency regulations due to end in 1950 remained in place, and governmental exhortations to collect yet more paper became a regular and increasingly strident presence. Pressures on local

---

[64] *Public Cleansing and Salvage*, October 1945, p. 150 gives 800,000 tons. However, see TNA, HLG 51/812, Interdepartmental Committee on Salvage, Interim Report 1947, where p. 6 suggests collections were between 700,000 and 750,000 tons annually. In addition, figures supplied by the UK's Confederation of Paper Industries (subsequently CPI) indicate 868,000 tons but with the caveat that data from both trade members and government agencies frequently show differences.

[65] CPI data compiled from members' and governmental records. There are no figures for imports of recovered paper before 1953.

[66] TNA, HLG 51/812, Interim Report, p. 6.

[67] Ibid., p. 7. Note that CPI data suggests ca. 3.48 million tons in 1938.

[68] Ibid. They were also required to do the same for "household bones and rags."

authorities continued because the paper industry itself was already recovering as much material as was feasible on its own. What is more, the significance of paper spread far beyond the publishing and stationery sectors. In 1945, the domination of the packaging medium in distribution of goods by paper products was nearly universal and they also featured extensively in industry, particularly in construction, where they often played a central role.[69] The expectation that wartime restrictions would be relaxed, prompting a return to something resembling a peacetime economy, led to fears in some quarters that a chronic shortage of paper and cardboard might have dire effects. In September 1945, the consequences of a prospective "famine in waste paper" were spelled out by Thames Board Mills Ltd (the "largest purveyors of waste paper in the British Empire") in a message to public cleansing practitioners. Recovery efforts, the company argued, needed to be stepped up because a shortfall in wastepaper would lead to unemployment in the paper industry itself. Moreover, the consequent lack of wrapping material would cause "serious difficulties" in distribution of food and other essentials, to the extent that even the national food rationing scheme "would break down," a calamity that had never occurred even in the worst days of the war.[70] Even if the company's message was self-serving, it nonetheless highlighted the severity of problems in providing adequate paper and cardboard output.

With imports of both timber and manufactured paper severely restricted, reclamation became even more of an issue in peacetime than it had been during the war, just as was the case with food. In contrast to kitchen waste, however, wastepaper could be sold by local authorities to "licensed waste paper merchants or mills" at whatever prices could be negotiated, subject to a maximum level.[71] National and local levels of demand thus largely determined prices paid by middlemen and mills, and prices fluctuated and regularly failed to cover collection costs. To encourage local authorities to collect, the Board of Trade therefore offered bonuses for tonnages sold above a set proportion of their previous year's figure,[72]

---

[69] Heavy-duty paper sacks were used for storing and transporting materials such as cement, lime, plaster, and whiting. In the absence of synthetic alternatives, distribution of these essentials was severely compromised.

[70] Advertisement in *Public Cleansing and Salvage* (September 1945), p. 7.

[71] MLG, Minutes of the Corporation of Glasgow, collection ref C1/3/112 (subsequently MLG/C1), "Report of the Special Committee on Salvage Operations," August 20, 1945, citing Ministry of Supply Information circulation letter number 120 of June 18, 1945.

[72] In 1945, this was set at £1 per ton "in excess of 80 percent of the weight sold in the corresponding period of the previous year." MLG C1/3/112, Report, August 20, 1945.

although not everyone was happy about this method. Glasgow's director of public cleansing, for instance, complained that the system favored previously inefficient cities and unfairly penalized his own, which, from the figures he had gathered, was one of most efficient wastepaper collectors in the country.[73] His suggestion that the scheme be revised to reflect performance relative to the national average was not taken up, however, perhaps because it was the least efficient cities that the Board really wanted to encourage.

In any event, government policy was effective insofar as substantial collections could be achieved in fiscal years 1947–1948 and 1948–1949. These years also marked a high point in postwar demand for wastepaper, during which, exceptionally, there was no real problem selling everything collected.[74] But even so, operating costs were only covered because the Board of Trade continued to pay subsidies. In August 1946, for instance, an indicated gross profit on Glasgow's recovery collections was chalked up as "entirely due" to such payments. Moreover, the following year the "principal reason" for an increased surplus was a bonus payment of £1,999 from the Board of Trade.[75] Birmingham's records, on the other hand, lump wastepaper recoveries in with other unspecified "salvaged sundries," but departmental reports suggest a similar situation. In November of the peak year 1947, revenue still only "approximately" equaled expenditure despite high levels of demand and prices approaching the ceiling set by the Board of Trade.[76]

These marginally cost-effective operations were, of course, inevitably ill suited to coping easily with any downturn in the market, let alone the catastrophic one that occurred in the second half of 1949 when, according to Glasgow's account, the market for wastepaper "vanished."[77] The proximate cause for this collapse of the market was additional Board of Trade intervention in late 1948. Given that restrictions on the use of paper and cardboard for packaging were to be relaxed imminently and the general export drive expanded, the board projected that a larger waste tonnage than ever would need to be collected. In the unlikely event of

---

[73] Ibid.

[74] At this time, the fiscal year ran from April 5.

[75] MLG/C1/3/116, Report, August 22, 1947.

[76] BCA, BCC, Salvage and Stables Committee Minutes, November 19, 1947, "Report on Recovery of Waste Paper."

[77] MLG, DTC 7/3/1 (5), Annual Report 1948–1949, p. 4. Although the reports covered the fiscal year ending in April, the accompanying notes were written later in the year and frequently acted as postscript to the data included in the document.

winter collections actually being larger than domestic demand, the board believed that any surplus wastepaper would find an export market. The government agency thus proposed a new basis of bonus payments to incentivize municipalities, a system to be established in conjunction with a national competition for collection organized by the Wastepaper Recovery Association on behalf of the paper trade. Duly motivated, cities increased their collections throughout a winter that was so free from seasonal disruptions that tonnages increased considerably. This very success, however, precipitated a crisis for local authorities.[78]

By the late 1940s and early 1950s, demand for paper was shifting to higher quality types that could not be made from the bulk of material that was collected because it varied both in nature and cleanliness. As a consequence, paper mills began increasingly to use new pulp, especially when supplies became more freely available. Their demand for mixed wastepaper thus diminished correspondingly and substantially. Makers of cardboard – board mills – continued to use mixed papers, but as collections increased and demand from paper mills declined, they became "inundated" and soon stopped taking deliveries, because supply now exceeded demand by some 2,000 tons a week. And for those cities without contracts from merchants or mills, sales temporarily ground to a halt. As the Board of Trade's director of salvage and recovery pointed out in 1949 to the professional institute's unhappy membership, "The laws of supply and demand [are] beginning to operate," and they "[are] fixed and inexorable." To make matters worse, hoped-for export sales had not materialized. There was substantial demand in the U.S.–occupied zone in Germany (which offered much-needed dollars in payment), but British mills were unable to supply the type required. France and Spain, meanwhile, were both desperate for lower-quality paper but lacked the sterling to pay for it. Consequently, local authorities had two choices: to hold on to stocks and hope for better times, or to sell now at whatever price they could find. The situation was "an embarrassment" to all, and the director concluded by pointing out that the lesson was that "everybody . . . was collecting too much of the wrong sort of paper."[79]

---

[78] The winter of 1947–1948 had been unprecedentedly severe, disrupting all waste collections, and it was feared that 1948–1949 might be similar.

[79] "A Statement from the Director of Salvage and Recovery," *Public Cleansing and Salvage* (August 1949), pp. 380–384. Most local authorities had "direct contracts" with mills whereby they were guaranteed sales, although not any particular price. The director had had no report that any board mill had "repudiated" a contract. See p. 383.

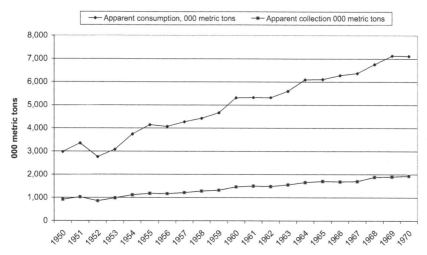

CHART 3.3. UK paper and board consumption and collection, 1950–1970. *Source:* data from Confederation of Paper Industries.

Practitioners, of course, had every right to be less than impressed by what the Board of Trade said to them. Despite recent "repeated assurances from the highest level that waste paper would be required for many years ahead," the market had in fact suddenly vanished, disrupting their "well planned organisation" for salvage recovery.[80] Not only had they been urged to increase efforts at a time when the responsible department of state must have known how the market was shaping up; to add insult to injury, wastepaper was also actually being imported at the same time.[81] Manchester's reaction was to halt wastepaper collection entirely as early as November 1948, when the situation was becoming clear, and not to resume collecting until two years later when the market had recovered and was apparently entering a period of some stability.[82] Glasgow, for its part, cut back its operations in late 1949, making a large number of its salvage workers redundant, and only started again in June 1950.[83]

The situation of 1949 highlighted the vulnerability of state-mandated operations in what was becoming, gradually but increasingly, a free market economy. Still, during the 1950s, when not only rationing but many import restrictions were removed, the market in wastepaper resumed operation (see Chart 3.3). Both paper consumption and recovery tonnages

[80] MLG, DCT 7/1/3 (5), Annual Report, p. 4.
[81] "The Waste Paper Crisis," *Public Cleansing and Salvage* (July 1949), p. 378.
[82] MCA, M595, Annual Reports, 1950–1951 and 1951–1952.
[83] MLG, DTC 7/1/3 (5), Annual Report 1949–1950, p. 11, and 1950–1951, p. 10.

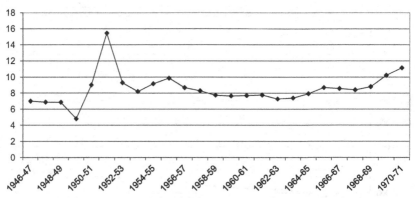

CHART 3.4. Glasgow: price realized for wastepaper, £ per ton, fiscal years 1946–1947 to 1970–1971. *Source:* extracted from Annual Reports, MLG DTC/7/3/1 (5).

increased between 1950 and 1970, although the proportion of salvaged paper being fed into the production process declined steadily, not least because the public's willingness to be frugal diminished substantially as economic conditions improved. Prices also increased dramatically over the levels of the 1940s and continued to fluctuate, sometimes considerably, but it has to be said that these fluctuations were modest compared to price movements of many other goods and services. On the other hand, the incidents of price collapse and market volatility in the late 1940s and early 1950s, modest as they might seem to those in other businesses, undoubtedly affected risk-averse municipal authority employees deeply (see Chart 3.4).

During most of this period, of course, prices for wastepaper were governed principally by the market. (See Figure 3.3.) Still, careful contract negotiations could provide some measure of insulation from these fluctuations, in the short term at least. For example, in December 1951, when prices were strong, Glasgow persuaded a wastepaper merchant to enter a five-year agreement that guaranteed the city the average price being paid for paper nationally, irrespective of local rates and with a minimum price assured regardless of market conditions. The rationale behind these terms was not just to maximize short-term income but to ensure the continued viability of salvage operations and avoid the debacle of 1949 that had disrupted the waste recovery structure then in place.[84] Faced with a decline in the market during 1953, however, the unfortunate "contract

[84] Ibid., Annual Report 1951–1952, p. 9.

FIGURE 3.3. Wastepaper "salvaging" by hand, Manchester, mid-1960s. Before paper could be sold to dealers, it first had to be sorted to remove foreign matter and heavily soiled material, which is being done in this photograph. It was then separated into different categories, which commanded various price levels, before being baled. Newspapers still made up the bulk of reclaimed materials at this time. Photograph courtesy of Manchester City Council.

partner" was paying the city a guaranteed £10 per ton against an average national market price of £6.50 and was obliged to enter into negotiations to seek a price reduction.[85] A compromise figure of £8.50 was set, with the contract being amended again the next year to give the city £2.00 per ton more than prevailing prices for the rest of the agreement's life. The Annual Report for 1955–1956 commented that it had been "a good year" for wastepaper, adding the following year that salvage provided benefits "not only to the city but to the nation as well."[86] A buoyant market certainly helped those local authorities that had organized themselves properly, and Glasgow was able to fix a new contract the following year that guaranteed a flat rate of £1 per ton more than prevailing market rates, plus a guaranteed minimum of £6 irrespective of current price levels.[87] Wastepaper thus seemingly continued to do well in the cleansing

[85] Ibid., 1953–1954, p. 10.
[86] Ibid., 1954–1955, p. 3, and 1955–1956, p. 4.
[87] Ibid., 1956–1957, p. 12.

department's estimation; the 1960–1961 report commented simply that "it had been a record year."[88]

The truth, however, is that in spite of all the hard bargaining by city officials, revenue was quite small relative to overall expenditure. In Glasgow's record year, the total budget for the cleansing department was £2.07 million, but wastepaper gross receipts amounted to only £115,000, or about 5.5 percent of turnover.[89] After allowing for operating costs, the monetary returns on wastepaper handling must therefore have been modest at best. Participation, moreover, became a matter of choice for local authorities after regulatory requirements were removed in 1949, and at first sight, it is not easy to understand the motivation for continuing operations that were scarcely (if at all) profitable. A comment made in a later report indicated, however, that there was in fact a pressing reason for continuing operations: although "little profit was now being made" from salvage, refuse disposal costs "would substantially increase" without receipts from salvage sales.[90]

Still, even if not separated and sold, the wastepaper would need to be collected and disposed of, something that would unavoidably incur handling costs and furthermore add either to the incineration load or landfill bulk. Separation and sale of the waste for salvage would help offset this. Thus, even if careful costing showed a deficit in operations, there might still be a beneficial effect on overall disposal costs. (See Figure 3.4.) Consultants scrutinizing the wastepaper organization in Westminster in 1964, for example, found that even though that operation ran at a loss, closing it down would result in an overall increase to the cleansing department's annual outlays of £20,000, considering the extra costs incurred elsewhere.[91] On the other hand, in some cases, wastepaper could not only be shown as a profit generator but also as making a substantial return on the capital invested. In fiscal year 1965–1966, Sunderland, a city with a population of 190,000, was able to show a net profit of 17 percent on its wastepaper sales of £46,350, which represented a return of 23 percent on the capital invested.[92] To be sure, Sunderland's experience may have been the exception rather than the rule, but it is clear that for all authorities

---

[88] Ibid., 1960–1961, p. 3.
[89] Ibid., 1960–1961, pp. 19 and 23.
[90] Ibid., 1962–1963, p. 6.
[91] Frank Flintoff and Ronald Millard, *Public Cleansing: Refuse Storage, Collection and Disposal; Street Cleansing* (London: MacLaren and Sons, 1968), p. 290.
[92] Ibid., p. 289. No details are given of the department's total costs or other income.

FIGURE 3.4. An early experiment in combining rationalization and paper salvage, Manchester, 1966. The city did trials to test the suitability of single-operator, electrically powered vehicles for collecting wastepaper bagged by shops and offices. Retailers and businesses paid for the paper to be collected, and the city subsequently sorted and sold it to wastepaper merchants. Photograph courtesy of Manchester City Council.

the benefits of wastepaper operations had a dimension transcending the simple balance sheet of their results.

Scrap metal constituted another long-standing salvage market, and it too was the subject of government intervention during wartime. Unlike waste food and paper, however, regulations mandating metal collection were rescinded very quickly with the return to peace because the Ministry of Supply decided that "the present and future position of these materials was satisfactory."[93] This judgement may well have been accurate since it is clear from the annual reports of Birmingham, Glasgow, and Manchester's cleansing departments that there was no postwar governmental pressure to gather up scrap metals of any sort. Rather, it was very much a speedy reversion to prewar practices, with the municipal economy rather than national necessity as the principal driver. The value of scrap metal to local authorities was generally smaller than for paper, partly because regular household disposal of metal tended to be more modest and partly because unit prices obtainable were almost

[93] BCA, BCC, Draft Annual Report for 1945–1946.

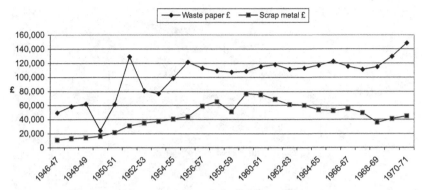

CHART 3.5. Glasgow: income from scrap metal and wastepaper sales, fiscal years 1946–1947 to 1970–1971. *Source:* extracted from Annual Reports, MLG DTC/7/3/1/5.

invariably lower than for paper. The detailed figures kept by Glasgow depicted in Chart 3.5 show the relative yields for wastepaper and scrap metals from 1945 to 1972.

Despite the observation in a 1950s textbook that the variety of metal in household waste was both considerable and varied,[94] the reality was that most of what was collected by cleansing departments was ferrous material in the form of empty food cans. In those cities that had operations geared to extracting metals from waste mechanically, however, recovering such metal scrap was a relatively simple capital-intensive rather than labor-intensive task, in contrast to wastepaper operations.

Glasgow, for instance, had a tradition of metal recovery dating back to the early 1900s. The city introduced magnetic extraction during the 1920s,[95] and unlike Birmingham and Manchester invested in modernization in its main treatment works after the war, even when planning a completely new plant.[96] Improved overhead magnetic separators such as those installed at Glasgow's Govan works in 1950 extracted all ferrous material quickly and efficiently, reducing labor time and increasing yields.[97] Glasgow recovered 5,702 tons of scrap in 1949, the year before

---

[94] Andrew Thomson, *Modern Public Cleansing Practice*, 3rd ed. (London: Technical Publishing Co. Ltd, 1951), p. 237.

[95] "The Govan Refuse Power Plant of the Glasgow Corporation," *Engineering* 125 (1928): 549ff.

[96] MLG, DTC 7/3/1(5), Annual Report 1947–1948, p. 9. The site was purchased that year as a matter of urgency as it was essential that "no delay takes place in the erection of these new works."

[97] MLG, DTC 7/3/1(5), Annual Report 1950–1951, p. 11.

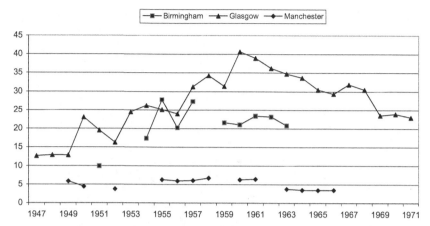

CHART 3.6. Scrap metal as percentage of all salvage income, Birmingham, Glasgow, and Manchester, fiscal years 1946–1947 to 1970–1971. *Source:* extracted from Annual Reports, Birmingham, BCC/BP 1919–1952 and 1953–1974; Glasgow, MLG DTC 7/3/1 (5); Manchester, MCA M595.

the new magnetic collectors were installed. This compared to 6,964 tons during the first full year of operations for the new collectors, an increase of approximately 22 percent. What is more, a rise in market prices of some 17.5 percent at the same time that salvage levels increased lifted income from £13,968 to £21,269 and raised scrap metal's share of the department's salvage sales from 12.83 percent to 19.53 percent.[98]

In contrast, neither Birmingham nor Manchester prioritized metals recovery, and where comparative figures are available it is clear that neither achieved results even close to Glasgow's (see Chart 3.6). In Birmingham, in 1950 (the first year for which figures are available), scrap metal sales were £11,054, or almost 8 percent of total salvage income. The following year, sales rose to £14,012, nearly 10 percent of all receipts. In the fiscal year ending in 1948, Manchester, on the other hand, sold 1,803 tons yielding just £3,216, or less than 6 percent of salvage income, and in 1951 the tonnage was down to 1,386 and income correspondingly decreased to £2,997, or about 3.5 percent of revenue.[99] (See Figure 3.5.) Unlike Glasgow, however, both English cities owned food-processing plants and, as recounted earlier, expended a good deal of energy in extracting saleable materials from food waste from 1945 through the 1960s and even into

[98] Ibid., Annual Reports 1948–1949 and 1950–1951.
[99] MCA, M595 Annual Reports, Salvage Reports 1948 and 1951.

FIGURE 3.5. Metal trash cans as salvage, Whalley Range, Manchester. This picture dates from 1952 but typifies the usual local authority practice of replacing worn-out containers with new ones as part of their cleansing services. The old zinc-plated steel cans were then sold to scrap metal dealers and the proceeds used to reduce the service's running costs. Photograph courtesy of Manchester City Council.

the early 1970s. Prioritization of efforts was presumably influenced by perceptions of local marketing potential.

In contrast, scrap metal sales in Glasgow rose steadily from the late 1940s to the late 1950s, although they were generally well below those for wastepaper. In fiscal year 1958–1959, the city's cleansing superintendent reported that it had been difficult to dispose of all the scrap metal recovered, commenting that the disbanding of "Scrap Campaign Committees" was a sign of severely diminished interest in recovering scrap metal.[100] Three years later, there was "little profit" to be made from salvaged metals. And a year after that, the annual report noted that the city's scrap contractor had closed down his operation completely, despite facing a £10,000 penalty for breach of contract. Another firm had in the meantime entered into a new contract at terms far less beneficial to the city, the price guaranteed being reduced from £7.64 to £4.53 per ton, or

---

[100] MLG, DTC 7/3/1(5), Annual Report 1958–1959, p. 3.

almost 41 percent.[101] The records show, however, that the actual prices realized in the following seven years never fell below £5.44 per ton, even in 1965, when, according to the cleansing superintendent, there was "no Scottish market" for the baled ferrous scrap being produced.[102]

In any event, both tonnages and income from scrap metal sales began to fall in Glasgow during the late 1960s, a national trend identified in the 1971 report of the government's Working Party on Refuse Disposal.[103] Although the data were incomplete and based primarily on estimates up to 1967, the figures that were reported showed a fall in scrap metal collections in England and Wales from 64,935 tons in 1963–1964 to 56,216 tons in 1966–1967, a decline of nearly 17 percent. Income meanwhile decreased by over 19 percent to £367,401.[104] Wastepaper, on the other hand, provided a stark contrast: tonnages were almost four times greater and their value six and a half times more than metals in 1966–1967.[105] The viability of scrap metal recovery as a municipal operation was therefore increasingly called into question, even taking into account the traditional argument that any income was useful in offsetting overall costs.

There were in fact significant problems with metal salvage that did not exist to the same extent with wastepaper. First of all, paper is relatively easy to collect separately from other household wastes, although as indicated earlier in this chapter, it was a labor-intensive operation that incurred sometimes significant overheads. Recovering ferrous metal from domestic rubbish, on the other hand, was only viable as part of a separation process geared primarily toward removing the dust and cinders created by domestic solid-fuel heating.[106] When the shift to central heating drastically curtailed the amount of house fire grate residues, there was henceforth "no necessity for this and, consequently, any separation must be justified on salvage grounds alone."[107] The high costs of plant and labor incurred through pre-separation of metals were thus now seen as unjustifiable in relation to the returns to be made, especially in view of the declining price trend for metals. New incineration plants already

---

[101] Ibid., Annual Report 1962–1963, and Annual Report 1963–1964, p. 22.
[102] Ibid., Annual Report, 1964–1965, p. 19.
[103] Department of the Environment, *Refuse Disposal: Report of the Working Party on Refuse Disposal* (London: HMSO, 1971). No data for Scotland were included in the Working Party's considerations.
[104] Ibid., p. 90, Table 1, Quantities.
[105] Ibid., p. 91, Table 1, Gross Income.
[106] Ibid., p. 92.
[107] Ibid.

commissioned and being built in the early 1970s were designed in anticipation of this development and consequently made no provision for separation. The only concession made for metal recovery, in fact, came in the form of magnetic sifting of incinerator residues.[108] Manual sifting of wastes was, apart from its questionable economics, no longer seen as a "desirable occupation."[109] Policy makers' thinking was clearly shifting to the conviction that existing methods of metal separation were rapidly becoming unviable.

In addition to the economic factors bearing directly on metal recovery, there were also technological and other factors affecting the market for scrap metals. From the 1950s, the scale and nature of demand for scrap from the metals industries changed, in part as a result of the growing availability of good-quality iron ore at "economic prices" and "increasingly stringent specifications" for scrap from steel makers. The supply situation, moreover, was expected to continue for "the foreseeable future," with the result that smaller tonnages of scrap would be needed.[110] In addition, because the scrap cans that made up the bulk of domestic metal refuse needed to be processed to remove their tin and solder constituents, they were considered "notably more intractable than new tinplate scrap" and consequently less attractive to trade buyers.[111] This combination of low prices for ores and greater selectivity on the part of smelters subsequently caused local authorities to reconsider their practices carefully, although again there was a need to balance the indirect benefits of reducing the total amount of space that might be saved at tips.[112]

As with wastepaper, judging the benefits of scrap metal salvage for local authorities was not necessarily straightforward. Efficiency in collection and the ability to package or bale it for easy removal by contractors were certainly important, as was the ability to enter into beneficial agreements with buyers. But no matter how well organized plants were and no matter how shrewd the negotiations, the inescapable fact was that metal dealing nationally was on a smaller scale in Britain than the wastepaper

---

[108] Ibid., See also MLG DTC 7/3/1(5), Annual Report 1966–1967, p. 10, noting that the city's new incinerator plant would work on the "direct incineration" method.

[109] Department of the Environment, *Refuse Disposal*, p. 92.

[110] Department of the Environment, *First Report of the Standing Committee on Research into Refuse Collection, Storage and Disposal* (London: HMSO, 1973), p. 10.

[111] M. E. Henstock, ed., *Disposal and Recovery of Municipal Solid Waste* (London: Butterworths, 1983), p. 73.

[112] Department of the Environment, *First Report of Standing Committee*, p. 11.

trade, and the contribution to cost reduction was thus inevitably less. By 1968, metal accounted for just 9 percent of the UK's municipal solid wastes by weight, compared to 37 percent for paper, which had become the single largest component of an average garbage can's contents.[113] No detailed costings for metal scrap comparable to those for wastepaper described earlier seem to exist, but the implication of these and other figures available must be that metal was far less important than paper to local authorities. The only real exception to this generalization may have been based on conservation of tipping space, and then possibly only on the grounds that metal takes far longer to decay than paper. In any case, it is clear that trends in metal salvage for the UK's public cleansing departments up to the end of the 1960s were, like those for paper, rooted in a combination of labor and scrap materials markets, technology, labor availability, and changing household waste streams.

Conclusion: The Role of Salvage in Postwar Public Cleansing Systems

There is no doubt that there were important markets and deep-seated traditions in salvage in both the United Kingdom and in Germany prior to the Second World War, especially in wastepaper and scrap metal, but the war led to an urgency to regularize and expand them, largely through state intervention. After the war, expanded wartime practices carried on in both countries for some time, owing mostly to postwar privation on the one hand, and the holdover of legislation from the war on the other. In Germany, however, perhaps because the wartime experience of salvage was much more draconian and was associated with National Socialist economic and racial policies, because Nazi policy had fatally undermined the prewar salvage business, because postwar privation was much more profound, and because recovery and resurgence of the economy was so rapid and sustained, wartime practices were jettisoned very quickly indeed, with salvage even in the form of the long-standing and highly institutionalized bottle deposit system under threat by the mid-1960s. In Britain, the departure from wartime practice was more gradual, perhaps because the disruption during and after the war was much less extreme, because long-standing salvage markets were not destroyed through government policy, and because the government was, if anything, strengthened rather than discredited by the outcome of the war. In addition, strong prewar national markets in Britain in the key areas of wastepaper and scrap

[113] Henstock, *Disposal and Recovery*, p. 118.

metal salvage could be resumed following the cessation of government restrictions in the 1950s.

In both cases, however, by the late 1960s, salvage practice, especially in the still-dominant municipal authority sector, was undermined or eliminated through a combination of economic vulnerability (in the form of market collapse and/or volatility, which may have been especially important to public-sector authorities), lack of public enthusiasm, and, especially in the case of Britain, changes in disposal practices. There are many ironies here, one of which is that a city like Glasgow, with a long and distinguished tradition of municipal salvage recovery, essentially began abandoning that tradition in the mid-1960s. In contrast, at about the same time and along with other West German cities, Frankfurt, a city whose weak traditions of municipal salvage were jettisoned practically entirely by the early 1960s, rediscovered the attractions of salvage, which became redefined as recycling. We now turn to an analysis of the causes, course, and consequences of these and other changes in waste in the next chapter, which is also the start of Part two, devoted to the period between the late 1960s and 1980.

PART II

GRAPPLING WITH CRISIS

From the 1960s to 1980

4

The Waste Flood

Introduction

For public cleansing as well as many other areas of British and West German politics, society, and the economy, much of the period from 1945 until the mid-1950s was characterized first by efforts at reconstruction and some reform and thereafter by a resumption of what many perceived as a return to some sort of "normality" after the extreme upheaval of the war, and prior to that the upheaval of the interwar period. However, even before the first postwar decade was over, there were clear signs that any notions of a return to pre-Depression and prewar normality amounted to a pipedream, whether that might be for better or for worse. Politically and economically, division of Germany, Europe, and indeed much of the world seemed not only permanent but also characterized by incessant hostility and tension.

On the other hand, by the second half of the 1950s, fears of a postwar recession or even depression receded, as both Britain and West Germany (along with the rest of the industrialized world) entered a golden age characterized by strong and steady economic growth, widespread employment, an emerging cornucopia of consumer goods, and steadily increasing buying power for most people. The intermingling of Cold War tensions, economic growth and competition, and consumerism was epitomized in the so-called kitchen debate of July 24, 1959, between Soviet leader Nikita Khrushchev and U.S. vice president Richard Nixon on the occasion of Nixon's visit to the USSR. In front of a kitchen exhibit featuring the latest gadgets at an American trade fair, the two men exchanged threats about potential missile deployment in close conjunction with – indeed, as a direct result of – claims and counter-claims about prosperity and consumer provision in capitalism versus communism.[1]

For British and German capitalism though, it is clear that sustained economic growth and prosperity translated into increased disposable income in both the United Kingdom and Germany, which led in turn to increased consumption and, perforce, to growing levels of household waste. Accommodating this growing waste stream was most assuredly a challenge to public cleansing professionals, but they were nevertheless generally optimistic that they would be able to cope with it at the local and/or regional level using a mixture of traditional practice and rationalization measures.

It might have been expected that this optimism would wane beginning in the late 1960s in tandem with the apparently rapid fading of the sheen and luster of the postwar economic golden age. Indications that the golden age was over started with "the end of the economic miracle" in Germany and much of the rest of the industrialized world, an ending conventionally dated in 1966;[2] an increasingly unviable Bretton Woods system; and eventually the energy crises and "stagflation" of the 1970s. But it is clear that, at least when it came to spending, getting, and throwing away, the optimism remained. In spite of economic crises, growth in household waste streams showed no signs of abating. Instead, the stream became a flood.

Opening the Floodgates: Changing Patterns of Consumer Behavior

The fundamental reasons for the explosion in volumes of household waste from the late 1960s were practically identical in Britain in Germany and did not so much involve revolutionary or even new developments as

---

[1] For a brief account of the "kitchen debate," see "1959: Khrushchev and Nixon Have a War of Words," BBC News, "On this Day 1950–2005," http://news.bbc.co.uk/onthisday/hi/dates/stories/july/24/newsid_2779000/2779551.stm (accessed January 28, 2011). More generally on the competition between the two countries and their respective blocs, see Nordica Thea Nettleton, "Comrade Consumer: Economic and Technological Images of the West in the Definition of the Soviet Future 1957–1969" (PhD thesis, University of Glasgow, 2006).

[2] Ferenc Jánossy, *The End of the Economic Miracle: Appearance and Reality in Economic Development* (White Plains, NY: International Arts and Sciences Press, 1971); Herbert Giersch et al., *The Fading Miracle: Four Decades of Market Economy in Germany* (Cambridge: Cambridge University Press, 1992); Tim Schanetzky, *Die große Ernüchterung. Wirtschaftspolitik, Expertise und Gesellschaft in der Bundesrepublik 1966–1982* (Berlin: Akademie, 2007), pp. 55–56.

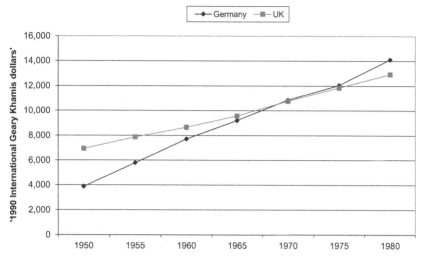

CHART 4.1. Per capita gross domestic product, Britain and West Germany, 1950–1980. *Source:* Angus Maddison, *The World Economy: A Millenial Perspective* (Paris: OECD, 2001), Table C1-c, pp. 276–277.

an intensification of ones that were already well underway. In essence, there were three interrelated causes. First, there was a continuation and heightening of trends involving more things bought, owned, and eventually discarded by more people. Second, beginning already in the 1950s, new ways of distributing and selling these things were extended and consolidated. And third, the additional things that flowed into the consumer society continued to change in composition, as did the packaging in which they were shipped to stores and sold to consumers, a trend that also had emerged during the 1950s.

More Things for More People
The story of the rapid rise in average incomes among those living in industrialized countries, including the United Kingdom and West Germany, is well known and need not detain us long here. Essentially, the story is this: in terms of gross domestic product (GDP) per capita, Britain, already relatively wealthy compared to most other countries in 1950, became nearly twice as wealthy per capita by 1980, while Germany, which had started out at about 57 percent as wealthy as Britain per capita at the beginning of that period, caught up with it by the early 1970s and outstripped the earliest industrializing nation over the course of the following decade and beyond (see Chart 4.1).

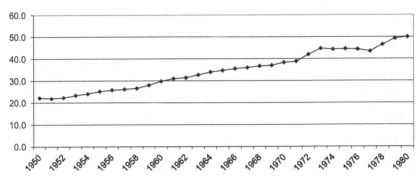

CHART 4.2. UK households' real disposable incomes 1950–1980 (2006 = 100).
Source: http://www.ons.gov.uk/ons/rel/naa1-rd/united-kingdom-economic-accounts/q1–2012/tsd-united-kingdom-economic-accounts-q1–2012.html (accessed July 11, 2012).

GDP per capita, however, is, of course, at once a very handy but also a very rough indicator of relative economic performance over time, because it says nothing about distribution of wealth or where or how it is being spent. Here, examination of indices of disposable income over time constitutes a useful next step. For the United Kingdom, there was a steady and steep rise in real disposable incomes (i.e., personal or household income, minus taxes and other mandatory charges, which can be spent for necessities and discretionary items) between 1952 and 1974 (see Chart 4.2, which shows an index of real disposable household income with 2006 set equal to 100). Owing to a combination of relatively lower prices for food and other necessities and increasing income, by the early 1960s, households had about half again as much disposable income as they had a decade earlier. By 1974, in fact, average British households had more than double the amount available to spend on things other than necessities compared to what they had in the immediate postwar period. There was some faltering of this upward trajectory in the mid-1970s, however, before real disposable incomes began moving upward again in 1978 and beyond.

We do not possess exactly equivalent data for West Germany for this time period, but those we do have indicate a similar upward trajectory. Real household income there in 1960 was just over a quarter of what it would be in 1980. That figure had grown to just over a third of the 1980 level by 1964, to just over half by 1970, and to well over two-thirds by 1974. What is striking here is that real household income in West Germany practically quadrupled in the two decades between 1960 and

1980, while real disposable income for households in Britain did not even double during the same period. This is another strong indicator of Germany catching up with – and eventually surpassing – Britain economically in the post–World War II period.[3]

It should also be borne in mind that these considerable increases in GDP per capita and real income per household occurred in the context of population growth in both countries. The population of Britain (i.e., England, Wales, and Scotland) grew by approximately 5 percent in the 1950s, 5.85 percent in the 1960s, and 0.78 percent in the 1970s, in all amounting to an increased population of almost 5.9 million compared to the beginning of the 1950s.[4] In Germany, the increase was even more dramatic. Owing to inflows of population from East Germany and elsewhere, increasing birthrates, and rising life expectancy, West Germany's population increased by more than 20 percent between 1950 and 1980, from about 50 million to just less than 62 million, a net increase of some 12 million people.[5] In other words, not only was there a lot more money floating about in both countries, there were many more people to spend it and thus a much larger consumer base for an expanding basket of products.

But what did this increasing population spend its growing income on? As previously suggested, there were important national differences between the United Kingdom and Germany in this regard. British city dwellers were probably more likely than their West German counterparts to own their homes than to rent them, for instance, which also probably entailed larger expenditures for elective do-it-yourself, furniture, and household decoration in Britain.[6] Both countries shared key characteristics as well. Automobile ownership, for instance, skyrocketed.

---

[3] German figures calculated on the basis of statistics in R. Rytlewski and M. Opp de Hipt, *Die Bundesrepublik Deutschland in Zahlen 1945/49–1980* (Munich: Beck, 1987), p. 118. For British figures, see Figure 4.2.

[4] Joe Hicks and Grahame Allen, *A Century of Change: Trends in UK Statistics since 1900* (London: House of Commons Library, 1999), p. 6, available at http://www.parliament.uk/documents/commons/lib/research/rp99/rp99-111.pdf (accessed July 12, 2012).

[5] Figures based on the German *Statistisches Jahrbuch* (*StJB*) and available at http://www.populstat.info/Europe/germanwc.htm (accessed September 29, 2011). Note that the remainder of citations from the *StJB* refer to the official published versions.

[6] Home ownership in Britain boomed in the 1950s as part of a rise in the rate of owner-occupation of homes from 23 percent of British households in 1918 to 57 percent in 1981. As a percentage of UK households, home ownership overtook the private-rented sector in 1961. See Andrew Heyward, *The End of the Affair: Implications of Declining Home Ownership* (Smith Institute, 2011), p. 6, available at http://www.smith-institute.org.uk/file/The%20End%20of%20the%20Affair%20-%20implications%20of

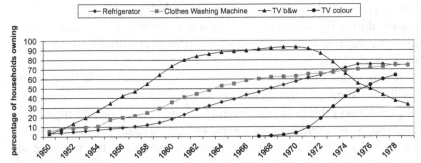

CHART 4.3. England and Wales; household diffusion of refrigerators, washing machines, and televisions, 1950–1979. *Source:* Sue Bowden and Avner Offer, "Household Appliances and the Use of Time: The United States and Britain since the 1920s," *Economic History Review*, New series vol. 47 (1994): 745–746.

In Britain, annual registrations of new private automobiles rose from less than 2 million in 1950 to 4.9 million in 1960. Car ownership then doubled to almost 10 million vehicles in 1970 and continued the upward trend in the following decade, rising to nearly 14.7 million in 1980.[7] Germans, on the other hand, owned fewer than a million cars in 1952. But by 1960, automobile ownership in West Germany had soared to 4.2 million, nearly catching up with the British in absolute terms. The Germans then surpassed the British in this area by 1970, with 12.9 million private cars on the road, a figure that rose again to 23.2 million, more than half again as many as in Britain, by 1980.[8]

Households in both countries were, however, even more likely to spend money on acquiring consumer durables, including televisions, washing machines, and refrigerators. (See Chart 4.3 for the British case.) The rapidity with which these consumer durables were adopted in the 1950s and 1960s is indeed breathtaking. In Britain, for instance, only 3 percent of households in England and Wales had a black-and-white television in 1950. By the late 1960s, by which time householders were increasingly choosing color televisions, the percentage of households with black-and-white televisions peaked at well over 93 percent. And color television's

%20declining%20home%20ownership.pdf; and BBC News Channel, "Home Ownership Dips to Decade Low," February 13, 2008, available at http://news.bbc.co.uk/1/hi/business/7242492.stm (both web pages accessed February 1, 2013).
[7] Figures available in Table VEH0103, "Vehicles Licensed Annually in UK." http://www.dft.gov.uk/statistics/tables/veh0103 (accessed 4 November 2011).
[8] *StJB* 1958, p. 352; *StJB* 1966, p. 366; *StJB* 1968, p. 322; *StJB* 1974, p. 338; *StJB* 1978, p. 263; *StJB* 1982, p. 278.

rise was even more meteoric. Just one-tenth of 1 percent of English and Welsh households had a color TV in 1967. But by 1978, two-thirds of them did. Comparable figures are not as readily available for West Germany, but here too it is clear that rates of ownership of televisions were rising steeply. In 1962, for instance, just over a quarter of German households had a television, but by 1980 that figure had risen to fully 97 percent.[9]

Other major consumer durables enjoyed even earlier widespread diffusion. Fewer than 10 percent of English and Welsh households had a washing machine in 1950. By the late 1970s, about three-fourths of English/Welsh households could machine wash their clothes at home. We do not have corresponding figures for Germany in the early period, but we know that by 1962 just over a third of German households had a washing machine. In 1980, the German figure for the proportion of households owing washing machines was at 91 percent – considerably higher than for Britain. Household refrigerator ownership, for another example, in 1950, was only about 5 percent in England and Wales, and in the early 1960s this had risen to about 20 percent. In West Germany, in 1962, in contrast, over half of all households already had a refrigerator. By the mid-1970s, around three-fourths had a refrigerator in England and Wales, while in West Germany the corresponding figure was 93 percent.[10] Additionally, of course, this increasingly widespread diffusion of "big ticket" items was accompanied by steep growth in ownership of smaller things such as cameras, transistor radios, electric can openers, and other consumer appliances.

Part of what was going on in both countries during this "golden age" was what Jan-Otmar Hesse has identified as "complementary consumption": for instance, the increasing numbers of people who purchased a television very often also bought a refrigerator, with which they could keep snacks and drinks cool for consumption while watching TV.[11] This is difficult to prove conclusively, but it is, for example, one plausible

---

[9] Sue Bowden and Avner Offer, "Household Appliances and the Use of Time: The United States and Britain since the 1920s," *Economic History Review*, New series vol. 47 (1994), pp. 745–746; Rytlewski and Opp de Hipt, *Die Bundesrepublik Deutschland in Zahlen*, p. 140.

[10] Bowden and Offer, "Household appliances," pp. 745–746; Rytlewski and Opp de Hipt, *Die Bundesrepublik Deutschland in Zahlen*, p. 140.

[11] Jan-Otmar Hesse, "Komplementarität in der Konsumgesellschaft. Zur Geschichte eines wirtschaftstheoretischen Konzeptes," *Jahrbuch für Wirtschaftsgeschichte* 30 (2007): 147–167.

explanation for the striking fact that in West Germany after the war the amount of bottled beer consumed rose rapidly.[12] Germans, that is, – along with British and citizens of other Western nations – increasingly changed their primary locus of consumption from public spaces such as the pub to private ones such as the living room and the kitchen, which in turn required that the household be outfitted with a range of new objects to support this new behavior.

Changing Patterns of Distribution, Retailing, and Consumer Behavior
The ever more widespread diffusion of consumer durables cannot be fully understood, however, without acknowledging that acquisition of these objects in part caused and in part was caused by new and different ways of purchasing these and other consumer goods. Two key developments stand out in this regard, both for Britain and for Germany. The first was the emergence of self-service retailing, especially in the food sector. The second was the growing importance of mail order. And both involved logistical issues in delivery from producer to store and producer/store to consumer that required the use of increasing amounts of packaging.

Traditional food and much other retailing in both Britain and Germany through 1945 involved staff dealing individually with customers. This practice was gradually but substantially replaced by larger stores that carried a vastly increased range of lines on open display, where customers served themselves and paid for the goods before leaving. Such self-service stores were extremely rare in Britain immediately after the war, but they became commonplace over the next quarter century.[13] It has been estimated that there were only 10 such stores in the United Kingdom in 1947, but by 1956 the figure was around 3,000, and by 1960 it had reached as many as 6,350.[14] In Germany, on the other hand, Herbert H. Eklöh opened the first self-service store in 1938 in Osnabrück in northern Germany, which ended in failure. But Eklöh did not give up and tried again in the late 1940s, this time successfully.[15] By 1950, others had followed his example, and there were already 20 self-service

[12] Lothar Ebbertz, *Die Konzentration im Braugewerbe der Bundesrepublik Deutschland: Entwicklung und Ursachen* (Frankfurt/M.: Peter Lang, 1992), pp. 43ff.

[13] G. Shaw, L. Curth, and A. Alexander, "Selling Self Service and the Supermarket: The Americanisation of Food Retailing in Britain, 1945–1960," *Business History* 46 (October 2004): 568–582.

[14] Ibid., 574.

[15] Jens Scholten, "Umbruch des genossenschaftlichen Förderauftrags durch Innovation und Wachstum: Nachkriegsentwicklung und Einführung der Selbstbedienung bei der

department stores in Germany. In 1970, the number of self-service shops had risen to 85,602 as a result of increasing numbers of department stores and a substantial move on the part of specialist shops toward self-service. By then, self-service stores amounted to fully 67.5 percent of all retail shops.[16]

In Britain, the first self-service stores were no more than conversions of existing businesses, usually in premises that were under 500 square feet and selling restricted ranges of foods such as fruit and vegetables or bakery items. By the early 1960s, however, when larger self-service stores were becoming widespread, the British concept of a supermarket was clearly defined as having a minimum sales area of 2,000 square feet and selling "all food groups... plus basic household requisites" such as laundry supplies, cleaning materials, and personal hygiene products.[17]

By the 1970s, this type of store began to dominate both British and German retailing, as both the number and size of large stores grew substantially. Shoppers steadily became habituated to self-service for the majority of their food purchases and many nonfood items as well. This change naturally occasioned the disappearance of the assistants who had advised and directed shoppers toward particular lines of merchandise. They were replaced by displays on customer-accessible open shelves that emphasized the various roles of packaging in protecting products, in giving the appearance of hygiene, and of promoting what was being offered, functioning in other words as a form of advertising.[18] Commodities that had previously been weighed and bagged by shop assistants were thus now prewrapped in standard packages. New materials such as plastic films were increasingly used to enhance the durability of paper-based materials or, with growing frequency, to replace them altogether. By the mid-1960s, indeed, a typical British self-service supermarket chain noted that all its lines were prepackaged – even its bakery products were in some

REWE Dortmund," in Jan-Otmar Hesse et al., eds., *Das Unternehmen als gesellschaftliches Reformprojekt. Strukturen und Entwicklungen von Unternehmen der "moralischen Ökonomie" nach 1945* (Essen: Klartext, 2004), pp. 167–200, especially pp. 173ff.

[16] Hans-Ulrich Wehler, *Deutsche Gesellschaftsgeschichte, Bundesrepublik und DDR 1949–1990*, vol. 5 (Munich: C. H. Beck 2009), p. 77. Note that the British figures apply just to self-service stores that sold food primarily, whereas the German ones also include specialist shops that made the transition to self-service.

[17] Shaw et al., "Selling Self Service," p. 574.

[18] Cf. Rainer Gries, *Produkte als Medien. Kulturgeschichte der Produktkommunikation in der Bundesrepublik und der DDR* (Leipzig: Universitäts-Verlag, 2003).

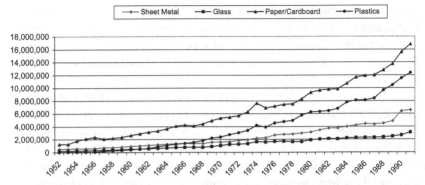

CHART 4.4. Gross production value of West German packaging industry (1000 DM). *Source:* Mathias Nast, *Die stummen Verkäufer. Lebensmittelverpackungen im Zeitalter der Konsumgesellschaft. Umwelthistorische Untersuchung über die Entwicklung der Warenpackung und den Wandel der Einkaufsgewohnheiten (1950er bis 1990er Jahre)* (Bern: Peter Lang, 1997), p. 345.

form of closed wrapping when on display.[19] German retailers for their part did not go quite this far, but here too, most goods were packaged in some way.

It was not just the sale of goods in self-service stores that required packaging, however. Supplying such goods to ever-growing numbers of ever-larger stores also necessitated transport in bulk, often over long distances. And to achieve economies of scale while making the distribution process more efficient and effective by minimizing damage and breakage, more and more packaging was required. Indeed, the ever-increasing deployment of packages is evident in the value of production for the West German packaging industry (see Chart 4.4).

Rising demand for packaging and the change in consuming habits did not stem exclusively from self-service retailing. Purchase of goods from mail-order outlets also grew apace in the postwar period in both the United Kingdom and Germany. These companies supplied a very large array of merchandise, from seasonal food hampers to clothing and footwear and from children's toys to hardware, bicycles, and lawn mowers. In Britain, the mail-order sector enjoyed substantial growth from the 1950s onward, proportionately even greater than other nonfood retailers. The newfound prosperity among broad swaths of the population became evident at this time, particularly in the form of "a meteoric growth" in this

---

[19] Peter Mathias, *Retailing Revolution: A History of Multiple Retailing in the Food Trades Based on the Allied Suppliers Group of Companies* (London: Longmans Green and Co., 1967), Plate 7.

relatively new form of consumer behavior, which was initially termed "home shopping."[20] Between 1961 and 1979, mail-order sales from the principal firms in the sector rose from 2.5 to 5.3 percent of the UK retail market, and their share of nonfood sales was even higher by then at fully 9.2 percent.[21] In West Germany, the growth of mail order sales was very similar to that in the United Kingdom. Starting almost from scratch, mail-order firms gained a market share of more than 5 percent of total department store sales by 1980, a share that has remained constant since then.[22]

All of this merchandise, of course, also had to be packed for safe transit. Although impossible to calculate precisely, we can get some inkling of the massive numbers of parcels sent from some of the data available. In the United Kingdom, in 1958, for instance, one of the main mail-order businesses, Grattans, was sending out 100,000 separate parcels each week, or approximately 5 million per year.[23] Assuming that the four other large firms in the sector were sending out similar numbers, this means that around half a million parcels per week, most of which contained more than one individually packaged item, were arriving at British homes.[24] Mail order's market share, moreover, grew threefold by the end of the 1970s, by which time around 1.5 million parcels, all protectively packed to prevent damage in transit, were being delivered weekly. Furthermore, because the mail-order businesses monitored their dispatch systems closely to govern costs, they constantly evaluated both materials and methods and were quick to adopt new products that were likely to improve their efficiency.[25] Plastics in the form of bags and tape thus became an integral part of their packing processes, although cardboard and paper continued to be heavily used also.

Materiality, the Consumer, and the Changing Waste Stream

Rising living standards in the United Kingdom and Germany in the period between 1950 and 1970 involved corresponding increases in ownership of consumer durables and changes in consumer behavior. These have been studied extensively by historians and other commentators. Virtually

---

[20] R. Coopey, S. O'Connell, and D. Porter, *Mail Order Retailing in Britain: A Business and Social History* (Oxford: Oxford University Press, 2005), p. 52.

[21] Ibid., Table 2.1, p. 53.

[22] Ralf Banken, "Schneller Strukturwandel trotz institutioneller Stabilität: Die Entwicklung des deutschen Einzelhandels 1949–2000," *Jahrbuch für Wirtschaftsgeschichte* 30 (2/2007): 117–145, especially p. 132.

[23] Coopey et al., *Mail Order Retailing*, p. 52 provides the figure, citing an unpublished manuscript prepared by the company itself.

[24] Ibid., Table 2.3, p. 68 provides indication of market share by company.

[25] Ibid., pp. 160–162.

nobody, however, has looked at this from the other perspective – that is, from the standpoint of consumerism as a form of waste production. Here, the effects of changing behavior were threefold. First of all, and most obviously, more things purchased meant more things thrown away, with packaging in particular finding its way almost immediately into the municipal waste stream. Second, and related to this, the consumer durables purchased, along with many other objects in the cornucopia of postwar consumerism, were subject to the inevitable end to useable life that any object experiences – an end frequently hastened by fashion and technological change. All of us are familiar with the latter, whether from the hastily changing formats of music reproduction from records to various types of magnetic tapes to compact discs and beyond, or from the rapid increases in computing speed and reliability that rendered machines obsolescent before they were physically worn out. To be sure, these are more recent examples of the phenomenon, but as already indicated, it also occurred in the period we are examining, such as in the rapid displacement of black-and-white by color televisions (see Chart 4.2 above for UK trends in television ownership).

The third way in which increasing numbers of objects and changing patterns of retailing and distribution had an impact on waste production related to the materiality of objects and the packaging in which they were delivered. Traditional materials continued to be widely used; paper and cardboard, for instance, still packaged many powder or granulated products such as flour and sugar. Glass, rather than plastic, also long remained the material of choice for jars and bottles, particularly for milk and soft drinks where there was a long-standing tradition of encouraging buyers to return them for reuse after sterilization. Some of the materials used to manufacture consumer goods and for packaging did not exist prior to the 1950s, however, or if they did, it was only in minuscule amounts.

The sheer number of new materials makes it unwise to try to examine them all. Instead, three classes of materials with particular relevance for the waste stream are highlighted here. First, many new consumer appliances required the use of batteries, and the rising demand that resulted from this was met not only with long-standing zinc-carbon and nickel cadmium technologies but also with new ones such as alkaline and mercury types developed on a large scale after the Second World War. Discarded batteries obviously added to the waste stream in weight and volume, but their disposal also involved concerns over real or potential toxicity. The second category of new material was semiconductors. The transistor was one such device. First developed after the Second World War, transistors were being used increasingly in consumer electronics design and manufacture by the middle to late 1950s. They were followed closely by a broader class of semiconductors and then in the mid-1970s by integrated circuits.[26] Again, besides adding to the weight and volume of the waste stream owing to the rapidity of technological change in the industry, these objects were environmentally problematic not just in the manufacturing but also in the disposal process.

The third class of material formed the most ubiquitous, visible, and ultimately controversial addition to the waste stream in the period from the end of the Second World War until 1980: synthetic materials, including synthetic fibers and thermoplastics. We focus on the latter in particular here. Plastics, of course, were by no means a creation of the 1960s. Synthetic materials such as Bakelite had been used for a range of molded products, ranging from electrical insulation components to automobile steering wheels and from telephone handsets and housings for radios to cameras and smokers' pipes, all dating back to well before the Second World War.[27] Cellophane was another such material. However, technological progress in the manufacture of synthetic polymers – stimulated significantly by the pressures of the war – transformed the qualities and capabilities of plastics in general, and after 1950 their use grew "at an explosive rate."[28] Widespread in all industrialized nations, the extent to which they were employed, however, varied from country to country. Britain, for example, consumed considerably less plastic material in the 1960s than did Germany, the United States, or Japan, but the rate of growth was still substantial. West Germany, on the other hand, was by the late 1960s by far the largest consumer of plastics per capita among rich industrial countries, with consumption rates well over twice those of Britain by 1969[29] (see Chart 4.5).

[26] Michael Tushman and Charles O'Reilly, "Ambidextrous Organizations: Managing Evolutionary and Revolutionary Change," *California Management Review* 38, No. 4 (1996), p. 9. More generally, see Ernest Braun and Stuart Macdonald, *Revolution in Miniature: The History and Impact of Semiconductor Electronics*, 2nd ed. (Cambridge and New York: Cambridge University Press, 1982).

[27] See W. E. Bijker, "The Social Construction of Bakelite: Toward a Theory of Invention," in W. E. Bijker, T. P. Hughes, and T. Pinch, eds., *The Social Construction of Technological Systems* (Cambridge MA: MIT Press, 1989), pp. 174–185.

[28] B. G. Reuben and M. L. Burstall, *The Chemical Economy: A Guide to the Technology and Economics of the Chemical Industry* (London: Longman, 1973), p. 34.

[29] In *Plastik und politische Kultur in Westdeutschland* (Zurich: Chronos, 2007), Andrea Westermann explores some of the political, cultural, and environmental dimensions of

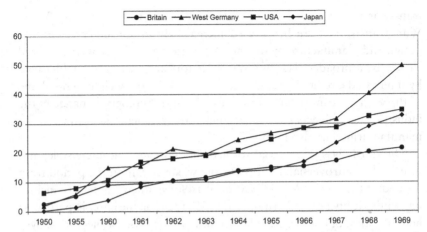

CHART 4.5. Per capita consumption of plastics, Britain, West Germany, United States, and Japan, 1950–1969 (kg per capita). *Source:* B. G. Reuben and M. L. Burstall, *The Chemical Economy: A Guide to the Technology and Economics of the Chemical Industry* (London: Longman, 1973), Table 2.4, p. 35.

If we look not at consumption but at production, UK growth was substantial, and indeed continued almost without interruption year to year until the end of the 1970s (see Chart 4.6).[30]

In Germany, on the other hand, production rates skyrocketed, with output rising by about two and a half times between 1950 and 1960 and then nearly doubling again between 1960 and 1965 before doubling yet again between 1965 and 1969. By the end of the 1960s, then, per capita German consumption of plastics was more than double that of Britain, while German production outstripped that of the United Kingdom by more than three times, indicating a high level of export (see Table 4.1).

One thing that has to be emphasized here in the context of the history of waste handling is that the term "plastics" refers to a wide variety of synthetic polymers with widely differing characteristics, including not only polyethylene, polypropylene, polystyrene, and polyvinyl chloride (PVC), but also mixtures and/or overlays of such polymers. The fact that they became so ubiquitous, combined with the wide variety of thermoplastics deployed and the fact that some of them were overlays of different plastic

---

this process of embracing plastics in West Germany using the case of polyvinyl chloride (PVC).

[30] Data from 1980 excluded some information submitted by the industry on the grounds of commercial confidentiality.

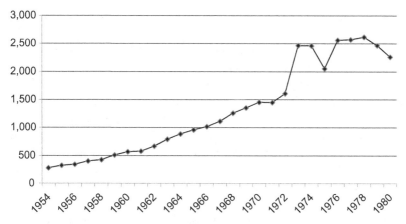

CHART 4.6. UK production of plastics materials, 1954–1980. *Source:* Central Statistical Office, *Annual Digest of Statistics* (London, HMSO): "Annual Production of Plastics Materials" (1954–1958) and "Annual Production of Synthetic Resins" (1959–1980).

types, soon posed enormous challenges for waste-handling professionals. We develop this point at greater length later in the chapter.

In any event, at this point it is important to note that the new materials, which began to appear from the 1950s, could be made more cheaply and with superior qualities of lightness, strength, and flexibility, which, taken together, permitted their use in a far wider range of applications than earlier types. Plastics could now be used for furniture, floor coverings, bathroom fittings, kitchen utensils, component parts in products from

TABLE 4.1. *Production of Plastics in West Germany, 1950–1969*

Year	Production of Plastics (million tons)
1950	0.379
1955	0.384
1960	0.982
1965	1.999
1969	3.963

Source: Deutscher Bundestag/Drucksache VI/1519 (December 4, 1970), BA Koblenz, B 106, 29370.

clocks to automobiles, and by no means least importantly, as packaging for almost anything.

Plastics, however, were introduced into consumer durable and other nonfood packaging for somewhat different reasons than in food-related industries. Nonfood products could be sealed in rigid, transparent plastic to enable attractive display of products, while at the same time protecting them from soiling and pilferage. Materials such as expanded polystyrene, moreover, offered the tempting advantages of being shock absorbing and easily molded to accommodate relatively delicate items irrespective of their size. The two-part clamshell close-fitting container, for instance, could protect goods in transit far more effectively than cardboard boxes, corrugated cardboard rolls, or even those traditional stalwarts of fragile-goods dispatchers, tissue paper and straw. Being very light, it could also substantially reduce transit costs, which in Britain were generally based on weight rather than volume. And, at least as importantly, it was inexpensive.

The photo-optical goods trade, many of whose products were highly sensitive to shock damage, well illustrates the extent to which these new materials displaced the old. By the late 1960s, not only were delicate items such as cameras almost universally cosseted in large volumes of molded, shock-absorbing polystyrene and foam rubber, but processing chemicals that had previously been delivered in glass bottles or metal canisters were now also presented in some type of plastic material. Powder chemicals, for example, were packed in polythene bags, while liquid ones came in plastic bottles or flexible sachets; sensitized materials acquired plastic containers as well. The leading maker of 35mm film, Kodak, which sold millions of film containers annually in the United Kingdom and elsewhere, began to replace the protective aluminum outer canisters with plastic ones toward the end of the 1960s. And by the end of the 1970s, synthetic packaging was the norm, biodegradable fiber materials being used for only a declining number of items.[31]

Many other categories of consumer goods benefited similarly from the perceived benefits of plastic packaging. From small objects such as wrist-watches to large and bulky items such as televisions, expanded shock-cushioning foam became the norm, even if a cardboard box usually still housed the ensemble. The arrival of S-shaped expanded polystyrene shock-absorbing packing chips in 1972 marked another milestone in the

---

[31] This paragraph is based on the personal experience of one of the coauthors of this book, Stephen Sambrook, who worked in the photographic trade during this period.

supplanting of natural fiber-based packing materials in distribution.[32] These loose polystyrene packing fillers, which soon appeared in other shapes as well, could indeed be described as ubiquitous chips. They enjoyed a rapid uptake in the distributive trades because they not only reduced the weight of parcels and added to protection in transit, they also made the packing of awkwardly shaped items quicker and easier for distributors and retailers.[33] Thus, although heavy-duty cardboard never disappeared from the world of outer packaging (and indeed would eventually see a resurgence in the 1990s), synthetics became the material of choice for the packaging industries during the 1970s, especially for inner packaging.

The Dimensions of the Problem

So, how did the combination of more goods for more people, changing patterns of consumer behavior, and the increased embrace of new materials affect the household waste stream in each of the two countries between the late 1960s and 1980? Before we answer that question directly, some background is needed. As noted previously, early statistics on waste were notoriously unreliable, and this did not change that much even in the 1970s when governments began serious efforts to try to collect them.[34] In Germany, initial efforts to measure waste "output" began with simply trying to discover how big the waste problem really was and how many different kinds of waste existed. In the early 1970s, for instance, the West German Ministry of the Interior ascertained for the first time that cattle excrement was the single highest category of waste production.[35] Additionally, there were varieties of toxic waste, atomic waste, industrial waste, trade waste, and household waste. In other words, it was not just the waste stream that grew; it was accompanied by a profusion of types and categories of waste. In addition to the problems of spotty and inconsistent returns (which were frequently based on estimates that often appear to have been plucked out of the air) and spiraling numbers of

---

[32] http://www.interpack.com/cipp/md_interpack/custom/pub/content,oid,10949/lang,2/ticket,g_u_e_s_t/~/Trends_in_Consumption.html (accessed February 22, 2011).

[33] For instances of the problems of packaging consumer goods for transit, see Coopey et al., *Mail Order Retailing*, pp. 158–163.

[34] For Germany, for instance, this began to be reported on a regular basis only beginning in the early 1980s. See, for instance, *StJB* 1983, p. 561; *StJB* 1993, p. 730.

[35] Programm "Umweltgestaltung – Umweltschutz" der Bundesregierung. Beitrag der Projektgruppe "Abfallbeseitigung," May 15, 1971, BA Koblenz, B 106, 29370.

categories, there is another issue with the statistics from this period: lack of comparability not only between Britain and Germany but also within each country and over time.

The best we can do to try to understand the extent of growth in output of waste and its changing composition is to look at snapshots at as local a level as possible. However, looking first at the three cities in the United Kingdom – Birmingham, Glasgow, and Manchester – there seems to be an inconsistency between what we might expect given the background outlined above and what actually happened, and this is a puzzle to explain. According to weight, based on the statistics that we have, the amount of waste in Glasgow in fact did not increase between 1964 and 1972 – it actually declined by about 25 percent! Birmingham's waste output by weight also declined, if not as dramatically, while Manchester's did not grow once it reached a peak in 1966 and began to decline. How can this be the explained?

To understand this, it is necessary once again to distinguish between weight of waste collected – which was the preferred method of recording used by local authorities in Britain (and also, as we shall see shortly, in Germany) – and volume of waste. Measuring by weight was conveniently accomplished by running loaded collection vehicles over a weighbridge or truck scale. Determining volume, however, was much more problematic, and because local authorities generally felt the need to measure the efficiency of their waste-handling services by relating costs to quantities handled, they naturally opted for the easiest available value, irrespective of whether it actually gave them an accurate picture of what was happening in the refuse stream. By the 1960s, it must be recalled, central heating systems were becoming more and more prevalent in both countries, resulting in a steep decline in the single heaviest component of the household waste stream – ashes and cinders and other fire-grate residues – and this trend was sometimes further emphasized by a decline in city populations. In Glasgow, for instance, the resettlement of those housed in high-density tenements to new towns outside the city boundary reduced the population from approximately 1,055,000 in 1960 to 898,000 a decade later.[36] Consequently, even though elimination of many coal fires meant that some paper and other wastes that previously would have been burned in the grate at home found their way into the municipal waste stream,

[36] Figures taken from Mitchell Library Glasgow, records of the City of Glasgow, Cleansing Department (subsequently MLG), DTC 7/3/1 (5), Annual Reports 1960–1961 and 1970–1971.

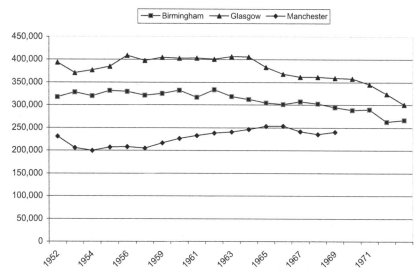

CHART 4.7. Refuse tonnages collected in Birmingham, Glasgow, and Manchester, 1952–1972. *Source:* extracted from Annual Reports, Birmingham BCC/BP 1919–1952 and 1953–1974; Glasgow MLG DTC 7/3/1 (5); Manchester MCA M595.

increasing its weight slightly, we would expect a severe plunge in tonnages collected. That this was not more severe is worth noting: as indicated in Chapter 3, a decrease in tonnages collected of as much as 65–70 percent might have been expected were fire-grate residues removed entirely from the waste stream.[37] The sheer amount of almost invariably lighter materials that kept tonnages collected from falling even further would thus suggest a vast increase in volume of waste collected in these British cities by the 1970s (see Chart 4.7).

Seen in this light, the startling decrease in tonnages collected in Glasgow between 1964 and 1972 appears dramatically different and is much more in keeping with what might have been expected given changes in consumer behavior and sales and distribution practices during the postwar period through about 1980. Thus, in addition to a slowly growing stream of relatively long lived consumer durables that had reached

---

[37] In Manchester, the summer proportion of "fine dust" and clinker could be as low as 25 percent, but in winter it was typically 65 percent or more. Figures extracted from Manchester City Archives, Records of Manchester City Council, Collection reference M595 (subsequently MCA M595), M595/2/2/61 Cleansing Department, Annual Report 1950–1951, tables detailing analysis of refuse from different classes of property. In Glasgow, the winter proportion could exceed 70 percent; see MLG, DTC 7/3/1 (5) Annual Report 1946–1947, analysis of refuse collected.

their end of life and/or had fallen out of fashion or behind technologically, practitioners were confronted with a substantial increase in the "instant wastes" of daily living, which were also now changing radically in makeup as well. Along with traditional household waste output, including uneaten food, discarded newspapers and magazines, small unwanted domestic artifacts, worn-out or redundant clothing, and household textile waste, plastics and other new materials were now finding their way into household refuse containers.

Before examining the specific ways in which these new materials affected waste collection and disposal, however, let us look briefly at the German situation, focusing on Dortmund and Mannheim. Dortmund, a city in the Ruhr district with plenty of disused mineshafts to fill with rubbish, estimated its collection based on the rather crude measure of the number of rounds each collection vehicle made multiplied by its capacity. Still, even though we have to take the figures thus compiled with a large portion of salt, the trend is unmistakable and impressive. It also seems to contradict the trend noted for the three British cities we looked at. Yet, there are ways in which the trend line exaggerates what was actually taking place in Dortmund. A large part of the growth through the 1960s, for instance, is an artifact of two factors: a substantial increase in service on the one hand and incorporation of surrounding communities on the other. In addition, two other factors were at work here. One was undoubtedly the low starting point for Dortmund and other German cities in the postwar period: probably "normal" – that is, prewar – levels of waste collection by weight were not reached until the mid-1950s. The rapid and unremitting increase thereafter may have been associated with the spectacular rise in living standards in Germany during the period of the "economic miracle," combined with the reluctance we noted in Chapter 3 to engage in the salvage practices so closely linked in the minds of the German populations with the privations of the war and postwar periods. Chart 4.8 gives a clear and unmistakable idea of what practitioners were faced with.

Mannheim's experience certainly confirmed the scale of the problem faced by West German cleansing practitioners in the wake of the "economic miracle," but the way that city collected data gives a different and much more nuanced picture of it. Until 1970, Mannheim, unlike any of the cities we have looked at so far, measured the waste it collected by volume rather than by weight. The vast increase in volume of more than two and a half times between the late 1950s and 1970 portrayed in Chart 4.9 is striking, and the increase cannot be explained by the

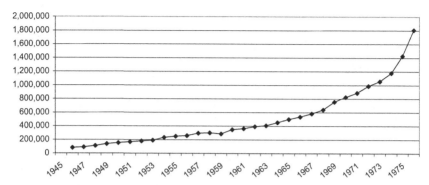

CHART 4.8. Waste tonnages collected in Dortmund, 1945–1978. *Source:* Jahresberichte Müllabfuhr, StA Dortmund, Bestand 190,8, "Dortmunder Statistik: Amt für Statistik und Wahlen," 77/III, p. 2.

incorporation of surrounding villages or extension of service because these were largely complete in the case of Mannheim by about 1960. From 1970 on, however, the local statistics office in the city changed its practices to measure the amount of waste, because in 1966–1967 the city acquired an incineration plant and, for incinerators, the weight of waste is far more important than its volume. Chart 4.10 illustrates the trend between the early 1970s and 1991 in weight of waste collected in Mannheim, which increased considerably in the first part of the period along the same lines as the trend experienced by Dortmund, probably for some of the same reasons. Thereafter, it leveled off by and large.

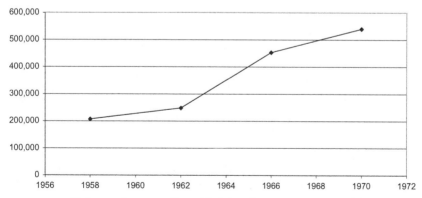

CHART 4.9. Volume of waste collected in Mannheim, 1958–1970 (cbm). *Source:* Stadtverwaltung Mannheim (ed.), *Statistische Übersicht auf dem Sachgebiet der Verkehrsplanung, des Tiefbauwesens, der Stadtreinigung, des Fuhrparks* (Mannheim: City of Mannheim, 1970), p. 20.

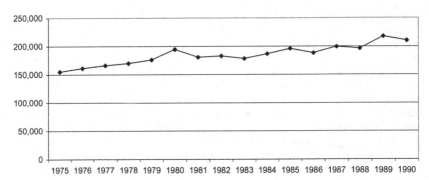

CHART 4.10. Tonnage of waste collected in Mannheim, 1975–1991. *Source:* Karl Pulver, "Von der Abfuhranstalt zum Eigenbetrieb. 125 Stadthygiene in Mannheim. Aus Verwaltungsberichten zusammengestellt von Karl Pulver" (Unpublished manuscript 2005, StA Mannheim), pp. 90ff.

But, again, even though the total weight eventually rose slowly, it is likely that the volume of waste rose much faster. Indeed, growing volume was probably an important factor in incineration becoming an attractive alternative to landfill during the 1960s.

All in all, then, the numbers that we have available, as incomplete as they are, would seem to confirm that the waste stream in the United Kingdom and Germany was growing substantially, in volume if not always in weight, during the 1960s and 1970s. Both countries experienced this general trend, but they differed in the timing of it. German cities appear to have witnessed continued growth in weight as well as volume, probably owing to later and much more rapid increases in the standard of living and also to the country's different wartime and postwar experience. In both countries, however, an important part of the increase in volume of waste collected involved new materials that posed new and different problems for waste practitioners. Let us now examine this by looking more closely at the case of plastics, which were certainly not solely responsible for changes in volume and composition of waste streams but played an important and highly visible role in that process. Because of the availability of a highly detailed professional report published in 1970 on the past, present, and future of plastics waste the United Kingdom, we focus in what follows on the British case, although there is no question that the general trends identified would have been similar in Germany, if not more pronounced by virtue of the greater usage of plastics in that country.[38]

---

[38] The report is J. J. P. Staudinger, *Disposal of Plastics Waste and Litter* (London: Society of Chemical Industry, 1970). On Germany, see Westermann, *Plastik und politische Kultur in Westdeutschland*, p. 126.

The findings of the 1970 study, undertaken under the auspices of the UK Society of the Chemical Industry, suggested that there would be long-term problems for waste disposal in Britain owing to the new material, something no doubt particularly telling given the interests of the sponsors of the study. The study found that packaging accounted for a substantial proportion of UK plastics consumption, estimated at between 20 and 25 percent. By weight, this amounted to some 250,000 tons in 1968, all of which was assumed to have become "instant waste."[39] Despite the assumption that all plastics packaging was discarded immediately, however, a sampling exercise conducted with the cooperation of Birmingham's Salvage Department in 1968 and 1969 estimated that only 46 percent of it found its way into household garbage cans. Although not further analyzed in the study, the remainder was almost certainly to be found in the trade collections done by the city, in the form of litter, or in the contents of public waste containers – in other words, it too would have eventually found its way to city landfills and/or incinerators. The Birmingham results also indicated that plastic waste in domestic refuse constituted approximately 1.2 percent of total weight, a value supported by other unidentified data that gave a corresponding figure of 1.15 percent for the rest of the country. For the chemists who did the study, the impact of plastic waste on local authorities' refuse disposal systems was still insufficient "to cause much concern," but they accepted that there was potential for future difficulties, particularly because the amounts entering the waste stream were certain to grow. The extent of that growth could not be accurately predicted, however. The figure forecast by the chemists in their study was 1.4 million tons by 1980. By then, they contended, plastics would make up 6.5 percent of all refuse collected. This was a far more modest estimate than that arrived at by A. E. Higginson of the Institute of Wastes Management, who predicted that plastic refuse levels (especially from packaging) would be at 3.5 million tons by 1980.[40] Whatever the eventual amount, though, the impact of this growth would be felt in both collection and disposal, because of plastic materials' physical characteristics and their chemical properties.

The physical characteristics of plastics in particular affected all stages in the "very complex" technology of refuse management.[41] Although the

---

[39] Staudinger, *Disposal*, p. xv; p. 3, Table 2 provides the quantitative data here and for the rest of this section unless otherwise indicated.

[40] Staudinger, *Disposal*, pp. 9–13 and 89; A. E. Higginson, "The Impact of Plastic Materials on Public Cleansing Services," *Public Cleansing* (January 1970), p. 15. Neither provides details about how the figures were determined.

[41] Staudinger, *Disposal*, p. 39.

weight of waste being handled formed the focus of municipal statistical returns, it was the relatively low density and high volumes of plastics that stood to exert the greatest effect on waste handling. This applied to both collection and disposal. In each case, low densities and high area-to-weight ratios meant plastic waste took up a disproportionate amount of space. Although accounting for less than 1.5 percent of weight in houses' refuse containers in the late 1960s, plastics were then estimated to take up 5 percent of the space, even though the use of rigid and semirigid containers was still far from extensive at the time. Plasticized cardboard, wrapping tape, and films were not necessarily any more bulky than traditional materials, but rigid expanded polystyrene packing was different. It not only occupied high volumes relative to the size of what it had protected but obdurately resisted volume reduction when thrown away. The typical polystyrene foam (also known by the brand name Styrofoam) packaging for a camera, for instance, had a volume of over 550 cubic inches for contents whose volume was scarcely a tenth of that figure. Other products followed a similar pattern. And breaking the polystyrene into small pieces produced only a small reduction in volume. Plastic containers, on the other hand, were usually made of polyethylene, and bottles in particular resisted manual crushing. What is more, because of their elasticity, they tended to revert to their original shape and volume to take up excessive space within household waste bins. Although still far from universal, the advantages they offered in terms of light weight and low cost were such that they were expected in the late 1960s to replace many of the "multi-trip" reusable glass bottles in the near future.

In Germany, this trend was also in evidence, if slower and ultimately less extensively than in Britain. In the mid-1960s, for instance, trading companies in Germany started a big advertising campaign for plastic drink bottles ("Ex und hopp"), highlighting how easy they were to dispose of.[42] But this provoked the first opposition against the growth of plastic packaging, something we return to in later chapters. Here, we simply note that further replacement of glass bottles by plastic ones was slowed down by the opposition of interest groups, especially the Deutscher Brauer Bund (German Brewers' Association). Thus, despite the fact that in the United States, for instance, the changing retail structure went along with the wide replacement of glass bottles by cans and, later on, plastic bottles,[43]

---

[42] Letter from Bürgermeisteramt der Stadt Stuttgart to Städteverband Baden-Württemberg (May 18, 1967), StA Mannheim, Zugang 52/1979,1463.
[43] Robert Friedel, "American Bottles: The Road to No Return," conference paper, Munich, June 2011.

in West Germany traditional bottle-deposit systems were saved. This did not stop plastics from gaining a bigger market share, but it was slowed down by institutional factors.[44]

In any event, the physical properties of important plastic materials such as polystyrene and polyethylene affected not only the storage of refuse at residences but also its collection and disposal. To some extent, volume-related problems in collection services were easily dealt with. The general decrease in density and increase in volume encountered in the 1960s, not all of which was from plastics, was largely managed by the introduction of compression vehicles whose ram or screw mechanisms forcibly reduced the space occupied by collected rubbish.[45] Disposal in landfills (controlled tipping), however, was likely to encounter a variety of problems once the level of plastic waste rose significantly from its late 1960s proportion of less than 2 percent. The level was predicted to grow to more than 6 percent by 1980, by which time significant difficulties were anticipated. First, the lightweight materials used to make film wrappings and cups, for instance, were liable to be scattered by even gentle breezes when tipped from delivery vehicles at landfill sites. Such materials were therefore likely to be blown away unless immediately covered with other matter, which was unlikely given that the covering process could be delayed by hours or even days depending on working practices at individual sites. And the prospect of a blizzard of brightly colored waste spreading across and outside landfill sites was something which waste-handling practitioners, the politicians who supervised them, and the general public were unlikely to relish.[46]

Although an embarrassing nuisance, however, the problem of wind-blown detritus would be of little consequence compared to the adverse effects of low-density waste with limited structural strength being placed along with other materials into the tipping strata. The plastics would take up more site space and also threatened to form "cavities, air pockets and loosely packed aggregates" in the layers of deposited refuse.[47] Furthermore, plastic films in large quantities were liable to form barriers affecting site drainage. And the resulting instability and inadequate drainage would mean that any subsequent buildings constructed on the

---

[44] Ebbertz, *Die Konzentration im Braugewerbe*, p. 566ff.

[45] G. E. Brown, "Development of Refuse Collection Vehicles and Thoughts on Future," *Public Cleansing* (October 1968), pp. 533–541.

[46] Staudinger, *Disposal*, pp. 44–46. The following paragraphs are also based on this source. Additional citations are simply to indicate individual page numbers for quotations from the study.

[47] Ibid., p. 44.

recovered land would be unsafe; landscaping for recreational use would be left as the only viable application.

Not surprisingly, the Society of the Chemical Industry thought that there were possible solutions to these problems. In its 1970 study, the society's spokesman, J. J. P. Staudinger, wrote on behalf of the chemists that volume reduction could be realized by compaction or by pulverization of refuse, either off- or on-site. Although adding to capital and operating costs, either form of mechanical treatment seemingly offered the benefits of higher landfill densities, less dispersed material, longer landfill life, and a more stable site for future development and building. Pulverization would constitute a preferred option because it reduced the volume by 50 percent or more, and in addition it improved site stabilization and drainage. In the chemists' opinion, the only reason for not adopting pulverization on a wide scale was its additional cost.

This was something with which municipal treasurers and accountants would no doubt have agreed. The waste managers who worked for them would have pointed out in addition that no single form of pulverization could cope with all types of mixed municipal wastes. Furthermore, some sort of segregation of different types of waste would be needed before feeding into the machinery – a major consideration, but something given little weight in the report. In any case, according to the chemists, a far better way to deal with the issue was to incinerate all the refuse gathered up by local authorities.

The chemists' enthusiasm for large-scale burning was, to say the least, considerable. It was "the most perfect and perhaps in the long term the only method" for ridding the environment of the ever-growing amount of rubbish being generated by society.[48] Landfill sites were bound to become ever more remote from cities, and even with the benefit of pulverization sanitary landfill was liable to create "hazards to health and environment'" from vermin, insects, and bacteria. And compared to incineration, burying refuse was inefficient and liable to become increasingly expensive. The chemists also pointed out that cremating waste was already a long-familiar part of waste disposal, and recent "great advantages in incineration technology" had produced "highly sophisticated plants," not least because furnace technologists had accepted that large-scale burning was "most likely to become an integral part of refuse management in large population centres."[49] Cities such as Birmingham and Glasgow

48 Ibid., p. 52.
49 Ibid., p. 53.

were indeed proponents of refuse incineration, although they might have reminded the chemists that it did not eliminate the solid waste introduced into the furnace altogether. Burning merely transformed the waste into other solid residues and gases, and thus it did not entirely relieve the land, while at the same time it transferred some of the problem into the air. To complicate matters still further, of course, the physical and in particular the chemical transformations that incineration caused severe side effects in the form of atmospheric and groundwater pollution.[50]

Despite these problems, for which solutions were largely still to be found, the chemists were – perhaps not surprisingly, given their interests and point of view – nevertheless optimistic about the future and confident that available incineration methods could "successfully cope" with burning plastic waste in amounts larger than likely to be encountered in the next two decades. And even if refuse practitioners shunned cremation and continued to bury municipal rubbish, processes such as pulverization could deal with "at least some" of the problems likely to come as a result of greater amounts of plastics in the waste stream.[51] Because packaging was the chief culprit in producing plastic waste, moreover, the society concluded that some words of advice should be given to all concerned in the chain of production and consumption. The packaging industry should consider developing strategies for the eventual disposal of what it produced in increasing quantities, avoid excessive material, and look for ways to minimize the "adverse effects" of plastics in disposal processes. One long-term but problematic solution suggested was the development of new plastics that would decompose once buried. Perhaps even less practical was the optimistic recommendation that families should compact or shred their own plastic waste, encouraged to do so by "suitable incentives" from local authorities, using equipment still to be developed by domestic appliance manufacturers whose opinions on the idea, like those of the municipalities, had not yet been sought.[52]

Conclusions

What is striking about the 1970 report of the UK Society for the Chemical Industry is not that those who wrote it were optimistic about technical solutions to the growing problems associated with plastic waste: they

[50] Ibid., especially pp. 55–56.
[51] Ibid., p. 90.
[52] Ibid., p. x.

were, after all, engineers who worked for the plastics industry. What is surprising, rather, is that they recognized or anticipated virtually all of the problems that eventually arose. These included increasing quantities of waste, increased volume, disruption to traditional practice, the need to invest in new equipment and more expensive operating procedures, and the potential toxicity of incinerated plastic waste. And each of them was indeed at least in theory amenable to engineering solutions, although the extent of understanding of toxicity associated with plastic waste disposal was not very full at the time, and thus the extent of the technical problems in rectifying it were undoubtedly underestimated. The main issue, however, was that this analysis and the associated recommendations for solving potential problems were made without any real engagement with the constraints of funding, practice, politics, public opinion, and legislation that public cleansing practitioners faced. In the next chapter, we consider this minefield by examining closely the politicization of public cleansing in the 1960s and 1970s.

5

Politicizing Household Waste

From Public Health Nuisance to Environmental Pollutant

Introduction

In many ways, public cleansing has been highly politicized from the outset. Creation of municipal services to collect and dispose of household waste in Britain and Germany in the last third of the nineteenth century came about at least in part through political pressure and action from broadly based public health and sanitation movements. What is more, to a greater or lesser degree depending upon time and circumstance, public cleansing professionals have been held accountable by elected politicians in local authorities. And in addition, the role of individuals or groups giving voice to complaints has been important from time to time, especially in cases where garbage dumps or incinerators were located near housing and produced noisome odors and/or attracted vermin.

Politicization of waste took on a completely different character and complexion beginning in the late 1960s, however, and this involved the interaction of three key dimensions. For one thing, public involvement in debates about waste and other environmental issues became a much more organized activity, not least through the formation of numerous new nongovernmental activist groups and through widespread concern with toxic waste in particular. The second closely related trend involved the ongoing "scientification" of public cleansing, which brought about new understanding of the social, medical, and environmental consequences of long-standing practice. And the third area, which resulted in part from the first two but also had independent causes, was the enactment of new national legislation with far-reaching consequences, as well as the establishment of new national governmental agencies with a much more focused and active remit in this area.

Although we deal with these three strands separately for analytical purposes, they were in fact intertwined. Scandals in waste disposal, for instance, led to public pressure on lawmakers for tighter legislation, which in turn needed to be underpinned by new scientific knowledge embodied in newly trained professionals operating in newly created organizations. Essentially then, this was a dynamic, evolving relationship that – especially in the course of the 1970s – was both caused by and resulted in a reconceptualization of household waste. Domestic waste had hitherto been seen variously as unsightly, a squandering of precious resources, and/or a potential danger to public health, but eminently controllable and therefore not particularly hazardous. Instead, it came to be viewed as an insidious form of environmental pollution that required effective regulation and coordination at the national level.

These trends occurred in both Britain and West Germany, mostly for the same reasons. As we have explored earlier, both countries experienced rapid and unprecedented increases in their standard of living, resulting in more consumption and consumption of different things, which had an impact on the size and composition of waste streams. Despite these powerful common drivers, however, by about 1980, the two countries remained as far apart as ever in societal attitudes toward household waste, in public cleansing practice, and in regulation of waste. We explore some of the reasons for this continued divergence throughout the chapter, but especially in the conclusion.

Waste and the "New Environmentalism"

Intermittent public protest has been a constant feature in the history of public cleansing, especially in relation to the disposal function. It has never been anyone's choice to live close to a landfill, and people who did so were frequently vocal about their sufferings. But the protests were generally unorganized, or if organized they were done on an ad hoc and temporary basis. Also, although public outcry occasionally met with success, it was sometimes not taken very seriously. When people in Aachen complained about the smell of the local dump in 1962, for instance, public authorities simply handed out spray cans of air freshener.[1]

---

[1] Volker Grassmuck/Christian Unverzagt, *Das Müllsystem: Eine metarealistische Bestandsaufnahme* (Frankfurt/M.: Suhrkamp, 1991), p. 39.

There was, however, also a long tradition in both the United Kingdom and Germany of organized environmental activism, some of which touched on the issue of household waste, but most of which focused primarily on conservation and preservation of "natural" surroundings in the face of industrialization, urbanization, and population growth. In 1895, for example, the National Trust for Places of Historic Interest or Natural Beauty (later simply "the National Trust") was founded to "promote the permanent preservation" of buildings and landscapes and their associated animal and plant life. The Society for the Protection of Birds (later the Royal Society for the Protection of Birds) was created in 1889,[2] and the Council for the Preservation of Rural England (later the Campaign to Protect Rural England) came into being in 1927.[3] In early-twentieth-century Germany, too, a number of analogous organizations were founded. Most of these *Naturschutz* (nature-protecting) organizations were conservative groups that combined campaigns for protection of the landscape with a harsh critique of civilization, which had allegedly alienated modern humans from their natural state of being.[4] An important exception, however, was Naturfreunde (Friends of Nature), a group affiliated with the Social Democratic Party of Germany.[5]

Many of these and other groups helped bring about some of the first major environmental legislation in the two countries, although the main focus into the 1960s was not household waste but rather the apparently much more pressing – and visible – problems of smoke and water pollution.[6] By 1956, for example, Britain enacted the Clean Air Act to

---

[2] http://www.rspb.org.uk/about/history/milestones.aspx (accessed July 2, 2012).

[3] For an overview of the evolution of these, see John Sheail, *An Environmental History of Britain* (Basingstoke, Hampshire: Palgrave Press, 2002), in particular Chapter 5.

[4] Frank Uekötter, *Umweltgeschichte im 19. und 20. Jahrhundert* (Munich: Oldenbourg, 2007), pp. 73–74; Almut Leh, *Zwischen Heimatschutz und Umweltbewegung: Die Professionalisierung des Naturschutzes in Nordrhein-Westfalen 1945–1975* (Frankfurt/M.: Campus, 2006), pp. 86ff.

[5] Jens Ivo Engels, *Naturpolitik in der Bundesrepublik: Ideenwelt und politische Verhaltensstile in Naturschutz und Umweltbewegung 1950–1980* (Paderborn: Schoening, 2006), p. 51; Ute Hasenöhrl, *Zivilgesellschaft und Protest: Eine Geschichte der Naturschutz- und Umweltbewegung in Bayern 1945–1980* (Göttingen: Vandenhoeck & Ruprecht 2010), pp. 85ff.

[6] On smoke pollution in Germany, see Frank Uekötter, *Von der Rauchplage zur ökologischen Revolution: Eine Geschichte der Luftverschmutzung in Deutschland und den USA 1880–1970* (Essen: Klartext, 2003); for the United Kingdom, see Howard A. Scarrow, "The Impact of British Domestic Air Pollution Legislation," *British Journal of Political Science* 2 (1972): 261–282. On water pollution, cp. Kai Hünemörder, *Die Frühgeschichte der globalen Umweltkrise und die Formierung der deutschen Umweltpolitik 1950–1973* (Stuttgart: Steiner, 2004).

attack the problem, which expanded on municipal legislation that had come into existence slightly earlier.[7] In Germany, the Wasserhaushalts-gesetz (Water Protection Law) was enacted by parliament in 1957 and came into effect – following a long delay – in 1960. This meant that for the first time, unified legislation that applied to the whole country came into force with the objective of protecting lakes, rivers, and groundwater.[8] Clearly, both of these examples of legislation had an impact on public cleansing – the former by causing diminished use of coal fires and a consequent decrease in discarded ash and cinders in Britain and the latter through governmental power to act if runoff from landfill endangered water supplies in Germany. Solid waste was not, however, the primary target of the legislation in either case.

This long tradition of environmentalism in both the United Kingdom and West Germany was marked by two important changes by the 1960s. First of all, the number, extent, and ambitions of the organizations promoting environmental protection grew at a rapid clip. Second, the intellectual basis for such action changed dramatically, and eventually this movement became known as the "new environmentalism." Still, household waste remained for some time the least problematic form of environmental "pollution," if in some ways also the most visible.

Most commentators would agree that the new environmentalism began, like many such movements, in the United States, with the publication of Rachel Carson's *Silent Spring* in 1962.[9] Carson's cautionary tale was well written and impassioned, articulating for the first time a range of emerging scientific concerns in an accessible way. In particular, it attacked the widespread use of pesticides, especially DDT, and their effects on the environment, and for several reasons the work represented a fundamentally new and different approach to understanding the impact of humans on the environment. First of all, the problem that Carson identified was caused by science-based industry and thus entailed a scathing and profound critique of an essential component of modern industrial society. Second, the threat she wrote about was largely invisible, and – unlike smoke pollution or sewage-laden water – incapable of being perceived by human senses on their own, unaided by technology. Third,

---

[7] Scarrow, "Impact of British Domestic Air Pollution Legislation."

[8] Hünemörder, *Die Frühgeschichte*. For an overview of this and other aspects of emerging environmental legislation, thinking, and activism in a global context, see Joachim Radkau, *Die Ära der Ökologie: Eine Weltgeschichte* (Munich: C. H. Beck, 2011), esp. pp. 124–164.

[9] Rachel Carson, *Silent Spring* (New York: Houghton Mifflin, 1962).

and partly for this reason, the critique was based on scientific under-standing and involved the deployment of sophisticated techniques and apparatus. Fourth, the problem identified had its primary effect locally, but at the same time it was also systemic, reaching regional, national, and even international levels, not least in the case of DDT and similar products by virtue of the multinational enterprises that manufactured and sold them. Finally, unlike smoke pollution in cities, for instance, which had sparked legislation on smoke abatement in Britain by 1956, the threat that widespread deployment of DDT would cause a "silent spring" was not immediate, but instead would occur over time, the result of accretion. As Martin Chick has pointed out, perceptions of time (as well as space) changed dramatically in regard to environmental aware-ness and policy over the course of the post–World War II period. Acid rain and later climate change, for instance, were and are issues transcend-ing borders as well as the immediate present, involving international and intergenerational considerations and requiring new and different kinds of coordinated action at a range of political levels to address them.[10]

The new environmentalism soon spread from the United States to Britain and Germany, and it eventually involved not just national but also international organizations. Friends of the Earth (FoE), for instance, was started in San Francisco in 1969; by 1971, an affiliate of the new organization committed to environmental awareness and activism had been established in Britain, Friends of the Earth UK (FoE UK). A similar German organization followed not long afterward. In summer 1975, the Bund für Natur- und Umweltschutz Deutschland (German Federation for the Protection of Nature and the Environment) was established. Renamed two years later to enable it to use the much more attractive acronym of BUND (the Bund für Umwelt- und Naturschutz Deutschland, same approximate translation), the organization eventually became known as Friends of the Earth Germany and also became part of an international network embracing FoE organizations in a number of countries.[11]

The early history of the Friends of the Earth UK provides an excellent example of the place of solid waste in its program of action as well as of the potential strengths and weaknesses of this new type of organization. In the early years of the organization's existence, issues associated with

[10] Martin Chick, "The Changing Role of Space and Time in British Environmental Policy since 1945" (unpublished manuscript, 2011). Our thanks to Martin Chick for his kind permission to cite this paper.

[11] http://www.bund.net/ueber_uns/geschichte/ (accessed December 8, 2011).

FIGURE 5.1. Friends of the Earth dump 1,500 nonreturnable Schweppes bottles at the front entrance to the company's headquarters in London. Photograph © Press Association, image ref. PA-10605062.

household or other types of solid waste rarely occupied top positions on its agenda. It is thus somewhat ironic that its first public relations coup came during its first year of existence in 1971 when FoE UK members dumped 1,500 nonreturnable Schweppes bottles at the front entrance to the company's headquarters in London – and 12,000 bottles in total at Schweppes depots around the country – as a critique of this symbol of the throwaway culture.[12] As can be seen in Figure 5.1, however, the reason for this was that consumer waste had the virtue, unlike some other more abstract environmental issues, of being both concrete and photogenic – something that would also be the case in Britain, for instance, later in the 1970s in the context of public sector industrial action that saw black plastic rubbish bags lying uncollected on city streets. (See Figure 5.2.)

---

[12] Charles Secrett, "Environmental Activism Needs Its Own Revolution to Regain Its Teeth," *Guardian* (June 13, 2011), available at http://www.guardian.co.uk/environment/2011/jun/13/environmental-activism-needs-revolution (accessed 21 June 2011). The figure of 12,000 bottles in total is in "Schweppes Chief Asks for Bottle Study," the *Times* (November 15, 1971), p. 2. A comparable demonstration took place in 1977 in front of the Federal Ministry of the Interior in Bonn, when activists disposed tons of aluminum and tin cans. BA Koblenz, B 106, 69733.

FIGURE 5.2. Uncollected refuse in Leicester Square, central London, 1979. Strikes by refuse collection workers during the "winter of discontent" disrupted schedules and led in many places to large accumulations of refuse. The Westminster City Council set up temporary refuse collection centers, the most publicized of which was the one in the heart of London's west end at Leicester Square. Photograph © Eugene Adebari/Rex Features.

It was, however, not yet something at the top of most people's thoughts about environmental "pollution."

The FoE UK action against Schweppes and its aftermath, however, illustrate the potential impact of an environmental group on policy and practice. The publicity surrounding it, for instance, not only inspired Yorkshire-based Versil Ltd. to develop a new process for turning nonreturnable bottles into glass fiber;[13] it also enabled the still very new environmental organization to gain direct access to the chairman of Cadbury-Schweppes, Lord Watkinson. Following a meeting with the chair of FoE UK, Graham Scarle, Watkinson commented publicly that "the Friends [are] doing a very sensible job. This is a general problem which includes wrapping papers, cans, bottles, the lot," and called for the government to

[13] Ronald Kershaw, "Glass Fibre Use for No-Return Bottles," the *Times* (March 7, 1972), p. 4.

set up a working party to look into the problem and possible solutions.[14] Shortly thereafter, the secretary of state for the environment announced the formation of such a working party, in conjunction with the Glass Manufacturers' Federation.[15]

The undeniable short-term effects of FoE UK on British industry and government, however, did not necessarily translate into long-term impacts, and there were two key reasons for this. The first was that FoE UK soon turned its attention to other matters, easing pressure on industry and government, mostly because the Glass Industry Liaison Working Party's report, by emphasizing the complexity underlying a seemingly straightforward issue, fell far short of endorsing FoE UK's campaign against nonreturnable bottles.[16] Once the pressure group's focus shifted, therefore, both the government and the glass industry were relieved of the need to act on the matter and – as predicted in the report – the presence of single-use glass containers continued to grow. A second factor explaining the lack of long-term impact of the FoE UK's action was far beyond the new group's control, and it involved the economic difficulties soon faced by Britain: inflation, high unemployment, soaring commodity prices, balance of trade problems, and labor unrest. As Campbell Wilson has pointed out in his examination of the early history of one of the key journalistic outlets for the new environmental movement, the *Ecologist* magazine, "The message of new environmentalism began [by the late 1970s] to sound shrill amid the darkness and queues."[17]

Germany was less affected by inflation, but it too experienced economic doldrums in the 1970s, with higher levels of unemployment and the difficulties of dealing with the oil shocks and their

---

[14] "Schweppes Chief Asks for Bottle Study," the *Times* (November 15, 1971), p. 2.

[15] "Non-Returnable Bottle Inquiry Planned," the *Times* (November 17, 1971), p. 2. The secretary of state, Mr. Walker, also noted discussions with a range of other industry and trade associations, including the Milk Marketing Board and the Plastics Institute. The article also refers to a parliamentary question that Walker answered by outlining ongoing cooperation with the Plastics Institute "on designing plastics for disposability and refuse."

[16] Glass Manufacturers' Federation, *The Glass Container Industry and the Environmental Debate* (London: Glass Manufacturers' Federation, n.d. [stamped 1974 by British Library]).

[17] Campbell Wilson, "*The Ecologist* and the Alternative Technology Movement, 1970–75: New Environmentalism Confronts 'Technocracy,'" *eSharp* 12 (2008): "Technology and Humanity," quotation p. 17. Available at http://www.gla.ac.uk/departments/esharp/issues/12winter2008technologyandhumanity/ (accessed 20 October 2011).

aftermath.[18] Germany did not, however, witness the same temporary downturn in the prominence of new environmental organizations as Britain. Instead, antinuclear protests against both civilian and military uses of atomic power in West Germany formed the focus for a constituency of environmental activists who were also interested in a variety of other environmental and social issues. Some of them participated in the founding the Green Party in 1980.[19] Soon thereafter, Germany's decentralized political system and its system of proportional representation enabled the nascent party to become a major force. First in local, then in state-level, and eventually in national politics, the Green Party had an impact on West German waste collection and disposal practice. This is something we return to in a later chapter.

Even in Britain, in spite of the temporary loss in prominence of the recently established environmental organizations, there is no question that there was rising interest in the environment among the general British population in the late 1960s and early 1970s, which continued throughout the decade and beyond. A 1976 study of coverage of a range of environmentally related themes in the *Times* newspaper between 1953 and 1973, for example, demonstrated the extent of this increased interest. Although the proportion of the newspaper's content dedicated to these themes actually declined by 23 percent from 1953 to 1965, between 1966 and 1973 coverage expanded to nearly two and a half times what it had been in 1953. And besides more news reports, readers' environment-related letters to the editor grew from an average of only three per year between 1953 and 1967 to thirty-nine in 1973. The authors of the 1976 report duly noted that the British new environmentalism seemed to be following a similar pattern to that in the United States and claimed that the environment was now a "recognizable concept in British politics." And they also pointed to important changes in the content of news reports and published letters devoted to the environment, which they claimed had emerged as "an issue-matrix," replacing the previous tendency to concentrate on specific local issues. Much of that material went beyond

[18] Tim Schanetzky, *Die große Ernüchterung: Wirtschaftspolitik, Expertise und Gesellschaft in der Bundesrepublik 1966–1982* (Berlin: Akademie, 2007), pp. 163–171.

[19] For German nuclear activism in the 1970s and 1980s, see Radkau, *Die Ära der Ökologie*, pp. 134ff; Silke Mende, *"Nicht rechts, nicht links, sondern vorn": Eine Geschichte der Gründungsgrünen* (Munich: Oldenbourg, 2011), pp. 289ff; Anne Stokes, *A Chink in the Wall: German Writers and Literature in the INF-Debate of the Eighties* (Bern: Peter Lang, 1995).

simply describing events. Indeed, it often went so far as to echo the views of concerned nongovernmental organizations.[20]

In West Germany, too, the environmental movement slowly gained momentum on the ground beginning in the mid-1960s, not surprisingly perhaps given the stronger organizational base there. It was at this time that the first public actions took place against large-scale measures to improve infrastructure, interference with natural landscapes (for tourism and economic development in particular), and so on. In 1965, for instance, people living near Lake Constance protested against a new pipeline that was supposed to run directly along the lake and threatened to contaminate the water,[21] while in Bavaria citizens protested at about the same time against the installation of new cable cars in the foothills of the Alps.[22] These activities were precursors to those of the 1970s when the environmental movement in Germany became a major force in society and politics. By the end of that decade, many people had organized themselves and/or joined various initiatives. Indeed, a 1979 study by the Federal Environmental Office entitled *Bürger im Umweltschutz* (Citizens Engaged in Environmental Protection Initiatives) counted more than 2,000 instances of organized activism in West Germany – mainly in cities, but in rural areas as well.[23]

For both countries, however, it must be emphasized that apart from a few of these initiatives that were specifically dedicated to opposition against landfills, solid waste in general and household waste in particular were vastly underrepresented in this wave of activism, especially in comparison to antinuclear and other more visceral environmental issues. Still, there were two key developments that attested to the growing importance of consumer waste in public consciousness, this in spite of the general neglect of these issues by the new environmental groups.

The two developments were hardly equal in stature, however. The first, a nascent recycling movement run by committed environmental activists working at a local level, was far more modest in its initial impact

---

[20] S. K. Brookes, et al., "The Growth of the Environment as a Political Issue in Britain," *British Journal of Political Science* 6 (April 1976): 245–255. See especially pages 246 and 247.

[21] Miriam Gassner, "Lokale Umwelt oder transnationale Chance? ENIs Reaktion auf die Protest gegen die CEL-Pipeline in den 1960er Jahren," *Zeitschrift für Unternehmensgeschichte* 57 (1/2012): 31–46.

[22] Hasenöhrl, *Zivilgesellschaft und Protest*, pp. 163ff.

[23] Umweltbundesamt (ed.), *Bürger im Umweltschutz: Nichtstaatliche Umweltorganisationen und Bürgerinitiativen* (Berlin: Umweltbundesamt, 1979).

than the second, which involved the profound effect of widespread public realization of the potential toxicity of solid waste disposal. The first of these developments is thus dealt with relatively quickly. Suffice it to say that local recycling initiatives were set up in both countries. Those who ran them were generally more driven by their environmental convictions than by business acumen, and they soon encountered the fundamental economic realities of this activity. First of all, of course, not all materials could be recycled, and some actually cost money to recycle. This, however, would not constitute a problem in principle if there were a system of cross-subsidization in place, and that was in fact the starting point for many of these projects. In practice, as we have seen in Chapter 3, those salvageables that were meant to subsidize the reclaiming of other materials (which were either less lucrative or actually required financial outlay) were subject to the vagaries of the market and could not be relied upon for cross-subsidy over time. Many of those who undertook such initiatives thus soon discovered to their chagrin that economic survival of the recycling operation was only possible by using one of two strategies. The first was for the recycling effort to be limited to one or two areas that were consistently (for the most part) capable of paying for themselves. Here, paper, glass, and metals were the only serious candidates, although markets for them fluctuated over time. Concentration on them alone also entailed forgoing the broader ideological project embraced by many of these alternative groups: recycling or reusing other things – or even *everything*. The other possibility for long-term survival of such broadly based recycling programs involved something beyond the capability of such groups on their own: nothing short of a government-led political – and economic – commitment to underwriting the inevitable economic nonviability of broad-based recycling programs. Until the end of the 1970s at the earliest, however, this was not in the cards. Indeed, it was not at all commonplace until much later in the century.

The second development in the 1960s and 1970s had a far more profound impact on public consciousness, prompting insistence on new and/or tighter legislation and regulations that had extensive impacts on public cleansing practice. There was growing realization of the potential toxicity of waste disposed in landfills, owing mainly to perceived or actual contamination of groundwater. The same was true of incinerators, primarily because of the production of dioxins from burning PVC. This meant that in spite of relative neglect of the solid waste issue by new environmentalist organizations, it became a central area of public concern and political action during the 1970s. Solid waste was transformed in public perception from a public health nuisance into a potentially deadly environmental pollutant. Growing scientific understanding of the problem was thus both cause and effect of increased public concern and activism.

The "Scientification" of Public Cleansing

Just as environmental activism has a long history stretching back to the middle to late nineteenth century, public cleansing too has a long and distinguished tradition of deploying scientific methods of various sorts. The origins of modern municipal public cleansing organization and practice in the nineteenth century were, after all, tightly linked to new medical understanding of potential dangers to public health protection. What is more, public health professionals in both Britain and Germany after 1945 were driven by the desire to rationalize practice, in part through deployment of new technologies for collection and disposal of solid waste. However, just as was the case for environmental activism, which in the form of the "new environmentalism" changed its character profoundly starting in the 1960s, scientific research into and understanding of the biological, chemical, and physical impact of waste disposal in particular grew by leaps and bounds from about the same time. Thus, this ongoing "scientification" of public cleansing starting in the late 1960s and early 1970s also represented a change not only in degree but also in kind.

Until the 1970s, public cleansing professionals used "science" primarily in the form of civil and mechanical engineering, as through the deployment of collection and handling machinery and in the design and construction of landfills and incinerators. And although a medical/public health understanding and rationale underlaid the efforts of these professionals, logistics was their key function and efficiency of service was their key aim. This began to change in the late 1960s, however, as scientific understanding of the potential dangers of sanitary landfills and of the by-products of incineration prompted extensive rethinking of existing practice as well as the inclusion of academically trained scientists in planning and design processes. Here too, then, solid waste moved fairly quickly from being viewed primarily as a public health nuisance to being seen as a form of environmental pollution.

In the United Kingdom, this increasing interaction among scientists, public cleansing professionals, and the science of waste disposal was more haphazard than it was in Germany, although even in Britain high-level commitment (at least, in principle) from the central government to the development of scientific understanding of pollution was apparent already in 1971 when it created the Department of the Environment (DOE) to oversee the control of air, water, and noise pollution, as well as to become involved in the "preservation of amenity" and the "protection of the coast and countryside." Notice here, however, that solid waste was not specifically identified as a major category of pollution, although clearly the "preservation" and "protection" mandates enabled action in this area as well. In any case, the document creating it was ambitious in a number of ways, warning for instance that tackling environmental issues successfully would need local, regional, national, and on occasion international action.[24]

To be sure, solid waste formed just one small aspect of the department's responsibility, but the DOE was nevertheless closely concerned with issues relating to it, in particular with toxic waste. Here, it could draw on the work of the Technical Committee on the Disposal of Solid Waste, which had been set up by the Ministry of Housing and published its report in August 1970.[25] There is indeed evidence that the committee's concern with toxic waste in particular affected the DOE's position on development of UK legislation to address solid waste issues between 1972 and 1974. The DOE wanted to "think in terms of a new system of control" that would subject the disposal of particular types of waste to specific authorization and impose penalties when the systems of control were breached. And in those cases where applications to dispose of "particularly noxious wastes" were refused, the new system would provide for local authorities to give "practical and positive help," because greater public service provision of facilities was expected to be embedded in future arrangements. To make that possible, however, local authorities would need to be in a position to invest in both plants and staff to develop the necessary specialized knowledge needed to dispose of toxic wastes without affecting water pollution or the area's geology.[26]

By the early 1970s, the practitioners' body, the Institute of Public Cleansing, had also come to the realization that it would be necessary to broaden its scope to take into account the increasingly scientific and technological aspects of waste handling. One sign of this was the institute's

---

[24] *The Reorganisation of Central Government, Cmnd 4506* (London: HMSO, 1970), p. 10.

[25] Great Britain, Technical Committee on the Disposal of Toxic Solid Wastes, *Disposal of Solid Toxic Wastes* (London: HMSO, 1970).

[26] The National Archives, Kew, London, subsequently TNA, records of the Department of the Environment (DoE), HLG/120/738, memorandum from N. Pryce, D of E, April 20, 1971, to Mr. Beddoe and Mr. Nafager, p. 1.

adoption of a new name in 1973 – the Institute of Solid Wastes Management – which, significantly, articulated explicitly the change underway in the profession from public cleansing to a much broader conception, that of *waste management*. Access to training for the institute's professional qualification, the Testamur, was also widened through providing courses taught at ten technical colleges distributed across England and Scotland. These covered not just the administrative and routine tasks of collecting refuse but also the composition of refuse, methods of processing and materials recovery, and problems associated with disposal in land. Cooperation between the institute and the government was substantially encouraged by the appointment of a former practitioner, James Sumner, as assistant director of wastes in the newly formed Department of the Environment. Sumner had been chairman of the government's Working Party on Refuse Disposal, whose 1971 report was influential in shaping reorganization of UK public cleansing practice, and he became the DOE's waste division director in 1974. According to the institute's own history, he was responsible not only for a substantial improvement nationally in waste handling standards but also for modernizing the institute's professional outlook generally.[27]

In Germany, interrelationships between science, scientists, and practitioners began earlier than they did in Britain, and they were also more closely intertwined and coordinated through persons and organizations. Already in the late 1950s, in response to growing crisis in the most densely populated German area, the Ruhr district, a working group on rubbish (Arbeitskreis Müll) was founded to help effect supraregional cooperation among cities.[28] This working group relied on external expertise, for instance, from the composting expert Professor Franz Pöpel of Stuttgart University and Otto Jaag of the ETH Zurich.[29] The latter figure and his university were particularly significant: smaller countries near West Germany – Switzerland, Denmark, and the Netherlands – were approximately as wealthy on average, yet far more densely populated than Germany and therefore had to struggle with scarcity of space. Because of this, they encountered the growing waste disposal problem earlier than elsewhere,

---

[27] Lewis Herbert, *The History of the Institute of Wastes Management 1898–1998* (Northampton: IWM Business Services Ltd, 1998), pp. 40–41.
[28] The official name was "Arbeitskreis Ruhr zur Sammlung, Beseitigung und Verwertung von Müll und Stadtkehricht," but it was commonly abbreviated as "Arbeitskreis Müll."
[29] Letter from Internationale Arbeitsgemeinschaft für Müllforschung (IAM) to Minister Niermann (MELF) (December 29, 1960), HStA Düsseldorf, Betand NW 354, 1096.

and they also pioneered in the development of alternative technologies of waste disposal.

The founding of the Arbeitskreis Müll was important not least because it was one of the first organizations to deal with the problem of waste scientifically. Thus, the working group outlined a concept for a central landfill for the Ruhr district (Großdeponie Emscherbruch) and also engaged in planning for a new incinerator in Essen-Karnap. Not long after this, in 1958, a pilot plant was built in Düsseldorf that became a model for similar efforts in other cities, including those in the Ruhr region, as they made plans to build central incinerators.[30]

The next important institutional development involved the establishment of supraregional agencies starting with the Zentralstelle für Abfallbeseitigung (ZfA; Central Office for Waste Disposal), founded in 1965 as part of the Wasser-, Boden- und Lufthygiene Institut (Institute for Water, Soil, and Air Hygiene) in Berlin.[31] The establishment of the ZfA went hand in hand with the creation of the Länder-Arbeitsgemeinschaft Abfall (LAGA; Working Party of the States for Waste), which organized cooperation among individual German states for discussing and finding solutions to disposal problems. The ZfA emerged in particular as a central contact point for cities and towns. The department used its scientific expertise to carry out surveys tailored to the specific conditions of particular cities. In 1970, moreover, the Zentralstelle published a general leaflet that defined standards for how to manage municipal waste.[32] Organizations such as the Arbeitsstelle für kommunale Abfallentsorgung (see Chapter 3), which represented an older, less scientific approach to the issue, were disbanded.[33]

---

[30] The Düsseldorf "system" provided a model for incineration plants in Rosenheim, Berlin, Hagen, Kassel, and even Tokyo, among others. "Der Müll wird gebändigt," *Energiewirtschaftliche Tagesfragen: Zeitschrift für die Elektrizitäts- und Gasversorgung* 17, 1–2 (1967), pp. 13–14, seen in LA Düsseldorf, NW 354, 589; Niederschrift über die Mitgliederversammlung des Arbeitskreises Ruhr zur Sammlung, Beseitigung und Verwertung von Müll und Stadtkehricht am 6.6.1963 (August 8, 1963), LA Düsseldorf, Bestand NW 354, 590.

[31] Schreiben Hösel an den Bundesfinanzminister (10.9.1968): Vertrag zwischen Bund und Ländern ZfA, BA Koblenz, B 106, 58708.

[32] Gemeinsames Amtsblatt des Innenministeriums, des Finanzministeriums, des Wirtschaftsministeriums, des Ministeriums für Ernährung, Landwirtschaft, Weinbau und Forsten und der Regierungspräsidien (September 22, 1970), StA Mannheim, Rechnungsprüfungsamt, Zugang: 40/1995, 269.

[33] Gottfried Hösel, *Unser Abfall aller Zeiten: Eine Kulturgeschichte der Städtereinigung* (Munich: Kommunalschriften Verlag Jehle, 1990), p. 194.

As these new organizations came into existence, new types of experts came to the fore. There was, of course, considerable continuity in spite of this development. Until they began to be challenged by private waste management companies in the 1970s, for example, the directors of municipal cleansing departments maintained their traditional responsibility for waste collection and were usually long-term public cleansing professionals. Still, responsibility for planning and decision making on political and technological solutions to problems associated with waste disposal in particular gradually moved to chemists and engineers who had no background in cleansing departments but who instead owed their positions to their scientific expertise.[34] The dominant figure in the Zentralstelle für Abfallbeseitigung, for instance, was Werner Schenkel, one of Franz Pöpel's pupils. Schenkel would become one of the leading experts in the field of waste management. And when scientific expertise on environmental questions was centralized at the federal level in 1974 with the foundation of the Umweltbundesamt (Federal Environment Agency), Schenkel became the head of the solid waste department, one of three divisions within the agency.

Scientifically trained experts also began to make an appearance in government ministries. Starting in the mid-1960s, for instance, a new generation entered responsible positions in the Federal Ministry of the Interior, which was the main driver of environmental policy from the early 1970s. The first thing these young ministry officials did was to identify the true extent and contours of the waste problem, and to this end they contracted the German office of the American Battelle Institute to act as consultants. Battelle, a not-for-profit research and development company, subsequently compiled a series of studies on composting, plastics, and wastepaper on the ministry's behalf.[35] These and other reports provided important preliminary background material for the development of West German federal waste legislation in the early 1970s. One of the young officials was Gottfried Hösel, who would later write a rather folkloristic history of waste from Roman times to the present.[36]

New institutions, new experts, and numerous specialized studies on waste meant, of course, that from the late 1960s the amount and the

---

[34] Referat U I 6 (Dr. Hösel). Betr. Sofortmaßnahmen der Bundesergierung zur Errichtung einer Bundesanstalt für Abfallwirtschaft (July 23, 1971), BA Koblenz, B 106, 58708.

[35] Bundesminister für das Gesundheitswesen: Niederschrift über die Besprechung am 2.7.1969 im Bundesministerium fuer Gesundheitswesen in Bad Godesberg (October 1969), BA Koblenz, 106, 29370.

[36] Ibid.; Gottfried Hösel, *Unser Abfall aller Zeiten.*

quality of available knowledge on waste in Germany grew exponentially. One impact of this was a dawning awareness of just how big the problem really was, as well as how many different kinds of waste actually existed. Officials in the Ministry of the Interior, for instance, were shocked to discover that the largest single type of solid waste in Germany was residue from industrial-scale livestock farming. They also became aware of the problems of scrap vehicles, ever-increasing amounts of plastic waste, and sewage sludge.[37] A further outcome of the studies was to make officials acutely aware of just how desperately they needed more sophisticated waste statistics to replace what had hitherto been extremely simplified and often highly idiosyncratic data compiled for individual cities, which in most cases simply counted the number of times their collection vehicles made their rounds and multiplied that by the vehicles' capacity.[38] The effect of this realization of the need for better data was an improvement, at least to some degree, in reporting during the years that followed. New research on waste produced knowledge and numbers, and urban statistical practice became more sophisticated as a result. In particular, cities with incinerators changed their statistical parameters, creating new categories of waste and privileging the measurement of weight of waste over volume.[39]

The most important result of all this systematic and scientific attention to the waste problem, however – and this applied both to West Germany and the United Kingdom – was that practitioners and the public began to realize just how poisonous some waste components really were. In 1965, for instance, the Bavarian government published a list of potentially dangerous substances with just eighteen entries.[40] Ten years later, the list had grown to a few thousand.[41] The toxic waste issue took on visceral and existential dimensions, however, as a result of a series of scandals

[37] Letter from Umweltbundesamt (Von Lersner) to Bundesminister des Inneren (July 22, 1975), BA Koblenz, B 106, 27094; Letter from Hessischen Ministers für Landesentwicklung, Umwelt, Landwirtschaft und Forsten to Bundesminister des Inneren (April 2, 1979), BA Koblenz, B 106, 70539.

[38] Letter from Hösel to Ministerialrat Menke-Glückert, BmI (January 27, 1971), BA Koblenz B 106, 29370.

[39] E.g., *Statistisches Jahrbuch der Stadt Frankfurt 1968* (Frankfurt: City of Frankfurt, 1969), p. 88.

[40] Anhang Bayerisches Staatsministerium des Inneren: Beseitigung von Hausmüll und ähnlichen Abfällen in kommunalen Anlagen (Sonderveröffentlichung Bayerisches Staatsministerium des Inneren, August 1965), StA Augsburg, 49/1473.

[41] Bericht über die Auswertung der Erfahrungen im Zusammenhang mit der Hanauer Giftmüllaffäre (January 1974), BA Koblenz, B 106, 65269.

in both countries (and indeed in all industrialized countries) beginning in the 1960s. These scandals were identified in part by virtue of scientific research, and they also had the effect of prompting still more research activity. In each of the two countries, it was a particularly notorious scandal in the early 1970s that galvanized public opinion and brought about new or enhanced legislation and regulation.

In Britain, the key incident occurred in 1971. Sustained media outcry following the discovery of a quantity of highly toxic cyanide waste dumped at a disused brick kiln near Nuneaton, Bedfordshire,[42] led to the creation of the Royal Commission on Environmental Pollution, which in turn rapidly produced a report calling for controls over dumping hazardous wastes. The drafting of a new law followed closely behind – indeed, in an unprecedented ten days – as did its almost equally rapid enactment by Parliament: the entire process took less than a month! In the same year in Germany, the infamous Hanauer Giftmüllskandal (Hanau Toxic Waste Scandal) also affected legislation and regulation by demonstrating shortcomings in existing laws, leading subsequently to substantial alterations. In this case, a private waste management company from Hanau disposed of toxic waste from chemical companies in normal solid waste landfills in the vicinity. The owner of the company was arrested and put on trial, but it turned out to be almost impossible to sentence him. Legislation proved ambiguous, and it became less and less clear in the course of the trial just who had been deceived in the affair. Most of the companies that had been "duped" by the contractor had in fact been well aware that he and his employees did not dispose of waste properly. The fundamental problem, in short, was the nonexistence of infrastructure to fulfill the requirements of new legislation,[43] which would eventually lead to adjustments to legal and regulatory frameworks. We return to these shortly.

The general result of such scandals in both Germany and the United Kingdom was a complete shift in how solid waste was perceived. What was dangerous was no longer what was generally known and could be perceived by the senses but rather what was unknown and could not be so perceived. Ironically, perhaps, the massive learning curve in all sorts of areas associated with the environment through systematic scientific research beginning in the 1960s led to a situation in which the general

---

[42] Stuart Bell and Donald McGillivray, *Environmental Law*, 6th ed. (Oxford: Oxford University Press), p. 560.

[43] Bericht über die Auswertung der Erfahrungen im Zusammenhang mit der Hanauer Giftmüllaffäre (January 1974), BA Koblenz, B 106, 65269.

public became convinced that knowledge on waste was almost always preliminary and inconclusive. Many had the impression that modern industrial production and the consumer society were full of invisible dangers, only some of which had been identified, and even these were only gradually and incompletely revealed.[44]

The Government Steps In

Not surprisingly, German and British politicians could not remain immune for very long to growing concerns about environmental issues. In both countries, and at about the same time, new and more powerful legislation was enacted at the national level that fundamentally changed the parameters within which public cleansing activities took place. In both cases, the legislation changed conceptualizations of the waste problem, although the new conceptualization in each case was different. The legislative action was related to the growth of environmental activism and increased scientific understanding of the waste problem, although establishing precise mechanisms of causation among the three is difficult. In the United Kingdom, there is no question that widespread public outcry over the 1971 toxic waste scandal in Bedfordshire was the proximate cause for new legislation.

The scandal, however, would probably not have had quite the same immediate legal impact had the government, the public, and scientists not already been thinking about the potential perils of solid waste. We have already mentioned the Expert Committee on the Disposal of Solid Waste, which published a report in August 1970. Six months before this report appeared, a standing Royal Commission was set up by the UK government "to advise on matters, both national and international, concerning the pollution of the environment," as well as the adequacy of research being done on the topic and the future dangers that might emerge. The commission's remit was broad: not only were its members to report on those specifics, it also had the authority to inquire into anything "on which we ourselves shall deem it expedient to advise." The first outcome of the commission's efforts, however, was modest and took the form of a short, forty-eight-page report that was published just a year after its creation; the disposal of domestic refuse on land occupied only

---

[44] Grassmuck/Unverzagt, *Müll-System*, p. 185; for the general background, see Ulrich Beck, *Risikogesellschaft: Auf dem Weg in eine andere Moderne* (Frankfurt/M.: Suhrkamp, 1986).

slightly more than one page. What is more, these comments amounted simply to a repetition of what was already well known and proffered no advice about future action, something generally true of the entire report.[45] Despite this, however, there was a considerable underlying significance in this overview of the nature and extent of pollution in Britain: for the first time ever, the national government formally recognized not only that pollution existed but also that it was essential to develop some means to control it.

That said, this report and another brief one published by a government working party in 1972 were indicative of the still very limited extent to which most solid waste was considered to be "pollution." In the 1972 report, for instance, the problems of disposing of motor vehicles and appliances such as stoves and washing machines were dismissed as "amenity" issues; in other words, such items were still considered more as general litter than as pollution. In short, British experts for the most part continued to hold the view that only a very small proportion of domestic waste was "indisputably hazardous." According to figures compiled for the Working Party, less than 1 percent of all the country's combined industrial and domestic waste belonged in that category, although the report also pointed out that because "so little information was recorded" on either the quantities or types of solid waste being produced, compulsory record keeping should be introduced as an urgent priority.[46]

There was, however, one major exception in all of these publications to the relatively relaxed view of solid waste's impact on the environment, and that was the area of toxic waste, which, of course, also turned out to be the precipitant of the first major change in UK waste legislation in 1972 in the form of a tentative Deposit of Poisonous Wastes Act.[47] As already noted, this piece of legislation was the product of hasty preparation and curtailed debate in the wake of a serious scandal. In spite of the flaws that would soon become apparent, however, the law was nevertheless highly significant for three main reasons. First, it was unprecedented in its criminalization of the depositing of any waste which was "poisonous, noxious or polluting [whose] presence on land is liable to give rise to an

---

[45] Great Britain, Royal Commission on Environmental Pollution, *First Report* (London: HMSO, 1971), pp. 1, 13, 14.

[46] *Nuisance or Nemesis? A Report on the Control of Pollution* (London: HMSO, 1972), pp. 43, 44. Refrigerators, which we now know to be at least potentially the most problematic of all kitchen appliances, were not even mentioned.

[47] *Deposit of Poisonous Waste Act 1972* (subsequently DPWA72). Elizabeth II, 1972, Chapter 21.

environmental hazard."[48] Second, it served as a model for other countries to act, being one of the first such controls introduced anywhere in the world.[49] Finally, and perhaps most importantly, it constituted the first concrete example of growing political will in the United Kingdom to regulate waste disposal for the whole country.

Not long after the hasty enactment of the law, its shortcomings were already clear, and it was soon replaced by the Control of Pollution Act 1974 (COPA74).[50] COPA74 was also shaped profoundly by another piece of apparently unconnected legislation from 1972, the Local Government Act 1972 (LGA72).[51] Establishing the connection between the two requires a slight diversion.

LGA72's origins lie in a white paper (which is an official publication setting out intended future governmental policy and giving opportunity for discussion) published by the new Conservative government in 1971. The white paper sketched out proposed changes to local government structures in England (Scotland and Wales were targeted in separate white papers, with different results) given that current arrangements had been "bequeathed" by legislation going back to 1888 when the population was scarcely half of what it had risen to in the meantime.[52] The white paper proposed to create new county councils (effectively regional bodies) and district councils (local bodies such as cities) in England with altered geographical boundaries and a logical division of responsibilities.[53] And public cleansing practice was one of the specific targets of the proposed legislation. Based in part on the finding of the Parliamentary Working Party on Refuse Disposal from the late 1960s that the "largely uncoordinated" disposal of solid wastes of all types should instead be controlled through a new system of Solid Waste Disposal Authorities,[54] the white paper proposed a separation of collection (which would remain the job of the district councils) from disposal, for which the new county councils were to be responsible on a regional basis. In Scotland, there were

---

[48] DPWA72, Section 1 (1).

[49] Bell and McGillivray, *Environmental Law*, p. 560.

[50] *Control of Pollution Act 1974* (subsequently COPA74). Elizabeth II 1974, Chapter 40.

[51] *Local Government Act 1972* (subsequently LGA72). Elizabeth II 1972 Chapter 20.

[52] *Local Government in England: Government Proposals for Reorganisation*, Cmnd 4584 (London, HMSO, 1971), pp. 5, 6.

[53] For a full list of those responsibilities, see *Local Government in England*, Appendix, p. 16.

[54] *Refuse Disposal: Report of the Working Party on Refuse Disposal* (London: HMSO, 1971), pp. 1, 132. Its remit was only to look at English practice, but the membership included both Scottish and Welsh MPs.

to be regional councils with district authorities within them, but there was to be no division of refuse collection and disposal functions; both would remain under the control of district councils.[55] The arrangements for Wales followed a generally similar pattern as Scotland's.

Faced with the prospect of separating collection and disposal functions in England, the practitioners' professional body, the Institute of Public Cleansing (IPC), began lobbying the Department of the Environment (DOE) in early 1971. It opposed the dismemberment of the unified structure of municipal refuse collection and disposal that had been the norm for almost a century. Noting in a letter to the minister for local government and development that the creation of the DOE was welcome evidence of the government's commitment to tackle environmental pollution, the IPC nevertheless reminded the minister that public opinion would be essential for success and that any new legislation must create the "best administrative machinery" to help secure it. With commendable tact (and some understatement), the IPC's letter indicated that the government's proposals suggested that "the practical operations of refuse collection and disposal are not fully understood." To separate them would be "a major error" because they actually formed two parts of a single process. The IPC was indeed absolutely unequivocal in asserting that "All cleansing services should be included in one organization in an authority of sufficient population, area and financial resources" to attain economies of scale in planning and operation. In any case, fragmentation of the two services was to be avoided in the interests of efficiency.[56]

Despite the vehemence of the IPC's arguments, practitioners failed to get their way. Although they put forward many practical suggestions about how to incorporate a collection role into upper-tier structures, the DOE paid them little heed, mainly because the department had a bigger and, from its perspective, much more problematic fish to fry. The overriding concern of the DOE was the threat from toxic wastes.[57] The department's position was made clear in mid-October 1972 in a letter to one of the local government bodies that had lobbied for the continued

[55] *Reform of Local Government in Scotland, Cmnd. 4583* (Edinburgh: HMSO, 1971), Appendix B, p. 28.

[56] TNA, Records of the Department of the Environment, HLG/120/738: "Local Government Reorganisation: Future Management of Refuse Collection and Disposal," letter from Institute of Public Cleansing (and attached document) to minister, January 11, 1971. Quotations from p. 1 (emphasis in original).

[57] TNA, HLG/120/738, memorandum from N. Pryce, DofE, April 20, 1971, to Mr. Beddoe and Mr. Nafager, p. 1.

integration of municipal refuse services. Having duly considered various expert reports, the DOE's position was that refuse collection was "a truly local service" that should be allocated to the new district councils, but that disposal was a completely different matter, with regional rather than local dimensions. Thus, it should become the responsibility of county authorities. The reasons cited involved a mixture of the economic, the administrative, and the environmental. The new county councils would have the financial resources to plan and operate large-scale waste disposal and so would "reap the benefits" accruing from such economies of scale in a way not possible if the task were delegated to smaller governmental bodies. But there was another perhaps more compelling reason. The government was now committed to a substantial extension of the provisions of the Deposit of Poisonous Wastes Act 1972, which would introduce further controls over the disposal of all waste on land. In the DOE's decided view, the new county bodies were the most appropriate ones to operate the proposed – though still unspecified – controls, especially because there was not only an anticipated requirement for the integration of domestic with industrial waste disposal, there was also a need to extend this to include toxic waste treatment and disposal.[58]

The DOE soon got its way, at least in England, with the Control of Pollution Act 1974 mentioned earlier, which duly divided collection and disposal responsibilities. It did not apply to Scotland and Wales, however, mainly owing to the belief that their very different distributions of population made the English model seem less than ideal for the Scots and the Welsh. Street cleansing, refuse collection, and refuse disposal outside of England thus remained lower-tier, local functions, substantially unchanged from earlier arrangements. The act proved highly significant, not least because it radically overhauled and extended existing law and produced the "first comprehensive system of controlling the disposal of waste" in the United Kingdom in a form that would continue without any major change until 1990.[59] Importantly, too, the new law introduced and established the concept of "controlled waste," which was defined as "household, industrial or commercial waste, or any such waste," a sufficiently broad categorization to permit inclusion of virtually everything discarded. Furthermore, waste was considered to be anything needing to

---

[58] TNA, HLG/120/738, letter October 13, 1972 from O. H. J. Pearcy, Dept. of the Environment, to N. C. Bizley, District No. 5 (Cumbria) Joint Committee, Town Hall, Westmorland. This supplies the source for the content and quotations in this and the succeeding paragraph unless otherwise noted.

[59] Bell and McGillivray, *Environmental Law*, p. 560.

be disposed of, whether a "material, effluent or substance arising from the application of any process." From now on, therefore, all contents of the typical domestic garbage can were to be elevated to a new, more meaningful status. Apart from a few strictly defined categories such as explosives and radioactive and medical wastes (for which separate regulations applied), the new collection and disposal authorities were now, for the first time in British history, legally obliged to deal with any waste generated within their jurisdiction.[60]

As might be expected, the law had little effect on waste *collection* practice, and the basis for recovering costs for this in all UK local authorities remained unchanged. *Disposal*, however, was different. Here the law's specification of new rules and regulations had a far greater impact on prevailing cleansing practices. The newly created disposal organizations were required to provide arrangements that were "adequate" to dispose of all the controlled wastes delivered to them, irrespective of origin. In addition, long-term plans had to be made indicating what kinds and quantities of controlled wastes were expected to be dealt with, as well as anticipating how much waste was to be transported out of the authority's area, either by the authority itself or by third parties. What is more, methods used to handle waste disposal had to be defined, including procedures for reclamation. All sites and plants had to be included and the costs incurred for everything within the plan estimated in advance.[61] Finally, and crucially, disposal licenses had to be held by anyone depositing controlled waste or using any plant or equipment relating to that, and all disposal or treatment sites had to be licensed by the disposal authority, which itself had to consult with the relevant collection or water authority before issuing the license.[62] This structure of interlocking licensing was meant to ensure the safe transport, handling, and disposal of waste and also the satisfactory location and operation of disposal sites and processing works, which had been difficult if not impossible to attain under previous legislation.

The underlying purpose of COPA74, then, was to control solid waste pollution through controlling the way it was deposited or disposed of, rather than through regulating its creation in the first place. It also did not place any controls on the storage or movement of waste by a license holder. On the other hand, the law's provisions hinted at a new conception related to environmental sustainability. In particular, it addressed – in

---

[60] *Control of Pollution Act 1974*, Section 30, Interpretation.
[61] Ibid., Part 1, Section 2 (1).
[62] Ibid., Section 3 (1) and Section 5 (1).

much more detail than earlier public health acts – the question of waste utilization through reuse or recycling. The 1875 and 1936 acts vested the right to collect waste – and any profit to be made from it – in the local authority. The duality of the new structure under COPA74, however, necessitated that the rights and responsibilities of each of the two tiers be spelled out explicitly. Thus, although the collecting bodies were obligated to pass material to the relevant disposal body, they were also permitted to retain waste to use it again in some way or to reclaim substances from it.[63] This meant not only that established salvage practices could be continued by municipal collection authorities such as those in Birmingham and Manchester (Glasgow, under different legislative and regulatory requirements, retained these as well); there was also encouragement of an expansion of activities in the recovery of economic value from refuse of all types. Specific provision was made for the generation of electricity by disposal authorities, for instance, either for their own use or for sale to third parties. And they were also authorized to use other fuels to assist the process if necessary.

This newfound emphasis on reclamation and reuse as official UK government policy was evident not just in COPA74 but also elsewhere. Hard on the heels of the Control of Pollution Act, the DOE published its green paper, *War on Waste: A Policy for Reclamation.*[64] The official designation of the document as "green" in this case, however, had nothing to do with the subject at hand: green papers are simply consultation and discussion documents meant to indicate the government's thinking on a particular topic and to allow both the public and members of Parliament to discuss and provide feedback on it. Still, there is no doubt that this one picked up at least part of the growing spirit of environmental awareness, proclaiming the need "for a new national effort to conserve and reclaim scarce resources."[65] Recovery and reutilization and conservation of resources were the emphases, with some stress laid on the recent law's requirement for local authorities to look at ways of promoting waste reclamation. They would have a "vital role" in winning the cooperation of the public, industry, and trade unions to achieve success in helping society to "learn, or re-learn, the habit of regarding waste material as

[63] Ibid., Section 14 (2). That the collectors had to obtain the agreement of the disposal authorities first seems to have been a legal necessity within the wording of the act, rather than an implication of a desire for salvage hegemony by the disposal authorities.

[64] *War on Waste: A Policy for Reclamation, Cmnd. 5727* (London: HMSO, 1974).

[65] Ibid., p. 1.

potentially valuable resources."[66] Despite the rhetoric and the implication that moving forward to the past was an essential prerequisite in the process of becoming a nation of salvagers, however, the green paper ultimately came down on the side of realism, noting that all this would amount to a "complex operation" in which there would be "no easy answers" to the problems involved.[67]

As in Britain, West Germany struggled during the late 1960s and early 1970s with the question of how to develop a functional and reliable legal framework to come to terms with the waste problem. Unlike Britain, however, legislation in Germany with a direct impact on public cleansing was restricted until the 1970s to the local level. Some national legislation before that was no doubt of indirect relevance to waste disposal, in particular the Wasserhaushaltsgesetz (Water Protection Law) that came into effect in 1960. The impact of this legislation, however, was ambivalent. On the one hand, it provided the main basis for efforts to protect water resources. On the other, it often proved impossible to implement or enforce, especially in the case of solid waste.[68] A good example of this was a 1963 initiative of the head (*Regierungspräsident*) of the Arnsberg district in the state of North Rhine Westphalia, a district that embraced the entire industrial area around the Ruhr River. He advised municipalities there to refuse to accept waste from industrial plants unless it could be demonstrated that there were no toxic substances in it. The measure provoked outcry from the companies involved, which insisted that they had no way of disposing of their waste given such restrictions.[69] And when numerous firms threatened to relocate to a state with more business-friendly waste policies, the ordinance was rescinded.[70] Just how many garbage dumps became "illegal" by virtue of the water protection law cannot be determined, but it must have been a very small number indeed, not least because expertise on the main issue that the legislation might have had an impact on – contamination of groundwater through toxic waste leaching from landfills – was sorely lacking.

[66] Ibid., p. 2.
[67] Ibid., p. 33.
[68] Vermerk Kau Betr.: Zentrale Müllbehandlung. Hier: Besprechung im Innenministerium am 18.9.1962 (September 18, 1962). LA Düsseldorf, Bestand NW 354, 586.
[69] Ministerieller Runderlass (January 21, 1963): Beseitigung fester Abfallstoffe, LA Düsseldorf, Bestand NW 354, 587.
[70] Letter from Bundesverband der Deutschen Industrie, Landesvertretung Nordrhein-Westfalen to the Minister für Landesplanung, Wohnungsbau und öffentliche Arbeiten des Landes NRW Joseph Franken (May 5, 1965), LA Düsseldorf, Bestand NW 354, 586.

Another problem of legislation on waste in West Germany through the 1960s was fragmentation – and sometimes overlapping – of responsibilities. In the 1950s and 1960s, the Ministry of the Interior in almost every state dealt with domestic waste, but the Labor Ministry dealt with atomic waste, owing to its role in overseeing the health and safety of workers. This fragmentation made it extremely difficult to create an effective and consistent set of organizations and practices for public cleansing, not only for Germany as a whole but also within individual states.[71] It is nevertheless striking that even as early as the 1950s, there was a broad exchange of *Kommunalordnungen* (municipal regulations) among German cities. This seems to be another example of the process of informal coordination we have already observed in the case of garbage cans and collection vehicles.[72]

In any event, by the early 1970s, it became clear to politicians and practitioners that new, less localized legislation was necessary to create a uniform and reliable legal framework and to prevent states with more lax waste policies from gaining advantages over those with more stringent ones. Hessen enacted the first state-level waste law in 1971, and neighboring Rheinland Pfalz followed suit shortly after. To follow the lead of these pioneering states at the national level, however, a change in the Basic Law, the West German constitution, was required, something that took place finally in summer 1972. This permitted the transfer of some responsibilities that had hitherto been the exclusive domain of states to the federal government. And a few months later, the parliament enacted the Abfallbeseitigungsgesetz (Waste Removal Law), which created a new legal framework for waste management.[73]

The law's most important clause was the requirement that, from now on, all municipalities would be responsible for dealing with all waste in their territory, a provision that was soon adopted in the British Control of Pollution Act of 1974. Unlike COPA74, however, the new German law did not separate responsibility for collection of waste from its disposal. Instead, it obliged cities to find a solution for both. The clause had one side-effect, however, which was that it invalidated contracts that many

[71] Niederschrift über die Besprechung am 9.6.1969 im Innenministerium Düsseldorf, LA Düsseldorf, Bestand NW 354, 877.

[72] See, for example, letter from Stadt Mannheim to Stadt Reutlingen, Bauratsschreiberei (January 2, 1958), StA Mannheim, Hauptregistratur, Zugang: 42/1975, 2402.

[73] For the history of the waste law, see "Änderung des Abfallbeseitigungsgesetzes: Die Novellierung stand von vornherein fest," *Zeitschrift Umwelt* 5/74, p. 17, seen in LA Düsseldorf, Bestand NW 354, 878.

private waste management companies had signed with (usually, quite small) municipalities, individual households in rural areas, or firms.[74] However, despite the fact that even today many people in private waste management characterize the Waste Removal Law as an "expropriation law" because of this unintended side-effect of the legislation, in practice any business "lost" by the private sector was soon made up. After all, because of the obligation of municipalities and towns to deal with their waste, and even more importantly because in most cases it would have been too expensive for them to establish their own comprehensive collection and disposal services, they had to hire private contractors to do some of the work.[75] During the 1970s, private waste management companies thus experienced substantial growth even though they had to pay a turnover tax (which public cleansing departments were exempt from). There is consequently no question: the Waste Removal Law did not harm private companies.[76]

There is also no evidence in surviving records that the clause was specifically written with the intention of pushing private waste management companies out of the business. The explanation put forward by later president of the Umweltbundesamt, Heinrich V. Lersner, is far more convincing. He noted that the legislators simply did not think about private business when preparing the law. Certainly, when the legislation was written and enacted, the waste problem was most visible and pressing in cities and industrial areas where the public sector had a virtual monopoly. Most private firms at the time, in contrast, did business in the countryside, which was not the primary focus of the legislation.[77]

There is a long-standing debate in German environmental literature over whether this and other laws such as the West German Clean Air Act of the early 1970s were merely a "summation" of legislation and

---

74 Bundesverband der deutschen Entsorgungswirtschaft (ed.), *1961–2001. 40 Jahre BDE. Von der Stadthygiene zur Kreislaufwirtschaft: Eine Zeitreise mit der Entsorgungswirtschaft* (Cologne, 2001), pp. 80–81.
75 Letter from Nordrhein-Westfälisches Ministerium für Landwirtschaft to Vorsitzenden des BT-Innenausschusses Friedrich Schäfer und Vorsitzenden der Arbeitsgruppe für Umweltfragen Klaus Konrad (November 4, 1974), LA Düsseldorf, Bestand NW 354, 878.
76 Stellungnahme Umweltministerium betr. Gespräch mit dem Bundesverband Privater Sonderabfallbeseitigung am 6.12.1979 (December 3, 1979), BA Koblenz, B 106, 70539. A different evaluation of the effects of the Abfallbeseitigungsgesetz can be found in Simon Meyer, *Die Entwicklungslinien des Rechts der Abfallentsorgung im Spannungsfeld von Recht und hoheitlicher Lenkung* (Frankfurt/M.: Peter Lang, 2010), pp. 63ff.
77 Bericht von der JHV des VPS in Berlin 10./11.10.1974, BA Koblenz, B 106, 69731.

regulation of the previous decades, or whether instead they marked a watershed in the development of German environmental policy.[78] In the case of the Waste Removal Law, however, there is no question that we can speak of a major breakthrough. There were certainly federal laws before the Waste Removal Law that affected waste management, including the Water Protection Law, for example. But it proved to be very difficult to implement previous legislation effectively owing to lack of knowledge, deficient infrastructure for waste disposal, competing waste policies of the individual states, and so on. What was decisive and different about the 1972 waste law, in contrast, was not only that it was enacted at the national level but that it was also accompanied by coordinated measures to bring its clauses into effect. State governments had to frame *Abfallwirtschaftspläne* (waste management plans) that divided the state into "disposal zones." And inside these disposal zones, authorities had to find suitable locations for central landfills that conformed to certain criteria.[79] This requirement was not unlike the plans required in Britain at about the same time, although they were acted upon more quickly in West Germany. This led to a centralization of disposal sites and a removal of numerous wild tips that had long been a nuisance in so many cities. In particular, the search for new landfill sites made intensive research on issues such as soil quality, groundwater, and so on necessary, which again shows how intertwined legislation and scientification were. All in all, then, the waste law involved nothing short of a major breakthrough, fundamentally changing the concept of the sanitary landfill.

The centralization of landfills, however, also had another effect: creating huge disposal sites in places where none (or only quite small ones) had previously existed often provoked public protests. Thus, many of the phenomena we describe in the first part of this chapter were often not caused by but were more the effect of policies aimed at finding a solution to the waste problem. For this reason, debates did not cease following the enactment of the Waste Removal Law; instead, the waste issue remained a controversial topic of public discourse in Germany.

Although in some ways the 1972 waste law represented a sea change, it was clear from the start that it marked only a first step toward more comprehensive national regulation of waste management. Just how

---

[78] Uekötter, *Umweltgeschichte*, pp. 73–74; Hünemörder, *Die Frühgeschichte der globalen Umweltkrise*, p. 305.
[79] Vermerk betr. Neuordnung der Abfallbeseitigung in den Planungsräumen Rhein Main Taunus und Untermain (December 10, 1971), HStA Wiesbaden, 509, 2331a.

provisional the law was soon became clear by virtue of numerous toxic waste scandals that happened (or were revealed) in the early 1970s.[80] The fallout from the infamous Hanauer Giftmüllskandal, for example, demonstrated shortcomings in the new legislation.[81] Hence, the Waste Removal Law had to be amended several times during the 1970s. In the course of this learning process, certainly, West Germany developed a sophisticated body of legislation to deal with household waste, toxic waste, and so on,[82] although here as in Britain it was one thing to legislate and another to enforce the law.[83]

Conclusion

Both Britain and Germany by the 1970s enacted legislation at the national level to address problems associated with the expanding and changing solid waste stream. In both countries, legislation went hand in hand with the growing influence of the "new environmentalism" and with growing scientific understanding of the dangers associated with all sorts of pollution, including solid waste, although the proximate cause for new or substantially strengthened legislation in both countries was toxic waste scandals. The result of the interaction of all of these developments was a clear change in fundamental conceptualization of the waste problem. This featured a gradual movement away from the narrower public health concerns that had dominated waste collection and disposal in British and German cities from the late nineteenth century and toward new, broader concerns with environmental health. Simultaneously, public cleansing gradually began to be reconceptualized as waste management, although the full flowering of this reconceptualization came after 1980, a story we take up again in Part three.

As noted, the two countries differed considerably in the ways they acted on this new focus on environmental health. For a number of reasons, German scientific investigation of waste and the influence of scientists on policy making were stronger than in Britain. Moreover, German

---

[80] "Umweltschutz, der vor dem Fabriktor endet: Die Arsenschlamm-Affäre zeigt das Leck zwischen Gewerbeaufsicht und der Kontrolle von Abfalltransporten," *Süddeutsche Zeitung* (August 3, 1971), seen in BA Koblenz, B 106, 29370.

[81] Bericht über die Auswertung der Erfahrungen im Zusammenhang mit der Hanauer Giftmüllaffäre (January 1974), BA Koblenz, B 106, 65269.

[82] Letter from Heinrich von Lersner to Bundesminister des Inneren (August 17, 1979), BA Koblenz, B 106, 70539.

[83] Renate Mayntz, *Vollzugsprobleme der Umweltpolitik: Empirische Untersuchung der Implementation von Gesetzen im Bereich der Luftreinhaltung und des Gewässerschutzes* (Stuttgart: Kohlhammer, 1978).

environmental activists were more likely by virtue of the combination of the West German federal system and proportional representation to be elected to office, with profound impacts on existing waste handling practice. German legislation from 1972, the first ever nationwide law in that country that specifically addressed municipal solid waste handling practice, therefore involved a step toward changing that practice fundamentally. This was in contrast to Britain, where 1974 legislation led to less rather than more coherent structures for handling waste, especially in England, which accounts for the largest proportion of the UK population by far. The differences between the two countries would become still more profound during the 1980s, a development that we explore in Part three. Before that, however, we examine in more detail the ways in which each country coped with the apparent waste crisis in the 1970s.

6

Coping with the Crisis

Introduction

Practitioners in the waste management industry in Germany and in the United Kingdom faced a raft of challenges between the late 1960s and the early 1980s. Not only had the household waste stream changed dramatically in terms of volume and composition; new scientific understanding of the hazards of some long-standing disposal practices also pushed practitioners toward reconsideration of their traditional ways of carrying out their duties. Added to this were new legislative requirements, especially at the national level, and increasing pressure from environmental activists. What is more, all of this upheaval took place in a context of economic turmoil as the "golden age" came to an abrupt end with the collapse of the Bretton Woods system, followed by oil crises, "stagflation," and rising levels of unemployment. In Britain, in particular, inflation raged at hitherto unseen levels, accompanied by high levels of industrial conflict.

In the first main section of this chapter, we examine the response of practitioners to this rapidly changing environment, dealing first of all with efforts to reorganize the delivery of service, in part through new technologies and work methods and in part through consideration of alternative service providers, in particular those drawn from the private sector. The second main section focuses on one key area that many came to view as a crucial part of the solution to managing the waste stream: the redefinition of what had previously been termed "salvage" as "recycling," which involved important changes not only to what was now being done and why, but also to who was doing it.

One of the key themes in both main sections of the chapter is once again the increasing divergence in practice between the United Kingdom and West Germany. Although the term "public cleansing" was very gradually giving way to "waste management," just as public health concerns were displaced by broader environmental health ones in both countries, West Germany took the lead in developing more coherent policies to integrate collection and disposal functions of waste handling. Germany was also one of the pioneers in implementing the reconceptualization of salvage as recycling. Both of these pathbreaking roles involved increasing participation of the private sector in waste management practice. Ironically, perhaps, privatization of aspects of waste handling began earlier and was much more widespread in Germany than in Britain, in spite of the fact that Margaret Thatcher and the Conservative Party gained power in the United Kingdom in 1979 with an ideological commitment to lessening the role of the public sector in British society and the economy. Because of this divergence, we deal for the most part separately with each country in what follows.

Reorganizing for the Delivery of Waste Management Services

In Britain, the comprehensive restructuring of local government through the Local Government Act of 1972 and the Control of Pollution Act of 1974 described in the previous chapter had a major impact on the delivery of municipal refuse services in England and Wales.[1] Although there were some changes to collection that we come to shortly, in many ways it remained much as it had been before in terms of organization and practice. Disposal, in contrast, was reorganized significantly, becoming the responsibility of new county councils that were to act as regional Waste Disposal Authorities (WDAs). The assumption here was that they would have the financial resources to achieve economies of scale and thus would also be better positioned to regulate and coordinate the disposal of waste by the private sector. The forty-six English WDAs thus started their work by having to coordinate waste disposal operations for a number of district councils using disposal facilities and infrastructure inherited from disparate local authorities. These varied widely in efficiency, previous organizational practice, and personnel.

---

[1] In Scotland, collection and disposal remained under the control of "unitary" authorities, although as in England and Wales these were also reorganized amalgamations of previous governmental bodies.

Still, even on the collection end, the creation of new district councils meant that long-established public cleansing departments were replaced with new organizations to cope with newly enlarged boundaries, and they were also often renamed, with the new names reflecting increasingly widespread concerns with environmental health. Thus, long-established designations such as "public cleansing" and "salvage" began to be replaced with "environmental services." In March 1974, when the outgoing City of Birmingham Council disbanded its Salvage Committee, it expressed the hope that the new Birmingham District Council's Environmental Services Committee would continue the policy of recovering materials from its waste collections.[2] The new district council of the City of Manchester also set up an Environmental Services Department but retained a Cleansing Department within it.[3] In Glasgow, as in the rest of Scotland, there was, of course, no division of collection and disposal services, and the newly enlarged City of Glasgow District Council continued to run its Cleansing Committee separately from that for Environmental Health.[4] Indeed, even when it was redesignated the Environmental Protection Committee in Glasgow in January 1977, its constitution and functions remained unaltered.

The reconfigured and/or renamed collecting agencies of district councils all faced changes in the amount and density of household wastes, although national figures prior to reorganization were based on often incomplete or estimated data supplied voluntarily by local authorities to nongovernmental bodies.[5] One benefit of the changes in 1974, however, was that more disposal authorities began systematically to weigh all their refuse, so the completeness and reliability of data improved substantially, although returns were still not compulsory and the overall picture given was at best indicative rather than definitive. (See Charts 6.1 and 6.2.)

² Birmingham City Archives, Records of the Salvage Committee and successors (subsequently BCA, BCC) Final meeting of Salvage Committee, March 20, 1974.
³ Manchester City Archives, Records of the Cleansing Department (subsequently MCA) M595, letter from chief executive to Greater Manchester County Council, April 25, 1978, and March 12. 1979.
⁴ Mitchell Library Glasgow, Records of the City of Glasgow (subsequently MLG), GDC 1/2: minutes of the City of Glasgow District Council meeting, August 13, 1974, and Rating Estimates, June 16, 1975. The Cleansing Department budget was £12.46 million compared to £1.49 million for Environmental Health.
⁵ A. E. Higginson, *The Analysis of Domestic Waste* (Northampton: Institute of Wastes Management, 1978), p. 6. The collating bodies were the Society of County Treasurers, the County Surveyors Society, and later the Chartered Institute of Public Finance and Accountancy.

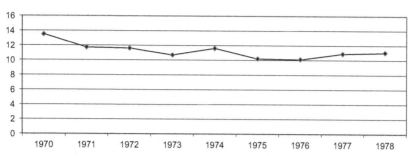

CHART 6.1. England and Wales: average weight in kilograms of domestic refuse per household per week, 1970–1978. *Source:* A. E. Higginson, *The Analysis of Domestic Waste* (Northampton: Institute of Wastes Management, 1978), p. 26.

What is most striking about these figures is that between reorganization in England and Wales in 1974 and the end of the decade, the average weight and density of a week's domestic refuse fluctuated only slightly. Probably for this reason, but also because of limited reorganization on the collection side, the 1970s were characterized more by tinkering at the edges than by fundamental reform of collection services. Collection agencies did fear that there might be a sustained increase in volume of waste that would require greater storage capacity at domestic premises to avoid overflowing garbage cans.[6] In a search for flexibility to deal with this potential problem, therefore, cities such as Birmingham and Glasgow moved toward replacing metal trash cans with plastic sacks that would hold greater volumes. But neither had much success. Birmingham, for instance, was initially unable to source the 3 million plastic bags it ordered to set up the scheme because the contractor, ICI, lacked the necessary raw materials.[7] Then the city's authorities ascertained that even if the bags were delivered, there was insufficient storage space for all of them. Thus, they had to be taken at the rate of 250,000 per month, presumably to match usage rates. Later that same year, furthermore, the city complemented the sacks by ordering 30,000 plastic "dustbins and lids," along with 3,000 traditional metal garbage cans with the usual capacity of 2.5 cubic feet.[8] The mixed economy of garbage containers in Birmingham reflected the fact that open fires continued to be used in many households. There was therefore a real risk of hot fire grate ashes setting plastic containers alight. At almost exactly the same time,

[6] Higginson, *Analysis of Domestic Waste*, p. 8.
[7] BCA, BCC, Environmental Services Committee report, July 9, 1976.
[8] Ibid., November 5, 1976.

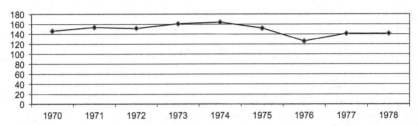

CHART 6.2. England and Wales: average density in kilograms per cubic meter of domestic refuse per household per week, 1970–1978. *Source:* A. E. Higginson, *The Analysis of Domestic Waste* (Northampton: Institute of Wastes Management, 1978), p. 26.

Glasgow too realized that the intended provision of one plastic sack per week per household was likely to be inadequate. Residents in one area of the city, for instance, complained that a week's refuse could not be accommodated because of "current bulky methods of packaging."[9] Like Birmingham, Glasgow thus featured a mixed economy of garbage containers, continuing use of metal containers as well as some plastic ones alongside their experiment with plastic sacks.

The introduction of new domestic refuse storage containers naturally had an impact on the type of collection vehicles that would be needed in the future. (See Figure 6.1.) Thus, in Glasgow, a vehicle replacement program ran between 1975 and 1979 at a cost of £622,500. It included research by the Cleansing Department in conjunction with manufacturers, experimenting on different types of vehicle bodies. This was done despite state-imposed limits on local authority spending increases of no more than 10 percent and the "increasingly adverse reactions from ratepayers" to any local expenditure that forced up local taxation.[10]

Collection was, however, not really the main problem in the United Kingdom. Perhaps the most challenging change for cleansing/ environmental health departments, especially in the new district authorities in England and Wales, lay in coordination with and division of labor between collection departments on the one hand and the relevant new regional WDA on the other. The potential problems of this division had been raised by the practitioners' professional organization from the start, but their importance had been minimized, or even disregarded, by

[9] MLG, GDC 1 / 2, Cleansing Committee meeting, July 5, 1976.
[10] MLG, GDC 1 / 2, City Council meeting, October 22, 1975.

FIGURE 6.1. Late 1970s British Dennis refuse collection vehicle with manual load-ing into a compression-system body intended to maximize the length of collection journeys. Photograph courtesy of Dennis-Eagle Ltd, Warwick.

policy makers. As it turned out, tensions and conflicts of interest emerged quickly, sometimes threatening to impede or even compromise the effect-ive disposal of refuse by the new WDAs.

One question might have been expected to be asked by any reason-ably competent planner: Who would be responsible for paying for any overlaps in the two functions? But the question seems to have cropped up only *after* the reorganization of local government took place. Answering it in turn slowed down preparation of long-term planning for regional waste disposal programs, one of the key tenets of reorganization. After restructuring, the district councils were no longer directly responsible for the disposal of the refuse they collected, but they were nevertheless legally required to deliver it wherever directed by their WDA.[11] Since the WDA was a regional rather than a local operation, however, its chosen disposal sites did not necessarily border directly on collection areas. Local author-ities soon objected that being required to transport waste outside their own boundaries would be likely to disrupt collection schedules and add to

[11] *Local Government Act 1972*: Elizabeth II 1972, Chap. 70 (London: HMSO, 1972), Schedule 14, Section 5 (2).

operating costs. To be fair, this issue had been anticipated to some extent in the legislation, and county councils were expected to make "a reasonable contribution towards expenditure reasonably incurred" by a district council in transporting refuse to sites nominated by the WDA. However, no definition of "reasonable" was given,[12] and arriving at an acceptable compromise could be a tortuous process that affected the efficiency of operations.

The interaction in the late 1970s between the West Midlands County Council – which served almost 2.8 million people and covered 346 square miles[13] – and the seven district councils for whose waste disposal it was statutorily responsible provides a good illustration of how all of this could play out. In January 1977, the county council was trying to resolve a long-standing dispute with its district councils over payments for transporting refuse over longer than normal distances.[14] The City of Birmingham District Council, the largest in the county, objected strongly to being directed by the WDA to deliver to sites outside its own boundaries. The reason was simple: Birmingham's area contained four modern incinerators as well as a new one nearing completion. They provided sufficient capacity for all the district council's refuse and were less than 2.5 miles from local collection rounds. Birmingham thus regarded delivering refuse to sites other than the closest as ill considered and an unreasonable imposition, adding needlessly to its costs.[15]

The county council, on the other hand, justified its policy by pointing to its need to maximize its total incinerator capacity to minimize the amount of residues sent to tipping sites, thereby conforming to the Control of Pollution Act's Waste Disposal Plan requirements.[16] Birmingham (and the other six district councils in the county) knew there was ultimately no way to avoid accepting this policy but held out in the short term for an acceptable compensation settlement before it could be implemented. The West Midlands County Council for its part wanted to impose a formula arrived at jointly by the three national associations of local authorities that

---

[12] Ibid., Section 6 (2).
[13] Figures extracted from Greater Manchester County Record Office, Manchester. Greater Manchester Council Minutes and Reports (subsequently GMCRO GMC Minutes), GMC 1264, Strategic Report February 14, 1978, Appendix C.
[14] BCA, BCC, Report of City Environmental Officer to Environmental Services Committee, January 7, 1977, p. 1.
[15] Ibid., p. 2.
[16] The Waste Disposal Plan had yet to be drafted because it was being held up by this very debate.

took into account various factors, including the "reasonable travelling distance" and average journey times.[17]

By March 1975, all parties except Birmingham City had accepted terms based on a notional 6 miles travel distance as standard and "reasonable."[18] Birmingham, however, insisted that the 2.5-mile distance typical of its own area should be its norm, not least since the slower speed of traffic in the city led to longer average journey times. As late as January 1977, therefore, Birmingham City was still in separate negotiations with the West Midlands County Council for better terms.[19] That tenacity was eventually rewarded in 1978 when the county agreed to accept all of Birmingham's demands, with the 2.5-mile distance also being applied as a standard "reasonable distance" to the county's other district councils.[20]

The county council's capitulation opened the way to development of a now long overdue long-term disposal plan for the West Midlands area. Even so, only in June 1980 was a draft plan published, and it attracted serious objections when it went for consultation to the district councils. Birmingham criticized its overreliance on acquiring landfill sites for dumping untreated waste rather than improving and modernizing existing incineration plants to reduce the volume of material to be buried. The city also bemoaned the plan for its failure to develop environmentally acceptable waste reduction methods for long-term conservation of landfill resources.[21]

Birmingham's complaints reflected the city's long-standing policies of extracting what had been called "salvage materials" for sale or reprocessing on the one hand and the large-scale incineration of collected refuse on the other. Those were practices that simultaneously generated income and reduced the volume of refuse, thus easing the city's problems in finding adequate local landfill capacity when it had been responsible

[17] BCA, BCC, Report of City Environmental Officer to Environmental Services Committee, January 7, 1977, p. 2. The bodies were the Association of Municipal Authorities, the Association of County Councils, and the Association of District Councils.

[18] Ibid. The formula was jointly devised by the Association of Municipal Authorities, the Association of County Councils, and the Association of District Councils. It included journey times.

[19] Ibid., p. 3.

[20] BCA, BCC, Report, "Transportation to Distant Disposal Sites," undated but probably 1978.

[21] BCA, BCC, Joint Report of the City Engineer, City Environmental Officer and City Planning Officer to the Environmental Health Committee, the Planning and Highways Committee and the General Purposes Committee on West Midlands County Council Waste Disposal Plan, October 20, 1982.

for disposal as well as collection. The City of Birmingham's comments led to the plan's redrafting a year later, followed by a "wide ranging Public Enquiry" after a change in political control at the West Midlands County Council. Even as late as October 1982, however, it had still to be finalized.[22]

Such problems of demarcation of duties and allocation of costs coverage were widespread in England in the wake of COPA74, and they took a long time to resolve. But the difficulties encountered in the West Midlands and other English counties were minor compared to those of the Greater Manchester County Council (GMC). These proved so severe that the council's refuse disposal system faced complete collapse within four years of being setting up. The route of the GMC toward crisis thus illustrates a worst-case scenario in the implementation of the new organizational forms and relationships mandated by the law.

The GMC was the second largest WDA in Britain, although only by a very small margin. By April 1974, it became responsible for integrating refuse disposal operations of ten newly created district councils whose populations ranged from 20,000 to more than 640,000 and that had been formed from seventy-one previously separate authorities.[23] Estimates based on figures compiled from the preexisting local authorities suggested that around 1.5 million tons of refuse would be handled annually, of which two-thirds would be domestic and "trade" waste,[24] plus a lesser unspecified quantity of industrial refuse, all of which was to be collected by the district councils. The remainder involved industrial waste for the most part that would be delivered directly to local authority disposal sites by the companies that produced it or by private collection services.[25]

Until reorganization, almost all local authorities in the new GMC area sent their refuse directly to their own local landfill sites without any sorting, reclamation, or treatment. There were eighty such dumps scattered across the region. Only 15 percent of waste was incinerated, with an even smaller proportion being recovered for sale or reprocessing.[26] In common

---

22 Ibid., p. 1.
23 GMCRO, GMC 1264, Strategic Report February 14, 1978, Appendix C. The largest WDA by population was the West Midlands, whose population was only 2.25 percent higher at 2.76 million.
24 That is, refuse collected directly from business premises such as offices, shops, restaurants, and workshops.
25 GMCRO, GMC Minutes, GMC 1264, County Engineer's Report, August 31, 1973, Para. 1.
26 Ibid., GMC 1268, note from J. J. Unsworth to chief executive, December 9, 1977.

with other new county councils, the GMC was therefore confronted with a number of difficulties in melding this diverse assortment into a cohesive operation. All faced a complex reorganization in the context of growing waste volume and on the basis of existing and sometimes deficient infrastructure. Each of these three areas – secular trends in waste production owing to the consolidation of the consumer society, inherited organization and infrastructure, and the effects of reorganization – was particularly problematic in Manchester County, however. Let us look at each of them in a bit more detail.

The GMC seems, first of all, to have experienced a particularly pronounced increase in household waste output. Part of the reason for this was probably a very bad set of estimates of the amounts of waste it would have to handle. When the GMC was formed, it used a 1972 estimate of 1.5 million tons annually as the basis for calculating the life expectancy of its landfill sites. New measurements made in late summer 1978 to check the earlier estimate's accuracy, however, revealed the startling news that annual inputs were now far higher: around 2.4 million tons, a 37 percent increase, which apparently indicated a substantial growth in domestic refuse.[27] This level was completely atypical of the rest of England and Wales, where the estimated totals of tonnages received by waste disposal authorities grew from 23.2 million tons in the fiscal year ending March 1975 to 24.7 million tons in 1978, an increase of just 6.5 percent – in other words, only one-sixth that of the GMC's.[28]

In a 1978 report on this and other problems encountered in the course of the reorganization, GMC's waste management team suggested two reasons for the increase.[29] One of them was a substantial growth in refuse from "civic amenity" sites, which were places where residents could discard household furniture and other items under the terms of the Civic Amenities Act.[30] This could not really explain much, because the trend applied across the United Kingdom as a consequence of the growth of the consumer society described in Chapter 4 and the attendant tendency to

---

[27] GMCRO, GMC Minutes, 1978 report on reappraisal of refuse disposal strategy by Resource and Policy Steering Group, September 22, 1978. Subsequently RPSG Report, p. 2, 3. The county engineer noted that it "had been felt for a time" that the original estimate noted above was too low.

[28] Society of County Treasurers, Annual Returns. The provision of figures by local authorities was voluntary.

[29] See Note 27.

[30] The duty to provide such facilities was laid down in the Civic Amenities Act 1967, partly to discourage indiscriminate urban dumping and partly to simplify the collection duties of local authorities.

replace possessions more frequently than before. The second explanation proffered was somewhat more convincing. The report pointed to a very substantial increase in trade and industrial waste being handled at GMC disposal sites. Again, this is likely to have been a UK–wide trend because handling such waste was a way for disposal authorities to raise money. Unlike household waste, disposal of which was paid for exclusively out of local taxes, authorities could charge directly for trade and industrial waste disposal services. Manchester, however, differed in the extent of growth, with such waste now estimated to be around 1 million tons a year, double the previously assessed figure. Increased industrial waste output and transport costs coupled with a declining number of privately operated disposal sites both in the GMC's area and the adjoining region because of tighter regulation meant that much nonmunicipal refuse that had previously been shipped out of the county was now brought directly to GMC sites, where it was accepted as a paid-for service. Income from that was substantial, rising from around 6.7 percent of the GMC WDA's total budget in 1974–1975 to 11.3 percent in 1976–1977.[31] While the increased income was no doubt welcome, however, the much larger than expected volume of waste posed a major problem for all English county councils – especially, Manchester.

The GMC also had to deal with a number of problems that it inherited from its predecessors. Again, this was not unlike elsewhere in the United Kingdom in principle, but the extent of historical neglect by the previous local authorities when they planned future provision of disposal facilities was such that, as noted in a May 1978 internal review, the GMC had "inherited a refuse disposal service which was extremely fragmented and seriously deficient." Lack of staff and facilities for maintaining essential transport vehicles meant that the GMC had to create a centralized servicing facility, although problems managing the project led to delays that left the authority struggling to maintain the trucks it depended on.[32] Plant and essential works such as incinerators were often in poor condition or unserviceable, primarily because maintenance standards had declined severely prior to reorganization.[33] For instance, nearly all incinerators that the GMC took over were at the end of their

[31] GMCRO, GMC Minutes, 1978 report on reappraisal of refuse disposal strategy, p. 3.
[32] GMCRO, GMC Minutes, County Personnel Department: Organisation and Method Unit, "County Engineer's Department, Review of Refuse Disposal Division" (subsequently OMU Report), May 1978, pp. 43, 44, para. 172, and 10.
[33] GMCRO, GMC Minutes 1268, Memorandum from J. Hayes to chief executive, April 15, 1977, p. 2.

serviceable lives.[34] Furthermore, poor quality record keeping by the previous authorities had hindered the integration of services.[35] Finally, as GMC began operations it found that numerous landfill sites had been – and were still being – filled beyond their intended capacity. This would entail a reduction in the number of dumps from eighty in 1974 to a projected twenty-three in spring 1979. Preliminary surveys of 332 potential alternative in-county landfill sites, moreover, showed that only two-fifths were worth investigating further. Even the most optimistic assessments indicated that available capacity would be inadequate beyond the short term.[36]

Although increasing amounts of waste and inherited and deficient infrastructure were problematic for the GMC, however, it is clear that the main refuse disposal issue faced by the new county council in the late 1970s stemmed from severe flaws in the way the reorganization of the disposal service was handled. The context was this: it was long-established precedent in Britain's largest cities that public cleansing should be a stand-alone department, and in 1967 the governmental Working Party on Refuse Collection recommended that such arrangements should apply to all authorities with a population of more than 100,000.[37] Nevertheless, the GMC's planners decided that refuse disposal for some 2.7 million people should be handled by the County Engineer's Department within the GMC Highways Division. From the outset, refuse management was, in the words of a subsequent internal inquiry, "not afforded the status required."[38]

For one thing, the county engineer who was given responsibility for running the service lacked both waste handling experience and an appropriate advisory team. A recommendation in 1972 to recruit a properly qualified waste disposal manager and staff was rejected because planners considered the "amount and nature" of the work insufficient to justify the appointments.[39] Staff thus occupied relatively junior positions in a structure where none of the senior officers were refuse specialists and that was

[34] Ibid., p. 1.
[35] The OMU Report added that systems for "monitoring the performance of plant and equipment" were "inadequate," p. 2 para. 4(i).
[36] GMCRO, GMC Minutes 1268, Memorandum from J. Hayes to chief executive, p. 1; GMC Minutes, Report of Highways Committee, March 13, 1978, Council Circular 2H, page 34.
[37] R. E. Bevan, director of cleansing, City of Manchester, "We Lead the World," *Public Cleansing*, May 1968, p. 282.
[38] GMCRO, GMC Minutes, OMU Report, p. 4 para. 12.
[39] GMCRO, Report of Joint Committee, April 16, 1973, p. 2.

200 The Business of Waste

not primarily focused on planning strategies for managing the constant generation of domestic and other wastes. The Engineering Department, on the other hand, did not originally expect to handle site acquisition because of the GMC's early intention to provide "some form of land agency" to identify and develop them. And when that failed to materialize, the department was forced to take on the task to remedy what the county engineer subsequently described as "unforeseen difficulties."[40]

Not surprisingly, the confluence of greater than anticipated increases in waste volume and costs, poor infrastructure and equipment, and ineffective organization led to crisis by 1978. In March, the GMC wrote to the Department of the Environment (DOE) and the chancellor of the exchequer warning of "the impending breakdown of the refuse disposal services in Greater Manchester" because of an acute shortage of landfill sites within the county.[41] Existing capacity would be exhausted within two years and, even if every other potentially suitable site in the county could be used, only five years' further capacity was predicted.[42] The GMC therefore sought financial and technical aid from the government to try to stave off impending disaster.

Between May and July 1978, the GMC and the DOE sparred with one another about the extent and type of aid that might be forthcoming, but, owing in part to financial stringency and in part to lack of sympathy with the plight of the GMC, the DOE's response was far from encouraging.[43] However, as costs continued to rise and other problems persisted, the GMC finally accepted that a new and more proactive waste disposal policy was needed along with major organizational restructuring and more vigorous senior management. Between January and September 1979, therefore, the GMC undertook a fundamental overhaul of both the organization and refuse disposal, clearing the way for effective measures of controlling the unsatisfactory situation. A new Refuse Disposal Committee was created with control of its own capital and revenue budgets.[44]

40 GMCRO, Memorandum from J. Hayes to chief executive, p. 1.
41 GMCRO, 1978, Refuse Disposal Division, similar letters from chief executive to chancellor of exchequer and secretary of state for the environment, March 7, 1978, p. 3. The responsibility for service provision ultimately lay with the elected members rather than the practitioners.
42 GMCRO, letter from chief executive to chancellor of exchequer, March 7, 1978, pp. 2 and 3.
43 GMCRO, letter from parliamentary under-secretary of State, Department of the Environment, to G. A. Harrison, chief executive, GMC, May 18, 1978, pp. 1–2.
44 GMCRO, GMC Minutes, report on the resolution of the role of the Refuse Disposal Committee, January 4, 1980, p. 61.

Further, the county engineer was replaced by someone "able to take an immediate hold on the longer term problems" facing the GMC.[45] This reconfiguration finally gave the service the status it lacked previously, and with that came both the professional energy and political will to move toward creating a refuse disposal strategy that would deal with immediate problems and prevent them from happening again in the future. It would also help with the preparation of the ten-year Waste Disposal Plan required by the Control of Pollution Act, on which (as in the West Midlands) virtually no progress had yet been made.

Although reforms might address the longer term, however, in the short term the council was forced to reveal publicly just how serious its waste disposal problems had become. In a detailed five-page information bulletin from October 1979 entitled "New Plans to Avert Crisis in Refuse Disposal Service," the GMC admonished district councils and the general public alike "to be realistic about the rubbish we all produce." The county was rapidly running out of landfill space in which to dispose of a problem that was "created by us all" and now needed everyone to cooperate in achieving a solution.[46] The ultimate objective of the plan was eventually "to eliminate the burial of raw refuse in the County completely"; for the time being, however, existing landfill practice would have to continue. The bulletin cheerfully asserted that modern management of landfills meant that they were "nothing like as horrible as people imagine," perhaps not exactly what their present and potential neighbors wanted to hear. Overall, the bulletin gave the impression that the GMC was firmly in charge of the current difficult situation and planning to ensure it could "take advantage . . . of all new developments in this field and maintain its refuse disposal performance at a reasonable cost" to its residents.[47]

In private, however, the GMC was far more frank and much less upbeat. The county council's chief executive confided to the district councils that it was not actually county policy to phase out all refuse dumps, even in the long term. The number could be reduced only "as far as is practicable" rather than totally eliminated. He made three main points. First, given the time needed to achieve large-scale bulk reduction, both the district and county councils must consider extending dump capacity and life expectancy despite local opposition, striking politically unsatisfactory

---

[45] GMCRO, GMC Minutes 1978, letter from chief executive to leader of the council, copied to chairman of highways committee, June 1, 1978.
[46] GMCRO, GMC Minutes, Information Bulletin, October 9, 1979.
[47] Ibid., pp. 2 and 5.

balances and compromises between public opinions, operational necessities, and environmental objectives.[48] This was a significant hardening of
previous attitudes. Second, the only way to reduce annual landfill intake
to a sustainable 1.5 million tons was by eliminating most industrial and
trade waste currently being accepted directly at sites. This was a new and
radical stance, signaling the GMC's willingness to sacrifice substantial
income in exchange for shedding the problems of handling such waste.
However, the GMC was constrained by having no legal basis for forcing
the district councils to do likewise. Indeed, they had discretionary powers
to accept waste from trade and industry provided they made appropriate charges (which of course provided an incentive for them to do so);
the GMC for its part was legally obligated to accept all refuse from the
district councils in its area.[49]

The third point in the letter marked another important policy switch:
disposal plans would now rely heavily on removal to remote locations,
something hitherto consistently rejected because of high transportation
costs. Negotiations were in fact already in progress to use privately owned
sites as far as 150 miles away, and road transport would be used only if
other means were "impracticable or uneconomic." Instead, rail was the
preferred method, and even canal transport would be used if "feasible
and economic." The whole argument obviously focused on economics
and logistics rather than the environmental advantages of rail or canal
over road use. Long-distance, large-scale transportation of waste was now
accepted as inevitable, the choice dictated by operational and economic
necessity.[50]

The county chief executive's letter signified a belated political will to
spend money to accomplish what needed to be done even if it might be
more than the public might normally be prepared to pay. But it also indicated the extent to which, nearly a decade into the process of local government reorganization and the consequent restructuring of waste handling
services, major issues were left unresolved as the details of the relationship between new collection and disposal authorities were worked out.
The situation in Manchester was particularly dire, but it was not unlike
the problems faced throughout England and Wales. Indeed, these organizational problems, combined with severe economic difficulties (which, of

---

[48] GMCRO, letter from chief executive GMC to chief executives of the district councils of
Greater Manchester, October 31, 1979.
[49] Ibid.
[50] Ibid., p. 2.

course, affected the whole of the United Kingdom), ensured that the 1970s represented a "lost decade" for British waste management. By the 1980s, the industry in Britain was characterized by policy incoherence, lack of clear lines of authority and responsibility, underinvestment, and the continued hegemony of the increasingly outdated "public cleansing" ethic. What is more, reorganization combined with increasing government regulation meant that the industry by the early 1980s was dominated by the public sector to an extent not seen since the mid-nineteenth century.

In certain respects, waste handling in West Germany in the 1970s was not that different from that in the United Kingdom. The combination of legislation (in the German case, the Waste Removal Law of 1972) and the growing technological and spatial demands of landfills led policy makers and practitioners to seek economies of scale through the establishment of larger, more centralized landfill sites that could accommodate the waste of a number of municipalities. As in Britain, the municipalities concerned frequently complained about the distances that their collection vehicles had to travel to reach the new sites, something that led to higher transportation costs. And in Germany, too, the planning of almost every new landfill was also accompanied by public protests, contradictory expert reports, and political quarrels.[51] Finally, German legislation, like that in the United Kingdom from about the same time, required the formulation of detailed plans (in this case, *Abfallwirtschaftspläne*, or waste management plans) that anticipated changes in the waste stream in the foreseeable future and made explicit provision for how these changes would be dealt with.

The German case differed from that of Britain in several key respects, however. For one thing, by the early 1970s, German cities had already made great strides toward rationalization of collection and transport of waste compared to those in the United Kingdom. (See Figures 6.2 and 6.3.) Second – although money was and is always a contentious issue in relation to waste handling and although Germany, too, experienced some economic problems during the 1970s (including levels of unemployment not seen since the early 1950s) – inflation there remained relatively low and economic growth was relatively stable. Money was therefore often available for additional investment, and existing equipment and plants were mostly of relatively recent vintage. Third, cooperation

[51] Ralf Herbold and Ralf Wienken, *Experimentelle Technikgestaltung und offene Planung: Strategien zur sozialen Bewältigung von Unsicherheit am Beispiel der Abfallbeseitigung* (Bielefeld: Kleine, 1993), pp. 12–13.

FIGURE 6.2. German Faun RotoPress refuse collection vehicle mechanism on a
British-made Bedford truck chassis, 1970s. Photograph courtesy of the Sammlung
aus Städtereinigung und Entsorgungswirtschaft (SASE), Iserlohn.

among cities in Germany – especially in relation to centralized disposal
sites – was facilitated by two apparently contradictory but actually complementary sets of organizations. The first was represented above all by
the Länder-Arbeitsgemeinschaft Abfall (Working Party of the States for
Waste, or LAGA), which encouraged cooperation between cities and
aided in the conceptualization of coordinated *Abfallwirtschaftspläne.*
The second took the form of private-sector waste handling firms, which
provided services in cases where municipalities could not cooperate
among themselves for whatever reason (something that happened especially frequently in areas where a large number of small to medium-sized
towns were located). Effectively, this led to indirect cooperation among
the municipalities involved because they were all customers of the same
private service provider. It also led to some scale economies. And the
result of the combination of all of these factors was that in most cases,
German *Abfallwirtschaftspläne* were actually completed and implemented in a timely fashion, in marked contrast to the situation in the United
Kingdom.

Despite these plans by German cities, a number of problems remained,
and they were far from completely solved even by the end of the decade.

FIGURE 6.3. A Faun RotoPress vehicle in operation during the 1970s with an MGB 1.1 container about to be coupled to the lifting mechanism. At the time, metal was still being used for the containers and had yet to be supplanted by plastics. Photograph courtesy of the Sammlung aus Städtereinigung und Entsorgungswirtschaft (SASE), Iserlohn.

One problematic area involved the political conflict that accompanied landfill planning. An extreme example was the intensive and lengthy battle over a landfill in the Grube Messel, a former opencast bituminous shale mine close to the city of Darmstadt. Despite being a famous archeological site, the Grube Messel was designated to become a sanitary landfill for Hessian household waste in 1971. More than twenty years of conflict between planners and protestors ensued before a technicality resulting from a bureaucratic error eventually led to abandonment of plans for the site in the 1990s.[52] The severity and length of the conflict demonstrated not only the perseverance of protesters but also how desperately public authorities sought disposal facilities for the still-growing waste stream. Eventually, the combination of the plans and their enforcement on the one hand and interaction of protesters and policy makers on the other led to pivotal changes in the disposal situation in West Germany, with the

---

[52] Manfred Raab, *Müll oder Fossilien? Der Kampf um die Erhaltung der Fossilienfundstätte Grube Messel: Eine historisch-politische Dokumentation* (Messel: Roether, 1996).

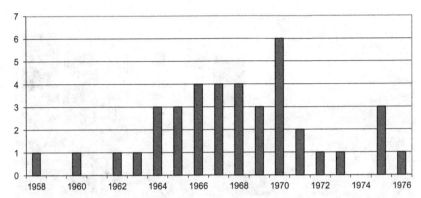

CHART 6.3. Number of new waste incinerators built in West Germany, 1965–
1976. *Source:* Aufstellung von Müllverbrennungsanlagen in der BRD (19.2.1975).
BA Koblenz B 106, 27094.

approximately 50,000 dumps existing there in the late 1960s radically
diminished over the course of the next decade.

Consolidation and rationalization of landfill sites did not, however,
solve the disposal problem in Germany in the 1970s, not least because
the volume of waste was still growing substantially. Thus, a second means
of addressing the issue – incineration – became an increasingly widespread
practice beginning in the early to mid-1960s and culminating in 1970,
when six new incinerators came on line (see Chart 6.3). Many cities
also expanded the capacity of existing incinerators. By the 1970s, then,
incineration was able to address some of the most urgent demand for
increased disposal. And unlike in Britain in the 1970s, most of the stock of
waste incineration equipment in Germany was new or of relatively recent
vintage and represented the culmination of ongoing efforts to improve
efficiency and lower costs associated with this technology.

That being said, incineration plants also became extremely controversial during the 1970s. A decade earlier the gravest concerns were about
the emission of hydrochloric acid by such plants.[53] By the early 1970s,
however, an increasing number of incidents demonstrated the dangers
in particular of incinerating polyvinyl chloride (PVC) plastics, which had
become an extremely important material for packaging as well as in other
applications. Workers in plastic-producing plants in particular began to
suffer from diseases that were soon traced to PVC, and it is thus no

[53] Vortrag Werner Schenkel: "Zukünftige Entwicklungslinien der Abfallwirtschaft" (May
30, 1979), BA Koblenz, B 106, 69732.

surprise that attention turned to the effects of burning it.[54] The public soon learned that incineration emitted dioxins, poisonous chemicals that became infamous in Europe following an accident in a chemical plant close to the Italian village of Seveso in 1976.[55] This incident increased public concern about the effects of the emissions from waste combustion. And here again, we can observe that people no longer perceived as dangerous only what they could see, smell, or feel, but they also became aware and suspicious of what their senses could not detect.

In spite of the growing concerns and protests, however, incinerators continued to be used, partly because of the ever-increasing levels of waste requiring disposal. But even this was not enough to deal with the growing volume, and so a third avenue – exporting garbage to the German Democratic Republic (GDR, or East Germany) – became more and more widespread beginning in the early 1970s. This was something that British municipalities did not have available: a neighboring country (albeit a former part of Germany divided after the Second World War) that could be accessed easily (given the political will to allow it) by road, rail, or canal and that was also increasingly keen to accommodate waste from the West since it was an excellent source of desperately needed hard currency. The first to take this path was West Berlin, which suffered especially acutely from lack of sufficient landfill space. Its authorities decided in 1972 to negotiate an agreement with the GDR, and in the same year the city began transporting part of its waste into the East.[56]

The practice became more and more common as the decade progressed, and West Berlin was joined by other West German cities (and by those in other parts of western and northern Europe) in using the GDR (and other eastern bloc states) as a dumping ground. This practice was especially problematic because it involved a deep contradiction: on the one hand, the West German government increasingly sought to enforce environmental standards to protect groundwater, soil, and the air; at the same time, it allowed municipalities to ship garbage to the GDR where enforcement of environmental standards was extremely lax. Despite the contradiction, however, the practice of shipping waste to the GDR not only became even more common during the 1980s, but West German state officials also started to use GDR dumps increasingly for disposing of toxic waste.

---

[54] Andrea Westermann, *Plastik und politische Kultur in Westdeutschland* (Zurich: Chronos, 2007), especially Chapter 4.

[55] Joachim Radkau, *Die Ära der Ökologie: Eine Weltgeschichte* (Munich: C. H. Beck, 2011), pp. 251–252.

[56] M. A. Jinhee Park, "Von der Müllkippe zur Abfallwirtschaft: Die Entwicklung der Hausmüllentsorgung in Berlin (West) von 1945 bis 1990," pp. 84ff.

The Schönberg landfill in northeast Germany, which started taking household and toxic waste from West Germany in 1978, is perhaps the best-
known example of this, although it is by no means the only one.[57]
   Thus, despite new legislation designed to help bring some measure
of discipline and control to public cleansing, partly through promoting
planning, reorganization, and rationalization of waste disposal processes,
West Germany remained largely mired in traditional practice. Even as late
as the early 1980s, for example, about two-thirds of household waste
was still disposed of in landfills, with the other third incinerated. Still,
the legislation and the plans that it required did bring about some innovation. One area in which that took place was the opportunistic, even
cynical practice of exporting the problem to its much poorer communist
neighbor. Others, however, represented the beginnings of real changes
that would characterize the development of waste management into the
twenty-first century, not just in West Germany but eventually everywhere
in the developed world. The first was the increasing presence of the private
sector in all aspects of waste handling and disposal. The second involved
the radical if gradual reconceptualization and reinvention of salvage as
recycling. We address the first by looking at the growing private sector participation in waste collection and disposal in the 1970s in West
Germany before turning to the emergence of recycling, which also had
significant private-sector dimensions.
   In the course of the 1970s, a newly potent force appeared on the waste
handling scene in West Germany. During this decade, the private sector
not only gained substantial market share (by 1980, it collected more
than half of West Germany's household waste), it also became "visible,"
establishing an influential trade organization and lobby group and coming
to terms with its workforce, in part through accommodation with trade
unions. In short, it became a player to be reckoned with.
   Private-sector involvement in waste handling, of course, was not new.
There was a long tradition of private-sector waste collection through the
end of the nineteenth century, although thereafter private contractors
often lost out to the public sector, at least in urban areas. Private-sector
firms were not viewed as being able to provide reliable and sustainable
service.[58] The creation of municipal waste collection services and public cleansing departments therefore soon meant that private companies

57 Matthias Baerens and Ulrich von Arnswald, *Die Müll-Connection und ihre Geschäfte*
    (Munich: Beck, 1993), esp. p. 88.
58 Peter Münch, *Stadthygiene im 19. und 20. Jahrhundert: Die Wasserversorgung,
    Abwasser- und Abfallbeseitigung unter besonderer Berücksichtigung Münchens*
    (Göttingen: Vandenhoeck & Ruprecht, 1993), pp. 234–235.

played almost no role in urban waste management, with the notable exception of Munich, where a private contractor collected the waste and carried it to a plant in Puchheim for sorting and salvage until just after the end of the war. In rural areas, however, and even in parts of cities outside of the very center, private waste handling firms continued to hold sway.[59]

Beginning in the 1960s, however, the situation started to change, with private firms regaining market share in urban waste handling. This change accelerated during the 1970s, and several factors were responsible for this. The first was the growing problem of industrial and other sorts of waste with which public authorities, especially smaller ones, were confronted. Municipal cleansing departments often simply did not have the facilities or expertise to deal with either the type or volume of new waste sources, such as the soaring number of scrapped automobiles, for instance. The same was true of waste disposal for the chemical industry: increased scientification of waste management required radical revision of decades-long practice. At the same time, however, it has to be emphasized that the new and challenging field of specialized industrial waste caused massive difficulties for private companies as well. The numerous toxic waste scandals that surfaced in the early 1970s affected the image of the profession severely, and much of the lobbying undertaken by the Verb- and Privater Städtereinigungsbetriebe (Association of Private Municipal Cleansing Companies, or VPS), founded in 1961, centered on trying to improve it.[60]

The second factor explaining private-sector growth involved changes in the countryside. The decline of agriculture, growing motorization, the exodus of city dwellers seeking respite from the hustle and bustle of urban life into rural areas, and the construction of shopping centers on the periphery of cities all meant that villages and small cities started to experience waste-related problems similar to those already affecting urban areas.[61] And as rural areas started to catch up with cities in the production of waste, it proved impossible to sustain traditional methods of waste disposal in the countryside (generally, burning or burying waste

[59] Ibid., pp. 71ff.
[60] For example, letter from VPS to federal labour minister (March 20, 1973), BA Koblenz, B 106, 69731.
[61] Bundesverband der privaten Entsorgungswirtschaft (ed.), *1961–2001. 40 Jahre BDE. Von der Stadthygiene zur Kreislaufwirtschaft: Eine Zeitreise mit der Entsorgungs-wirtschaft* (Köln: BDE, 2001), p. 74; Michael Wildt, "*Am Beginn der Konsumgesell-schaft": Mangelerfahrung, Lebenshaltung, Wohlstandshoffnung in Westdeutschland in den fünfziger Jahren* (Hamburg: Ergebnisse, 1994), pp. 188ff.

at each household), necessitating establishment of regular waste collection service, something which in turn required complicated and expensive organizational capabilities.[62] To create a functioning and rational service, small and medium-sized municipalities would have to cooperate to share the costs for collection vehicles, disposal facilities, and so on, cooperation that often proved a challenge owing to local quarrels, organizational difficulties, and above all else, legal problems. Here, private companies provided an attractive solution by offering economies of scale without forcing the municipalities to cooperate formally. If they proved their reliability over time, it would become easier for small and medium-sized cities, villages, and towns to arrange long-term contracts with them. This was one of the most important reasons why the toxic waste scandals of the 1970s were so embarrassing for private companies.[63]

A third factor explaining the growth of the private sector involved the changes in legislation in 1972 that we have already discussed. By requiring establishment and implementation of waste disposal plans, the new legal environment reinforced the trend toward small and medium-sized towns and cities contracting out waste services to the private sector. Again, the key issue driving this was the inability or unwillingness of the towns and smaller cities to invest both in equipment and in the development of organizational capabilities that would be essential to carrying out the work now required by law.

A fourth factor in the rise of the private sector in German waste management in the 1970s was related to technological change: the introduction and diffusion of plastic garbage cans and dumpsters. Even in the late 1950s, it was broadly accepted among practitioners that the plastic bin represented the future of waste collection, despite long-standing concerns about the material's stability and durability. And the "future" began to arrive in 1964, when Freiburg became the first German city to introduce plastic garbage cans.[64] Although their adoption elsewhere in Germany was gradual because most cleansing departments were fully equipped with sheet metal bins and immediate replacement was hard to justify, diffusion of plastic dumpsters was faster, as we demonstrated in Chapter 2

---

[62] Abfalltechnik GmbH, "Studie über Maßnahmen zum Schutz der Gewässer vor Verunreinigungen durch häusliche und gewerbliche Abfallstoffe im Planungsraum Starkenburg (Südhessen)," August 1971, HStA Wiesbaden, 509, 2323a.

[63] Open letter from Schulte (chairman of VPS) to president of the German Bundestag Renger and president of the German Bundesrat Filbinger (May 28, 1974), BA Koblenz, B 106, 69731.

[64] Article, "Die Mülltonne aus Kunststoff kommt," *ÖTV-Magazin* (October 1965): 24.

using the example of the MGB 1.1, which held 1.1 cubic meters of rubbish.[65]

The type of plastic garbage can that most affected private firms, however, was the smaller 220/240-liter wheelie bin, which quickly became standard in the countryside and smaller towns and also in some cities. The "MGB 240" resulted from development work undertaken by the Edelhoff Company in Iserlohn starting in the late 1960s. It was deliberately tailored to solve the disposal problems of most municipalities by offering sufficient space for most needs and, at the same time, ease of handling. Edelhoff cooperated with the plastic garbage can producer SULO, which began serial manufacture of the new type in 1972.[66] Public cleansing departments in both smaller and larger municipalities quickly adopted the new design; the City of Mannheim, for example, bought its first 3,000 units in 1973. By the mid-1980s, the MGB 240 had replaced the 110-liter bin as standard.[67]

The fifth and final factor explaining the rise of private companies in the German waste-handling sector involved the country's economic problems in the 1970s, in particular the return of significant levels of unemployment after many years of extremely low rates. Compared to the unemployment experienced in Germany during much of the 1990s and the early part of this century, levels in the 1970s may seem relatively low, but increased unemployment compared to the years of the "economic miracle" nevertheless made labor supply both more flexible and cheaper. Private firms could thus afford to hire unskilled workers, mainly from *Sonderschulen* (special schools), who were particularly disadvantaged in the new job market.[68] They were also able to recruit young workers who wanted to stay in the area that they hailed from, something that was a major issue in rural areas and small towns. The problem of the turnover

---

[65] For instance, Münch, *Stadthygiene*, pp. 324–325; Vortrag Bernhard Irmisch (Direktor des Stadtreinigungsbetriebes der Stadt Mannheim und Vorsitzender der Landesgruppe Baden-Württemberg im VKS Mannheim), June 3–6, 1975, BA Koblenz B 106, 27094. MGB stands for *Mullgroßraumbehälter*, or large-capacity garbage container.

[66] Dirk Wiegand, "Die Entwicklung der deutschen Städtereinigung, der NKT und die Normung des MGB 240 – eine Erfolgsgeschichte," conference paper, Bochum, 2010, pp. 25ff.

[67] Karl Pulver, "Von der Abfuhranstalt zum Eigenbetrieb: 125 Jahre Stadthygiene in Mannheim," unpublished manuscript, Mannheim 2005, p. 118, StA Mannheim.

[68] ÖTV (ed.), *Rationalisierung und ihre Auswirkung im Bereich der Stadtreinigung (Müllabfuhr)* (Stuttgart: ÖTV, 1983). The union, however, lamented that this hiring practice would made it almost impossible to recruit higher positions from the staff.

taxes to which the private firms (unlike the public sector) were subject was therefore to some degree counterbalanced by lower wages.

It should be clear from this discussion of the factors bringing about the rise of the private sector in German waste handling during the 1970s that they started off and were initially most successful in the countryside and in small and medium-sized cities. Usually beginning with just a single truck and offering services to small groups of farmers or to a single industrial firm, these mostly family businesses often grew and professionalized during the decade. Until the late 1980s, however, larger cities with long-standing waste collection services continued to be dominated almost exclusively by the public sector,[69] although this dominance in large cities did not go unchallenged. Indeed, as early as the late 1960s, private firms made their first attempts to secure the regular waste collection of bigger cities. Mannheim's public authorities, for instance, received numerous letters from the Altvater Company, which from 1963 was a subsidiary of plastic garbage can producer SULO. Altvater's managers notified Mannheim that their firm was running waste services in the small cities of Geisslingen and Nördlingen, as well as in some other minor municipalities in southern Germany. They asked if they could do the same for Mannheim,[70] but the city's public cleansing authorities doubted that a company such as Altvater was in any position at all to provide a regular service to a major city with approximately 300,000 inhabitants.[71]

Altvater's letters may have been meant more as provocation than as a serious offer, but to a certain degree it was a harbinger of a new era: from now on, public cleansing departments had to take private firms seriously even in larger cities. After all, by about 1980, the VPS, the private sector's trade association, represented the interests of more than 400 companies. And the member companies handled about half of all household waste and nearly 80 percent of trade waste in West Germany.

One of the key factors enabling consolidation of the position of private firms in the West German waste handling sector was the gradual resolution of differences between these companies on the one hand and labor unions on the other. For a long time, private companies rejected wage agreements with unions completely. In 1975, however, the VPS came to an agreement with the public-sector employees' trade union, the ÖTV,

---

[69] Federal Ministry of the Interior, Interne Notiz (March 1979), BA Koblenz, B 106, 69732.
[70] Letter from Altvater & Co. Transporte to Stadtverwaltung Stadtkämmerei (February 16, 1967), StA Mannheim, Zugang: 52/1979, 1463.
[71] Letter from Verband kommunaler Fuhrparks- und Stadtreinigungsbetriebe (Baumann) to City of Ludwigshafen (April 11, 1967), StA Mannheim, Zugang: 52/1979, 1463.

primarily owing to the initiative of VPS chairman Gustav Edelhoff, who owned one of the largest private waste management firms and was also a strong supporter of the center-left Social Democratic Party. However, there was opposition within the VPS with some private companies stepping out of line and rejecting the tariff agreement.[72]

In the long run, however, the dissident private firms were unable to maintain this strategy, although the relationship between private waste management companies and the powerful ÖTV remained anything but easy during the 1970s and beyond. A statement from a 1983 ÖTV publication is illustrative of the ongoing tensions and the reasons for them: "A comparison with private waste management companies reveals that the average worker's age is lower there. This mirrors the common practice of private firms: they hire young workers who are able to perform at an extremely high level for a short time period, but after a few years are so worn out that they cannot meet their daily targets and have to leave the firm. Older workers are therefore hard to find in such businesses."[73]

In spite of this and other criticisms of the private sector, however, there is no question that it was becoming increasingly central to public cleansing and waste management in Germany, in direct contrast to Britain, where this trend was much less pronounced through 1980. There were also significant differences between the two countries in the development of a new weapon in the arsenal for fighting against growing waste output: recycling.

From Salvage to Recycling

Before we examine the contrasting paths taken by the United Kingdom and Germany toward recycling, it is essential to make a general point:

---

[72] ÖTV (ed.), *Qualitatives Wachstum 1. Umweltschonende und rohstoffsichernde Abfallwirtschaft: Vorschläge der Gewerkschaft ÖTV für die Entwicklung der Müllbeseitigung zur Abfallwirtschaft* (Stuttgart: ÖTV, 1985), p. 15; ÖTV (ed.), *Geschäftsbericht 1976–1979* (Stuttgart: ÖTV, 1980), p. 486.

[73] ÖTV (ed.), *Rationalisierung und ihre Auswirkung*, p. 26: "Ein Vergleich mit privaten Müllabfuhrunternehmen lässt erkennen, dass das Durchschnittsalter dort niedriger ist. Hier spiegelt sich die heute gängige Praxis privater Unternehmen wider: Es werden nur junge Arbeitnehmer eingestellt, die kurzfristig in der Lage sind, extrem hohe Leistungen zu erfüllen. Schon nach wenigen Jahren ist ihre Arbeitskraft allerdings so verschlissen, dass sie ihr Tagessoll nicht mehr erfüllen können und den Betrieb verlassen müssen. Ältere Kollegen lassen sich aus diesem Grund in solchen Betrieben kaum finden." In public cleansing departments, on the contrary, the staff was dominated by workers aged between thirty and sixty: Rolf Jansen and Reinhard Rudat, *Stadtreinigung der Bundesrepublik Deutschland* (Bremerhaven: Wirtschaftsverlag NW, 1978), p. 33.

in all industrialized countries, the 1970s represented a pivotal period in which one long-standing practice, salvage, was reconfigured into another, recycling. It was, moreover, far more than just a change in name. After all, although time-honored salvage practice associated with separation and reprocessing of waste materials (especially metals, glass, and paper) into useful goods would be subsumed under the new "recycling" rubric, recycling from its beginnings involved much more than that. And for that reason, too, applying the neologism to past salvage practice is an anachronism – an understandable one perhaps, but an anachronism nonetheless.[74]

Consider this: a search in the excellent online catalog of the National Archives of the United Kingdom (TNA) using the keywords "scrap" and "salvage" on the one hand and "recycling" on the other turns up two very different sets of results.[75] The two former words appear in documents throughout the twentieth century, especially those produced during wartime, and this usage is confirmed in the *Oxford English Dictionary* (*OED*), which indicates that "scrap" was used for the first time as a noun in the sense of reuse of materials in 1902, although as a verb in this sense already in the mid-nineteenth century. "Salvage," meanwhile, was first used in this sense in 1918, while it was used most heavily in and after the Second World War.[76] In contrast, however, with just three exceptions – one wartime entry, some entries during the 1950s that refer to a type of "recycle" engine, and some early material on nuclear fuel recycling issues – all of the recycling entries in the TNA catalog date from the 1970s and beyond. What is more, only these entries from the 1970s and beyond use the word as we would today.

---

74 This is done routinely. For an early example, see, for instance, Richard A. Wines, *Fertilizer in America: From Waste Recycling to Resource Exploitation* (Philadelphia: Temple University Press, 1985). This revised PhD dissertation looks at the process by which "waste recycling" was gradually replaced by chemical fertilizer in the United States during the nineteenth century. The idea is to look at this industry as a "complex technological system" and to examine changes in it, and it is successful in this attempt. The use of the term "recycling" in the subtitle and in the text is somewhat anachronistic, however. And, although in his introduction Wines explicitly states that the term was not developed until the twentieth century, he does not problematize the fact that it did not exist earlier at all.

75 http://www.nationalarchives.gov.uk/catalogue/search.asp (accessed 10 July 2012).

76 For "scrap," see http://dictionary.oed.com/cgi/entry/50216613?query_type=word& queryword=scrap&first=1&max_to_show=10&sort_type=alpha&search_id=LJwP-NNIcF5-4279&result_place=1 (accessed 2 March 2006); for "salvage", see: http://www.oed.com/view/Entry/170270?rskey=EIgroX&result=1#eid (accessed 12 September 2011).

Let us take a moment to unpack this last point briefly, again with the aid of the *OED*. "Recycle" in the sense of reusing materials in some way or another was first used as a noun and as a verb in the mid-1920s in connection with petroleum refining. The word's use remained restricted to what we would now term high-tech industries – petroleum refining, chemical production, aviation, and eventually nuclear power – until the late 1960s or later, with explicit usage of the term in the broader, more modern sense of "recycling household waste" beginning only in the 1970s.[77]

This is perhaps an interesting set of observations for word history buffs, but how is it important in this context? It is our contention that the new word "recycling" became essential to replace "salvage" (and not just in English, but also in German and many other languages) for several reasons. First of all, scrap and salvage, in peacetime at least, were activities firmly rooted in the market: whether they were carried out or not depended on whether there were buyers for the waste. Admittedly, during wartime, the market was less important, but even then salvage was used in the sense of "rescuing" materials from what might otherwise be discarded, something especially important when the nation was fighting for its very existence.

Recycling, in contrast, involved a broader conception, one which, while tied to the market in important ways, also recognized that there were ongoing noneconomic factors. In particular, there was an overriding concern for environmental well-being – the need to determine whether or not discarded materials should be used again in some form or other. Second, and related to this, there was an important sociological dimension that required the use of a new word. Those who carried out scrap and salvage work were, for the most part, on the *economic fringes* of society, although the processors of that scrap might be more mainstream companies. As we have seen, established municipalities were involved in this work to some degree, but the role of the public sector in salvage operations as a whole was quite limited, even during wartime. Recycling operations, on the other hand, tended to be carried out initially for the most part by people on the *political fringes* of society. These were members of the counterculture and early environmental movement starting in the late 1960s and early 1970s, with activities becoming more and more mainstream as time went on and with an increasingly vital role for city governments.

---

[77] See http://dictionary.oed.com/cgi/entry/50199849?query_type=word&queryword=recycling&first=1&max_to_show=10&single=1&sort_type=alpha (accessed 2 March 06). This produced results for "recycle" as a noun and a verb and for "recycling."

Finally, it is probably no accident that the term "recycling," as it has come to be widely used and understood, had high-tech origins. Salvage of traditional materials such as metals, glass, and paper may have been time consuming, labor-intensive, and dirty at times, but it was also relatively low tech and straightforward. Recycling of the new materials that were coming into the waste stream en masse by the 1960s, however, was not.

The importance of all three of these reasons for the adoption of a new term for what appeared an old activity is perhaps best exemplified in relation to plastics recycling. It was, after all, only with the realization of the sheer volume of plastic packaging and other plastic products being discarded and of the acute problems presented by the disposal of these items – either in landfills or, even more so, by incineration – that thoughts turned seriously in the direction of trying to recover the material in some way or another. This proved to be a massive challenge, however, both economically and technologically.

The problem was not necessarily the reuse of the material itself. The early thermoplastics industry pioneered in taking "rejected parts, trim, and flash from the fabrication operations" that could then be "ground, blended with virgin material, and molded into acceptable parts." Indeed, until the end of the Second World War, most scrap plastic was reused in the industry itself, although there was also a market for clean plastic waste among scrap dealers and independent reprocessors through much of the 1950s. What happened after that was again a function of economies of scale and increasing affluence. Thermoplastics, initially high-price, low production run items, became low-cost commodities. By the 1960s, "virgin plastic" prices had declined precipitously, and not surprisingly, profit margins for reprocessors faded to nothing.[78] Most of the fast-growing plastic waste stream therefore ended up in landfills or being burned in incinerators, again with rapidly obvious and frequently unpleasant consequences. The reaction of practitioners to this state of affairs, which could not be addressed through traditional salvage practice because there was no economic basis for it, differed considerably between the United Kingdom and West Germany. Let us look at the response in each country in turn.

Although there were plenty of voices in Great Britain in the 1970s calling for greater use of recycling as a key component of the solution

---

[78] R. J. Ehrig and M. J. Curry, "Introduction and History," especially pp. 8–14, in *Plastics Recycling: Products and Processes* (Munich: Hanser, 1992); quotation p. 8. Here, too, "recycling" is used anachronistically in relation to the pre-1970 period.

to growing waste streams and difficulties with landfill and incineration, a variety of factors – including the contested and unresolved reorganization of waste services in England, the costs associated with broadly based recycling, and/or alternative techniques for disposal – meant that they were for the most part ignored. The result was that even in cities having a long and distinguished tradition of salvage and reclamation, such practices were largely discarded. The process by which this occurred differed by city, however, and it is therefore worthwhile to look briefly at two contrasting cases: Manchester and Glasgow.

In the late 1970s, a "mammoth new plan" announced by the Greater Manchester County Council (GMC) to address the area's disposal problems provoked sharp criticism from prominent local and national politicians.[79] For example, a local member of Parliament, who was also the minister at the DOE responsible for dealing with the GMC, urged that refuse separation by the authority and individual households should be undertaken, asking whether these methods had even been "seriously considered" as a means to reduce the volume of waste.[80] Another local member went still further in his criticism, finding the new plans "extremely depressing and lacking in imagination" because they omitted any proposals for "drastically" reducing the overall amount of refuse that would have to be buried. In his opinion – based on having "looked at three tips" – at least half the waste was paper, cans, or glass bottles, all of which could be recycled in one way or another. Of the other refuse, "a large percentage" was polythene bottles whose recycling problems he claimed would "soon be solved" and that could all be dumped at one location so as to be ready for reprocessing when it became feasible.[81]

The GMC's response to this particular letter indicated the gulf that existed between the member of Parliament and waste handling practitioners. The politician doubtless reflected the views of many of the general public, whereas practitioners were less convinced that avoiding production of waste on the one hand and recycling on the other were viable tools for tackling disposal problems. The GMC conceded the fact that half the landfill material was potentially recyclable and that reducing the amounts received would indeed enable substantial savings in space and expenditure. But large-scale recovery posed serious problems for waste

---

[79] "Backing Urged for £54m Rubbish Plan: Warning to Local Councils," *Oldham Evening Chronicle*, December 27, 1979.
[80] GMCRO, GMC Minutes, letter from Ken Marks MP to chief executive, GMC, December 12, 1979.
[81] GMCRO, letter from Andrew Bennett MP to chief executive, GMC, December 6, 1979.

disposal authorities. The GMC already extracted ferrous material at its incineration plants and planned to extend the process as new incinerators came into use, but selling the metal was problematic because markets were unstable and the economics of recovery uncertain. Paper for recycling needed to be free of contamination, which could be achieved only by precollection separation. It also had to be sorted into grades before it could be sold, and waste disposal authorities lacked legal powers to organize paper collection or to direct district councils to do so. The latter were in any case generally uninterested in recovering paper because of the unpredictable economics. Glass, on the other hand, was usually broken and there was neither any practical way to extract it from other trash nor any commercial market for it. And with regard to plastics, the GMC claimed to be unaware of any possibility of recycling polythene bottles; nor did it have the space to store the estimated 400,000 cubic meters of bottles delivered to its disposal sites every year. No matter how desirable recycling might be, therefore, the problem for waste disposal authorities was that once waste had been received, recovering materials was neither technically nor financially viable.[82]

Responding in turn to the GMC's justifications for its actions, the parliamentarian who had written the particularly critical letter found it disappointing that the legal division of responsibilities between the collecting and disposal agencies meant nothing could be done to promote recycling by the GMC. Nevertheless, he urged that "a system of cooperation" for recovery be worked out between the county and district councils, with the GMC offering "a cash incentive" to facilitate this.[83] Perhaps wearying of what seemed to practitioners to be a mismatch between enthusiasm and understanding, the chief executive replied that it was "difficult to indicate to people who are interested [in recycling] the extent and nature of the problem." The restricted financial climate, moreover, meant that progress toward ending the increasingly unacceptable method of simply dumping crude refuse had to be done in stages, in which "careful study" was being given to recycling. Cooperation between collection and disposal agencies was going on, but there were limitations imposed by lack of money, manpower, and dependable markets for reclaimed materials.[84] What is more, the GMC's comments were very much in tune with

[82] GMCRO, briefing memorandum from county engineer to chief executive, GMC, December 20, 1979. The actual letter is not present in the records.
[83] GMCRO, letter from Andrew Bennett MP to chief executive, GMC, January 29, 1980.
[84] GMCRO, letter from GMC chief executive to Andrew Bennett MP, February 6, 1980.

contemporary observations and experiences in the rest of England. In 1979, for instance, the president of the professional practitioner body called recycling the "most potent frustration" in municipal waste handling. On the one hand, the recent rapid growth in public opinion endorsing the recognition of the need for resource conservation could hardly be ignored; but market forces, he argued, continued to inhibit the "total exploitation of the theoretical opportunities for salvaging."[85] His use of the term "salvaging" was yet another indication that British practitioners in the 1970s had not fully taken on board the still new concept of recycling.

The situation in Glasgow was considerably different from that in Manchester and elsewhere in England. As a Scottish local authority, Glasgow retained both collection and disposal functions, which facilitated an integrated approach to materials recovery and ensured continuity of market knowledge and negotiating expertise. A wastepaper contract made in 1976 guaranteed a minimum price for one year, irrespective of market conditions, a continuation of long-established practice.[86] Moreover, metals recovery went beyond easily extracted ferrous materials, even to the extent of sourcing a buyer in the same year for "loose enamel ware." Here, the city's long-standing firm – even aggressive – approach to salvage operations (see Chapter 3) was very much in evidence. The hapless enamelware purchaser claimed a typographical error had caused his firm to offer £18 per ton rather than the £8 intended, but the council refused any concession.[87] And as for glass, which the GMC had written off as a hopeless case, Glasgow negotiated contracts with a local glass container maker to sell him both clear and colored glass in 1978 and set up six collection sites to encourage public participation.[88] Sales of all of these recovered materials continued through the end of the decade and beyond, in a continuation of a long-established policy of generating income to offset operating costs. For Glasgow, the economic factors that constrained other local authorities were, apparently, repeatedly overcome successfully, thus encouraging rather than discouraging the notion of resource recovery.

Regardless of this continued embrace of some types of salvage, Glasgow was similar to Manchester in that there was little evidence that either

[85] Frank Flintoft, "New Year Message," *Public Cleansing* (January 1979), p. 5.
[86] MLG, GDC 1/2, Council Minutes 1975–1976, Cleansing Committee, November 24, 1976.
[87] MLG, 1977–1978, Environmental Protection Committee, October 6, 1977.
[88] MLG, April 6, 1978. The company was U. G. Glass Containers Ltd.

city's activities in this area were informed by or transformed into a full-fledged program of recycling. The market remained at the core of salvage practice, which led to continuation and even intensification of traditional methods of disposal, if sometimes carried out using new techniques. In the case of Glasgow, local circumstances formed part of the explanation for both continuity and change. In 1973, the Scottish city's large separation and incineration plant at Polmadie suffered a catastrophic fire that destroyed half its capacity. The city had long been totally committed to a policy of maximizing reduction of refuse volume because of the shortage of local dumping space, and replacement was therefore urgent. However, economic and environmental factors led to major rethinking. Because of changes in composition, municipal refuse no longer burned unassisted once it was ignited, and supplemental oil firing of furnaces had become commonplace. Rising fuel prices and maintenance costs, moreover, made it "obvious" even before the fire that some alternative reduction system was desirable to contain costs, while complaints about grit emissions from those residing in local housing meant that "environmental aspects" also had to be addressed.[89]

Here, Glasgow faced a situation not unlike that faced by the GMC. But in contrast to Manchester, which took from 1974 until 1979 to even decide on which volume reduction option to follow, Glasgow moved quickly. Practitioners surveyed the alternatives, identified high-density baling as the most likely solution to its problems, sent an investigatory team to the United States to see the sole plant operating in the world at that point, committed itself to a decision, obtained the necessary £1.7 million funding, and had the new works going by November 1976. Costs were then minimized by installing the facility on the burned-out part of the Polmadie site, enabling better utilization of the infrastructure that had remained intact after the fire. Volume reduction, moreover, was claimed to be close to the level of 10:1 previously achieved by incineration,[90] and the new process seemed superior to furnaces in that refuse from normal household waste right up to the size of vehicle body shells could be processed. The new technique essentially allowed Glasgow

[89] "Glasgow Drops a 'Brick' – and Makes a 'Bomb,'" *Public Cleansing*, April 1977, p. 171. Similar complaints had been made in the 1950s about the works at Govan, encouraging the construction of the Polmadie plant in a less densely populated area. But by 1973, residential development had surrounded the works leading to the recurrence of similar complaints.

[90] Attained levels varied from the 90 percent claimed at Glasgow down to only 60 percent.

to continue with landfill and some incineration, which were supplemented with a small amount of old-fashioned salvage. As was the case in Manchester and the rest of the United Kingdom, recycling as a fundamentally new way of dealing with waste disposal was thus not embraced in Glasgow by the public sector, which here, as in most cities, continued to control almost all waste-handling services. Nor was it mandated by government.

The German case provided a stark contrast to that of the United Kingdom. In 1975, the federal government published the *Abfallwirtschaftsprogramm* (Waste Management Program), which outlined the future goals of waste management policy. Besides providing some solutions to disposal problems and dealing with the toxic waste issue, one of the main agendas behind the program was promotion of recycling – not merely to reduce the waste stream but also as a means to save energy, a highly sensitive topic in Germany, especially in the wake of the oil crisis of 1973–1974. In addition, the reduction of packaging waste (especially made of plastics) was proclaimed as a major goal.[91]

The Waste Management Program was, however, not just pie-in-the-sky "future music" with regard to recycling and waste reduction. In an earlier chapter, we noted that the traditional German bottle deposit system, threatened with elimination through competition from one-way bottles, was saved following a wave of protests, not least from the powerful brewing industry (in contrast to beverage distributors, who favored one-way bottles). There was also opposition to one-way bottles from German cities, which claimed that the abandonment of the deposit system would cause an increase in the amount of waste of up to 30 percent from one day to the next, a growth that could not be handled by Germany's new incinerators because they were not optimized to burn glass.[92]

The West German federal government, too, had started to embrace recycling even before it announced its Waste Management Program. In preparing the Waste Removal Law of 1972, for instance, government officials identified recycling as a way both to diminish the amount of waste and at the same time to save much of the energy that was, from their point of view, squandered in plastics manufacturing. Moreover, in 1973, the

---

[91] Abfallwirtschaftsprogramm 75 der Bundesregierung. Umweltbrief 13, Bonn (BMI), 1976.

[92] "Wohin mit dem Wohlstandsmüll? Einwegflaschen kosten Stadtreinigung zusätzlich mehrere Millionen," *Mannheimer Morgen* (April 12, 1969), seen in StA Mannheim, Bauverwaltungsamt, Zugang 52/1979, 940; letter from Tiefbauamt to Dezernat VII (June 29, 1967), StA Mannheim, Bauverwaltungsamt, Zugang 52/1979, 1463.

Ministry of the Interior launched a recycling initiative that later became part of the more comprehensive 1975 Waste Management Program.[93] For a society with growing awareness of the likely consequences of an ever-growing waste stream and a developing sense that better environmental protection was essential, recycling appeared to be the main alternative to traditional ways of waste disposal.[94]

Practical implementation gained momentum slowly, however, and it is worth exploring the gradual evolution of practice from salvage to recycling concretely, focusing for the most part on the case of paper. In 1969, church organizations started a widely regarded campaign to collect telephone books. This was an example of the third sector (i.e., charities, voluntary groups, social enterprises, cooperatives, and other community and self-help organizations) engaging in environmental action for noneconomic reasons. And soon after, in the 1970s, they were joined by much more powerful players, including cities such as Mannheim and Frankfurt, all of which contracted commercial operators to collect wastepaper from private households. Here, although there was clearly a market for the wastepaper, the cities did not gain financially from it at all. Instead, their involvement was for noneconomic reasons; essentially, they facilitated the private sector to ensure that the paper did not go into landfill. At first, no collection points were provided; instead, householders were required to bundle their wastepaper and to leave it outside their homes. For glass, however, which quickly followed wastepaper as a collectable and reclaimable commodity, installation of collection points proved necessary.[95] Within a few years, between 1974 and 1977, the tonnage of scrap glass recovered in Germany more than doubled (see Table 6.1). Remember, too, that this was in the context in which most glass bottles were still likely to be recovered through the deposit system.

From their start in the early 1970s, these services were provided by private contractors. Indeed, the field of recycling provided an opening for private companies to penetrate more and more deeply into the business

---

[93] Referat UB I 6. Ergebnisvermerk Recyclingprogramm der Bundesregierung. Bezug: Sitzung am 11.7.1973 (July 16, 1973), BA Koblenz, B 106, 58783.

[94] Ecosystem, Gesellschaft für Umweltsysteme mbH: Vorstudie Abfallwirtschaftsprogramm der Bundesregierung im Auftrag des Bundesministerium des Innern, Bonn (December 1973), BA Koblenz, B 106, 58783; Konrad Peil, "Wie eine Bürgerinitiative eine große Umweltzerstörung verhinderte: Mülldeponie Dreihausen. Dokumentation," Marburg (Marbuch), 1981, p. 134.

[95] Letter from Stadtreinigungsamt to Dezernat VII (May 21, 1974), StA Mannheim, Zugang: 52/1979, Lfd.-Nr.: 950.

TABLE 6.1. *Recovery of Scrap Glass in Germany*[96]

Year	Recovery of Scrap Glass
1974	150,000 tons
1975	200,000 tons
1976	260,000 tons
1977	310,000 tons

traditionally dominated by municipal public cleansing departments. Here, as would be the case in other areas of waste management later, they benefited from the fact that on the one hand there was more and more pressure on local authorities from the general public, legislation, and government to do more to minimize incineration and landfill, while on the other hand there were no extra funds available to cities to carry out these additional responsibilities. Private-sector involvement was the only solution.

One result was that, in spite of the fact that production and consumption of paper and cardboard grew faster than the growth of the German gross national product during the 1970s, the technology of paper recycling became more energy efficient and achieved improved results in quality. On the other hand, because of price fluctuations the market proved extremely shaky and unpredictable (see Tables 6.2 and 6.3).[97]

One reason for these fluctuations, of course, was that many factors influenced the price of wastepaper: overall demand, market relations, transport costs, number of suppliers, general paper prices, and the appearance of new competitors in the world market. A second reason, however, was that paper collection fell prey to its own success, an effect that would later also cause teething problems for the so-called dual system (or *Grüner Punkt*, green dot-system) of recycling that was introduced in 1990. The widespread adoption of paper collection in Germany naturally led to a rise in wastepaper supply, and depending upon demand this could often lead to a fall in prices. Thus, sometimes the collection of wastepaper was profitable and sometimes not.

[96] Memorandum des Bundesverbandes der deutschen Industrie zu den Entwicklungslinien der deutschen Abfallwirtschaftspolitik vor dem Hintergrund des deutschen Abfallwirtschaftsprogramms (July 1978), BA Koblenz, B 106, 69723.

[97] Wolfgang Schneider, "Sekundärrohstoff Altpapier: Markt und Marktentwicklung in der Bundesrepublik Deutschland" (PhD dissertation, University of Dortmund, 1988), p. 157.

TABLE 6.2. *Prices for Wastepaper*
in Germany, 1968–1973[98]

Year	Price Index (1962 = 100)
1968	109.2
1969	117.3
1970	138.6
1971	99.9
1972	92.6
1973	106.3

In many ways, this situation was not very different from earlier ones centered on the market. Price fluctuations in secondary markets were accompanied by the lack of well-structured systems, as only a small number of collection points and a few special containers for paper and glass existed. Practitioners were keenly aware that "bring-to systems" – ones in which people had to take their waste to a certain place so that it could be reclaimed – suffered from a lack of acceptance and convenience. They also caused social problems when containers were set on fire or even at times formed a focal point for small riots.[99] Collections were, moreover, often infrequent and covered only certain areas. By the late 1970s, therefore, it became clear that market solutions were insufficient to deal with an issue that had become a political and social one as well.

If broad-based and continuous recycling rather than simple salvaging was going to be achieved, the only alternative was for the state to step in. In 1979, the president of the Federal Environmental Agency (Umweltbundesamt), Heinrich von Lersner, wrote to the minister of the interior that waste recovery through salvage and recycling was no "self-runner" – that is, it could not happen on its own accord through reliance on the market and the private sector. In his opinion, it was necessary to issue "strategic directives" to encourage public authorities in their efforts to install permanent services.[100] His statement illustrates clearly that the breakthrough of modern recycling could not come about solely as a result of voluntary behavior and market forces. On the contrary, it was

---

[98] Rationalisierungs-Kuratorium der deutschen Wirtschaft, *Verpackung und Recycling* (Frankfurt/M: RKW, 1975), pp. 17–18.

[99] "Große Pleite mit Sperrmüllbehältern," *Rhein-Neckar-Zeitung* (May 12, 1966), seen in StA Mannheim, Hauptregistratur, Zugang: 42/1975, 1084.

[100] Letter Umweltbundesamt, from Heinrich von Lersner to Bundesminister des Inneren (August 17, 1979), BA Koblenz, B 106, 70539.

TABLE 6.3. *Prices for Wastepaper in Germany, 1978–1984*

Year	Price Index (1980 = 100)
1978	58.5
1979	82.6
1980	100
1981	61.6
1982	59.4
1983	59.6
1984	81.2

inextricably linked to state-sponsored installation of recycling infrastructure, including the establishment of multiple collection points, price guarantees to contractors, and so on. Obviously, this was a move predicated on nonmarket considerations, which, however, involved not only the public sector but also the market and the private sector.

The first concrete step to make this happen was to guarantee prices. Many German cities hired contractors in the late 1970s, pledging to make up the difference should the price fall below a certain level. On the other hand, if the price rose over this level, the contractor could pocket the difference. Through such guarantees, cities created an incentive to set up and maintain regular service,[101] and private firms were well prepared for this task. Furthermore, they had built up their own infrastructure, including landfills, incinerators, and recycling facilities.[102] These were the preconditions for recycling becoming a regular service in the 1980s. During this time, all larger cities in Germany either installed collection points for paper or started the regular collection of waste paper.[103]

Simultaneously, moreover, consumer behavior showed signs of change. For a long time, practitioners assumed that people would not accept new technologies of waste collection and thus avoided introducing them. They had good reason to believe this: several attempts to rationalize waste

[101] Pulver, "Von der Abfuhranstalt zum Eigenbetrieb"; Volker Grassmuck and Christian Unverzagt, *Das Müllsystem: Eine metarealistische Bestandsaufnahme* (Frankfurt: Suhrkamp, 1991), p. 99; Protocol Sitzung VPS – UBA am 5.4.1979 im UBA (June 11, 1979), BA Koblenz, B 106, 69732.
[102] Protocol Sitzung 28/6/1978 Umweltbundesamt (August 16, 1978): Zusammenarbeit zwischen VPS und dem UBA, BA Koblenz, B 106, 69732.
[103] See reports in StA Mannheim, Zugang 52/1979, Nr.1463; Park, "Von der Müllkippe zur Abfallwirtschaft," pp. 111ff.

collection in the past had failed because of people's "misbehavior."[104] But with recycling, it was different. People proved willing to sort their waste and to carry their glass and other items to collection points. This was almost certainly the result of greater ecological awareness over the course of the two decades starting in the mid-1960s. Recycling was thus particularly significant because it offered an opportunity for the general public to engage actively in environmental protection, in direct contrast to air and water pollution and *Waldsterben* (death of forests through acid rain), which seemed to be beyond the power of individuals. Partly, too, this was a result of local authority efforts to educate people to behave responsibly.[105]

Conclusion

The 1970s were a critical decade in the development of waste-handling services in the United Kingdom and West Germany. Both countries established pathbreaking national legislation at the beginning of the decade that shaped changes in existing practice. As the decade proceeded, these and other factors – perhaps most importantly Britain's considerable economic distress and Germany's relative stability and wealth, along with differences in political systems and gradually emerging differences in public attitudes – led to considerable divergence in the two systems. Both were in the process of moving from a traditional public cleansing ethic in waste handling toward a conception of waste management, although Britain's system of waste services, especially in England, was less coherent than that in Germany. What is more, throughout the United Kingdom, the prevailing provider of services remained municipal or regional government; in contrast, growing prominence of the private sector characterized West Germany during the same period.

The divergent development of the two countries in waste-handling practice in the 1970s was nowhere more in evidence than in the contrasting role of the new concept of recycling in each country. West Germany,

---

[104] "Große Pleite mit Sperrmüllbehältern." Another example: Letter from Residents Maudacher Straße 4, 6, 8, 10 to Städtisches Tiefbauamt, Direktor Borelly (March 15, 1958), StA Mannheim, Hauptregistratur, Zugang 40/1972, 291. Ecosystem, Gešellschaft für Umweltsysteme mbH.

[105] Arbeitsgemeinschaft Fichtner/ifeu, Stuttgart/Heidelberg im Dezember 1989: Abfallwirtschaftliches Gesamtkonzept für die Stadt Dortmund (StA Dortmund). For a critical point of view, see Sonja Windmüller, *Die Kehrseite der Dinge: Müll, Abfall und Wegwerfen als kulturwissenschaftliches Phänomen* (Münster: Lit, 2004), pp. 43–44.

unlike Britain, played a major role in the gradual emergence of modern recycling, something characterized, first of all, by the extension of markets. Earlier, paper and metals had been sold on small and regional markets, mostly to local traders; modern recycling in contrast depends on much bigger markets. This has led eventually to today's globalized markets for secondary raw materials. The second difference from salvage was that recycling was no longer driven by the absolute scarcity of raw materials but rather was shaped by price levels guaranteed by the state or municipalities. And the third key difference from prior practice, closely related to this, was not only the decisive role of the state but the crucial participation of the private sector as well. To diminish the amount of waste and also to secure the objective of environmental protection, cities fostered markets by guaranteeing prices. The business of recycling thus became sustainable. They did not, however, generally go about organizing recycling activities themselves, leaving this to private firms for the most part. By virtue of this, recycling became one of the first major industries featuring widespread privatization in the West German economy during the period after the Second World War, ironically because of the very prominence of the role played by the state.

PART III

RECONCEPTUALIZING WASTE AND
CONCEPTUALIZING WASTE MANAGEMENT

From 1980 to the Present

7

Framing Waste

Measurement, Regulation, and Legislation in the 1980s

Introduction

Growing environmental awareness starting in the late 1960s certainly had an impact on some aspects of public cleansing practice by the 1970s. But it did not translate into lower levels of waste in the decade that followed, although the amount produced by UK and German households during the 1980s seems to have stabilized following decades of rapid growth. Nevertheless, the 1980s were a decade in which there was a growing sense of crisis, in part because of an emerging conviction among many in the general public and among practitioners that, for all sorts of reasons, it was essential not merely to stop the waste stream from increasing but to shrink it radically. The sense of crisis was also fueled by the fact that the waste stream was becoming simultaneously more complex in its material makeup than it had been before. Ironically perhaps, the waste stream was also becoming increasingly uniform, not only regionally but also nationally and even, to an ever-increasing extent, internationally.

The response to the dual challenge of needing to decrease sharply the volume of household waste and of increased material complexity led in both countries to a range of measures aimed at defining the scale of the problem and refining the regulatory and legal context within which it might be addressed. Both Germany and Britain undertook these measures at the national level, although national-level decisions in both were increasingly affected by European-level regulations and legislation. Once again, however, in spite of common drivers, problems, and even constraints upon national action in the form of European intervention, the two countries had by 1990 become even less alike than ever before in their fundamental approach to the emerging field of waste management. This chapter explores this undeniable divergence in the face of apparently irresistible pressures toward convergence. It begins with a brief consideration of what we can ascertain about apparent quantitative changes to the waste stream during the 1980s and the very different measurement techniques that were used in each country to try to establish the extent of these changes. We then turn to more extensive investigation of the ways in which, despite an apparent end to growth in output of household waste in both countries, there was a well-founded sense of crisis in Germany and the United Kingdom, although the assessment of the crisis and the ways of dealing with it differed fundamentally. Then we examine national-level regulatory frameworks and legislation during the decade, with the aim of establishing the fundamentally different conceptualizations for addressing issues associated with waste collection and disposal that emerged in the two countries in spite of the beginnings of European legislation. And in the penultimate section, we look briefly at the impact of these differing conceptualizations in practice, mainly in relation to the ever-increasing role of the private sector, before outlining some brief conclusions at the end of the chapter.

Society's Unremitting Waste Stream: Slowing Growth?

Although there *appears* to have been no significant downturn in the amount of household waste produced in the United Kingdom and Germany during the 1980s, the rate of growth *seems* to have declined to close to zero in both countries. The truth is, however, that we just do not know, because reliable statistics are virtually impossible to come by until the 1990s and arguably remain problematic even in the new century.[1] Additionally, in the rare cases where they can be found, it is still impossible to construct an accurate time series for the decade owing to definitional changes. Still, it is worth examining the figures that are available and how

---

[1] Waste management practitioners from the public, private, and third sectors attending a workshop held at the Centre for Business History in Scotland on June 10–11, 2010, agreed that even then the only category of waste for which accurate statistics were available was still household waste, which, as we have seen, is only a small proportion of the total waste stream. For information on the workshop, "The Business of Waste: Past, Present and Future," see http://www.gla.ac.uk/schools/socialpolitical/eventsseminars/ economicsocialhistory/eventsarchive2007-11/headline_213375_en.html (accessed 26 September 2012).

they were compiled to try to establish trends in collection and disposal during the 1980s.

For Britain, statistical trends are particularly difficult to ascertain for the decade, and to the extent they can be, the figures apply only to England and Wales. There are a number of reasons for that, two of which are particularly important. First of all, until the 1990s there was still no legal requirement for local authorities to quantify accurately and identify precisely the refuse they handled. The Department of the Environment (DOE) had expected that the 1974 Control of Pollution Act's requirement for local authorities to produce waste disposal plans would make much more quantitative data available without any additional legislation, but little such information was forthcoming in the years that followed, owing in no small part to delays in development of the plans themselves.[2] The second major reason for the poor to nonexistent data on waste output in the United Kingdom during the 1980s lay in the extraordinary lack of clarity over who might be responsible for the compilation of the data, coupled with an astonishing lack of cooperation from those who might supply it.

Well into the 1960s, the Ministries of Health and of Housing and Local Government published data on quantities of waste and associated costs on the basis of voluntary questionnaires completed by local authorities in England and Wales, although no such data were collected in Scotland, where the numbers were compiled – or not – by local authorities. The ministries' data were certainly incomplete and often little better than seat-of-the-pants estimates, but they were at least something. The Ministry of Housing and Local Government, however, eventually stopped publishing the data in the late 1960s, for reasons that remain unclear. It is equally uncertain whether data continued to be gathered during this period, and if so by whom. In any case, the large-scale reorganization of local government in 1974 and the introduction of the Control of Pollution Act led to data for England and Wales again being published annually under the auspices of an initiative involving the DOE, the Welsh Office, and two nongovernmental associations, the Chartered Institute of Public Finance and Accountancy (CIPFA) and the Society of County Treasurers (SCT). This was probably in anticipation of more detailed record keeping that was supposed to result from the separation of collection and disposal functions, although regrettably, there was still no legal

[2] Department of the Environment, *Waste Management Paper No. 1: A Review of Options* 2nd ed. (London: HMSO, 1992) p. 7.

obligation for local authorities to provide data to the new collecting bodies. Returns were thus no better than those to the government departments previously. Consequently, although CIPFA (which acted as publisher) considered that the data represented a "reasonably comprehensive" picture of waste management activity and spending, the reality was that information was always incomplete.[3]

CIPFA, moreover, soon discovered that the task became increasingly difficult to carry out effectively. Not all local authorities responded, and of those that did only a minority actually weighed all the refuse they handled. Thus, most figures for weights handled were usually at best estimates and often little more than guesstimates. And things got even worse as the decade proceeded. Following reunification of collection and disposal services in England and Wales in 1985, numbers of returns from local authorities declined precipitously, so much so that in its report for fiscal year 1986–1987, CIPFA warned that the data it received were of such poor quality that it was "unwise to speculate" on possible trends in municipal refuse handling: only 61 percent of questionnaires that CIPFA sent out had been returned, and many of these were incomplete.[4] An important reason for this was an unintended consequence of local government reform in England and Wales undertaken in the mid-1980s by the Conservative government led by Margaret Thatcher. Owing to the impending requirement to put their refuse collection services out to tender starting in 1989, many local authorities simply refused to complete their returns; the CIPFA summary for 1987–1988 noted that some of the authorities had declined to submit figures as a matter of policy on the grounds that the information was now regarded as confidential because it might be "useful to competitors."[5]

The problems caused by the increasingly restricted submissions from local authorities led CIPFA to discontinue publication of definitive collection and disposal figures in 1987.[6] A new series that was started in 1991–1992 intended to avoid publishing details that might be commercially

---

[3] "Commentary," in *Waste Collection and Disposal Statistics, 1996–96: Actuals* (London: CIPFA, 1997), unpaginated (first page).
[4] *Waste Collection Statistics, 1987/88: Actuals* (London: CIPFA, 1988). The term "actuals" refers to the figures submitted by local authorities, irrespective of whether estimated or determined by weighing.
[5] Ibid., "Commentary," p. 2.
[6] Personal communication from CIPFA statistics manager to Stephen Sambrook, September 21, 2012, confirmed that there were no definitive data sets for 1988–1989 and 1990–1991 and only estimated figures for 1989–1990.

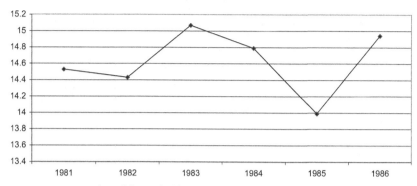

CHART 7.1. Weight of household and commercial waste collected in England and Wales, financial years 1980–1981–1985–1986, in millions of tons. *Source:* Chartered Institute of Public Finance and Accountancy, *Waste Collection Statistics: Actuals* (published annually, 1980–1981–1985–1986).

sensitive, as well as to cater better to new requirements under the 1990 Environmental Protection Act and European Economic Community (EEC) waste regulations. The surveys now permitted local authorities to compare their activities with one another and to measure progress in relation to legislative requirements, and in particular they highlighted the levels of waste recovery and recycling achieved.[7]

This background is essential for understanding just how carefully we must approach the data presented in Charts 7.1 and 7.2, and why only part of the decade is depicted in these graphs. It also helps explain why there is a massive discrepancy between the amounts collected and the amounts disposed of: reporting irregularities abounded. Nevertheless, the trends in both cases are clear: there was remarkably little volatility and certainly no trend toward growth in the annual statistics on collection and disposal of household and commercial waste in the England and Wales from fiscal years 1980 through 1986. Also, the astonishingly steady trend line for disposal between 1980–1981 and 1984–1985 suddenly dropped considerably in 1985–1986, probably because of reporting effects that accompanied implementation of extensive local government reforms in England and Wales. In any event, in the following year the figure returned to the previous steady state seen in the earlier part of the decade.

For Germany, trends in collection of waste during the 1980s appear to be similar to those for England and Wales. Here, the data were more systematically and reliably collected, but they are not much more suitable for

7 See note 3.

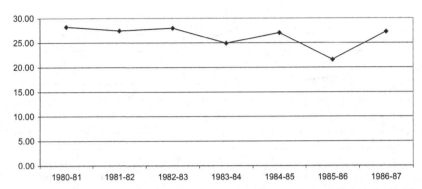

CHART 7.2. Weight of household and commercial waste disposed of in England and Wales, financial years 1980–1981–1986–1987, in millions of tons. *Source:* Chartered Institute of Public Finance and Accountancy, *Waste Collection Statistics: Actuals* (published annually, 1980–1981–1986–1987).

rigorous time series analysis than the British numbers owing to changes in definition over time. Nor are figures available for trends in *disposal* for Germany. Regardless, the systematic collection of data resulted from legislation. The 1975 Federal Law on Environmental Statistics (Umweltstatistikgesetz) required the Federal Statistical Office (Statistisches Bundesamt) to measure and report amounts of waste collected within German borders, and corresponding statistics were published beginning in 1981.[8] Thus, we can construct a graphic representation of apparent trends for the whole decade for the country (see Chart 7.3).

In Germany, too, it appears that there was remarkable stability in amounts of waste collected during period 1982–1987, and after an apparently substantial short-term increase in 1988–1989, amounts of waste collected returned to approximately the level that had prevailed throughout the earlier years of the decade. Two things in particular require further elaboration here, because both of them reflect the ongoing struggle of statisticians and practitioners to understand the problems they were dealing with. The first involves the odd formulation in the title of Chart 7.3. "Commercial waste similar to household waste," or "*hausmüllähnlicher Gewerbeabfall,*" referred to waste coming from restaurants, small shops, and so on, which was quite similar in composition to normal household waste although it was produced by commercial operations. Both were handled by public cleansing authorities, and so they were grouped

[8] Michael Homberg, *Die Abfallwirtschaft in unterschiedlich strukturierten Räumen: An Beispielen aus Westfalen* (Bochum: Brockmeyer, 1990), pp. 6–7.

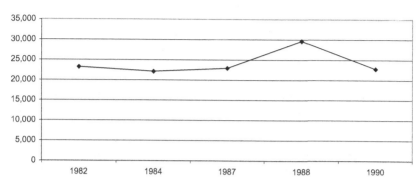

CHART 7.3. Weight of household waste, "commercial waste similar to household waste," and bulky waste collected by public waste management services in Germany, 1982–1990, in thousands of tons. *Source:* Statistisches Bundesamt, *Statistisches Jahrbuch der Bundesrepublik Deutschland 1982* (Wiesbaden, 1983), p. 561, and Statistisches Bundesamt, *Statistisches Jahrbuch 1993* (Wiesbaden, 1994), p. 730.

together in the statistics, demonstrating once again the ambiguity of many waste classification categories.

The second point requiring elaboration also refers to definitions, but it also helps explain the aberration in the trend line for 1988 and 1989. In 1986, the German parliament enacted a new Waste Management Law (Abfallwirtschaftsgesetz), which we examine in more detail later in this chapter. What is important to highlight here is that the law required public authorities to deal with new kinds of waste, such as the so-called basin business *(Muldengeschäft)* – that is, construction waste.[9] Initially, the new types of waste were simply incorporated into overall household waste figures, but because it clearly did not belong there, it was quickly removed.[10] In other words, there was almost surely no real increase in the weight of household (and household-similar) waste collected by German municipalities in the late 1980s: it was simply a result of a change in definitions and methods of measurement. This illustrates once again the efforts among statisticians and public cleansing practitioners starting in the mid-1970s and continuing into the following decade and beyond to

---

[9] Karl-Heinz Pörtge, and Michael Mehlhase, "Die Entwicklung der Müll- und Abfallbeseitigung im südlichen Niedersachsen seit 1970," in: *Göttinger Jahrbuch* (1989), pp. 175–188, 182.

[10] *Statistisches Jahrbuch der Stadt Frankfurt 1990* (Frankfurt/M: Frankfurt City, 1991), p. 164.

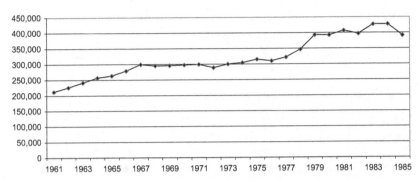

CHART 7.4. Tonnage of wastes collected in Frankfurt/Main, 1960–1985. *Source:*
Statistisches Jahrbuch der Stadt Frankfurt (Frankfurt/M: Frankfurt City, various
years): 1955–1956, p. 124; 1965, p. 95; 1968, p. 88; 1971, p. 88; 1974, p. 89;
1977, p. 90; 1980, p. 91; 1983, p. 92; 1990, p. 164.

come to terms with what they feared was a growing volume, but what
they were absolutely sure was a growing complexity of waste.[11]

Dimensions of the Crisis

In spite of this apparent stabilization of the amounts of household waste
produced annually in Britain and Germany during the 1980s, the general
perception that had developed in both countries starting in the 1960s
continued: that society would have to find a way of coming to terms with
a constantly growing waste stream. The notion of a "waste avalanche" – a
phrase used by some in West Germany from the 1960s onward – gradually
gained widespread currency, and it was especially scary to some because
it seemed that the avalanche would never stop. It is in any case not
surprising that people in the 1980s thought in these terms, because the
previous decades had indeed involved massive growth in quantities of
rubbish discarded by households. Chart 7.4, for example, indicates in
relation to long-term developments in the German city of Frankfurt that
the amount of waste collected practically doubled between 1960 and
1980. The graph also indicates, however, that in Frankfurt, as was the
case also for Germany as a whole and for England and Wales, the 1980s
represented a decade in which actual growth in waste output seems to
have slowed or even stopped.

---

[11] Werner Schenkel, "Mengen und Zusammensetzung von häuslichen und gewerblichen
Abfällen," in: Jochen Vogel et al. (ed.), *Handbuch des Umweltschutzes* (Landsberg a.
Lech: Ecomed, 1987).

Still, even if growth in waste output apparently leveled off, there were three key reasons why the sense of crisis during the 1980s was well founded. The first involved the simple fact that although waste output appeared not to be going up, it was also most certainly not going down. This meant in turn that landfill space would continue to run out and/or incinerator capacity would continue to be taxed.

The second factor centered on growing knowledge about the dangers of certain types of rubbish, knowledge generated by the ongoing scientification of waste management. In Britain, the effect of this was far more limited than in West Germany. In the United Kingdom, there was, of course, recognition that landfill/incineration could be dangerous, but the overall impression in primary sources was that British practitioners and policy makers believed that everything was well under control. Indeed, there were some who argued, for instance, that landfill capacity was not running out at all. One commercial operator in fact contended in a British practitioner journal that the country's mineral extraction industry was every year creating voids "several times" large enough to bury all of the wastes produced in the United Kingdom for the foreseeable future. Moreover, he went on, since the 1970s both central government and the private waste industry "had spent enormous sums of money on research and field trials to improve techniques and [had thus] shown how safe modern methods are."[12] We explore some of the ramifications of this type of thinking shortly.

In Germany, in contrast, starting in the 1970s more and more brownfield sites (*Altlasten*) where dangerous kinds of waste had been disposed of in the previous decades were discovered. The former central dump of the city of Frankfurt, the Monte Scherbelino, had been closed in the mid-1960s and then was transformed into a romantic park for young couples. In the late 1970s, however, this "park" had to be closed when scientists found out how contaminated the former dump actually was. One of them simply called the site a "witch's kitchen,"[13] and in Germany, like Britain, the brownfield issue proved especially problematic when dwellings were built on such sites after the dumps had been closed. This happened, for instance, in Dortmund-Dorstfeld and also in Bielefeld-Brake, where a chemical company for a long time had disposed of toxic substances. Not unlike the famous case of Love Canal near Niagara Falls in 1979, after

---

[12] John Holmes, "The Waste Disposal Options," *Wastes Management* (June 1987), p. 378.
[13] Justus Bender, "'Monte Scherbelino,' Der Müllberg wird abgedeckt und begrünt," *Frankfurter Allgemeine Zeitung* (August 30, 1984).

which the United States passed "superfund" legislation to fund cleanup of massive environmental degradation caused by industrial waste,[14] these incidents provoked a huge scandal, forcing cities and states in Germany to spend enormous sums to remediate the mess.[15]

The third major factor fostering the sense of crisis that was shared by the United Kingdom and Germany was the growing realization of just how much more complex the household waste stream was becoming, posing new and in the short term apparently insolvable environmental challenges. We have already discussed the impact of thermoplastics on public cleansing. Invented in the 1930s to 1950s and mass-produced from the 1950s onward, these new materials and their steadily increasing ubiquity caused dramatic changes in the waste stream. But by the 1980s, plastics were becoming in some ways the least complicated materials to deal with, because many of them were easily recycled, a process that the American Society for the Plastics Industry's 1988 resin identification code (RIC) eventually simplified still further. The RIC was introduced by private industry in response to demand from recyclers and also to legislation from some U.S. states that set mandatory recycling targets, but it also had international impact, being recommended for instance by the British Plastics Federation.[16] A similar system was adopted in Germany.

By the 1980s, moreover, thermoplastics were joined by increasing amounts of composite materials used in the production of consumer goods such as sporting items (e.g., golf clubs), clothing, and electronics, among other things. Composite materials had been around for some time, with fiberglass and Plexiglas, for instance, already in existence well before the Second World War. Starting in the 1960s and gaining pace over the next decades, however, composite materials such as carbon fiber and improved resins increased in number, volume, and applications.[17]

---

[14] Chris Magoc, *Environmental Issues in American History* (Westport, CT: Greenwood Press, 2006), pp. 247ff.

[15] Christian Möller, "Abfallpolitik und Entsorgungstechnik im 'ökologischen Zeitalter'" (University of Bielefeld, master's thesis, 2010), pp. 38ff.

[16] "SPI Resin Identification Code: Guide to Correct Use," http://www.plasticsindustry. org/AboutPlastics/content.cfm?ItemNumber=823 (accessed September 14, 2012). Scholarly research on the origins and impact of this code is needed. For British adoption, see http://www.bpf.co.uk/sustainability/plastics_recycling.aspx#identifyingplastics markingsystemsforplasticsproducts (accessed 25 September 2012).

[17] A. Brent Strong, "History of Composite Materials: Opportunities and Necessities" (Brigham Young University, n.d.), available at: http://strong.groups.et.byu.net/pages/ articles/articles/history.pdf (accessed September 14, 2012); Tim Palucka and Bernadette

Recycling of many of these new and ever more ubiquitous materials proved virtually impossible, at least until relatively recently, with obvious implications for the waste stream in highly developed countries such as Britain and Germany by the latter part of the twentieth century.

Complexity of the waste stream was heightened still further when, to an ever-increasing degree, households began consuming even greater quantities of electronic goods. Some of these were made of the composite materials just mentioned, but all of them contained increasingly sophisticated electronic components that were not only difficult to impossible to recycle but also, if they were discarded, could introduce toxic chemicals into landfill and from there into the water table. Electronic waste, however, was only one of many categories of household waste making it more complex through the 1980s and beyond: think, for instance, of batteries, household chemicals, and a range of other items in ever-increasing use by consumers. And, ironically, because most of these electronic and other products were developed, manufactured, and distributed by multinational enterprises that sold them in both the United Kingdom and Germany (and elsewhere), the growing complexity of the waste stream simultaneously led to increased uniformity of waste in and between these and other industrialized countries.

All other things being equal, it would seem logical that these shared factors in the growing sense of crisis about waste management in the 1980s might lead to a common perception in both countries about the crisis and how to deal with it. This was not the case, however, because of a fundamental difference between the two in the identification of the most important factor or factors that had led to the crisis. On the one hand, mainly because of the general sense among British practitioners and policy makers that all of the environmental and logistical problems associated with waste handling were either under control or *could* be mastered, the still new Thatcher government viewed the key issue at stake in the 1980s as one involving organization and governance. Specifically, Thatcherites identified local government and overreliance on the public sector as the primary problem. In contrast, the German federal government under Chancellor Helmut Kohl (who took power in 1982 and remained there until 1998), along with German state and local governments, did not view the public sector per se as a key problem. Instead, the Germans in

Bensaude-Vincent, "Composites: An Overview" (California Institute of Technology, n.d.), available at: http://authors.library.caltech.edu/5456/1/hrst.mit.edu/hrs/materials/public/composites/Composites_Overview.htm (accessed 14 September 2012).

the 1980s saw the key issue at stake as an environmental one. So, let us examine each of them separately.

In the United Kingdom, the main factor exerting a constant and often unsettling influence on municipal waste organization and practice throughout the 1980s was that the Conservative government of Margaret Thatcher, which was formed in 1979, was committed above all else to securing improvements in local government by reducing spending and improving service efficiency. It sought to do this in two ways: first, by encouraging local authorities to allow the private sector to take over some of their environmental services and second, by revisiting the changes in local and regional government structures that had been carried out in the mid-1970s, described in the preceding chapter. For waste handling, this involved reconsideration of the separation of the collection from the disposal function. Both aspects of the new government's agenda were important, although the one aimed at reorganization of local and regional governmental structures exerted influence from the second half of the decade. In contrast, the Thatcher government's focus on drawing commercial operators into refuse collection and disposal work was present almost immediately starting with the government's election in 1979, and it retained its influence into the 1990s.

The Thatcher administration's determination to drive through what it saw as essential improvements in the cost-effectiveness of local government was emphasized already in 1980 when the Department of the Environment commissioned an independent study by management consultants Coopers & Lybrand into how environmentally related services were organized and priced by local government authorities in England. The two foci were on how services were provided (i.e., directly by a local authority or through some form of outside contracting) and the policies for determining costs and charges made for services. The investigation was, however, hardly all encompassing. Only 24 case studies of refuse collection and waste disposal out of a possible 450 authorities were carried out, although they did cover a cross-section of collection and disposal bodies of varying sizes. In any event, the published findings identified shortcomings in the efficiency of the organization and provision of services throughout England.[18]

---

[18]   Coopers & Lybrand Associates Ltd, *Service Provision and Pricing in Local Government: Studies in Local Environmental Services* (London: HMSO, 1981), p. iii. The company described itself as "management consultants" but was also a major business in the accountancy field. The report covered not only refuse handling but also cemeteries, small farms, sports centers, swimming pools, golf clubs, theatres, and markets. About half of the final report dealt with refuse matters.

At the time the report was written, local authorities were spending £374.8 million annually on their refuse collection costs, which amounted to 17.5 percent of their total expenditure of over £2.1 billion on environmental services. And based on information they had gathered about the United States, the consultants suggested that private contractors could do the work at least as well as local authorities. Many municipalities, they pointed out, were still using long-established operating practices and workers' bonus schemes that both inhibited cost-efficient operations and excluded possibilities for introducing technical improvements. Because of political factors, in particular local labor relations and trade union resistance to change in organization and pay, relatively few district councils had seriously embraced the idea of opening up collection services to competition. And in those cases where councils had requested tenders from commercial firms, the report went on, accurately evaluating bids was frequently complicated by authorities not knowing what their own real costs were. The report found disposal a more complex field than collection to evaluate, not least because it had "more of the characteristics of an industry than a public service." This was mainly owing to the fact that there was a very large commercial sector dealing with the disposal of nonmunicipal wastes of all types, often handling greater weights than local authorities themselves, while at the same time also being involved with them in various ways. Here, too, the report found that the private waste disposal industry could "in principle" help in the transfer of new technologies to local authorities, although Coopers & Lybrand gave no real indication of how or by what means.[19]

Tellingly, the report focused almost exclusively on cost savings. In doing so, however, it made no serious attempt to assess just how much saving could be made through greater reliance on the private sector. Moreover, it completely ignored the issue of how effectiveness might be measured outside of an accounting context. More significantly, in light of growing ecological awareness, it skated over virtually all environmental aspects of refuse handling. The relative merits of landfill versus incineration were expressed solely in terms of investment and operating costs. The desirability of developing "new disposal methods" was similarly located exclusively in possible benefits to cost efficiency. And "optimal solutions" were divorced completely from likely ecological impact. In fact, in a revealing comment, the authors pointed out that because metropolitan waste disposal problems had intensified and become more costly,

---

[19] Coopers & Lybrand, *Service Provision*, especially pp. 54, 79, and 80. Quotations from p. 80. No details of the U.S. evidence mentioned were given in the report.

planning and environmental objections to sites had become less limiting than they had been five years previously.[20] The implication was that the licensing measures introduced by the Control of Pollution Act in 1974 and designed to tighten up requirements for site location and suitability were not having the intended effect.

The commissioning of the report was, of course, not universally welcomed by those being scrutinized. Nor did they accept its observations and conclusions uncritically. In the Greater Manchester County Council, which had had its share of dealings previously with the DOE, both the county planning officer and the county engineer were "increasingly sceptical" on the eve of the report's publication of the way its recommendations might be used.[21] And for his part, the county treasurer concluded in the aftermath of its publication that it was "difficult to see how some of the conclusions and recommendations are supported by the text," and that the document's usefulness was "reduced by its superficial nature, suspect methodology and emotive style."[22]

Those sentiments reflected perhaps some of the problems recently experienced in public-sector refuse handling. The 1974 Control of Pollution Act (CPA) and the 1975 Local Government Act (LGA) had inundated municipalities with new duties, but financial constraints still prevented recruitment of enough staff to deal with them properly. This naturally created backlogs, particularly in producing the long-term assessment and disposal plans that were at the heart of the CPA's strategy for managing waste on a national scale so as to bring environmental benefits. Even more compellingly, as R. F. Adams, president of the Institute of Public Cleansing, expressed it in 1979 on behalf of many practitioners, the "preoccupation with disposal" had "overshadowed the ... vital public health and environmental aspect of waste management services – that of storage and collection," on which 70 percent of taxpayer spending still went.[23] Adams thus reiterated the traditional core values of British municipal refuse handling in which efficiency was measured principally by adhering to budgets set on the basis of a combination of expenditure in previous

---

[20] Ibid., pp. 110–111.

[21] Greater Manchester County Record Office (uncataloged collection) (hereinafter GMCRO), GMC Chief Executive's Department administrative files, memo from county planning officer to Committee Administration section, January 28, 1981. For details of the GMC's prior experiences with the DOE, see the preceding chapter.

[22] GMCRO, Report of the County Treasurer on the Coopers & Lybrand Report, April 14, 1982.

[23] R. F. Adams, "Presidential Address," *Solid Wastes* (August 1979), p. 365.

years on the one hand and any current constraints on spending on the other. This philosophy, however, was soon challenged not only by a central government bent on reforming public-sector spending but also by some within waste management itself,[24] although ironically the legislation of the mid-1980s that constituted the concrete manifestations of these sentiments reinforced aspects of long-existing policy and practice. We return to this later in the chapter.

In Germany, cost was, of course, a consideration, too, as was the potential for incremental organizational improvement, but here environmental issues were much more important in shaping the sense of crisis. Part of this had to do with public opinion. Between 1978 and 1984, German contentment with current levels of environmental protection dropped precipitously in polls, from 40.4 percent to 22.2 percent, while at the same time the proportion of discontented people rose from 38.7 percent to 58.3 percent.[25] Germany's political system involved a combination of strong individual federal states on the one hand and proportional representation in legislatures at all levels on the other, which allowed smaller parties to enter and/or to influence state and federal parliaments. And this also played a role in bringing environmental issues to the top of the agenda. In 1980, the German Green Party was founded, the result of collaboration among a rather strange assortment of environmental activists from the far right to the far left. The Greens nevertheless managed to become a major political force within a relatively short period of time.[26] Already in 1983, delegates from the party entered the Bundestag for the first time. In 1985, Joseph "Joschka" Fischer (who would later serve among other things as Germany's foreign minister) became the first Green Party minister in the state of Hessen. Environmentalists were thus not just on the back benches or in opposition; they were now in government. In many ways, then, the 1980s marked a heyday for environmental debate in West Germany, in contrast to Britain. And the Germans perceived it not only as a policy issue. Many people also tried to adjust their lifestyles to conform more closely to the tenets of environmentalism. Organic food from local providers gained market share, for instance, and the popular slogan,

---

[24] J. Sumner, "Waste Disposal in the United Kingdom," *Waste Disposal* (June 1980), p. 302.
[25] Wolfgang Glatzer and Wolfgang Zapf, "Die Lebensqualität der Bundesbürger," in *Aus Politik und Zeitgeschichte (Beilage zur Wochenzeitschrift das Parlament)* 3.11.1984, pp. 3–25, especially p. 17. (Seen in Landesarchiv Berlin, B44/84.)
[26] E. Gene Frankland and Donald Schoonmaker, *Between Protest and Power: The Green Party in Germany* (Boulder, CO: Westview Press, 1992), pp. 78ff.

"Jute statt Plastik" (jute instead of plastic) expressed not only fundamental social criticism but also a willingness to change individual consumption patterns.[27] But the newfound status of environmentalism was not restricted to Greens and other alternative groups and individuals. Even governmental bureaucrats showed heightened awareness. In 1986, for instance, Werner Schenkel, director of the federal environmental office's waste section, publicly expressed the hope that there would soon be a change in Germany from a "throwaway society" to a "sorting society."[28]

This emerging societal – and political – consensus in Germany on the centrality of environmental concerns shaped policy and practice in relation to household waste handling. In other words, Germans were especially sensitive to the three key aspects of generalized crisis discussed earlier in this chapter. But there were additional indicators of crisis in 1980s Germany that would have required urgent attention and action even if Germans had not been quite so sensitive. Moreover, some of them in fact led to behaviors demonstrating that even Germans could be less than environmentally caring. Here, the most important issue was that Germany's disposal infrastructure, which had been aggressively extended and modernized during the 1960s and 1970s, nevertheless reached its limits and was threatened with collapse. Many landfills, for instance, were exhausted in the course of the 1980s, which meant even greater pressure on remaining sites. The Buchschlag landfill in Hessen, for instance, which took some of Frankfurt's waste, thus partially replacing Monte Scherbelino, had already exceeded its official rated capacity in the mid-1970s. Nevertheless, out of necessity, it remained in use almost fifteen years after it was "full." And when Buchschlag was finally closed down in 1989, it caused a "waste emergency" (*"Müll-Notstand"*) for large parts of Hessen.[29] This was one reason why officials were so eager to push through the approval of the Messel landfill (see Chapter 6) in spite of serious environmental and archaeological concerns. The long planning cycle for approval of new landfill facilities created a path dependency,

---

[27] Jens Ivo Engels, "Umweltschutz in der Bundesrepublik: Von der Unwahrscheinlichkeit einer Alternativbewegung," in Sven Reichardt and Detlef Siegfried (eds.), *Das alternative Milieu: Antibürgerlicher Lebensstil und linke Politik in der Bundesrepublik und Europa 1968–1983* (Göttingen: Wallenstein, 2010), pp. 405–422.

[28] Werner Schenkel, "Ziele künftiger Abfallwirtschaft," *Müll und Abfall* (2/1986): 41–47.

[29] "Der wundersame Müllschwund: Die Schließung einer Großdeponie in Hessen und ihre Folgen," *Die Zeit* (August 3, 1990)], seen in StA Frankfurt, Sammlung Ortsgeschichte S3/V, 19.107.

which in turn meant that practitioners had strong incentives to persist with their decisions even in the face of well-founded arguments against them, because any changes would cost too much time and money. Incineration in Germany, moreover, was not much better off. Many facilities erected during the 1960s and 1970s were antiquated, worn out, or no longer fulfilled the requirements of environmental legislation, especially the TA Luft (technical specification for pollution control of the air, officially Technische Anleitung zur Reinhaltung der Luft), which had originally been enacted in 1964. Regulations associated with the law were repeatedly tightened from the 1970s onward. But a revised version of TA Luft from 1986 placed particularly stringent limits on emissions.[30] This regulation resulted in large part from a reaction to greater knowledge about the toxicity of dioxins.[31]

The process of scientification of waste management and public initiatives aimed at influencing planning of new sanitary landfills also made the modernization of the disposal infrastructure much more complicated and, of course, more expensive. In Dortmund, in the late 1980s, for example, it proved necessary to remediate two landfills at Huckarde and Greve after their capacity was exhausted. In the meantime, until the establishment of a new landfill for the city, domestic waste had to be "exported" to a dump in the German Democratic Republic (GDR), something justified not only on grounds of a particularly parochial form of environmental protection but also on grounds of cost.[32]

Practitioners reacted to the disposal crisis not only by sending waste to the GDR but also by championing adoption of new technologies to make landfills safer and to reduce the emissions of incineration plants. Possible chemical reactions inside landfills were examined, for instance, and plans were developed to prevent groundwater contamination through implantation of plastic foil linings. But such efforts were not enough, and the general public remained skeptical or even hostile toward new disposal facilities.[33] Thus, practitioners were forced to think about new

---

[30] Frank Uekötter, *Von der Rauchplage zur ökologischen Revolution: Zur Geschichte der Luftverschmutzung in Deutschland und den USA 1880–1970* (Essen: Klartext, 2003), pp. 470ff.; brochure, "Saubere Zukunft jetzt!" StA Frankfurt, KS 2810, p. 7.

[31] Volker Grassmuck and Christian Unverzagt, *Das Müll-System: Eine metarealistische Bestandsaufnahme* (Frankfurt: Suhrkamp, 1991), pp. 234ff.

[32] Hermann Josef Bausch, *Es herrscht Reinlichkeit und Ordnung hier auf den Straßen: Aus 400 Jahren der Stadtreinigung und Abfallentsorgung in Dortmund. 111 Jahre kommunale Abfallwirtschaft/10 Jahre EDG* (Dortmund: EDG 2001), pp. 117ff.

[33] Martin Runge, *Milliardengeschäft Müll: Vom Grünen Punkt bis zur Müllschieberei. Argumente und Strategien für eine andere Abfallpolitik* (Munich: Piper 1994), p. 167.

ways of planning facilities to avoid provoking public protest. It may be a slight exaggeration to interpret the ever-increasing inclusion of the public into the planning process as an example of "experimental technological design" (*experimentelle Technikgestaltung*), but there is no doubt that this approach was certainly a reaction to ongoing protests against disposal facilities. And it was particularly necessary in places where the public was exceptionally sensitive owing to previous waste scandals.[34]

In some cases, however, when the waste infrastructure finally reached its limits, new facilities were still in the planning process, still not finished, or under reconstruction, desperation proved the only way out. In 1990, for instance, the city of Frankfurt faced a tense situation. The city's incinerator, one of the oldest in West Germany (it opened in 1964), had to be refurbished and was therefore shut down for one year. Alternative disposal opportunities did not exist in the immediate vicinity – remember that the Buchschlag landfill had been closed down in 1989 – so the city decided to ship the waste, once again, to the GDR, where ever-growing quantities of West German rubbish were being disposed of in exchange for valuable deutsche marks throughout the 1980s.[35] However, for Frankfurt's head of the environment protection department (Umwelt-dezernent), prominent Green Party representative Tom Koenigs, this was particularly embarrassing. And his statement in defense of the policy – that although shipment of waste to the GDR was the only solution to the city's waste problems, it should be transported by barge rather than by truck as this reduced emissions – did not make things much better.[36] With the reunification of Germany, however, the GDR soon disappeared and East Germany became part of the restored German state, subject to its laws, so the "solution" was short lived.

This and earlier cases of waste transfer to the GDR, sometimes involving toxic waste as well, were widely viewed as a demonstration of the inability of mass-consumption society to deal with the residues of wealth. And it made clear to many Germans that a fundamental transformation of existing disposal infrastructure was necessary to avoid such emergency situations in the future. Concentration of disposal into a

---

[34] Ralf Herbold and Ralf Wienken, *Experimentelle Technikgestaltung und offene Planung: Strategien zur sozialen Bewältigung von Unsicherheit am Beispiel der Abfallbeseitigung* (Bielefeld: Kleine 1993), p. 111ff.; Möller, "Abfallpolitik und Entsorgungstechnik im 'ökologischen Zeitalter,'" pp. 68ff.

[35] Matthias Gather, "Hundert Jahre Müllnotstand: Der lange Weg wiederkehrender Ratlosigkeit in Frankfurt am Main," *Die alte Stadt* (4/1991): 358–369.

[36] "Der wundersame Müllschwund."

relatively few facilities made landfill extremely vulnerable, and it caused higher costs for cleansing departments, which had to spend a lot of time transporting the rubbish to centralized sites. But the eventual solution embraced in Germany during the 1990s – large-scale incineration of waste – was in fact far from the one environmental activists and concerned citizens had hoped for during the 1980s.[37]

Reconceptualizing Waste at the National Level

Although there were significant shared factors promoting a sense of crisis in relation to waste handling in Britain and Germany in the 1980s, crucial differences in the assessment of the key issue at stake drove legislation and policy in each country in divergent directions. Viewing the issue as primarily related to local government profligacy, trade union obstinacy, and, more generally, an overly large and inefficient public sector, Britain's Conservative government concentrated on reforming local government and encouraging entry of the private sector into what had previously been a virtual public sector monopoly in most local authorities. In the process, any moves in the direction of greater incorporation of environmental considerations into policy were for the most part rolled back, with "efficiency" reinforced as the dominant objective, although that word took on a different meaning from the way it had historically been understood in British public cleansing. In contrast, West German legislation and policy were underpinned primarily by increasing attention to environmental considerations. As a result, German law on the one hand and government policy and practice on the other developed fundamentally new conceptualizations of waste and of the industry that handled it. We will thus look at the legal/policy dimensions in each country in this section before considering their impact on practice in the next.

As we saw in Chapter 6, dramatic changes to the organization and operation of public cleansing were undertaken in the mid-1970s in England and Wales, involving in particular the concentration of what had been mostly local disposal authorities into larger regional ones, effectively decoupling what had been a unitary local authority collection and disposal service. Understandably, therefore, practitioners and politicians did not take long to criticize these changes for failing to meet their original goals, and both major political parties accordingly promised revisions in

---

[37] Jörg Fischer, *Die Konzentrationsprozesse in der deutschen Entsorgungswirtschaft* (PhD diss., Freie Universität Berlin, 1999), p. 39.

their election manifestos during 1979.[38] In 1980, however, soon after coming to power, the new Conservative administration began planning changes based once again on the main motivation for their behavior – securing greater financial efficiency, mainly through greater private-sector involvement. By 1983, after much discussion and publicity, the government thus published its proposals for more changes in England and Wales. These centered on abolishing the six very large "metropolitan" county councils created in the mid-1970s. They also called for a general return of responsibility for most of the county councils' functions to district councils, including refuse disposal. Abolishing the "fundamentally unsound" structures created during the mid-1970s would bring savings and "remove a source of conflict and tension" between local government tiers by placing most local services under the control of a single authority.[39] Thus, when the Local Government Act of 1985 was eventually put in force, waste disposal once again became a local rather than a regional matter. And the irony was that this proposed reform, done in the name of efficiency and cost savings, had virtually the same rationale as the previous one seems to have been lost on the new government.

Despite the earlier trenchant opposition of practitioners to the concentration of disposal services in regional authorities, however, they did not necessarily welcome the proposed reintegration of collection and disposal at the local level. This was in part owing to the view that the "traumas of reorganisation" would once more be visited on its members within local authorities,[40] and in part because the consequences of such reforms were unclear. Nevertheless, in contrast to its stance on the reforms of the mid-1970s, the practitioners' professional organization, the Institute of Wastes Management (IWM, which was the new name for the Institute of Public Cleansing from 1981), proved unwilling to be as vocal in its opposition as it had been before. Instead of lobbying for any particular outcome, by mid-1985 the professional body committed itself to avoiding any advocacy that could be seen as politically inclined. Instead, its policy

---

[38] John Sheldrake, *Modern Local Government* (Aldershot, UK: Dartmouth Publishing, 1992), p. 19.

[39] Department of the Environment, *Streamlining the Cities: Government Proposals for Reorganising Local Government in Greater London and the Metropolitan Counties* (House of Commons, Cmnd. 9063, 1983). The Greater London Council, which had a separate identity from the metropolitan counties, was also included among the bodies scheduled for abolition. Quotation is from p. 5.

[40] "Editorial Reflections," *Wastes Management* (June 1985), p. 275.

was now to be professionally detached from external debates and neutral on both reorganization and growing pressure to open up municipal services to the private sector.

This major shift in tactics seems to have been rooted in two considerations. First, the proposed changes would actually have the effect of recreating a unified structure of waste collection and disposal under the control of a single authority, which, after all, is what many practitioners had expressly advocated prior to the earlier restructuring. Second, the IWM was aware of and concerned about the tendency for waste management roles to become politicized within some local authorities, which wanted senior public cleansing officials to identify publicly with their corporate identities. The IWM viewed such politicization as a potential source of friction in carrying out professional duties. It would also have the effect of weakening the position of practitioners vis-à-vis council supervising committees in the event of party-political changes in control of local government.[41]

Irrespective of such thinking, however, there were some dissenters from the government's proposals and the institute's policy of detachment. Claims were made that the post-1975 structure had enabled more operational and environmental improvements in waste handling than in the rest of the industry's history because the county councils' detachment from purely local issues had allowed them to take "courageous if unpopular decisions" in disposal planning. Moving back from regionalization would thus potentially lead "eventually to a state of shambles" resulting from "petty parochial issues" among the newly reintegrated, smaller-scale waste management authorities. Moreover, these governmental bodies would never achieve the economies of scale and attendant benefits that regionalization offered.[42]

In general, however, published objections were relatively few, and the reshuffling of municipal refuse organization in England and Wales went through without the major trauma feared by some. Waste disposal authorities naturally increased in number when the large county councils were dismembered, although sometimes the diminution in size was scarcely noticeable. Such was the case with the successor body to the Greater Manchester Council, the Greater Manchester Waste Disposal Authority, which actually became Britain's largest single waste disposal

---

[41] Ron Stanyard, "Facing the Facts," *Wastes Management* (August 1985), p. 415.
[42] G. Holmes, letter entitled "No Blunder," *Wastes Management* (December 1985), p. 752.

organization, serving a population of 2.3 million and handling 1.4 million tons of domestic waste annually.[43] This may have been why the new Waste Disposal Authority in Manchester seems to have avoided any repetition of the trials and tribulations attending the creation of its predecessor described earlier. For the new organization, it was business as usual, carrying on from where the former GMC had left off.[44]

In Germany, in contrast, changes in law and policy during the 1980s had much more far reaching effects. Not long after the Waste Removal Law (Abfallbeseitigungsgesetz) came into effect in 1972, practitioners knew that it would not be the last word in regulating the domestic management of waste. As we have seen in Chapter 6, the Hanau toxic waste scandal (among others) and its legal aftermath quickly demonstrated the shortcomings of the 1972 law.[45] Thus, in 1976, it was amended for the first time, and two further amendments followed in 1982 and 1985, as lawmakers tried to keep the provisions of the law up to date.[46] The three changes mainly dealt with problems of toxic waste and with the issue of waste transport.[47]

All these amendments, however, had only minor impacts on the ways municipalities and private companies dealt with "normal" household waste. Throughout, the basic definition of waste remained the same, something that practitioners took much pride in. The definition had both subjective and objective dimensions. Waste thereby consisted not only of transportable items that the original owner simply wanted to get rid of, it also included items for which controlled disposal was required in the public interest or for purposes of environmental protection. Municipalities were thus responsible for ensuring proper collection and disposal of waste, but they were permitted to transfer this responsibility to a third party. These were the basic tenets of the 1972 waste law and its three revisions through 1985.

A "fourth amendment" to the 1972 law, undertaken in 1986, constituted a different matter altogether, however. Lawmakers decided that

---

[43] "What Britain's Biggest Waste Disposal Authority Does," *Wastes Management* (July 1986), p. 376.

[44] "Business as Usual," *Wastes Management* (June 1986), p. 337.

[45] Bericht über die Auswertung der Erfahrungen im Zusammenhang mit der Hanauer Giftmüllaffäre (January 1974), BA Koblenz, B 106, 65269.

[46] Philip Kunig, Gerfried Schwermer, and Ludger-Anselm Versteyl, *Abfallgesetz: AbfG*, (Munich: Beck 1988), p. 67.

[47] Kunig et al., *Abfallgesetz*, l.c., pp. 7–8.

the new version should not merely be an update, but that it should incorporate fundamentally new thinking. In the end, quite logically, it was not called an "amendment" to existing legislation but instead was given its own name. The Waste Removal Law (Abfallbeseitigungsgesetz) became the Waste Management Law (Abfallwirtschaftsgesetz). The new designation was significant because it highlighted the fact that the focus of activity should no longer be restricted to waste removal and disposal – it also should increasingly incorporate recycling and reuse. The basic definition of waste stayed more or less the same, but it was supplemented by a clause indicating that waste remained waste only until it or substances recovered from it were reintroduced back into the economy. In other words, it explicitly recognized that waste might have economic value. This change clearly represented an attempt to resolve broad and intense debates about the differentiation between "waste" and "economic good" that had led to numerous lawsuits during the 1970s.[48]

The reorientation toward waste management rather than simple removal or disposal found expression in other passages of the new law as well. Even if only symbolically to begin with, it was nevertheless significant that the legislation established a waste management hierarchy. Reuse of things took priority over recycling, and recycling had priority over disposal. The law itself, moreover, reiterated the general obligation of local authorities to ensure effective waste collection and disposal,[49] but it simultaneously abandoned the principle of municipal self-government (*kommunale Selbstverwaltung*) concerning waste handling. Instead, it recommended that municipalities create joint waste management authorities.[50] The legalese may have been convoluted and opaque at times, but the implications were not lost on private-sector firms in Germany, which would be the primary beneficiaries of both the new conceptualization of waste management and of the new vision for municipal waste handling. In effect, it would all lead directly to the German "Packaging Law" (Verpackungsgesetz) and the creation of the privately run "Green Dot" system of the early 1990s, which are covered in Chapter 8.

---

[48] Nicole Pippke, *Öffentliche und private Abfallentsorgung: Die Privatisierung der der Abfallwirtschaft nach dem Kreislaufwirtschaft- und Abfallgesetz* (Berlin: Duncker & Humblot, 1999), p. 78; Andreas Kersting, *Die Abgrenzung zwischen Abfall und Wirtschaftsgut* (Düsseldorf: Werner, 1992).

[49] Kunig et al., *Abfallgesetz*, pp. 94–95.

[50] Ibid., pp. 104ff.

We return later to some of the implications of new legislation in the 1980s for waste management practice in the United Kingdom and Germany. First, however, it is important to note the gradual appearance of another actor on the stage: the European Economic Community (EEC). Starting in the 1970s, the EEC began issuing directives on how member states – including Germany and, from 1973, the United Kingdom – should deal with waste-related issues, mainly to ensure that varying levels of environmental protection regulation in member states would not distort competition and so impede the creation of a common market. Some scholars see this as the start of the EEC's own "interventionist environmental policy."[51] But this is very much an exaggeration for two reasons. First of all, EEC directives related to environmental protection were in fact extraordinarily weak at first because they were not legally binding on member states, which could thus decide when, how, or even *if* to comply with them. Certainly this was rectified by the Single European Act of 1986, which gave directives legal force, allowed the introduction of measures aimed at protecting the environment in its own right, and required that environmental considerations be a mandatory component of decisions in all policy areas for member states.[52] But even then, the EEC's sway over law, policy, and practice was limited by virtue of the fact that many of its member states were already far down the road of environmental legislation. Thus, the effects of initial EEC directives on waste in West Germany were minimal because many were formulated on the basis of German law (or that of other environmentally progressive member states such as the Netherlands).[53] The EEC was in fact more a follower than a leader in its early directives on waste management even in relation to Britain, where many of the initial principles of EEC regulation were already incorporated into the 1974 Control of Pollution Act. Even so, in the process of carrying out their responsibilities for ensuring legal and orderly disposal of all wastes, UK and German waste handling authorities were drawn increasingly into direct contact with European law. That contact would become especially important in the 1990s when European Community/European Union legislation started to have a direct impact not just on the management of particularly dangerous waste but also on the established methodologies of dealing with general domestic rubbish.

---

[51] Susan Wolf and Anna White, *Environmental Law* (London: Cavendish, 1995), p. 57.
[52] Ibid., p. 73.
[53] Pascale Kromarek, *Vergleichende Untersuchung über die Umsetzung der EG-Richtlinien Abfall und Wasser* (Forschungsbericht Umweltbundesamt, November 1987), p. 103ff.

The Changing Structure of the Industry

The identification of the root causes of the waste handling crisis of the 1980s differed in Great Britain and in Germany, and attempts to solve them through legislation and policy making were correspondingly different. But there is no doubt that one of the main outcomes in each case was strikingly similar: that is, the greater participation of the private sector in municipal household waste handling, even if there were important distinctions in the way in which this occurred.

For the United Kingdom, owing in large part to the ideological tenets of the ruling Conservative Party, the issue of privatization exerted an increasingly strong influence on municipal waste handling in the course of the 1980s. Indeed, even before the Coopers & Lybrand study on service provision discussed earlier was completed in 1981, a particularly high-profile test case of the new doctrine of favoring the private over the public sector was taking place. In 1980, the Conservative-controlled authority of Southend-on-Sea in Essex became the first mover in contracting out municipal household collection services to a commercial company, ostensibly to reduce costs and improve the standard of service to residents.[54] Controversy surrounded Southend's handling of the affair, with allegations of political rather than economic motivation by the local workers' trade union, the Transport and General Workers Union,[55] while the council's Labour Party opposition claimed that the tendering process breached EEC rules.[56] In the end, the legal challenge was rejected on narrow technical grounds,[57] but other aspects of the objections were harder for the government to ignore.

The government was keen for Southend's privatization to proceed because the council "was carrying the flag for local government

---

[54] The National Archives, Kew, London (subsequently TNA), Records of the Ministry of Housing and Local Government, HLG 120/3055, "Contracting Out: Southend's Experience," letters from A. R. Barnes to private secretary of Lord Belwin, January 13 and 15, 1981.

[55] TNA HLG 120/3055, letter from Lionel Murray, general secretary, Trades Union Congress, to secretary of state for the environment, April 29, 1981.

[56] TNA HLG 120/3055, letter from Lindsay Coombs to private secretary of Lord Belwin, January 14, 1981.

[57] Ibid. The Labour Party group had claimed that the alleged breach of EC rules (failing to advertise the contact throughout the EC and failing to accept the lowest tender) required a general audit of Southend Council's affairs, but the DOE insisted there was no causal link and dismissed the complaint solely on that ground.

generally."[58] Still, growing controversy in the months following led to a mood of increased caution. Following a nationally broadcast news feature on the process of privatization at Southend on BBC television in February 1982,[59] a confidential DOE memo to the secretary of state warned that sustained adverse criticism of claims about savings at Southend might prejudice other local authorities' decisions to move toward privatization of collection services. The DOE claimed that assessing the extent of the savings likely to result from contracting out the collection service had actually been "difficult," and DOE officials were therefore concerned that they would not be nearly as large as originally claimed by Southend Council. If this were shown to be the case, it would discredit "much of the effort [recently made] to encourage contracting out." In view of all this, the secretary of state's political advisors warned that "extreme caution" was essential so as to ensure that figures would stand the strictest scrutiny. This, he claimed, would help avoid any further embarrassment to either local authorities or the central government.[60]

Practitioners were not necessarily opposed to employing the private sector in some capacity, although they were often reticent about advocating it publicly. In any case, they did not necessarily endorse privatization policies uncritically. After all, it was clear to them that contracting out services could be tantamount to complete closure of a city's refuse collection department. Thus, even if ultimate responsibility for the work remained with the local authority, existing municipal operational infrastructure – including the workforce, plant, and most professional staff – would have to be dispersed to make room for the private sector. One consideration that weighed on local elected politicians (and even more so on practitioners), however, was this: What would happen if a contractor failed to deliver the promised standards of service or, even worse, went out of business? In the mid-1970s, British local authorities became legally responsible for the collection and disposal of domestic refuse, which meant that contractor default in the 1980s and beyond had serious potential implications both for the authority and individual councilors. Being forced to look for a company to take over refuse collection would

---

[58] TNA HLG 120/3055, letter from P. N. Bristow to secretary of state and others, summarizing meeting with members of Southend Council, January 15, 1981.

[59] For transcript, see HLG 120/3055, "BBC 1, Nationwide, 15 February 1982, 18.20 GMT."

[60] TNA HLG 120/3055, memo from H. G. Dormer to secretary of state and others, March 15, 1982, p. 1.

hardly put a council in a strong bargaining position, and reestablishing the service in-house would be costly and protracted.

By mid-1983, however, in spite of such potential problems, local authorities slowly moved toward contracting out collection work. Fourteen English municipalities had already made the change by then, to the general satisfaction of the government.[61] For its part, the professional body, the IWM, embraced the reality of growing commercial presence in the industry by enrolling members from the private sector, some of whom had migrated there following service in local authorities. The organization even provided a platform for private-sector views. In 1983, for instance, the institute's journal printed a lengthy article by the managing director of Waste Management Ltd., K. Bury, stressing the growing importance of companies like his and the collaborative role that they could play with the public sector. Bury claimed that the public and private sectors shared commitment to professionalism and service quality and were well aware of the public's adverse reaction to breakdowns in service delivery. Major capital projects in waste disposal, he pointed out, were already being undertaken jointly between the largest waste disposal authorities such as the Greater Manchester and West Midlands County Councils on the one hand and private firms on the other, few if any of which could have happened without such cooperation. In collection, contracting out had the potential to solve "the inability of some authorities to extricate themselves from the costly web of restrictive [read: trade union] practices" currently causing discontent among politicians, practitioners, and the public alike.[62]

In spite of such sentiments, however, scarcely a year later the movement toward privatization seemed already, in the words of the IWM's president, "to have run out of steam."[63] Of approximately 480 UK district councils, just 80 had seriously considered contracting out, and only half of those had actually invited tenders, from which just 25 contracts had been awarded. Most of them, moreover, were clustered in the southeast of England in Conservative-controlled areas.[64] By June 1985, only three more contracts had been placed with private firms, the total value of

---

[61] Michael Ancram, "The Government View," *Wastes Management* (August 1983), p. 390.
[62] K. Bury, "Privatisation: Private Sector View," *Wastes Management* (December 1983), pp. 640–643. The paper was presented to a meeting of the institute in February but only appeared in print at the end of the year.
[63] Ron Stanyard, "Facing the Challenge," *Wastes Management* (August 1985), p. 415.
[64] Ibid., p. 418.

which came to £19.66 million, with each contract thus worth approximately £702,000. These in turn were shared out among eight companies,[65] hardly a substantial penetration of a market worth an estimated £626 million annually. Despite this, however, local government restructuring starting in 1985 gave the private sector new heart, no doubt reinforced by a recent Audit Commission Report on refuse collection that favored greater commercial involvement. Commercial firms also knew that the government was intent on opening up public service provision generally to more competition.[66]

Thus, in May 1986, the practitioners' journal printed more papers from commercial companies urging the wider acceptance of the private sector by both individual practitioners and local authorities. A former senior municipal public cleansing officer who had become a consultant to Cleanaway Ltd., one of the largest UK private-sector waste companies, reminded his old colleagues (perhaps unnecessarily) that legal responsibility for waste management was vested in local authorities, and there could be no question of it being taken away from them. Although the responsibility could not be delegated, however, the actual work could, and at the last count 24 English authorities (which was, of course, slightly down from the 25 from a year earlier) had already turned to commercial operators to take over collection services completely. Another 51 used private contractors to assist with such work, while 28 used private companies to aid in disposal. Indeed, Cleanaway alone was disposing of 2.2 million tons of waste annually from all its contracts, which was claimed to be more than any single local authority. The total being handled by all private-sector firms had in fact doubled in the previous five years from 2.7 to 5.4 million tons. Even more significantly, however, there was a growing palette of benefits that large private waste companies could offer the public sector. Private firms, he noted, now employed graduate civil engineers, chemists, hydrogeologists, and other university-educated, waste-dedicated specialists not normally found in local authorities. These specialists could work in multidisciplinary teams able to cooperate with the public sector in handling site negotiations and designing disposal schemes that would meet the requirements of all aspects of the Control of Pollution legislation.[67]

---

[65] "Privatisation: The Facts. Awards to the Private Sector as of June 1985," *Wastes Management* (June 1985), p. 541. Contracts usually ran for three years.

[66] Audit Commission for Local Authorities in England and Wales, *Securing Further Improvements in Refuse Collection* (London: HMSO, 1984).

[67] R. Millward, "The Private Sector Involvement," *Wastes Management* (May 1986), pp. 21–23.

While the Cleanaway consultant was clearly evangelizing, his latter point highlighted one aspect of waste management where the public sector indubitably found itself at a disadvantage compared to large commercial operators. Recruitment of refuse practitioners into local government was still rarely done from among university graduates. Instead, admission to the profession usually came through general entry into local government service, and training was carried out both on the job and through part-time programs created and supervised by the IWM that were delivered regionally at ten technical colleges.[68] As noted earlier, these offered courses geared toward preparation for the institute's qualifying examination, the Testamur, and had been created in the 1960s. Even in the 1980s, however, the exam remained focused primarily on the general practice of refuse handling, emphasizing "a breadth of knowledge and plenty of common sense" rather than scientific training, which, particularly in the environmental aspects of disposal planning, was becoming more important. Commercial companies, in contrast, were prepared to invest in hiring graduates as technically qualified staff to work alongside ex-public-sector officials who understood how local government bodies worked to facilitate substantial market penetration into domestic waste handling through offering what was presented as a superior combination of skills. And that became progressively more important as attention focused increasingly on particularly problematic wastes and as the former boundaries between municipal, commercial, and industrial waste disposal became less clearly defined.

In Germany, on the other hand, one of the technical manuals published to facilitate implementation of the 1986 Waste Management Law explicitly recommended hiring private waste management firms if they could do the job more efficiently. This was reinforced by the major administrative directive for the implementation of the 1986 Waste Management law, the *TA Abfall*, which came into effect in 1991. The technical manual/directive decreed that waste utilization should have priority over disposal, especially if there was a market for recovered materials. Furthermore, it stated that a market could be created through the assignment of responsibility for recycling of waste to a third party. Not wishing to leave this open to interpretation, the *TA Abfall* also explicitly recommended the use of private companies.[69] It was thus clear that the gradual inroads

---

[68] Lewis Herbert, *The History of the Institute of Wastes Management 1898–1999* (Northampton: IWM Business Services Ltd, 1998) p. 41. Not until the 1990s did universities begin to offer specific degree courses in waste management.

[69] Zweite allgemeine Verwaltungsvorschrift zum Abfallgesetz, TA Abfall (March 12, 1991), GMBl. I S. 139, ber. GMBl, p. 469.

made in Germany by the private sector into the previous monopoly over cleansing services by municipalities that began in the 1970s would soon be cemented further. Private companies were no longer perceived by the state as dubious exploiters, threatening city hygiene in pursuit of cost efficiency, but instead as reliable partners that could relieve pressure on municipal administrations. The growing presence of the private sector was also a function of the establishment of numerous joint waste management authorities.[70]

There were also other factors at work, however, in the increase in private-sector involvement in German waste management. One involved a political change. In 1982, the socialist-liberal governments previously led by Willy Brandt and then Helmut Schmidt, which had been in power since 1969, were followed by a conservative-liberal coalition government led by Helmut Kohl, who would remain chancellor for the next sixteen years. Kohl had promised a "spiritual-moral turn" (*geistig-moralische Wende*) toward conservative values and increased self-responsibility. Privatization and free-market policies per se were nevertheless far less important in Kohl's Germany than in Thatcher's Britain or in the United States under Reagan, certainly in the eighties. Still, the idea that a partial retrenchment of the state was a desirable goal gained some traction in West Germany, too.[71] And given that the field of waste management served as a forerunner to more general privatization in West Germany, it is not surprising that moves toward greater private involvement were often welcomed, especially by government officials and those supporting their aims. Nevertheless, the most important factor in the greater involvement of the private sector in Germany during the 1980s was the Waste Management Law's emphasis on recycling. This gave private companies a significant market advantage on account of the extensive infrastructure they had erected during the 1970s, as well as the private sector's broad general experience in that field. Both aspects matched the requirements of new legislation. In other words, when lawmakers emphasized recycling, private companies had a significant advantage over the public sector.

This private-sector advantage also stemmed in part from measures taken from the late 1970s onward by public authorities to address the problem of massive volatility of prices for glass and paper mentioned in

---

[70] Bundesverband der deutschen Entsorgungswirtschaft (ed.), *1961–2001, 40 Jahre BDE. Von der Stadthygiene zur Kreislaufwirtschaft. Eine Zeitreise mit der Entsorgungswirtschaft* (Cologne: BDE 2001), p. 72.

[71] Andreas Wirsching, *Abschied vom Provisorium, 1982–1990: Geschichte der Bundesrepublik Deutschland*, vol. 6 (Munich: DVA 2006).

the last chapter. The Bavarian State Office for Environmental Protection (Bayerisches Landesamt für Umweltschutz) outlined the nub of the problem in 1978. In 1974, the average price for wastepaper peaked at 120 DM per ton. Two years later, the price had fallen to just 16.50 DM/ton, less than 14 percent of the peak. And a year after that, in 1977, the price had risen to about 20 DM/ton, while in 1978 it ranged between 50 and 60 DM/ton.[72] Clearly, it was very difficult to build up a viable commercial wastepaper recycling business given such fluctuations. And it *needed* to be viable: environmental activists, for instance, feared that people's willingness to separate paper, glass, and other recyclable materials would dissipate if the service was intermittent rather than constant and predictable.

The only solution, all finally agreed, was to guarantee a minimum price that would make providing this service on an ongoing basis attractive to the private sector. The sweetener was that, while the minimum price ensured profitability, if the price went above that level private firms could pocket the surplus. The recycling business in Germany thus essentially became a "cash cow" with very low risk, obviously attractive to the private sector. But it was simultaneously of little interest to the public sector, for two main reasons. First of all, German cities, strapped for cash in this period, had no appetite for hiring the extra staff and developing the specialist capabilities that would have been required. They therefore saw the private sector as a flexible alternative. Second, in contrast to the public sector, private firms had distinct advantages because they could construct supraregional (and eventually international) recycling infrastructures, and they also had much more experience in the sector and therefore better understood markets.

During the 1980s, recycling activities intensified in Germany. The city of Dortmund, for instance, increased the amount of collected paper and glass substantially between 1979 and 1989, as indicated in Chart 7.5.

These efforts were facilitated by development of "pick-up systems" in the case of wastepaper as opposed to "bring-to systems," which proved to be less effective. For glass, on the other hand, private firms developed containers with different slots for green, white, and brown glass as a result of experience with containers for mixed and other glass, which proved to be not very promising.[73] After recyclable materials were

---

[72] Letter from Bayerisches Landesamt für Umweltschutz to Augustana-Hochschule Neuendettelsau (January 16, 1978), HStA Munich, Landesamt für Umweltschutz, 141.

[73] Cf. HStA Munich, Landesamt für Umweltschutz, 142.

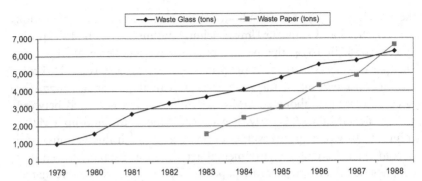

CHART 7.5. Tonnage of wastepaper and glass collected in Dortmund, 1979–1989. *Source:* Stadtreinigungsamt Dortmund (ed.): *Partner für mehr Umweltschutz. Abfallwirtschaft in Dortmund* (Dortmund: Dortmund City, 1989), p. 16.

collected, cleansing departments and recycling firms then worked together to improve sorting facilities. This was a significant and ongoing topic for debate from the 1970s onward, although attempts to develop mechanical replacements for sorting by hand in most cases ended up a failure in these early years, despite the engagement of big companies like Krauss-Maffei from Munich.[74] The Trienekens Company from the Rhineland, however, established Europe's largest sorting facility in 1985 located near the city of Kerpen, where the volume of household waste was allegedly reduced by 66 percent through the separation of various types of recyclable materials from other waste and from each other.[75]

Another technology, composting, returned to the agenda in Germany during the 1980s. As we have seen in previous chapters, this had long seemed unviable as a solution for cities' disposal problems. With increasing criticism of the harmful effects of landfills and incinerators, however, composting became an interesting alternative again. Environmental groups protesting against new or existing disposal facilities, for instance, championed composting, if only to forestall accusations that environmental activists were simply rejecting establishment of an incinerator or landfill in their neighborhood on the basis of the classic "not in my

---

74 Schreiben Bayerisches Landesministerium für Landesentwicklung und Umweltfragen an das Bayerische Landesamt für Umweltschutz (October 8, 1975), HStA Munich, Landesamt für Umweltschutz, 109.
75 Eric Schweitzer, *Ordnungspolitische Probleme der Abfallwirtschaft: Die historischen Ursachen, eine komparative Analyse und der Versuch einer differenzierten, wettbewerbspolitischen Neustrukturierung der unterschiedlichen Bereiche der Entsorgungswirtschaft* (Berlin: Self-published dissertation, 1990), p. 119.

backyard" principle. But although scientific efforts to refine compost-ing techniques were also intensified in the 1980s, the research concluded that composting could at best process only organic and food waste. At about one-third of total German waste output in the first half of the 1980s, organic and food waste amounted to a substantial proportion of all household refuse. But not everything in this category could be com-posted, and even if it all were disposed of in this way, at least two-thirds of household waste would still have to be contended with.[76]

Conclusions

The rapid upsurge in household waste output that gathered pace in the 1960s and continued growing steeply in the 1970s in both Britain and Germany appears to have leveled off during the 1980s. Growing environ-mental awareness in both countries may have been part of the explanation for this, although it is likely that part of the explanation, given that output was generally measured in terms of weight, involved the continuing move in consumption toward items made of plastics and other new materials such as composites, which in turn made household refuse lighter. These complex materials were simultaneously more or less difficult to dispose of safely. And related to this, greater scientific and popular awareness of the long-term environmental implications of landfill or incineration, the two most important forms of waste disposal, and other factors such as running out of appropriate landfill space, especially in Germany, entailed a quite justified sense of crisis in both countries. When we add to this the fact that both countries were members of an increasingly powerful and act-ivist European Economic Community, we might have expected that they would react in similar ways to the crisis. The opposite happened, however. Britain remained wedded by and large to long-established notions of how and why public cleansing should be carried out – that is, as an exercise in logistics and cost minimization. Germany, on the other hand, redefined public cleansing decisively as waste management and then enlarged on

---

[76] Marion Bieker, "Getrenntsammlung und Kompostierung von organischen Hausmüll-bestandteilen in Stadt und Landkreis Göttingen," in Das bessere Müllkonzept Bayern (ed.), *Müll vermeiden, verwerten, vergessen? Kommunale Aufgaben – ökologische Pflichten* (Ulm: Universitätsverlag 1991), pp. 47–60, 59; Gerlach Hans and Bernhard Irmisch, "Abfallwirtschaftsbericht: Bericht über die gegenwärtigen Formen, Möglichkeiten und zukünftigen Konzeptionen der Abfallwirtschaft in Mannheim" (Unpublished manuscript, March 1985), p. 5, in StA Mannheim; Homberg, *Abfall-wirtschaft in unterschiedlich strukturierten Räumen*, p. 298.

that concept considerably: waste handling was henceforth not merely as organized collection and disposal but instead focused on recycling and resource recovery as crucial (and high-priority) alternatives. The question is, What accounts for this difference?

The potential of the EEC to bring about convergence is most easily explained away here. EEC directives had no force of law until after 1986, and for some time after that Germany and to some extent even Britain led rather than followed the EEC in environmental policy, in particular with regard to waste management. Instead, the key factor in explaining the growing divergence seems to have been differences between the two countries in the prevailing identification of the main issue at stake in the crisis and how to address it. In Britain, the main issue was identified, especially by the powerful central government under the Conservative Party after 1979, not as a fundamentally environmental one, but rather one that involved perceived public sector inefficiency. In Germany, on the other hand, a much less powerful federal government (owing to more or less powerful state governments as well as to multiple parties operating in each owing to proportional representation) identified the main issue as environmental protection.

The Conservative Party's ideological position that the private sector did things better and more cheaply was one thing at work here. But, as we have seen, the right-center government that came to power under Helmut Kohl in 1982 was certainly not averse to embracing privatization. This was perhaps not as fervent an embrace at first as was the case in Thatcherite Britain, but it certainly took wings by the late 1980s, in particular in the massive privatization of the former East German economy undertaken by the Treuhandanstalt starting in June 1990.[77] Rather, the most important explanation for divergence does not seem to be ideology so much as identification of and action upon the perceived root cause of the crisis. The result was legislation that involved yet another round of government reform in the United Kingdom and that embodied in Germany in contrast a completely new conceptualization of public cleansing as activist waste management. And yet, ironically, the greater involvement of the private sector in waste handling that resulted in both countries was arguably much more extensive and effective in Kohl's Germany than in Thatcher's Britain. For the former, identification of recycling as one of the key issues in managing waste opened up the field still further to the private

---

[77] Wolfram Fischer et al., *Treuhandanstalt: Das Unmögliche wagen* (Berlin: Akademie-Verlag, 1993).

sector, which already possessed – and developed still further – its capabilities in this regard. For the United Kingdom, avoidance of mandated recycling combined with an unwillingness to resolve the dilemma (in the case of collection in particular but also of disposal) of what might be done to ensure that there would be a waste handler of last resort if waste handling were left to private firms ensured that private-sector inroads into the waste-handling sector in Britain were much more tentative than in Germany.

8

The Waste Management Industry Since 1990

Introduction

German waste management legislation and regulation in the 1990s included the Verpackungsordnung (Packaging Directive) of 1991 and the Kreislauf- und Abfallwirtschaftsgesetz (Recycling [literally, "circulation and waste management industry"] and Waste Management Law) of 1994. In many ways, these represented a logical culmination of trends in public cleansing policy and practice that had started in Germany in the mid-1960s and intensified in the following decades, and their organizational consequences were seen in the creation and operation of the Dual System of Germany (DSD). But if the gradual embrace in Germany of a new conceptualization of waste management as resource recovery was the result of evolution, the effects of this were revolutionary. By 2010, Germany sent less than 3 percent of its total municipal solid waste to landfill, which represented less than 2 kilograms of solid waste per capita, whereas the proportion of *total* waste sent to landfill (including not only household but also construction and other waste) amounted to less than 20 percent. On the other hand, close to 70 percent of total German waste was recovered in some way or another through recycling, reuse, or other means. And energy recovery through incineration accounted for more than 8 percent of waste disposed of, while all in all incineration eliminated more than 11 percent of the total.[1]

---

[1] Additional information comes from Antonio Massarutto, "The Municipal Waste Management Sector: Shifting Boundaries between Market and Public Service," presented at Bocconi University, May 11, 2012. Our thanks to Professor Massarutto for making his slides and other relevant material available to us.

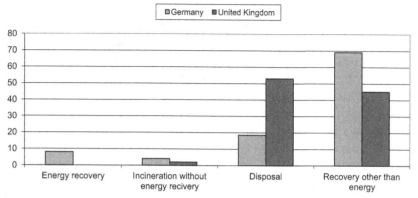

CHART 8.1. Percentage of waste disposed of by key methods in Germany and the UK, 2010. *Source:* Calculated on the basis of data supplied by Eurostat, available at http://epp.eurostat.ec.europa.eu/statistics_explained/index.php/ Waste_statistics (accessed October 31, 2012).

This emergent German waste management regime featured extensive public-private partnerships, widespread citizen participation, and elaborate collection and processing systems.[2] It also facilitated a form of industrial policy in that it stimulated German manufacturers to develop environmentally friendly products, packaging, and processes. And this in turn made the goods and services they produced more competitive internationally, especially in light of growing environmental awareness and increasingly strict waste management legislation and regulation in Europe – where Germany counted among the leaders in defining emergent European direction – and around the world.

In contrast, the United Kingdom, which in the mid-1960s embarked on an alternative path to that of Germany in developing its own waste management regime, had arrived at a very different place by 2010 (see Chart 8.1). In spite of the growing influence of European-wide legislation and regulation – where the United Kingdom was more follower than leader – and in spite of increasing environmental awareness, especially in relation to the causes and impact of climate change, which had in fact combined to begin pushing Britain toward adoption of many long-standing German waste management practices, Britons sent on average more than a hundred times as much municipal solid waste per

---

[2] The concept of waste regime is developed by Zsuzsa Gille in *From the Cult of Waste to the Trash Heap of History: The Politics of Waste in Socialist and Post-Socialist Hungary* (Bloomington: Indiana University Press, 2007).

capita to landfills as their German counterparts. Indeed, landfills in 2010 still accounted for well over half of *all* solid waste disposal (including construction and other waste). To be sure, great strides had been made in direct and indirect materials recovery, but "recovery other than energy recovery" still represented only about 45 percent of waste processing, or two-thirds the German rate. Incineration, in fact, accounted for less than 2 percent of the total, with energy recovery at about 0.5 percent – so miniscule as to be invisible in Chart 8.1. Also, although the British waste management regime relied on the private sector, it did so to a lesser degree than did the German one, something perhaps remarkable given the political and ideological emphasis in Britain from 1979 onward on private-sector solutions, an emphasis that continued even after the Conservatives lost power to New Labour in 1997. There was also more reliance on the third (charitable and nongovernmental) sector and growing citizen participation in schemes to promote increased recycling and reuse, even if this was still less enthusiastic than in Germany.

In this chapter, we try to explain this continued divergence in practice between these two European countries. Naturally, part of the explanation is historical, involving path dependencies that resulted from a number of factors, something we have considered at length earlier in this book. But part of the explanation has to do with fundamental differences in approach. Here, unlike the 1980s, which formed the focus of Chapter 7, the two countries did not differ in their assessment of the key issues at stake. Growing European Community/European Union activism and increased awareness and acceptance of the role of waste in environmental degradation and climate change were two key reasons that there was widespread agreement in both countries about the central problems to be addressed. Instead, persistent differences between Germany and the United Kingdom from the 1990s onward seem to have stemmed in large part from the fundamentally different tools used to address them. In what follows, we explore some of the drivers, dimensions, and implications of these contrasting outcomes during the period from 1990 to the present. We start with the German case, with a focus in particular on examining in detail that country's leadership in the paradigm shift from recycling to resource recovery and the changes in waste management policy and practice that resulted.

From Recycling to Resource Recovery: The Case of Germany

In an earlier chapter, we sketched out the significance of the shift in public cleansing and waste management beginning in the 1970s from salvage to recycling. The former was driven in peacetime exclusively by the market, although in wartime (or in cases of extreme poverty or lack of sufficient foreign exchange), materials shortages represented the main driver. Salvage was a relatively low-tech process pursued for the most part by those on the fringes of society and generally by the private sector (except in wartime or extreme materials shortages caused by political factors other than war). In contrast, recycling was driven less by the market (although market forces continued to be important) and more by political will and legislation. It often involved more sophisticated technologies for collection, sorting, and processing, and it was pursued to an ever-increasing degree by those in society's mainstream economically and otherwise. Finally, it involved an enhanced role for the private sector, although always in partnership with the public sector. This was, then, more than just a change in terminology.

The same holds true with the movement from recycling to resource recovery. In essence, recycling extended and enhanced older salvage practices in important new ways, in the process changing them fundamentally. Resource recovery did the same with recycling, refining it substantially as a concept. This was accomplished, for example, by distinguishing between "downcycling" (i.e., recycling a material to make something of lesser quality or value) and "upcycling" – recycling to maintain or enhance original quality and/or value.[3] At the same time, resource recovery subsumed recycling within a range of more or less sophisticated ways and means to minimize the amount of solid waste that was completely discarded and therefore essentially lost. Instead, resource recovery sought and seeks to maximize the amount that is used again for production of materials, products, or energy. By the first decade of the twenty-first century, this trend had crystallized into serious articulation of aspirations for a "zero waste" society.[4]

Germany was one of the pioneers in this transformation, which resulted from evolutionary development during the preceding decades but also from the challenges attendant upon reunification of Germany (the former West German Federal Republic and the East German Democratic Republic).

The year 1989 brought about decisive changes for West Germany when the people in East Germany started a peaceful revolution, resulting

---

[3] For an example, see the international paper and printing industry's Down to Earth entry, "Issue: Is Recycled Paper the Best We Can Do?" available at http://www.international paper.com/apps/d2e/down2earthonline/rp-03.html (accessed April 3, 2013).

[4] See, for instance, the "Zero Waste Scotland" Web site available at http://www.zerowaste scotland.org.uk/ (accessed October 31, 2012).

eventually on November 9 in the opening up of the previously highly restricted border between the divided nation. By summer of the following year, East and West had moved to unite their currencies under the aegis of the deutsche mark, and on October 3, 1990, they were united again as a single country. These events, of course, exercised a profound impact on German politics. New administrations and institutions had to be built up, the GDR's planned economy had to be liquidated, and so on. These developments were anything but easy and caused a lot of friction and bitterness, especially among people in former East Germany.[5]

In the field of waste management, these events also had an impact, posing the difficult task of integrating considerable additional territory into West Germany along with increasing the population considerably. And the task was made more challenging by virtue of the fact that waste collection and removal in the former GDR was in many respects backward: in spite of a first-rate resource recovery operation in the form of the Secondary Raw Materials organization (Sekundärrohstoff) and notionally stringent environmental laws, the GDR, as we have seen, was so strapped for cash that it was willing to flaunt those laws mercilessly, not least in the acceptance of more or less dangerous waste from West Germany and other Western European countries. A second challenge came in the form of a new waste management system for both the former East Germany and the territory of the Federal Republic. In 1990, the same year as reunification, the Duales System Deutschland (Dual System for Germany, DSD) or Grüner Punkt System (Green-Dot System) was announced, which aimed to create a widespread infrastructure for collection and recycling of packaging in particular, with producers of packages responsible for operating it. This system lent a further dynamic to the development of the private sector in waste management. A third decisive change, also posing challenges for practitioners and citizens alike, was related to the technology of waste disposal. After the millennium, German politicians decided essentially to halt disposal of household waste in sanitary landfills, opting instead for incineration as the fundamental means of waste disposal. Let us look at each of these developments in turn.

Reorganizing Municipal Waste Handling in Germany in the Wake of Reunification

After the Berlin Wall came down, there were two main problems for waste management practitioners. First, they had to establish a system of

---

[5] For instance, Dirk Laabs, *Der Goldrausch: Die wahre Geschichte der Treuhand* (Munich: Pantheon Verlag, 2012).

waste collection for former East German cities based on what existed already in the western part of the country. Second, they had to try to come to grips with the disastrous situation of waste collection and disposal in the former communist country. After all, the system of waste handling was in the throes of massive difficulties even before the peaceful revolution, problems that formed one reason for growing resistance of East Germany's citizens to state authorities.[6]

But authorities had to deal with another problem after 1990, too: how to come to terms with rapid increases in the amount of waste in the former East Germany. In the GDR, reusable packaging was ubiquitous, and a considerable proportion of rubbish was burned in the coal ovens that remained the predominant form of heating in the GDR.[7] The introduction of West-German style retailing and packaging combined with the gradual replacement of coal ovens with central heating systems meant that the "new federal states" of the former East German territory experienced within just a few short years what had taken well over two decades in the aftermath of the Second World War to occur in West Germany. The situation in the former East Germany was further exacerbated by the rapid dismantling of the GDR's flagship secondary raw materials (SERO) system. Introduced in the early 1980s, SERO had overseen collection, reuse, and salvage of large quantities of waste, reducing waste output in the GDR by an estimated 40 percent.[8] It largely disappeared, however, immediately after reunification, although it lived on in a handful of places, with the work continued by private firms. Given these developments, it should come as no surprise that waste output in the newly rejoined German states converged rapidly with that in the western states.[9]

---

[6] Martin Krischok, *"Zur Transformation der ostdeutschen Presse anhand der Berichterstattung über die gefälschte DDR-Kommunalwahl vom 7. Mai 1989"* (master's thesis, Universität der Bundeswehr Munich), pp. 34ff.

[7] Susanne Hartard, M. Huhn, and A. Kötter, "Zusammenfassende Abschlussbilanz des SERO-Systems der DDR, BMFT Forschungsvorhaben," in Klaus Wiemer et al. (ed.), *Weniger Abfall: Entwicklungen in der Abfallwirtschaft nach der Verpackungsverordnung* (M.I.C. Baeza-Verlag 1991), pp. 103–178, esp. pp. 119ff.

[8] See, for instance, Raymond G. Stokes, *Constructing Socialism: Technology and Change in East Germany, 1945–1990* (Baltimore, MD: Johns Hopkins University Press, 2000), chapter 7; Jacqueline Ferkau and Günter Lelgemann, *Entwicklung der Abfallwirtschaft in Ostdeutschland unter besonderer Berücksichtigung des Landes Brandenburg* (Fachhochschule Bochum, Schriften Nr. 15), p. 9; Jakob Calice, "'Sekundärrohstoffe – eine Quelle, die nie versiegt': Konzeption und Argumentation des Abfallverwertungssystems in der DDR aus umwelthistorischer Perspektive" (master's thesis, University of Klagenfurt, 2005), pp. 8ff.

[9] Klaus Rick, *Zur Konstruktion, Implementation und Wirkung des Dualen Systems in der Abfallwirtschaft. Eine umweltökonomische Analyse* (Regensburg: Transfer Verlag, 1998).

The tendency toward increased dependence on private businesses in waste management (which we dealt with in previous chapters) was naturally given added impetus by the reorganization of waste handling in the former GDR. Just as was the case for other fields, perhaps most notably electricity generation and distribution, fierce competition broke out among existing western German firms for the rights to provide waste collection services in the east. While many cities there opted to follow the classic path by founding municipal cleansing departments, others turned to the private sector. The result was a so-called *Gebietskampf* (struggle for territory), as contemporary waste management practitioners called it. And when all was said and done, private companies were much more important in servicing former East German municipalities than in the west, with the important exception of Berlin.

At the same time, it is worth noting that in western German cities privatization was on the rise as well. Whereas it was rare for a city simply to transfer its collection services to a private firm, many a city hived off its cleansing departments as an arms-length, privately organized *Gesellschaft mit beschränkter Haftung* (limited liability company, or GmbH), which might be owned by the city on its own or by the city in partnership with a private company. This resulted not least from the attempt to organize waste collection more efficiently and cost effectively. The city of Dortmund, for instance, decided to become involved in a public-private partnership (PPP) in 1991.[10] The city of Frankfurt did the same in 1995 when it signed a contract with the Rethmann Company from Westphalia; under the new name of Remondis, it is currently the biggest private German company involved in the waste management and recycling business. In Mannheim and Augsburg, on the other hand, cleansing departments were reorganized but remained entirely city-owned operations.

It would be an exaggeration to speak of absolute private domination of municipal waste collection services in Germany, because many German cities continue to provide them. Still, the inroads of the private sector have been substantial. On the basis of market research commissioned by the private sector's trade association, the Bundesverband der deutschen Entsorgungswirtschaft (the Federal Trade Association of the Waste Management Industry [BDE], successor organization to the Verband des privaten Statdreinigungsgewerbes, the Association of Private City

[10] Stadt Dortmund, *Es herrscht Ordnung und Reinlichkeit hier auf den Straßen: Aus 400 Jahren Geschichte der Stadtreinigung und Abfallentsorgung in Dortmund* (Dortmund: Dortmund City, 2001), pp. 118–119.

Cleansing Providers [VPS]), about 30 percent of all German household waste is still collected by communal waste management operations.[11] In other words, 70 percent of the activity is carried out by private firms, alone or in partnership with the public sector. Moreover, private firms place considerable pressure on local cleansing departments to act more efficiently or at least at lower cost. A recent interview with a practitioner in Mannheim revealed that the threat of privatization is sometimes used as a weapon in city politics to resolve conflicts between politicians and the city cleansing department.[12]

The combination of steadily rising levels of private sector intrusion into the field of urban waste management and the ever-increasing importance of recycling saw increased levels of employment among private waste management companies. While in 1980 the branch employed about 140,000 people, in 1990 employment levels had increased to about 165,000, and by 1995 nearly 200,000 were employed in the industry by the private sector.[13] Such growth prospects attracted the attention of big energy supply companies such as RWE and VEBA, which viewed investment in waste management companies as a form of related diversification: not only would it be profitable in its own right, but because newly built incinerators were designed from the outset as waste-to-energy plants, they would feed into the core business.[14] Waste management, however, turned out to be much more complicated than the managers of energy companies initially thought, and after the millennium most of them divested their interests. But by then a fundamental concentration process had taken place in the private sector of the industry: it was now dominated by very large players with interests extending beyond Germany. These included the Berlin-based ALBA company, Remondis, and Veolia (the former SULO company), all of which became multinationals.

There are divergent views about how to evaluate this development. The BDE, not surprisingly, is unstinting in its trumpeting of the achievements

[11] Trend:research, *Gutachten: Auswirkungen der Auflösung des Umsatzsteuerprivilegs in der Abfallentsorgung* (2010), available at http://www.bde-berlin.org/wp-content/pdf/2010/umsatzsteuergutachten2010.pdf (accessed November 5, 2012).

[12] Statement of Karl Pulver, worker at the waste management operation of the City of Mannheim (Interview May 4, 2008).

[13] Rick, *Zur Konstruktion*, p. 201.

[14] Jörg Fischer, *Die Konzentrationsprozesse in der deutschen Entsorgungswirtschaft und ihre Konsequenzen für die Volkswirtschaft* (PhD diss., University of Berlin, 1999), p. 134.

of private firms in promoting economic and technological efficiency as well as secure disposal (*Entsorgungssicherheit*).[15] Others, however, have expressed concerns that the ongoing concentration movement has had the effect of creating a "silent oligopoly," essentially eliminating any real price competition.[16] Indeed, events such as the infamous "paper war" of 2007, when companies were, among other things, accused of removing the wastepaper collection bins of other operators, seem to suggest that competition is still very much alive in the sector, although perhaps not always particularly attractive or economically efficient.[17]

Recycling on the Advance

One of the most important developments in the sector in Germany was the steady growth in levels of recycling and reuse that started in the 1970s and gained momentum in the 1980s. In the 1990s, however, the recycling of household waste climbed to a new level, amounting eventually to something new: resource recovery. We have already discussed the proportion of waste that is recovered in Germany, either as materials or energy (see Chart 8.1), but a poignant symbol of this new state of affairs is that in every German city as many as five color-coded bins stand in front of private houses and apartments, each with a separate function for holding organic waste, paper, plastics, and so on.

The introduction of the Duales System Deutschland (DSD) that took place in 1990–1991 was a major factor in this. DSD's establishment anticipated by one year the enactment of the Verpackungsverordnung (Packaging Regulation). Both were initiated by conservative environmental minister Klaus Töpfer (CDU), whose environmental initiatives in general earned him approval even from the political opposition. The DSD represented in the first instance an attempt to lower quantities of waste produced that resulted in the hotly debated "waste crisis" covered in the last chapter and thus to relieve pressure on overstrained landfill and

---

[15] Axel Schweitzer and Eric Schweitzer, "Der Wandel: Private Entsorgungs- und Recyclingwirtschaft im Spiegel der Zeit," in Peter Kurth (ed.), *Ressource Abfall: Politische und wirtschaftliche Betrachtungen anlässlich des 50-jährigen Bestehens des BDE* (Neuruppin: TK-Verlag, 2011), pp. 166–176.

[16] Hans-Georg Baum, "Privatisierung vs. Kommunalisierung: Argumentationspapier widerstreitender Interessen," in Peter Hoffmeyer, Martin Wittmaier, and Karl J. Thomé-Kozmiensky, *Privatisierung in der Abfallwirtschaft* (Neuruppin: TK-Verlag, 2000), pp. 69–76, esp. p. 73.

[17] "Der Papierkrieg tobt jetzt fast überall," *Augsburger Allgemeine Zeitung* (December 27, 2007).

incinerator capacity.[18] Even if many environmental associations criticized the Duales System as halfhearted and not suitable to get a grip in particular on the problem of plastic packaging,[19] it unquestionably represented a first step in tackling waste, especially from packaging. In this context, its name was telling: the term "dual system" referred to the establishment of a second system of waste collection and disposal to complement the other one involving traditional collection and disposal of household waste.[20]

To establish the DSD, a nonlisted joint-stock company was established (the Duales System Deutschland AG) that collected license fees from firms that wished to use the green-dot symbol on packaging. The symbol – a green circle with two arrows pointing in opposing directions, which now appears on much European consumer-goods packaging – does not necessarily indicate that the package on which it appears can be recycled but rather that the firm producing the consumer goods in question has paid for use of the trademark. DSD AG in turn used these funds to pay private companies to collect recyclable packaging in characteristic "yellow sacks" or from collection points. From the beginning, moreover, the DSD guaranteed a certain recycling quota for the glass, paper, and plastics it collected.

In its initial years, the dual system was not exactly a success story. It struggled owing to insufficient recycling capacity and fraud, but also because the German passion for waste collection and separation for recycling and reuse wildly exceeded all expectations. The Verpackungsverordnung intended that the Green-Dot System would be voluntary for consumers, but enthusiasm was such that supply of "waste" for recycling and reuse soon exceeded processing capacity. This eagerness diminished considerably, however, when it became known that much of the plastic and paper waste collected under the scheme was eventually burned rather than recycled because there were insufficient processing facilities at that time. In 1993, furthermore, the DSD AG faced severe financial difficulties that necessitated its reorganization. Only additional reorganizations and

---

[18] Eckhard Willing, "Ziele und Inhalte der Verpackungsverordnung," in Wiemer et al., *Weniger Abfall*, pp. 25–52, 34–35.

[19] A. Fußer, "Duale Abfallwirtschaft: Ein öffentlich-privates Tandem mit ungewissem Kurs, Stellungnahme BUND," in Wiemer et al., *Weniger Abfall*, pp. 13–23.

[20] Irina Bremerstein, "Die Entwicklung und Arbeitsweise des Dualen Systems – insbesondere auf dem Gebiet der Sortierung von Leichtverpackungen," in Roland Ladwig (ed.), *Recycling in Geschichte und Gegenwart: Vorträge der Jahrestagung der Georg-Agricola Gesellschaft in Freiberg (Sachsen)* (Freiberg: TU Bergakademie Freiberg, 2003), pp. 127–144, esp. p. 127.

extensive financial investment eventually enabled the DSD to fulfill targets for recycling on an ongoing basis.[21]

In 1994, the new Kreislaufwirtschafts- und Abfallgesetz (Recycling and Waste Management Law) was enacted, which further strengthened recycling efforts. It differentiated, among other things, between "waste for valorization" and "waste for disposal" (*Abfälle zur Verwertung; Abfälle zur Beseitigung*). The law also reinforced the priority of recycling over disposal, but it went beyond that through the new concept of "valorization," which implied not only recycling but a broader conception of resource recovery.[22] What is more, recycling technologies got a further push when Helmut Kohl's long-standing conservative/liberal government was replaced in 1998 by a coalition of the Social Democratic Party and the Green Party under Gerhard Schröder. This was the first time that the Green Party took over responsibility in government at the federal level. The new Green Party environment minister Jürgen Trittin thereafter managed to become one of the most hated German politicians over the seven years of the "red-green" coalition, at least in some quarters, partly because he turned out to be a stubborn advocate of stringent environmental policies.

One of Trittin's controversial initiatives was to introduce an obligatory deposit on cans and other nonreturnable beverage packaging in 2002, which came into effect one year later.[23] The measure provoked an outcry from various interest groups, and especially from the retailing industry. When the attempt to oppose the deposit failed, however, the *Dosenpfand* (literarily "can deposit") became law. Today, vending machines that accept what were previously nonreturnable bottles and cans from consumers and return their deposits are obligatory in department stores and larger supermarkets, another example of technological innovation associated with legislated recycling.[24] At the same time,

---

[21] Christian Thywissen, *Die Abfallwirtschaft in der Bundesrepublik Deutschland* (Frankfurt/M: Peter Lang, 1995), pp. 128ff.; Agnes Bünemann, "Duales System Deutschland: Ein Rückblick über die Entwicklung in Deutschland," in Kurth, *Ressource Abfall*, pp. 18–31.

[22] See Peter Queitsch, *Kreislaufwirtschafts- und Abfallgesetz (KrW-/AbfG): Rechtsverordnungen mit kommentierender Einführung zum KrW-/AbfG, einschl. der Entsorgergemeinschaftenrichtlinie* (Cologne: Bundesanzeiger, 1997).

[23] Gerd Rosenkranz, "Pfand-Debatte: Dosenlobby bläst zur Entscheidungsschlacht," *Der Spiegel* (August 20, 2003).

[24] Christoph Schlautmann, "Millionengewinne durch Einwegpfand," *Handelsblatt* (July 26, 2012); see also Finn Arne Jørgensen, *Making a Green Machine: The Infrastructure of Beverage Container Recycling* (New Brunswick, NJ: Rutgers University Press, 2011).

however, the new law brought with it a resurgence of street collectors. After all, many people are willing to forego the deposit they have paid because throwing the container away is more convenient. It is now common on German streets to see people fishing bottles and cans out of public garbage containers for return en masse. Indeed, there is even a celebrated homeless man who funds not only his subsistence but also a yearly pass on the German railways (he spends his nights traveling) by collecting deposit bottles and cans at rock concerts, football matches, and other events that he attends.

Part of the reason that recycling has become more prominent over time is because of technological improvement. During the 1970s and 1980s, for instance, development of sorting technology proved more or less fruitless despite the involvement of large firms such as Krauss-Maffei and others. Beginning in the 1990s, however, traditional recycling of waste plastics, which essentially involved making the same plastics again, was complemented by already known but hitherto not widely used chemical methods that transformed plastic materials into industrial intermediates such as oils or kerosene.[25] Sorting plants also reached an advanced level, using scanning technologies, sophisticated grates, air blowers, and so on.[26] These machines and apparatus have in the meantime developed to such a point that a discussion has emerged about whether Germany should abandon the system of color-coded garbage cans and instead let sorting plants do the job.[27] Such a development is unlikely in the near term, however, because of the costs already invested in the existing system and the simple fact that people seem to have embraced recycling as their very own individual contribution to environmental protection and well-being.

Government efforts to improve rates of recycling and other waste-related environmental measures have indeed caused highly emotional debates among the German public, but what is remarkable is that discussion has often died down in the aftermath of their introduction. The DSD has constantly been criticized for acting inefficiently and/or failing to reach its environmental goals, although it seems to have bedded in over time. Deposits on nonreturnable beverage packaging, extremely controversial when first introduced, have in the meantime become almost

---

[25] Alexandra Göschl, Bernhard Hartleitner, and Siegfried Kreibe, *Die Entwicklung des Grünen-Punkt-Systems: Verwertungstechnik, politischer Druck und Innovation durch Worte* (Augsburg: Bayerisches Institut für Abfallforschung, 2001), pp. 11–12.

[26] Bremerstein, *Die Entwicklung und Arbeitsweise des Dualen Systems*, pp. 131ff.

[27] Dirk Asendorpf, "Gegen den Trennt," *Die Zeit* (March 19, 2007).

an article of faith. To conduct a full assessment of the actual effects of these measures on business, society, or even the environment, however, is a difficult task.

The Long Farewell to Landfilling in Germany

Although there were problems in developing a waste collection system for the former GDR, the biggest single challenge following German reunification was almost certainly dealing with the disastrous situation of waste disposal there. This had two aspects. First, as noted in previous chapters, West German cities and West Berlin had been using the GDR as a dumping ground to "solve" their local disposal problems for some time. Thus, when it disappeared and the territory it used to occupy was suddenly subject to West German law, the disposal crisis in the old federal states came to a head once again. The second aspect of the waste disposal situation in the former GDR relates to the fact that the situation there in 1990 was comparable to that of West Germany in the 1960s. East Germany had about 13,000 disposal tips, of which 11,000 were dedicated to household waste and 2,000 were intended for industrial waste. Only 120 of the former, however, were – at least officially – declared to be sanitary landfills. A further 1,000 landfills had the status of controlled dumping sites (*kontrollierte Ablagerungen*), although this classification meant only that they were regularly staffed and that the sites were demarcated by a fence.[28] The vast majority of dumps, therefore, were essentially wild tips, not meeting any fundamental safety requirements.[29]

The application of West German environmental standards meant that most of these tips had to close down in the years following reunification. Furthermore, public authorities were faced with a huge task of brownfield cleanup to remediate them. It was not possible to follow this policy to its logical conclusion, however, since some of the landfills were desperately needed to dispose of incoming garbage even if they did not meet the German Federal Republic's safety standards. This was especially the case with the Schönberg landfill in Mecklenburg-Vorpommern, which has been mentioned previously. After reunification, the landfill continued to be used for all kinds of waste, especially toxic industrial waste. In the early 1990s, moreover, rumors spread that numerous "garbage black

---

[28] Ferkau and Lelgemann, *Entwicklung der Abfallwirtschaft in Ostdeutschland*, p. 15.
[29] Steffen Hentrich, Walter Komar, and Martin Weissheimer, "Umweltschutz in den neuen Bundesländern: Bilanz im zehnten Jahr deutscher Einheit," Diskussionspapier, Institut für Wirtschaftsforschung Halle (December 2000), p. 26.

FIGURE 8.1. Demonstrators at the Schönberg landfill site in Mecklenburg-Vorpommern, Germany, protesting against the alleged dumping of toxic wastes there by "garbage black marketeers" (*"Müllschieber"*). Photograph courtesy of Bundesarchiv Koblenz.

marketeers" (*"Müllschieber"*) had made false declarations and disposed of dangerous kinds of waste in Schönberg and elsewhere.[30] And there was indeed something to the rumors: in the early 1990s, those politicians in the state of Mecklenburg-Vorpommern responsible for the practice had to resign. In the meantime, waste exports from the west to the east did not stop immediately after 1989 but continued for some years afterward. And Schönberg (under the name Deponie Ihlenberg), in fact, still operates as a toxic-waste landfill for all of Europe. (See Figure 8.1.)

Nevertheless, the most important development in waste handling in Germany since 1990 has been the triumph of incineration over landfilling. In some ways, this is quite astonishing, because in the competition between landfilling and incineration from the 1960s onward, the latter generally lost out badly, especially once the dangers of dioxins were known. One of the factors involved was public opposition: if protests against landfills were fierce, protests against new incinerators were usually

---

[30] Matthias Bärens and Ulrich von Arnswald, *Die Müll-Connection: Entsorger und ihre Geschäfte* (Munich: C. H. Beck, 1999), p. 116.

even fiercer. Thus, as late as 1990, 70 percent of West German household waste was disposed of in landfills. Today, as we have seen, the situation is completely reversed: almost all household waste that is not recycled in one way or another is burned in incinerators.

So, why did Germany opt for this? One explanation can be found in the extremely large problems that the huge sanitary landfills constructed from the 1970s onward caused. The base seals of landfills proved very difficult to maintain. Leaking landfills did not just pollute soil and groundwater, they also caused air pollution by emitting methane gas, which some eventually linked to climate change.[31] Furthermore, a disposal infrastructure based on centralized sanitary landfills had the clear disadvantage that the distance between place of collection and place of disposal was considerably farther than would be the case for a decentralized structure based on incineration. Traveling these distances to landfill cost time and money, but it also produced additional air pollution from the vehicles that took the waste there. Over time, it became clear that problems of landfills were almost impossible to solve. And in the meantime, filter and other technologies for treating incinerator off-gases made considerable progress. Beginning in the 1980s, it thus proved possible to use such technologies to eliminate dioxin pollutants, although it took some time for all plants to be fitted out with this technology.[32]

This technological change was accompanied by new regulations and directives, beginning in 1993 with the *Technische Anleitung Siedlungsabfall* ("Technical Specification for Household Waste"), which tightened requirements for waste disposal sites. The "*TASI*," as the directive was known, was in large part a reaction to the problems of contamination through seepage and landfill gas.[33] In the years that followed, regulations were constantly sharpened. From 2005 on, for instance, disposal of untreated waste on landfills was forbidden, although dumps, of course, continue to be necessary for the disposal of residues from incineration, for instance.[34]

---

[31] Heinz Steffen and Marc Joachim Prabucki, "Risikoabschätzung bei der Planung neuer Deponien," in Peter A. Wilderer, *Die Deponie des 21. Jahrhunderts* (Munich: Gesellschaft für Wassergütewirtschaft, 1992), pp. 53–73.

[32] Göschl, Hartleitner, and Kreibe, *Die Entwicklung des Grünen-Punkt-Systems*, pp. 60–61.

[33] See Lars Krause, *TA Siedlungsabfall (TASI), Einführung und Kritik* (Berlin: VWF Verlag, 1999).

[34] Verordnung über Deponien und Langzeitlager (Deponieverordnung), Bundesgesetzblatt (BGBl.), I S. 900.

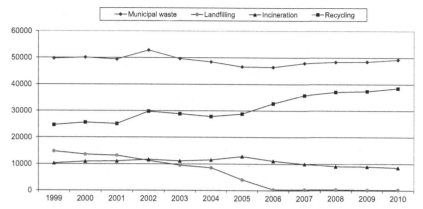

CHART 8.2. Amounts of municipal waste collected in Germany and amounts disposed of by landfill, incineration, and recycling, 1999–2010, in thousands of tons. *Source:* http://www.umweltbundesamt.de/abfallwirtschaft/abfallstatistik/ index.htm; http://www.destatis.de/DE/ZahlenFakten/GesamtwirtschaftUmwelt/ Umwelt/Umwelt.html (accessed October 25, 2012).

Chart 8.2 demonstrates that the amount of waste burned did not change very much between 1999 and 2010, partly because amounts of recycled rubbish grew dramatically. Nevertheless, new, more modern facilities were built, and their number rose from fifty-two in 1995 to seventy-two in 2007.[35] This naturally cost a tremendous amount of money, and the vast flows of cash almost inevitably caused some scandals. In 1999 the Trienekens Company of Cologne, which had pioneered in large-scale sorting of waste, paid millions of deutsche marks to bribe local politicians to ensure that the firm's tender for an incineration plant in the city's Niehl district was accepted. The oversized plant was eventually built for 820 million deutsche marks, but Helmut Trienekens and the former director of the City of Cologne's limited liability waste recovery company, Abfallverwertungsgesellschaft, were convicted in the end.[36]

The side effect of this building boom is that, when the effects of ever-higher rates of materials recovery through recycling are factored in,

---

[35] German Ministry for Environment, Nature Conservation, and Nuclear Safety, "Waste Incineration: A Potential Danger?" (September 2005), p. 2, available at http://www.bmu. de/files/english/pdf/application/pdf/muellverbrennung_dioxin_en.pdf (accessed October 31, 2012).

[36] Eva Maria Thoms, "Köln, wie es stinkt und kracht," *Die Zeit* (May 13, 2004); Eva Maria Thoms, "Der Mann, der Müll, die Korruption," *Die Zeit* (February 17, 2005).

Germany now has a considerable overcapacity for waste incineration.[37] This was the reason, for instance, why operators of incineration plants were eager to burn waste from Naples when the city was in danger of drowning in a pile of rubbish in 2008.[38] On the other hand, many Germans complain that waste collection fees are relatively high compared to those in other European countries, not least because of expensive incinerators.

All in all, the waste management industry in Germany has clearly changed dramatically since the 1980s. Recycling has gained considerably in importance, incineration has largely replaced landfilling of household waste, and the privatization of waste management has also advanced markedly. The industry, moreover, now focuses primarily on resource recovery rather than traditional collection and disposal through public cleansing. Nevertheless, the changes can also be seen as a continuation of some key developments in the field of waste handling in Germany since the 1960s involving ongoing scientification, the replacement of salvage with recycling, and privatization.

Until the late 1980s, discussion in West Germany focused on the country's waste crisis, which was generally acknowledged to be caused by the fact that disposal facilities – landfill and incinerators – were scarce. At the same time, however, landfill and incineration were also contested because they were often dangerous (or perceived to be so). More recently, discussion has shifted to other problems that are perceived as more urgent, especially climate change. One of the reasons that this shift in the focus of public debate toward more abstract, longer-term, and more global issues has been able to take place is that public authorities, using challenging targets and in cooperation with private companies, have managed to establish an institutional solution to manage the problems of waste disposal to a reasonable extent within the limitations of technological possibilities. And this outcome came about in part by virtue of a considerable extension of recycling, which is perceived by many as one of the very few examples of successful environmental politics, whether in Germany or elsewhere.

37 Udo Ludwig and Barbara Schmid, "Germany's Booming Incineration Industry: Burning the World's Waste," *Spiegel*, 8/2007 (February 21, 2007), available at http://www.spiegel.de/international/spiegel/germany-s-booming-incineration-industry-burning-the-world-s-waste-a-467239.html (accessed October 31, 2012).
38 Roberto Saviano, "Warum versinkt Neapel im Müll?" *Die Zeit* (May 18, 2011); Michael Brockerhoff, "Müll aus Italien in Düsseldorf," *Rheinische Post* (April 28, 2008).

Struggling to Catch Up: Britain from 1990 to the Present

The period after 1990 saw major transformations in British municipal waste management. Indeed, this period has witnessed the greatest changes in attitudes and methods of dealing with household waste since the late nineteenth century. The drivers for such radical revision were not dissimilar to those at work in Germany and also had parallels with those of the Victorian era: the perception of waste as a serious threat to the common weal, combined with the political inclination to tackle the menace as it was understood.

At the same time, however, crucial differences separated the Britain and Germany of the 1990s from the Britain and Germany (and other industrialized and industrializing countries) of the Victorian era. The common weal was no longer the improvement of public health but the safeguarding of the environment – not just locally, regionally, or nationally but internationally as well. Also, the political will to engage with the problem was shaped by a more complex set of factors than those of the nineteenth century: a sustained desire to rationalize public-sector service delivery by involving private contractors; growing environmental awareness and activism among the citizenry; and, for Britain in particular (which followed rather than led in this area, unlike Germany), the growing need to conform to European Union legislation and regulation. The latter imposed new and inescapable obligations on the sovereign British state. The environmental and political components of the pressure to change were closely linked, even if originating from separate roots, and in concert they opened the door to the acceptance of a fundamental change in conceptions of household waste. By the end of the new century's first decade, the de facto monopoly of local government in refuse handling was consequently a thing of the past, and the role of British practitioners was increasingly to facilitate reduction, reuse, and recycling of discarded materials, even if local authorities remained legally the waste handlers of last resort.

By the early part of the twenty-first century, in other words, the United Kingdom, like Germany, was guided increasingly by notions of resource recovery rather than those that had shaped waste collection and disposal in traditional public cleansing practice or in the private sector. Real differences remained between the two, however, not least in the vastly lower levels of recycling and energy recovery through waste incineration in Britain compared to Germany. One of the main reasons for these persistent differences must be found in differing political systems, which in the

British case involved highly centralized governmental authority and the virtual lack of environmentally focused political parties in Parliament, let alone government. The other key reason has to do with the choice of tools to implement policy and to try to bring about change in the industry and in consumer behavior: to a much greater degree than in Germany, British governments used tax policy as their primary lever, and it proved in many cases to be a very blunt instrument indeed.

The evolution of British municipal waste management after 1990 was driven to a great extent by legislative changes aimed at securing a greater level of environmental protection. Some of these measures were of domestic origin and others emanated from the European Union, but all espoused publicly the aim of regulating the level of waste creation and its impact on the environment, principally by reducing the amount of material that would eventually require disposal.

Let us start with the UK's Environmental Protection Act 1990 (EPA 90), which marked a key step in enlarging the rationale behind waste handling from protecting the public's health to safeguarding the whole environment. It also demanded changes both to practices in handling municipal waste and to related organizational structures that went well beyond those already made during the 1980s. Described by one commentator as "reflecting the multi-faceted nature of environmental law as it [was] developing in the 1990s," the new legislation embraced everything from handling complex, highly polluting wastes down to "the collection of abandoned supermarket trolleys," with the overall aim of integrating all aspects of pollution regulation by local authorities.[39] The law brought into force a three-tier system. First, new waste regulation authorities (WRAs) were responsible for licensing, supervision of activities, and publication of annual reports. Second, waste collection authorities (WCAs) that had been established in the 1980s continued broadly, as under previous legislation, as locally based and accountable to the local electorate. Indeed, not much had changed here over the course of the past century. Finally, the third tier in the system was the waste disposal authority (WDA), to which the WCAs delivered waste they collected.

Under the 1990 law, much remained of WDA structures as they had been revised less than five years earlier, but there were two key changes. The first was removal of their previous regulatory function, which not surprisingly now went to the WRAs. Thus, regulation was separated from

39 Stephen Tromans, *The Environmental Protection Act 1990: Text and Commentary* (London: Sweet and Maxwell, 1991), p. vii.

operations to avoid conflicts of interest within authorities. The second change was that the new WDAs would not be directly responsible for operations either. Instead, they were tasked with developing long-term strategy and ensuring that disposal work was properly done. Actual day-to-day disposal operations, however, were now carried out by separate "arm's-length" organizations designated as waste disposal contractors and defined as "companies formed for the purpose of collecting, keeping, treating or disposal of waste in the course of a business."[40] But this did not amount to the compulsory privatization of disposal services. Instead, the legislation specifically allowed local authorities to create waste disposal companies that would then compete for business "on equal terms" with the private sector.[41] This was very much in keeping with the ethos of the Conservative government in encouraging competition for local government services. And as with previous legislation, Scotland and Wales were covered by separate schedules that provided for their different arrangements for local authorities, although they often led to very similar outcomes.

Even as the 1990 UK Environmental Protection Act was being phased in over the course of the three years following its passage, the European Community/European Union was revisiting its directives on waste and the environment, a process that continued through 1996. The original Waste Directive Framework of 1975 was revised in 1991 and again in 1996, culminating in a demand that all EU members formulate national waste strategies regarding the types, quantity, and origins of material to be recovered from the waste stream, as well as the appropriate means for their disposal. Owing to the Single European Act, these requirements could no longer simply be ignored, and the 1996 revision was particularly significant because it established a formal hierarchy of waste. At the top was waste minimization in manufacturing processes, followed in descending orders of merit by reuse of materials in their original form (e.g., glass bottles), recycling of materials such as plastics by processing, and energy recovery from incinerating wastes and through combustion of landfill gases.[42] What was particularly important for existing British practice in the 1996 decree, however, was that landfill was assessed as the least desirable method of treating refuse. This was significant because

[40] Environmental Protection Act, 1990, Section 30 (7) and Section 30 (5).
[41] Tromans, *Environmental Protection Act*, p. 43.
[42] Paul Williams, *Waste Treatment and Disposal*, 2nd ed. (London: John Wiley & Sons, 2005), p. 9.

that year, an estimated 90 percent of the country's municipal waste was going into dumps.

A 1993 report by the Royal Commission on Environmental Pollution also decried landfill as dangerous in the long term, partly owing to greenhouse gas emissions associated with it. The report also supported the idea of moving away from the practice by imposing full economic costs on those disposing of waste in that way.[43] The EU directive, however, placed the United Kingdom in an uncomfortable position. After all, for one thing, British practitioners and politicians agreed almost unanimously that landfill was the most efficient method of disposal, combining the lowest cost on the one hand with the benefit of an acceptably low level of threat to the environment on the other.[44] Incinerators as an alternative had gradually fallen from favor starting in the 1970s, owing to sharply rising costs of fuel that had to be added to maintain waste incineration, but even more so because of the growing threat of air pollution from incineration, especially of many plastics. Thus, no new municipal waste incinerators had been built in Britain between the mid-1970s and 1994, when one new combined heat and power plant was finally completed in southeast London. And this was compounded by the fact that the introduction of an EU Municipal Incineration Directive in 1996 featuring still more stringent emission requirements led to more closures among those still surviving from the 1970s.[45] By the mid-1990s, then, the United Kingdom was effectively committed to landfill as its sole disposal method.

Faced with this quandary, the government decided to use taxation as its primary tool, as suggested in the 1993 Royal Commission report, although discouraging landfill through taxation also posed political problems. Local authorities objected that they would face a virtually unlimited liability as a result of having no practical means of persuading households to curtail their refuse generation. Moreover, the requirement in the 1875 Public Health Act that charges for refuse-related services be levied indirectly and generally through local taxation continued to hold sway as late as 1990. Levying individual charges related to the amount of waste produced individually or by each household was thus entirely precluded until then. Local authorities would therefore have to pay the tax on whatever amounts of refuse their populations put out for ultimate disposal. But the

---

[43] Antony Seely, *Landfill Tax: Introduction and Early History* (House of Commons Library, Standard Note SN/BT/237, 2009), pp. 2 and 3.

[44] Williams, *Waste Treatment and Disposal*, pp. 172 and 173.

[45] Lewis Herbert, *The History of the Institute of Wastes Management* (Northampton: IWM Business Services, 1997), p. 46.

option of raising local taxes across the board would simultaneously be unpopular while providing no incentive for individual reduction of refuse generation. And so any efforts to promote recycling would certainly rely on a voluntary response that was unpredictable.[46]

The government, however, overrode these objections and went forward with landfill tax legislation because it was convinced that it would achieve many things at the same time by doing so. First, according to the Customs and Excise Department, which would collect the tax, waste producers would now be forced to look for new ways to reduce the amount of waste they generated, encouraged by these "non-regulatory" economic measures also to promote reuse of materials and to recover value from a greater variety of waste. Second, Customs and Excise promoted the tax as harmonizing with EU policy: it was an important move away from taxing employment toward taxing resources, an area in which the United Kingdom now laid claim to leadership in implementing policy in Europe.[47] And finally, on a more pragmatic level, the new tax regulations declared that not all wastes were equally harmful to the environment, and consequently two different rates of taxation were applied. A lower one was levied on "inert" waste such as construction rubble, while a higher one was reserved for "active" materials, which covered food, paper, plastics, and wood.[48]

The strength and depth of the government's inclination to foster more environmentally sound waste policies, however, can be gauged from its intended use of the revenue likely to be generated through the landfill tax and also by its limited commitment to developing alternatives. Fourfifths of anticipated income from the tax – estimated at £5 billion – was to be used to reduce the level of taxation that all British employers levied on their workforces on behalf of the government,[49] in the hope that more jobs would be created, thus bolstering the economy generally.[50] There does not appear to have been any thought given to the idea of using at least part of the expected landfill tax to finance research into

[46] *Landfill Tax: Report on Responses Received to Consultation Paper*, September 1995, pp. 4–5 (cited by Seely, *Landfill Tax*, p. 4).
[47] HM Customs & Excise press notice, "Less Waste – More Jobs," September 30, 1996.
[48] The Customs and Excise Authority published precise details of what qualified as inactive wastes, as well as a third category of "exempt" wastes that comprised dredging from waterways, natural waste from mines and quarries, and waste from the reclamation of historically contaminated land.
[49] This was the "National Insurance" levy of approximately 10 percent of each employee's earnings.
[50] House of Commons speech by Chancellor Kenneth Clarke, November 28, 1995.

waste-related problems. Revenue generation within an overall policy of deregulation characterized the exercise, rather than the creation of investment directed toward waste reduction and extending recycling and related technologies. Additionally, there was also little evidence that the government considered any alternative solutions to the landfill problem beyond the new tax; implicitly, then, it continued to recognize that landfill would be the primary means of waste disposal in the country.

Some work on incineration processes had been carried out by the government's environmental research center, the Warren Spring Laboratory (WSL), when the potential dangers of releasing toxins had become clear, but that institute was closed down in early 1994, and no successor was created by the state. In any event, the WSL's research efforts over the years before it was shut down had concluded that public-sector municipal incinerators were unsuitable for adaptation to meet more stringent emission controls and that the high cost of building new ones was a deterrent to their more widespread use, whereas landfill seemed to offer enough advantages to outweigh any drawbacks.[51]

But did the tax have the desired effect of reducing waste going into landfill? Although the data available after the introduction of landfill tax are as usual sometimes incomplete and/or inconsistent, it seems clear that at least initially it had little or no such effect. Based on voluntary returns from local authorities in England and Wales in the fiscal year 1995–1996 before the tax was introduced, the total of household waste gathered by waste collection authorities was nearly 12 million tons, or 345 kilograms per capita. In the tax's first year, 1996–1997, however, the total gathered rose to 12.82 million tons, or 354 kilograms per person. A bit of good news followed in fiscal year 1997–1998, when the total of household waste collected fell to 11.84 million tons (although at 377 kg per capita, it was still higher than before introduction; just why the per capita level increased so substantially is unclear). In 1998–1999, on the other hand, the data returns from local authorities were processed to take into account missing values and nonresponding authorities to provide a more representative picture for England and Wales, and the result was that tonnages recorded increased dramatically. Total household collections rose to 21.11 million tons, or 403 kilograms per person covered by the survey. And in 1999–2000, both values went up again, to 21.76 million tons (410 kg per capita). At the same time, however, recycling from domestic

---

[51] See Web site at http://adlib.everysite.co.uk/adlib/defra/content.aspx?id=000IL3890W.
16NTBYQ9OMA1YM (accessed October 15, 2012).

refuse was improving. In 1995–1996, just 5.35 percent of domestic waste collections was recycled, with paper materials and glass accounting for three-quarters of the total. But by 1997–1998, the proportion recycled had increased to 7.3 percent, more than two-thirds of which was paper and glass.[52]

In October 1997, the Conservative government was replaced by a Labour administration committed to "environmentally sustainable" growth and promising to "increase incentives to reduce environmental damage." Again, however, the lever to be used by the new Labour government was environmental taxation, something generally in line with its predecessor's policy.[53] One month later, Friends of the Earth UK (FOE UK) published a report on the workings of the tax thus far, which pointed out that its impact on industry was quite limited, largely because the average addition to costs caused by the landfill tax had been less than 1 percent. In addition, the report argued that local authorities' hands were largely tied because they lacked any means to enforce either reduction of waste output or recycling.[54] And in the following month a survey by accounting firm Coopers & Lybrand (which had previously prepared reports on waste management for the Thatcher government) was even less encouraging. The firm (like FOE UK) found that most waste producers had made no effort to reduce their generation of taxable wastes as result of the tax. Furthermore, illegal dumping of waste had increased, and (in the one area of disagreement with FOE UK's claims) the accountants claimed that the tax was adding to business costs, results that were "diametrically opposed" to the original intention of the tax.[55]

The government's response to these criticisms was to commission an inquiry by the Customs and Excise Department (rather than the Department of the Environment) into the environmental impact of the tax. Again, the priority given to fiscal rather than environmental issues was very clear and not unlike the emphases set by the previous Conservative government. In his 1998 budget statement, the chancellor of

---

[52] CIPFA Statistical Information Service, *Waste Collection and Disposal Statistics Actuals,* 1995–1996, 1996–1997, 1997–1998, and 1998–1999, Table 1 in each issue and page 2 of last one. There is no explanation for the increase in the per capita figure, although it probably arises from differences in the populations of responding authorities. The cohort of responders also varied from year to year.

[53] HM Treasury press notice, "Tax Measures to Help the Environment," July 2, 1997.

[54] Seely, *Landfill Tax,* p. 11.

[55] Ibid., p. 9.

the exchequer announced that the standard tax rate to be charged for landfill would increase from £7 to £10 per ton in 1999, with the proviso that in the light of "the new emerging national waste strategy" and new European targets for reducing landfill, further increases might be needed to help meet them.[56] At the same time, however, inert wastes used for reclaiming landfill sites and quarry workings were to be exempt from tax because their previous nonexemption had resulted in a shortage of materials.[57] Then, in the following year's budget, it was announced that the standard rate for landfill would be subject to an annual escalation of £1 per ton. According to FOE UK, along with the twenty-two other "green measures" this would generate a net income of £8.4 billion over the next five years. Despite its pleasure in what it described as the "greenest ever" budget, however, FOE UK reminded its audience that British governments, of whatever color, had a long track record of failing to invest in the infrastructure needed for an environmentally friendly society.[58]

The need to find some means to reduce landfill was further sharpened by the promulgation of the EU Landfill Waste Directive 99/31EC, which was scheduled to take effect in 2001. The directive included mandatory targets for reducing the amounts of biodegradable municipal waste going to landfill. And for the United Kingdom, that meant slashing the quantities of such wastes sent to the dump in 1995 by fully 75 percent by 2010.

As far as household waste was concerned, there were by the turn of the century finally some noticeable changes in output of waste and recycling levels in Britain. CIPFA suggested in its annual reports that the increase in waste collected witnessed around the mid-1990s had resulted from the growing use of the 1.1-cubic liter wheelie bins. Local authorities that were still using a mixture of refuse storage methods also reported that the per capita content of wheelie bins was generally higher than that in disposable sacks or the smaller traditional British dustbin. And the increase in waste collected in the mid-1990s did in fact correlate with the rise in wheelie bin usage: in 1995–1996, for instance, approximately 35 percent of properties had wheelie bins, whereas by 1997–1998 the figure had risen to 42 percent, and it increased further to 45 percent in 1999–2000. (See Figure 8.2.) After this, however, the evidence of the "wheelie bin effect" is less convincing: although diffusion of the bins

---

[56] HM Customs and Excise Budget press notice C&E19, March 17, 1998.
[57] Seely, *Landfill Tax*, p. 13.
[58] FoE press notice, "It Was Greener Than You Think," March 17, 1999, cited by Seely, *Landfill Tax*, p. 19.

FIGURE 8.2. "Wheelie bins" on the sidewalk outside a cafe near Great Western Road, Glasgow, 2012. Separation of waste for recycling and use of color-coded plastic wheelie bins have now become as common in Britain as in Germany. Authors' photograph.

continued apace (in 2004–2005 the proportion of households having them had risen to 55 percent), the output of household waste eventually began to decline.[59]

In June 2001, the Department of the Environment, Transport and Regions was merged with the Ministry of Agriculture, Fisheries and Food to create the Department for the Environment, Food and Rural Affairs (DEFRA), and the new ministry subsequently began publishing an increasing amount of data, including a more comprehensive range of waste statistics. The need for accurate, comprehensive, and timely data resulted eventually in the creation of WasteDataFlow, a Web-based system that started in 2004 for municipal waste data reporting by local UK authorities directly to government.[60] Echoing some of the problems experienced by CIPFA, however, the transition to the new reporting system led to such an incomplete return in the first year that no recycling

[59] CIPFA *Actuals*, 1995–1996, p. 3.
[60] See http://www.wastedataflow.org/ (accessed October 16, 2012). WasteDataFlow provides open access information freely to the public. CIPFA continues to collate material of particular interest as management tools for local authorities that is also available, but on a fee-paying basis.

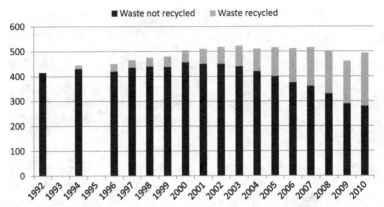

CHART 8.3. England and Wales: weights in kilograms of waste recycled and not recycled, fiscal years 1991–1992 to 2009–2010. No data available for 1992–1993 and 1994–1995. *Source:* http://webarchive.nationalarchives.gov.uk/ 20130123162956/ http:/www.defra.gov.uk/statistics/environment/waste/wrfg04-hhwastrecyc/ (accessed May 30, 2013).

rates could be published.[61] But figures issued by DEFRA and other agencies between 1991 and 2010 show that the per capita output of household waste increased gradually up to 2003–2004, after which a decline began. Regardless, assuming that the early figures are actually reliable, at approximately 470 kg per capita in fiscal year 2009–2010, household waste output was still higher by almost 15 percent than in the early 1990s (see Chart 8.3).

Nevertheless, as Chart 8.4 shows, the amount of refuse from all household sources being handled by waste collection began to decline in absolute terms between fiscal years 2000–2001 and 2010–2011. Moreover, the proportion of household waste being recycled climbed from 7.2 percent in 1996–1997 to 17 percent in 2003–2004, and then to nearly 40 percent in 2010–2011. And, in the area of recycling, the largest growth was experienced in composting, whereas the traditional twin stalwarts of recovery – paper and glass – went up as well, but much more modestly. Separate figures were issued by the Scottish Environmental Protection Agency (SEPA), which acts as the environmental regulator for Scotland, and by the Welsh Assembly, which performs a similar function for Wales. They too indicate considerable increases in recycling, although there are considerable disparities as well. In fiscal year 2009–2010, for instance, Scotland's recycling of household waste ran at nearly 25 percent, much

---

[61] See "Household Recycling by Material Type," note 4, available at www.defra.gov.uk/ statistics/environment/waste/wrfg23-wrmsannual/ (accessed October 15, 2012).

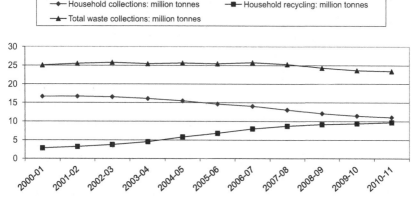

CHART 8.4. England: tonnages of household waste collected by local authorities from homes and civic amenity sites. *Source:* Compiled from "Household Recycling by Material Type," available at www.defra.gov.uk/statistics/environment/waste/wrfg23-wrmsannual/ (accessed October 15, 2012).

lower than for England, whereas household waste recycling in Wales, at 45 percent, was higher.[62] The reasons for these regional disparities are unclear, in particular the relatively low rate for Scotland.

Although legislation, regulation, and in particular taxation played key roles in the British approach toward more environmentally sensitive handling of waste, political philosophy played an equally important part in restructuring the organizational frameworks that actually provided waste management services. Whereas the public sector continued to be legally responsible for ensuring adequate service delivery, its virtual monopoly over waste handling, which had started in the late nineteenth and early twentieth centuries and continued well into the 1980s, was finally removed through a combination of legislative change and market forces. In the decades that followed, the private sector achieved widespread penetration into both collection and disposal services. The commercial side of the industry also transformed itself from a structure featuring predominantly small companies operating on a local basis to one characterized by large firms operating nationally, which were often owned by foreign multinationals or owned foreign subsidiaries themselves.

The 1988 Local Government Act described in the previous chapter started the ball rolling by requiring local authorities to put waste handling and other services out to Compulsory Competitive Tendering (CCT),

---

[62] For Scotland, see SEPA, *Waste Data Digest* 12, p. 12. For Wales, see http://wales.gov .uk/topics/statistics/headlines/environment2011/111103/?lang=en (accessed October 18, 2012).

with the private sector eligible for submitting tenders alongside public authorities or public-private companies. The act also required councils to provide a "level playing field" so as to avoid privileging bids from their own direct-labor organizations.[63] In fiscal year 1984–1985, prior to the introduction of CCT, fewer than 10 percent of local authorities contracted out their collection services to commercial operators either in whole or part, but a greater proportion was already working with the private sector through leasing landfill capacity and using private carriers to haul waste to disposal sites.[64] After 1988, however, councils increasingly handed over at least some of their collection operations to contractors, particularly in handling of waste deposited by residents at "civic amenity sites," which were waste collection depots that local authorities were obliged to provide for the deposit of things like old furniture, garden waste, and other items not generally collected as part of the regular service.

After the 1990 Environmental Protection Act came into force, the proportion of collecting authorities using contractors increased even more substantially. By 1992–1993, 101 did so, up from just 28 a decade earlier. And by 2004–2005, 266 councils in England and Wales were using private contractors, amounting to fully 71 percent of all collection authorities.[65] According to one commentator, the introduction of CCT "made the UK waste management market very attractive to large multinationals," and there is some evidence for this. In 2005, for instance, four such companies – Onyx, Cleanaway, Sita, and Biffa – controlled 27 percent of municipal collection contracts by weight, although it must be kept in mind that this figure included trade waste handling as well as domestic collection.[66] CIPFA's 2004–2005 returns, furthermore, show that the main areas of contracting out of waste handling services to private providers involved removal of abandoned vehicles and handling of clinical wastes and recyclables. At that time, 65 percent of councils retained direct control over household waste collections.[67]

---

[63] Steve Davies, *Politics and Markets: The Case of UK Municipal Waste Management* (Cardiff: School of Social Sciences, 2007), p. 8. Unsuccessful bidders had complained that some councils had insisted on contractors integrating their operating and control systems into those of the local authority while failing to provide necessary information on grounds of confidentiality.

[64] CIPFA *Actuals*, 1995–1996, Section 1: Waste Collection.

[65] CIPFA *Actuals*, 2004–2005, p. 4.

[66] Davies, *Politics and Markets*, p. 13.

[67] Material collected in street cleansing is classed as household waste under UK legislation.

Disposal was also affected. The requirement for local authorities to separate their regulatory function from their operational activities opened up all aspects of their disposal functions to competitive bidding, which tended to push the private sector's involvement a stage further. Many waste disposal authorities did create arm's-length (yet still authority-owned) local authority waste disposal companies, but one study has suggested that "[political] pressure to sell these companies was intense," with the result that over time "most waste disposal... [was] controlled by the private sector."[68] Whatever the cause of the tendency toward greater private-sector involvement in waste disposal services, however, there is no doubt that it was extensive. By 1995–1996, in fact, local authorities had already virtually withdrawn from solo operations, with less than 5 percent conducting the work entirely on their own. Two-thirds of authorities carried out their waste disposal work jointly with private firms, while the remaining 30 percent or so contracted disposal out entirely to the commercial sector.[69] By 2005, moreover, only nine local authority waste disposal companies remained in Britain. On the other side of the equation, nine private firms were responsible for disposing of 78 percent of UK waste by weight.[70]

Between 1990 and the end of the first decade of the twenty-first century, then, the British waste regime, like that in Germany, changed dramatically. Spurred on in part by the European Union and in part by growing awareness of environmental threats, in particular climate change, the British government has intervened to force changes in municipal solid waste handling that had not seen any fundamental improvements between the public health reforms of the late nineteenth century and the 1980s. Recycling rates soared, and absolute amounts of waste going into landfill finally began to decline in the new century. A final change in the British waste regime was that the private sector has become increasingly involved in all aspects of waste handling.

Conclusions

In spite of the similarities in many aspects of the British and German waste regimes today, profound differences continue to exist between Britain and its large European neighbor. Materials recovery in the United Kingdom

---

[68] Davies, *Politics and Markets*, p. 13.
[69] CIPFA *Actuals*, 1995–1996.
[70] Davies, *Politics and Markets*, p. 13.

has lagged persistently behind that in Germany, and landfill usage continues to be the largest single disposal method in Britain. Germany, in contrast, has all but done away with landfill. And finally, the private sector, although heavily involved in aspects of British waste management, still lags behind the German commercial sector in terms of influence and activity.

As we have seen, there are many reasons for these differences. Germany's fervent embrace of expensive, high-tech incineration technology, for instance, along with the country's apparent obsession with recycling, are two factors that go far toward explaining why landfill has virtually disappeared there. And the increasingly heavy emphasis on recycling in Germany also helps explain the prominence of the private sector there. But the origins of these enormous differences in practice also need to be explained. Here, three key factors stand out. First, German municipalities could charge directly for providing waste handling services to households, which enabled them to make different decisions, such as about funding the expensive running costs of incinerators and other capital equipment. Second, although it is an open and perhaps unanswerable question whether German people might be more environmentally conscious than the British, there is no question that the German political system allows Germans to express their desire for action on environmental concerns much more effectively. Proportional representation enabled the fledgling Green Party eventually to become a national force in Germany, unlike in Britain, while the German federal system allowed political pressure to develop, which led to changes in policy and practice at the regional, state, and then national levels.

Finally, and related to this, although both countries relied on legislation and tax policy to push the industry in the direction of greater environmental responsibility and increasing privatization of services, the German federal government embraced a completely different set of policy levers than did the centralized British administration. Even before there was a Green environmental minister, the government set challenging targets for the industry and left it to its public *and* private components to work out how to meet them. One result was the Dual System, which was a significant factor leading to skyrocketing rates of recycling. In contrast, the British government, whether Conservative or Labour, focused almost entirely on tax policy to try to achieve its aims, with disappointing results at first.

Still, there have been some signs of convergence. In 2010, for instance, the Scottish government announced a "Zero Waste Plan," the title of which indicated precisely the ultimate, extremely challenging goal, which would be met according to planners by a combination of smarter packaging, reuse, sophisticated materials recovery, and waste-to-energy schemes. Achieving it would, crucially, require high levels of cooperation among the public, private, and third sectors, as well as active engagement from the general public.[71] And for its part, the German Parliament has recently passed the Kreislaufwirtschaftsgesetz (Recycling Management Law, literally the "Circulation Industry" Law), which came into effect on June 1, 2012, and replaced the old Kreislauf- und Abfallwirtschaftsgesetz from 1994. What is particularly striking here is that for the first time in Germany, the term *Abfall* (waste) is not mentioned in the law's formal name. This seems to imply that, just as in the United Kingdom, the idea of "zero waste" has become a key objective of German environmental politics, and similar means to achieving it are envisioned. It has to be admitted, however, that one of them is through creative redefinition: for example, classifying incineration as thermal recycling (or thermal valorization) (*thermische Verwertung*).

In both of our cases and in those of many other nations that have embraced "zero waste" as an objective, however, profound doubts remain about its achievability. As long as people throw more and more things away, particularly new products such as electronic devices, more sophisticated batteries, composite materials, and so on, it is difficult to think of how the waste stream will dwindle to zero.[72] In light of this, the real achievement of waste management in recent times has not been to *solve* the problem of waste disposal but to develop institutional frameworks capable of *managing* it. This, of course, may hold true only for as long as practitioners know (or think they know) what the problem actually is.

---

[71] Ray Stokes and Stephen Sambrook, "Centenary Stories," *Chartered Institute of Wastes Management Journal (CIWM)* (December 2010): 16–17. See also the "Zero Waste Scotland" Web site available at http://www.zerowastescotland.org.uk/ (accessed October 31, 2012).

[72] Heike Holdinghausen, "Auf Deponien, in Strudeln und Schornsteinen: Der lange Weg vom Müll zur Ressource," *Politische Ökologie* (June 2012): 30–35.

Summary, Conclusions, and Reflections

Between the end of the Second World War and the early 1970s, the United
Kingdom and Germany, like many other industrialized countries, experienced a golden age of economic growth that translated into dramatic
increases in per capita wealth. In the process, they moved from being
societies of want to societies of plenty. Consumer goods became more
and more widely available, and this involved more than just a quantitative
change. Often designed for fashion and/or rapid obsolescence, the goods
were increasingly constructed of new materials, which made not only for
larger but also more challenging waste streams. One side of this equation –
increasing wealth and the emerging consumer society in Britain and West
Germany during the postwar period – has been the subject of numerous
studies by contemporary commentators and by historians. The flip side of
the equation, however, is not usually considered: dramatically improved
standards of living, consumerism, and planned obsolescence inevitably
resulted in increasing levels of garbage, and new materials caused the
composition of consumerism's castoffs to change markedly. Both trends
continued more or less unchecked into the 1990s, and some would argue
that household waste output and ever more complex waste streams pose
extremely difficult – and possibly insurmountable – challenges even in
the present, when many are talking seriously of the objective of a "zero
waste society."

Focusing on growing and changing household waste streams in Germany and Britain between 1945 and the present, this book has explored
how those responsible for dealing with the seemingly unremitting output of refuse in the two countries responded to it. Initially, we argue,
they were not very well equipped to do so. Waste handling practice

in both the United Kingdom and Germany at war's end and well into the 1960s was shaped fundamentally by the desideratum of preserving public health in urban areas, which had its origins in late-nineteenth-century municipal reform movements. Thus, in both countries, collection of household refuse was almost exclusively a public-sector activity, a state of affairs few considered challenging in any major way until the 1970s and 1980s.

Disposal, on the other hand, was more complex from the start, with considerable private-sector involvement in salvage of wastepaper and metals in particular and, especially in Britain, in haulage and in ownership of what we would now call landfill sites. Still, the public sector dominated the disposal of household waste, too. Also, although motorized vehicles were increasingly used in the decades following the end of the war to collect and transport household waste, the technologies and infrastructure of waste collection and disposal remained in many ways unchanged from the late nineteenth century to the 1960s. Storage of waste at urban households for later collection, for instance, was in garbage cans that were fashioned from iron or steel to provide safe, heavy-duty, fireproof storage until collection took place. Indeed, the latter two characteristics in particular formed crucial design criteria for the receptacles, the contents of which until the 1960s were mostly cinders and ash from coal fires. That is also why, aside from discarded food that would eventually decay into (alleged) harmlessness, household rubbish through the 1950s was mostly inert and could be disposed of relatively easily and safely. To be sure, the decaying food might cause unpleasant odors to those living near the dump where the garbage was taken, but such dumps were for the most part considered benign. And while this was less true for the other major method of disposal – incineration – the pollution was almost surely much less dangerous in the 1950s than it became later, once new materials such as thermoplastics entered the waste stream. For all of these reasons, waste handling practitioners in what were almost universally called "public cleansing departments" from the late nineteenth century until the 1980s – indeed, in many cases well into the 1990s – thought of their work as a form of logistics that involved deployment of people and other resources to move waste from the household to its ultimate destination. In addition, it was work that was organized, financed, and carried out at the local level, although national-level legislation affected it more and more from the 1970s onward.

This orientation toward logistics is one key reason why those in the industry thought of themselves as needing to be "businesslike" in their behavior, which explains in large part why we treat public cleansing (and eventually waste management) in this book as an industry that lends itself well to a business history approach. Businesslike behavior indeed had a number of dimensions, even in the public sector. Besides managing large workforces and some equipment from the start of the postwar period, over the course of the next decades public cleansing professionals also undertook programs involving mechanization, automation, and rationalization that entailed a shift toward greater capital intensity. And this in turn required greater attention to investment and planning. Greater use of large collection vehicles was one example of this, as was the creation of integrated systems involving standardized garbage containers and specialized vehicles, something known as "dustless collection." Managers and engineers employed by local authority public cleansing departments, moreover, behaved in a businesslike, professional way through active participation in associations. And finally, another area of the industry, salvage, involved even the public sector directly in commercial markets (except in wartime, where other values drove salvage efforts) in which private-sector companies were key actors.

This traditional approach to and structure of the industry, however, was challenged fundamentally from the early 1960s onward, eventually requiring adoption of even more businesslike practices in the public sector and involving the private sector to an increasing extent in collection, disposal, and salvage operations. Increases in amounts of waste produced by households formed one part of this challenge, which was exacerbated by the widespread replacement of open fires with central heating, a trend that was in turn the product of increasing affluence and the enactment of smoke-abatement legislation. Household waste thus became not only more plentiful but also lighter, because cinders and ash from coal fires were no longer a major part of the waste stream. At the same time, however, new materials, in particular thermoplastics, made household waste output both more voluminous and more dangerous to dispose of, especially through incineration but also through seepage of runoff containing incinerator residues and other materials from landfill into groundwater.

These dangers were certainly not anticipated. Indeed, they were not even known for a time, although scientific investigation eventually uncovered them. Greater public awareness then followed, leading to political pressure for even more scientification of waste handling practice. And finally, growing evidence that suitable landfill space was not only potentially dangerous but also running out, combined with general concerns that the "limits to growth" had been reached,[1] also led to demands from the public and public cleansing professionals for legislation to control production and disposal of waste.

The result of all these developments was a set of important changes. For one thing, although collection and disposal continued to be run at the local level for the most part and as a mainly logistical operation, national-level legislation now came into play to shape waste handling. Dealing with plastic waste in particular helped usher in another significant change: the reconceptualization of the long-standing practice of "salvage" as "recycling." Although the two terms are often used interchangeably, this reconceptualization entailed far more than a simple name change. For one thing, scrap and salvage, in peacetime at least, were activities firmly rooted in the market; that is, whether they were carried out or not depended on whether or not there were buyers for the waste. Recycling, on the other hand, involved a broader conception. While it was naturally tied to the market in important ways, it also recognized that there were noneconomic factors such as concern for environmental well-being that should determine whether or not discarded materials should be used again in some form or other. Second, and related to this market aspect, the change in terminology implied an important sociological dimension that the replacement of the old with the new term captured to some degree. Those who carried out scrap and salvage work were mainly on the economic fringes of society, whereas recycling operations tended to be carried out initially for the most part by people on the *political* fringes of society – that is, by members of the counterculture and early environmental movement starting in the late 1960s and early 1970s. Activities became more and more mainstream as time went on, not least owing to growing national and European legislation and regulation, with an increasingly vital role for city governments and the private sector. Third, it is probably no accident that the term "recycling," as it has come to be widely used and understood, had high-tech origins.[2]

---

[1] E. F. Schumacher, *Small Is Beautiful: A Study of Economics as if People Really Mattered* (London: Abacus, 1974); Club of Rome, *The Limits to Growth* (London: Earth Island, 1972); on the history of climate change awareness generally, see, for instance, http://www.direct.gov.uk/en/Environmentandgreenerliving/Thewiderenvironment/Climatechange/DG_072901 (accessed April 17, 2012).

[2] It was first used in the nuclear power and chemical industries. See the entry in the *Oxford English Dictionary*, available at http://dictionary.oed.com/cgi/entry/50199849?query_type=word&queryword=recycling&first=1&max_to_show=10&single=1&sort_type=alpha (accessed March 2, 2006). This link produces results for "recycle" as a noun and a verb and for "recycling."

Salvage of traditional materials such as metals, glass, and paper may be time consuming, labor intensive, and dirty at times, but it was also fairly straightforward. Recycling of the new materials coming into the waste stream en masse by the 1960s, however, was and is most definitely not so straightforward. The expertise and equipment involved required even more skill and acumen than had previously been the case in the industry. Markets for recycling also tended to be national and/or international, ensuring that private firms were at a distinct advantage in this new part of the industry. Cooperation between the private and public sectors was of course also required, such as in the form of price guarantees given by the latter to the former.

If the reconceptualization of salvage as recycling provided a major opportunity for greater private-sector involvement in public cleansing, however, it also entailed the gradual reconceptualization of "public cleansing" as "waste management," a name change that neatly captures the requirement and the desire of those in the industry to be even more businesslike. But recycling was not the only factor promoting greater private-sector involvement in the industry; nor was it the only factor in the emergence of the concept of waste management. Politics and ideology were also at work. In particular in Great Britain under the government of Prime Minister Margaret Thatcher between 1979 and the early 1990s, but also under the center-right coalition in Germany under Chancellor Helmut Kohl from the early 1980s to the mid-1990s, moves were made to promote greater private-sector provision of public services. This included waste management, with the result that private firms, often multinationals by the new century, played a prominent role in the industry.

Increasingly stringent national and international legislation, greater use of recycling, improvements in incineration technology, greater private-sector involvement, and a number of other developments through the 1980s, however, did not solve the waste problem. It was also perceived by many as being not very well managed. In response, Germany pioneered through legislation, regulation, and other means in the development of a new and important reconceptualization, "resource recovery," which extended the idea of recycling in significant ways. By the 1990s, in Germany and somewhat later in the United Kingdom, the realization of the concept of resource recovery involved waste avoidance becoming a watchword, while at the same time any "waste" remaining was to be deployed in some way as a resource insofar as possible.

Our general overview of the development of the household waste industry between 1945 and the present, then, applies to both Germany and the United Kingdom, and it is summarized in Table 9.1.

TABLE 9.1. *A Typology for the Development of Waste Management in Germany and the United Kingdom, 1945 to Present*

Period	Designation	Key Driver	Key Provider of Waste Services	Dominant Conceptualization of Industry	Key Level of Policy Making and Decision Making
Late 19th century to 1960s	Public cleansing	Public health	Public sector	Logistics/efficiency	Local/regional
1970s to 1990s	Public cleansing/ Waste management	Environmental health	PUBLIC/private	Logistics/efficiency	National
1990s to present	Waste management	Environmental health and climate change	public/PRIVATE	Resource recovery	International

If, however, household waste handling in both countries developed in similar directions at about the same times and with similar effects, there were nevertheless important differences between the two from the out-set, differences that grew more rather than less pronounced through the 1990s, and some of which remain. West Germany, for instance, pion-eered in the rationalization of waste collection technology in the 1960s to a far greater degree than the United Kingdom. And even now, rates of resource recovery are much higher and landfill usage much lower there than in Britain. These differences, we would argue, are not the result of in-built cultural factors. Indeed, as late as the mid-1960s, Glasgow con-tinued its proud tradition of salvage and also used incinerators to produce electricity. Waste going into the city's landfills was consequently largely inert and harmless to the environment, thus representing perhaps an early version of resource recovery. In Frankfurt, from the 1950s to the mid-1960s, on the other hand, virtually all waste collected went into landfill, and very little salvage was recovered. The two cases are, in short, the opposite of what we might expect given the way waste handling behavior in the two cities looks now.

Things changed dramatically from the mid-1960s onward, however, when Glasgow along with other UK cities abandoned previous practice owing to volatility in the salvage market, development of sanitary land-fills, and the fact that sales of electricity to local power companies were no longer possible because of the full realization of the British national electricity grid that had been completed and nationalized in the 1950s. At about the same time, Frankfurt and other German cities moved in the opposite direction. In the case of Frankfurt, this was mostly owing to the fact that the city's landfill ran out of space, but it was also because of the greater ability of the environmental movement to influence policy there due to Germany's federal and voting systems. The latter indeed allowed the election of Green Party politicians, first at the local, then the regional and state, and finally at the national level. And these politi-cians eventually exercised considerable power. But another by no means trivial factor that must be mentioned in the case of Frankfurt was that it was possible for the city and other West German cities through 1989 and even to some degree afterward to "export" some of their household waste problems by paying for it to be disposed of in the German Democratic Republic, or East Germany. In other words, what is at work in these two cases and many others are factors such as historical contingency and political structures rather than any sort of innate cultural predilection.

In the final analysis, it is not just the parallel development of the waste handling industry in the two countries that is striking but some of the clear policy implications of our investigation as well. First, it is clear from what we have described throughout this book that the formulation of waste policy requires active engagement with markets (and market failure) as well as an appreciation of the respective roles of the public and the private sectors in waste management. The history of public cleansing/waste management in the United Kingdom and Germany after 1945 provides countless examples of both good and bad practice in this regard. Second, and more importantly, it is clear from our study that the implementation of policy relating to sustainable waste management through resource recovery must rely heavily on the technical, logistical, and organizational capabilities of the private sector, with important input in Britain in particular from the third sector as well. At the same time, however, private-sector involvement at the levels that currently exist in Germany and Britain would be unthinkable without a simultaneous and equally significant role for the government in the form of legislation, regulation, subsidies and other market interventions, and the operation of waste-management services as the collector/disposer of last resort. In sum, it is clear that the successful operation of waste management under the conceptualization of resource recovery requires that social and political values take precedence over narrow economic ones as well as close cooperation among the public, private, and third sectors, which is overseen and directed by the state.

Bibliography

Primary Sources: Manuscript

Bayerisches Hauptstaatsarchiv München (Bavarian State Archive, Munich).
Bayerisches Landesamt für Umweltschutz.
Birmingham Archives and Heritage Service, Central Library, Birmingham:
Records of the Salvage and Stables Committee: BCC/BP 1919–1952.
Records of the Salvage Committee: BCC/BP 1952–1974.
Records of the Environmental Services Committee: 1974–1990.
Bundesarchiv Koblenz (Federal Archive Koblenz):
Bundesinnenministerium (B 106).
Glasgow City Archives, Mitchell Library, Glasgow:
Records of Glasgow City Council: DTC 7/3/1, 1945–1974.
Records of the City of Glasgow Council: GDC 1/2, 1975–1990.
Greater Manchester County Record Office, New Cross, Manchester:
Records of the Greater Manchester County Council:
Chief Executive's Department Administrative Files, 1972–1989.
Legal Department Committee Services Papers, 1974–1989.
Hessisches Hauptstaatsarchiv Wiesbaden (Hessian State Archive Wiesbaden):
Bestand 509 (Innenministerium).
Institut für Stadtgeschichte Frankfurt (Frankfurt City Archive):
Bauverwaltung.
Magistrat.
Sammlung Ortsgeschichte.
Stadtkämmerei.
Stadtplanungsamt.
Tiefbauamt.
Landesarchiv Berlin (State Archive Berlin):
Deutscher Städtetag (B Rep 142).
Manchester City Library, Deansgate, Manchester:
Records of the Cleansing Department: M595, 1948–1974.

307

National Archives, Kew, London:
Department of the Environment records: AT 29 and AT 32.
Department of Scientific and Industrial Research records: AY 28.
Ministry of Health and successors, records: HLG 51, HLG 100, and HLG
120.
Ministry of Technology records: FV 12.
Privy Council Office records: PC15.
Nordrhein-Westfälisches Landesarchiv Düsseldorf (North Rhine-Westphalian
State Archive Düsseldorf):
NW 132.
NW 354 (Gesundheitsministerium, Innenministerium).
Stadtarchiv Augsburg (Augsburg City Archive):
Bestand 49.
Stadtarchiv Dortmund (Dortmund City Archive):
Stadtreinigungsamt.
Unterlagen Verwaltungsberichte.
Stadtarchiv Mannheim (Mannheim City Archive):
Amt für Wirtschaftsförderung.
Bauverwaltungsamt.
Dezernatsregistratur.
Hauptamt.
Hauptregistratur.
Hochbauamt.
Ordnungsamt.
Rechnungsprüfungsamt.
Tiefbauamt.
Stadtarchiv München (Munich City Archive):
Amt Bürgermeister (Mayor's Office).

Primary Sources: Printed

Chartered Institute of Public Finance and Accountancy. *Waste Collection and Disposal Statistics; Actuals.* London: CIPFA, annually but with some omissions.
Department of the Environment. *Refuse Disposal: Report of the Working Party on Refuse Disposal.* London: HMSO, 1971.
_____. *Streamlining the Cities: Government Proposals for Reorganising Local Government in Greater London and the Metropolitan Counties.* London: House of Commons Library, 1983.
_____. *Waste Management Paper No. 1: A Review of Options.* London: HMSO, 2nd ed., 1992.
"The Govan Refuse Power Plant of the Glasgow Corporation." *Engineering* 125 (1928): 549–551.
Great Britain Ministry of Health. *Local Government Financial Statistics, England and Wales, 1936–37.* London: HMSO, 1939.
_____. *Public Cleansing (Refuse Collection and Disposal; Street Cleansing) Costing Returns for the Year Ended 31st March, 1938.* London: HMSO, 1939.

Great Britain Ministry of Housing and Local Government. *Clean Air Act 1956.* London: HMSO, 1956.
———. Working Party on Refuse Storage and Collection. *Report.* London: HMSO, 1967.
Great Britain Parliament. *Control of Pollution Act 1974.* London: HMSO, 1974.
———. *Environmental Protection Act 1990.* London: HMSO, 1990.
———. *Local Government Act 1972.* London: HMSO, 1972.
———. *Public Health Act, 1848.* London: HMSO, 1848.
———. *Public Health Act, 1875.* London: HMSO, 1875.
———. *Public Health Act, 1936.* London: HMSO, 1936.
Great Britain Technical Committee on the Disposal of Toxic Solid Wastes. *Disposal of Solid Toxic Wastes.* London: HMSO, 1970.
Local Government in England: Government Proposals for Reorganisation, Cmnd 4584. London: HMSO, 1971.
Nuisance or Nemesis? A Report on the Control of Pollution. London: HMSO, 1972.
Public Cleansing and Salvage, various issues and dates.
Reform of Local Government in Scotland, Cmnd 4583. Edinburgh: HMSO, 1971.
The Reorganisation of Central Government, Cmnd 4506. London: HMSO, 1970.
Statistisches Bundesamt. *Statistisches Jahrbuch der Bundesrepublik Deutschland,* Wiesbaden, *various issues and dates.*
Statistisches Jahrbuch der Stadt Frankfurt. Frankfurt: Stadt Frankfurt, annually.
Wastes Management, various issue and dates.

Secondary Sources

Abelshauser, Werner. *Deutsche Wirtschaftsgeschichte seit 1945.* Munich: Beck, 2004.
R. F. Adams. "Presidential Address." *Solid Wastes* (August 1979): 365.
Aird, Andrew. *Glimpses of old Glasgow* (1894). Available at: http://gdl.cdlr.strath.ac.uk/airgli/airglio114.htm, accessed December 1, 2009.
Ancram, Michael. "The Government View." *Wastes Management* (August 1983): 390.
"Änderung des Abfallbeseitigungsgesetzes: Die Novellierung stand von vornherein fest." *Zeitschrift Umwelt* (May 1974): 17.
Asendorpf, Dirk. "Gegen den Trennt." *Die Zeit.* March 19, 2007.
Audit Commission for Local Authorities in England and Wales. *Securing Further Improvements in Refuse Collection.* London: HMSO, 1984.
AWB, Köln, ed. *111 Jahre Abfallwirtschaft in Köln.* Cologne: Stadt Köln, 2001.
Banken, Ralf. "Schneller Strukturwandel trotz institutioneller Stabilität: Die Entwicklung des deutschen Einzelhandels 1949–2000." *Jahrbuch für Wirtschaftsgeschichte* 30 (February 2007): 117–145.
Bärens, Matthias, and Ulrich von Arnswald. *Die Müll-Connection: Entsorger und ihre Geschäfte.* Munich: C.H. Beck, 1999.
Barnhart, Michael A. *Japan Prepares for Total War: The Search for Economic Security, 1919–1941.* Ithaca, NY: Cornell University Press, 1987.

Baum, Hans-Georg. "Privatisierung vs. Kommunalisierung: Argumentation-spapier widerstreitender Interessen," in Peter Hoffmeyer, Martin Wittmaier, and Karl J. Thomé-Kozmiensky, *Privatisierung in der Abfallwirtschaft*. Neuruppin: TK Verlag, 2000.

Bausch, Hermann, et al. "Es herrscht Reinlichkeit und Ordnung hier auf den Stra-ßen," in *Aus 400 Jahren Geschichte der Stadtreinigung und Abfallentsorgung in Dortmund: 111 Jahre kommunale Abfallwirtschaft, 10 Jahre EDG*. Dortmund: EDG, 2001.

BBC News Channel. "Home Ownership Dips to Decade Low," February 13, 2008, available at http://news.bbc.co.uk/1/hi/business/7242492.stm (accessed February 1, 2013).

Bell, Stuart, and Donald McGillivray. *Environmental Law*. 6th ed. Oxford: Oxford University Press, 2006.

Bender, Justus. "'Monte Scherbelino,' Der Müllberg wird abgedeckt und begrünt." *Frankfurter Allgemeine Zeitung*, August 30, 1984.

Benidickson, James. *The Culture of Flushing: A Social and Legal History of Sewage*. Vancouver: University of British Columbia Press, 2007.

Bevan, R. E. "Controlled Tipping of Solid Urban Refuse and Suitable Indus-trial Waste." *Aquatic Sciences: Research across Boundaries* 31 (1969): 378–379.

Bieker, Marion. "Getrenntsammlung und Kompostierung von organischen Hausmüllbestandteilen in Stadt und Landkreis Göttingen." In Das bessere Müllkonzept Bayern (ed.), *Müll vermeiden, verwerten, vergessen? Kommu-nale Aufgaben – ökologische Pflichten*. Ulm: Universitätsverlag, 1991.

Bijker, W. E. "The Social Construction of Bakelite: Toward a Theory of Inven-tion." In W. E. Bijker, T. P. Hughes, and T. Pinch (eds.), *The Social Construc-tion of Technological Systems*. Cambridge, MA: MIT Press, 1989.

Black, H. J. *History of the Corporation of Birmingham, vol. 6: 1936–1950*. Birmingham: Birmingham Corporation, 1950.

Bond, Jon R. "The Scientification of the Study of Politics." *Journal of Politics* 69 (2007): 897–907.

Bowden, Sue, and Avner Offer. "Household Appliances and the Use of Time: The United States and Britain since the 1920s." *Economic History Review*, New Series 47 (1994): 745–746.

Breer, Ralf, et al. *Asche, Kehricht, Saubermänner, Stadthygiene und Städtere-inerung in Deutschland bis 1945*. Selm: SASE, 2010.

Bremerstein, Irina. "Die Entwicklung und Arbeitsweise des Dualen Systems – insbesondere auf dem Gebiet der Sortierung von Leichtverpackungen." In Roland Ladwig (ed.), *Recycling in Geschichte und Gegenwart: Vorträge der Jahrestagung der Georg-Agricola Gesellschaft in Freiberg (Sachsen)*. Freiberg: TU Bergakademie Freiberg, 2003.

Brockerhoff, Michael. "Müll aus Italien in Düsseldorf." *Rheinische Post*, April 28, 2008.

Brookes, S. K., A. G. Jordan, R. H. Kimber, and J. J. Richardson. "The Growth of the Environment as a Political Issue in Britain." *British Journal of Political Science* 6 (April 1976): 245–255.

Bundesverband der privaten Entsorgungswirtschaft (ed.), *1961–2001. 40 Jahre BDE. Von der Stadthygiene zur Kreislaufwirtschaft: Eine Zeitreise mit der Entsorgungswirtschaft.* Köln: BDE, 2001.

Bünemann, Agnes. "Duales System Deutschland: Ein Rückblick über die Entwicklung in Deutschland." In Peter Kurth, Anne Baum-Rudischhauser, and Klaus Töpfer (eds.), *Ressource Abfall.* Brandenburg: TK-Verlag, 2011.

Bury, K. "Privatisation: Private Sector View." *Wastes Management* (December 1983): 640–643.

Calice, Jakob. *"Sekundärrohstoffe – eine Quelle, die nie versiegt": Konzeption und Argumentation des Abfallverwertungssystems in der DDR aus umwelthistorischer Perspektive.* Master's thesis, University of Klagenfurt, 2005.

Carson, Rachel. *Silent Spring.* New York: Houghton Mifflin, 1962.

Chick, Martin. "The Changing Role of Space and Time in British Environmental Policy since 1945." Unpublished manuscript, 2011.

Cooper, Timothy. "Burying the 'Refuse Revolution': the Rise of Controlled Tipping in Britain, 1920–1960." *Environment and Planning A* 42 (2010): 1033–1048.

———. "Challenging the 'Refuse Revolution': War, Waste and the Rediscovery of Recycling, 1900–1950." *Historical Research* 81, no. 214 (2008): 710–731.

———. "War on Waste? The Politics of Waste and Recycling in Post-War Britain, 1950–1975." *Capitalism Nature Socialism* 20, no. 4 (2009): 53–72.

Coopers & Lybrand Associates Ltd. *Service Provision and Pricing in Local Government: Studies in Local Environmental Services.* London: HMSO, 1981.

Coopey, R., S. O'Connell and D. Porter. *Mail Order Retailing in Britain: A Business and Social History.* Oxford: Oxford University Press, 2005.

Corporation of the City of Glasgow. *Municipal Glasgow: Its Evolution and Enterprises.* Glasgow: Robert Gibson & Sons Ltd, 1914.

Crawford, Robert. "Glasgow's Experience with Municipal Ownership and Operation: Water, Gas, Electricity, and Street Railways," *American Academy of Political and Social Science* 27 (1906): 1–19.

Davies, Steve. *Politics and Markets: The Case of UK Municipal Waste Management.* Cardiff: School of Social Sciences, 2007.

"Der Papierkrieg tobt jetzt fast überall." *Augsburger Allgemeine Zeitung,* December 27, 2007.

"Die Mülltonne aus Kunststoff kommt." *ÖTV-Magazin* (October 1965): 24.

Ebbertz, Lothar. *Die Konzentration im Braugewerbe der Bundesrepublik Deutschland: Entwicklung und Ursachen.* Frankfurt/M.: Peter Lang, 1992.

Economides, Nicholas. "The Economics of Networks." *International Journal of Industrial Organization* 14 (1996): 673–699.

Edgerton, David. *Britain's War Machine: Weapons, Resources, and Experts in the Second World War.* Oxford: Oxford University Press, 2011.

Ehrig, R. J., and M. J. Curry. *Plastics Recycling: Products and Processes.* Munich: Hanser, 1992.

Engels, Jens Ivo. *Naturpolitik in der Bundesrepublik: Ideenwelt und politische Verhaltensstile in Naturschutz und Umweltbewegung 1950–1980.* Paderborn: Schoening, 2006.

————. "Umweltschutz in der Bundesrepublik: Von der Unwahrscheinlichkeit einer Alternativbewegung." In Sven Reichardt and Detlef Siegfried (eds.), *Das alternative Milieu: Antibürgerlicher Lebensstil und linke Politik in der Bundesrepublik und Europa 1968–1983*. Göttingen: Wallenstein, 2010.

Erhard, Heinrich. *Aus der Geschichte der Städtereinigung*. Stuttgart: Kohlhammer, 1954.

Fairlie, P. D. *A Review of Public Cleansing in Glasgow: From 1868 to 1968*. Glasgow: Corporation of the City of Glasgow, 1968.

Ferkau, Jacqueline, and Günter Lelgemann. *Entwicklung der Abfallwirtschaft in Ostdeutschland unter besonderer Berücksichtigung des Landes Brandenburg*. Fachhochschule Bochum, Schriften Nr. 15.

Fischer, Jörg. *"Die Konzentrationsprozesse in der deutschen Entsorgungswirtschaft und ihre Konsequenzen für die Volkswirtschaft."* PhD thesis, Berlin, 1999.

Fischer, Wolfram, et al. *Treuhandanstalt: Das Unmögliche wagen*. Berlin: Akademie-Verlag, 1993.

Flintoff, Frank, and Ronald Millard. *Public Cleansing: Refuse Storage, Collection and Disposal; Street Cleansing*. London: MacLaren and Sons, 1968.

Fourastié, Jean. *Le grand espoir de XX siècle*. Paris: Gallimard, 1963.

Frankland, E. Gene, and Donald Schoonmaker. *Between Protest and Power: The Green Party in Germany*. Boulder, CO: Westview Press, 1992.

Friedel, Robert. "American Bottles: The Road to No Return." Conference paper, Munich, June 2011.

Frilling, Hildegard, and Olaf Mischer. *Pütt un Pann'n: Geschichte der Hamburger Hausmüllbeseitigung*. Hamburg: Stadt Hamburg, 1994.

Fußer, A. "Duale Abfallwirtschaft: Ein öffentlich-privates Tandem mit ungewissem Kurs, Stellungnahme BUND." In Klaus Wiemer and Michael Stern (eds.), *Weniger Abfall: Entwicklungen in der Abfallwirtschaft nach der Verpackungsverordnung*. Vitzenhausen: M.I.C. Baeza-Verlag, 1991.

Gassner, Miriam. "Lokale Umwelt oder transnationale Chance? ENIs Reaktion auf die Protest gegen die CEL-Pipeline in den 1960er Jahren." *Zeitschrift für Unternehmensgeschichte* 57 (January 2012): 31–46.

German Ministry for Environment, Nature Conservation, and Nuclear Safety. "Waste Incineration: A Potential Danger?" (September 2005), p. 2, available at http://www.bmu.de/files/english/pdf/application/pdf/muellverbrennung_dioxin_en.pdf (accessed October 31, 2012).

Giersch, Herbert, et al. *The Fading Miracle: Four Decades of Market Economy in Germany*. Cambridge: Cambridge University Press, 1992.

Gille, Zsuzsa. "Actor Networks, Modes of Production, and Waste Regimes: Reassembling the Macro-Social." *Environment and Planning A* 42 (2010): 1049–1064.

————. *From the Cult of Waste to the Trash Heap of History: The Politics of Waste in Socialist and Postsocialist Hungary*. Bloomington: Indiana University Press, 2007.

Glasgow Corporation, Cleansing Department. *A Review of Public Cleansing in Glasgow from 1868 to 1968*. Glasgow: Corporation of the City of Glasgow, 1968.

Glass Manufacturers' Federation. *The Glass Container Industry and the Environmental Debate.* London: Glass Manufacturers' Federation: ca. 1974.

Göschl, Alexandra, Bernhard Hartleitner, and Siegfried Kreibe. *Die Entwicklung des Grünen-Punkt-Systems: Verwertungstechnik, politischer Druck und Innovation durch Worte.* Augsburg: Bayerisches Institut für Abfallforschung, 2001.

Grassmuck, Volker, and Christian Unverzagt. *Das Müllsystem: Eine metarealistische Bestandsaufnahme.* Frankfurt/M.: Suhrkamp, 1991.

Gries, Rainer. *Produkte als Medien: Kulturgeschichte der Produktkommunikation in der Bundesrepublik und der DDR.* Leipzig: Universitäts-Verlag, 2003.

Hartard, Susanne, M. Huhn, and A Kötter. "Zusammenfassende Abschlussbilanz des SERO-Systems der DDR, BMFT Forschungsvorhaben." In Klaus Wiemer and Michael Stern (eds.), *Weniger Abfall: Entwicklungen in der Abfallwirtschaft nach der Verpackungsverordnung.* Vitzenhausen: M.I.C. Baeza-Verlag 1991.

Hasenöhrl, Ute. *Zivilgesellschaft und Protest: Eine Geschichte der Naturschutz- und Umweltbewegung in Bayern 1945–1980.* Göttingen: Vandenhoeck & Ruprecht, 2010.

Henstock, M. E. (ed.). *Disposal and Recovery of Municipal Solid Waste.* London: Butterworths, 1983.

Hentrich, Steffen, Walter Komar, and Martin Weissheimer. *Umweltschutz in den neuen Bundesländern: Bilanz im zehnten Jahr deutscher Einheit.* Diskussionspapier, Institut für Wirtschaftsforschung Halle. December 2000.

Herbert, Lewis. *The History of the Institute of Wastes Management, 1898–1998: Celebrating 100 Years of Progress.* Northampton: IWM Business Services Ltd, 1998.

Herbold, Ralf, Kämper Eckard, and Wolfgang Krohn. *Entsorgungsnetze: Kommunale Lösungen im Spannungsfeld von Technik, Regulation und Öffentlichkeit.* Baden-Baden: Nomos, 2002.

Herbold, Ralf, and Ralf Wienken. *Experimentelle Technikgestaltung und offene Planung: Strategien zur sozialen Bewältigung von Unsicherheit am Beispiel der Abfallbeseitigung.* Bielefeld: Kleine, 1993.

Hesse, Jan-Otmar. "Komplementarität in der Konsumgesellschaft: Zur Geschichte eines wirtschaftstheoretischen Konzeptes." *Jahrbuch für Wirtschaftsgeschichte* 30 (2007): 147–167.

Heyl, John. "The Construction of the *Westwall*, 1938: An Exemplar for Nazi Policymaking." *Central European History* 14 (1981): 63–78.

Heyward, Andrew. "The End of the Affair: Implications of Declining Home Ownership," The Smith Institute, 2011, p. 6, available at http://www.smith-institute .org.uk/file/The%20End%20of%20the%20Affair%20-%20implications%20 of%20declining%20home%20ownership.pdf (accessed February 1, 2013).

Hicks, Joe, and Grahame Allen. *A Century of Change: Trends in UK Statistics since 1900.* London: House of Commons Library, 1999. Available at http:// www.parliament.uk/documents/commons/lib/research/rp99/rp99-111.pdf (accessed July 12, 2012).

Higginson, A. E. *The Analysis of Domestic Waste.* Northampton: Institute of Wastes Management, 1978.

HM Customs & Excise. "Less Waste – More Jobs." Press Notice, September 30, 1996.

HM Treasury. "Tax Measures to Help the Environment." Press Notice, July 2, 1997.

Holdinghausen, Heike. "Auf Deponien, in Strudeln und Schornsteinen: Der lange Weg vom Müll zur Ressource." *Politische Ökologie*, June 2012.

Holmes, G. "No Blunder." *Wastes Management* (December 1985): 752.

Holmes, John. "The Waste Disposal Options." *Wastes Management* (June 1987): 378.

Homberg, Michael. *Die Abfallwirtschaft in unterschiedlich strukturierten Räumen: An Beispielen aus Westfalen*. Bochum: Brockmeyer, 1990.

Hösel, Gottfried. *Unser Abfall aller Zeiten: Eine Kulturgeschichte der Städtereinigung*, 2nd expanded ed. Munich: Kommunalschriften-Verlag J. Jehle, 1990.

Hounsell, David A. *From the American System to Mass Production: The Development of Manufacturing Technology in the United States*. Baltimore, MD: Johns Hopkins University Press, 1984.

Huchting, Friedrich. "Abfallwirtschaft im Dritten Reich." *Technikgeschichte* 48 (1981): 252–273.

Hünemörder, Kai. *Die Frühgeschichte der globalen Umweltkrise und die Formierung der deutschen Umweltpolitik 1950–1973*. Stuttgart: Steiner, 2004.

Jánossy, Ferenc. *The End of the Economic Miracle: Appearance and Reality in Economic Development*. White Plains, NY: International Arts and Sciences Press, 1971.

Jansen, Rolf, and Reinhard Rudat. *Stadtreinigung der Bundesrepublik Deutschland*. Bremerhaven: Wirtschaftsverlag NW, 1978.

Jørgensen, Finn Arne. *Making a Green Machine: The Infrastructure of Beverage Container Recycling*. New Brunswick, NJ: Rutgers University Press, 2011.

Kalt, Anton. "Haltet die Straßen sauber! Wiederaufbau der Stadtreinigung und des Fuhrparkes." In *Von der toten zur lebendigen Stadt: Fünf Jahre Wiederaufbau in Dortmund*. Dortmund: Mayer, 1951.

Kaupert, Walter. "Moderne Städtereinigung, eine Ingenieursaufgabe." *Der Städtetag* (October 1958): 487–489.

Kellett, J. R. "Municipal Socialism, Enterprise, and Trading in the Victorian City." *Urban History* 5 (1978): 36–45.

Kershaw, Ronald. "Glass Fibre Use for No-Return Bottles." The *Times*, March 7, 1972.

Kersting, Andreas. *Die Abgrenzung zwischen Abfall und Wirtschaftsgut*. Düsseldorf: Werner, 1992.

Krause, Lars. *TA Siedlungsabfall (TASI), Einführung und Kritik*. Berlin: VWF Verlag, 1999.

Krischok, Martin. "Zur Transformation der ostdeutschen Presse anhand der Berichterstattung über die gefälschte DDR-Kommunalwahl vom 7. Mai 1989." Master's thesis, Universität der Bundeswehr, Munich.

Kromarek, Pascale. *Vergleichende Untersuchung über die Umsetzung der EG-Richtlinien Abfall und Wasser*. Berlin: Forschungsbericht Umweltbundesamt, 1987, p. 103 ff.

Kunig, Philip, Gerfried Schwermer, and Ludger-Anselm Versteyl. *Abfallgesetz – AbfG*. Munich: Beck, 1988.

Kurth, Peter, Anne Baum-Rudischhauser, and Klaus Töpfer (eds.). *Ressource Abfall*. Brandenburg: TK-Verlag, 2011.

Laabs, Dirk. *Der Goldrausch: Die wahre Geschichte der Treuhand*. Munich: Pantheon, 2012.

Leh, Almut. *Zwischen Heimatschutz und Umweltbewegung: Die Professionalisierung des Naturschutzes in Nordrhein-Westfalen 1945–1975*. Frankfurt/M.: Campus, 2006.

Ludwig, Udo, and Barbara Schmid. "Germany's Booming Incineration Industry: Burning the World's Waste." *Spiegel*, 8/2007 (February 21, 2007), available at http://www.spiegel.de/international/spiegel/germany-s-booming-incineration-industry-burning-the-world-s-waste-a-467239.html (accessed October 31, 2012).

Maddison, Andrew. *The World Economy: A Millennial Perspective*. Paris: OECD, 2001.

Magoc, Chris. *Environmental Issues in American History*. Westport, CT: Greenwood Press, 2006.

Massarutto, Antonio. "The Municipal Waste Management Sector: Shifting Boundaries between Market and Public Service." Presentation at Bocconi University, May 11, 2012.

Mathias, Peter. *Retailing Revolution: A History of Multiple Retailing in the Food Trades Based on the Allied Suppliers Group of Companies*. London: Longmans Green and Co., 1967.

Mayntz, Renate. *Vollzugsprobleme der Umweltpolitik: Empirische Untersuchung der Implementation von Gesetzen im Bereich der Luftreinhaltung und des Gewässerschutzes*. Stuttgart: Kohlhammer, 1978.

Medina, Martin. "Waste Picker Cooperatives in Developing Countries." Paper prepared for WIEGO/Cornell/SEWA on membership-based organizations of the poor, Ahmebabad, India, January 2005. Available at http://wiego.org/sites/wiego.org/files/publications/files/Medina-wastepickers.pdf (accessed September 16, 2011).

Meikle, Jeffrey. *American Plastic: A Cultural History*. New Brunswick, NJ: Rutgers University Press, 1995.

Melosi, Martin. *Garbage in the Cities: Refuse, Reform, and the Environment*. Pittsburgh: University of Pittsburgh Press, 2004.

———. *The Sanitary City: Environmental Services in Urban America from Colonial Times to the Present*. Baltimore, MD: Johns Hopkins University Press, 2000.

Mende, Silke. *"Nicht rechts, nicht links, sondern vorn": Eine Geschichte der Gründungsgrünen*. Munich: Oldenbourg, 2011.

Meyer, Simon, *Die Entwicklungslinien des Rechts der Abfallentsorgung im Spannungsfeld von Recht und Hoheitlicher Lenkung*. Frankfurt/M.: Peter Lang, 2010.

Millward, Robert. *Private and Public Enterprise in Europe: Energy, Telecommunication and Transport, 1830–1990*. Cambridge: Cambridge University Press, 2005.

_____. "The Private Sector Involvement." *Wastes Management* (May 1986): 21–23.

Möller, Christian. "Abfallpolitik und Entsorgungstechnik im 'ökologischen Zeitalter.'" Master's thesis, University of Bielefeld, 2010.

Mosca, Manuel. "On the Origins of the Concept of Natural Monopoly: Economies of Scale and Competition." *European Journal of the History of Economic Thought* 15 (2008): 317–353.

Münch, Peter. *Stadthygiene im 19. und 20. Jahrhundert: Die Wasserversorgung, Abwasser- und Abfallbeseitigung unter besonderer Berücksichtigung Münchens.* Göttingen: Vandenhoeck & Ruprecht, 1993.

Nast, Mathias. *Die stummen Verkäufer: Lebensmittelverpackungen im Zeitalter der Konsumgesellschaft: Umwelthistorische Untersuchung über die Entwicklung der Warenpackung und den Wandel der Einkaufsgewohnheiten (1950er bis 1990er Jahre).* Bern: Peter Lang, 1997.

Nettleton, Nordica Thea. "Comrade Consumer: Economic and Technological Images of the West in the Definition of the Soviet Future 1957–1969." PhD thesis, University of Glasgow, 2006.

Osnos, Evan. "Wastepaper Queen." The *New Yorker* (March 30, 2009): 49.

ÖTV (ed.). *Geschäftsbericht 1976–1979.* Stuttgart: ÖTV, 1980.

_____. *Qualitatives Wachstum 1: Umweltschonende und rohstoffsichernde Abfallwirtschaft: Vorschläge der Gewerkschaft ÖTV für die Entwicklung der Müllbeseitigung zur Abfallwirtschaft.* Stuttgart: ÖTV, 1985.

_____. *Rationalisierung und ihre Auswirkung im Bereich der Stadtreinigung (Müllabfuhr).* Stuttgart: ÖTV, 1983.

Palucka, Tim, and Bernadette Bensaude-Vincent. "Composites: An Overview." Cal Tech, n.d., available at http://authors.library.caltech.edu/5456/1/hrst.mit.edu/hrs/materials/public/composites/Composites_Overview.htm (accessed September 14, 2012).

Park, M. A. Jinhee. "Von der Müllkippe zur Abfallwirtschaft – Die Entwicklung der Hausmüllentsorgung in Berlin (West) von 1945 bis 1990." PhD thesis, Berlin, available at http://opus.kobv.de/tuberlin/volltexte/2004/517/pdf/park_jinhee.pdf (accessed November 13, 2012).

Pawlowski, L. "Historical Overview on Water Management in Berlin." N.d. (ca. 2003).

Pfister, Christian. "Energiepreis und Umweltbelastung: Zum Stand der Diskussion über das 1950er Jahre-Syndrom." In Wolfram Siemann (ed.), *Umweltgeschichte, Themen und Perspektiven.* Munich: C. H. Beck, 2003.

Pippke, Nicole. *Öffentliche und private Abfallentsorgung: Die Privatisierung der der Abfallwirtschaft nach dem Kreislaufwirtschaft- und Abfallgesetz.* Berlin: Duncker & Humblot, 1999.

Pörtge, Karl-Heinz, and Michael Mehlhase. "Die Entwicklung der Müll- und Abfallbeseitigung im südlichen Niedersachsen seit 1970." In *Göttinger Jahrbuch* (1989): 175–188.

Pulver, Karl. "Von der Abfuhranstalt zum Eigenbetrieb: 125 Stadthygiene in Mannheim: Aus Verwaltungsberichten zusammengestellt von Karl Pulver." Unpublished manuscript, 2005, StA Mannheim.

Queitsch, S. Peter. *Kreislaufwirtschafts- und Abfallgesetz (KrW-/AbfG): Rechts-verordnungen mit kommentierender Einführung zum KrW-/AbfG, einschl. der Entsorgergemeinschaftenrichtlinie.* Cologne: Bundesanzeiger, 1997.

Raab, Manfred. *Müll oder Fossilien? Der Kampf um die Erhaltung der Fossili-enfundstätte Grube Messel: Eine historisch-politische Dokumentation.* Messel: Roether, 1996.

Radkau, Joachim. *Die Ära der Ökologie: Eine Weltgeschichte.* Munich: C. H. Beck, 2011.

Reuben, B. G., and M. L. Burstall. *The Chemical Economy: A Guide to the Tech-nology and Economics of the Chemical Industry.* London: Longman, 1973.

Rick, Klaus. *Zur Konstruktion, Implementation und Wirkung des Dualen Sys-tems in der Abfallwirtschaft: Eine umweltökonomische Analyse.* Regensburg: Transfer Verlag, 1998.

Rosenkranz, Gerd. "Pfand-Debatte: Dosenlobby bläst zur Entscheidungs-schlacht." *Der Spiegel,* August 20, 2003.

Rossberg, Hans. "Kompostwerk Duisburg-Huckingen ein Jahr in Betrieb." *Der Städtetag* (April 1959): 188–190.

Runge, Martin. *Milliardengeschäft Müll: Vom Grünen Punkt bis zur Müll-schieberei: Argumente und Strategien für eine andere Abfallpolitik.* Munich: Piper 1994.

Rytlewski, R., and M. Opp de Hipt. *Die Bundesrepublik Deutschland in Zahlen 1949/49–1980.* Munich: Beck, 1987.

Sabel, Charles, and Michael Piore. *The Second Industrial Divide: Possibilities for Future Prosperity.* New York: Basic Books, 1984.

Sabel, Charles, and Jonathan Zeitlin. "Historical Alternatives to Mass Production: Politics, Markets, and Technology in Nineteenth-Century Industrialization." *Past and Present* 108 (1985): 133–176.

———(eds.). *World of Possibilities: Flexibility and Mass Production in Western Civilization.* Cambridge and New York: Cambridge University Press, 1997.

Saviano, Roberto. "Warum versinkt Neapel im Müll?" *Die Zeit,* May 18, 2011.

Scarrow, Howard A. "The Impact of British Domestic Air Pollution Legislation." *British Journal of Political Science* 2 (1972): 261–282.

Schanetzky, Tim. *Die große Ernüchterung: Wirtschaftspolitik, Expertise und Gesellschaft in der Bundesrepublik 1966 bis 1982.* Berlin: Akademie-Verlag, 2007.

Schenkel, Werner. "Mengen und Zusammensetzung von häuslichen und gewerb-lichen Abfällen." In Jochen Vogel et al. (eds.), *Handbuch des Umweltschutzes.* Landsberg a. Lech: Ecomed, 1987.

———. "Ziele künftiger Abfallwirtschaft." *Müll und Abfall* (February 1986): 41–47.

Schlautmann, Christoph. "Millionengewinne durch Einwegpfand." *Handelsblatt,* July 26, 2012.

Scholten, Jens. "Umbruch des genossenschaftlichen Förderauftrages durch Inno-vation und Wachstum: Nachkriegsentwicklung und Einführung der Selbst-bedienung bei der REWE Dortmund." In Jan Otmar Hesse et al. (eds.), *Das Unternehmen als gesellschaftliches Reformprojekt.* Essen: Klartext, 2004.

Schweitzer, Axel, and Eric Schweitzer. "Der Wandel: Private Entsorgungs- und Recyclingwirtschaft im Spiegel der Zeit." In Peter Kurth (ed.), *Ressource Abfall: Politische und wirtschaftliche Betrachtungen anlässlich des 50-jährigen Bestehens des BDE.* Neuruppen: TK-Verlag, 2011.

Schweitzer, Eric. *Ordnungspolitische Probleme der Abfallwirtschaft: Die historischen Ursachen, eine komparative Analyse und der Versuch einer differenzierten, wettbewerbspolitischen Neustrukturierung der unterschiedlichen Bereiche der Entsorgungswirtschaft.* Berlin: Self-published dissertation, 1990.

Secrett, Charles. "Environmental Activism Needs Its Own Revolution to Regain Its Teeth." *Guardian* (June 13, 2011), available at http://www.guardian.co.uk/ environment/2011/jun/13/environmental-activism-needs-revolution (accessed June 21, 2011).

Seely, Antony. *Landfill Tax: Introduction and Early History.* London: House of Commons Library, 2009.

Shane, Matthew. "Real Historical Gross Domestic Product (GDP) Per Capita and Growth Rates of GDP Per Capita for Baseline Countries/Regions, 1969–2010" (in real 2005 US$ per capita), September 22, 2010, available at http://www. ers.usda.gov/Data/Macroeconomics/ (accessed October 20, 2010).

Shaw, G., L. Curth, and A. Alexander. "Selling Self Service and the Supermarket: The Americanisation of Food Retailing in Britain, 1945–1960." *Business History* 46 (2004): 568–582.

Sheail, John. *An Environmental History of Britain.* Basingstoke, Hampshire: Palgrave Press, 2002.

Shearer, J. Ronald. "Talking about Efficiency: Politics and the Industrial Rationalization Movement in the Weimar Republic." *Central European History* 28 (1995): 483–506.

Sheldrake, John. *Modern Local Government.* Aldershot: Dartmouth Publishing, 1992.

"SPI Resin Identification Code: Guide to Correct Use." Available at http://www. plasticsindustry.org/AboutPlastics/content.cfm?ItemNumber=823 (accessed September 14, 2012).

Spoerer, Mark. *Zwangsarbeit unter dem Hakenkreuz: Ausländische Zivilarbeiter, Kriegsgefangene und Häftlinge im Deutschen Reich und im besetzten Europa 1939–1945.* Stuttgart: DVA, 2001.

Stadt Frankfurt (ed.). *100 Jahre Stadtreinigung in Frankfurt am Main 172–1972.* Frankfurt: Stadt Frankfurt, 1972.

Stadtreinigungsamt Dortmund (ed.). *Partner für mehr Umweltschutz: Abfallwirtschaft in Dortmund.* Dortmund: Stadt Dortmund, 1989.

Stadtverwaltung Mannheim (ed.). *Statistische Übersicht auf dem Sachgebiet der Verkehrsplanung, des Tiefbauwesens, der Stadtreinigung, des Fuhrparks.* Mannheim: Stadt Mannheim, 1970.

Stanbridge, H. H. *History of Sewage Treatment in Britain.* Maidstone: Institute of Water Pollution Control, 1976.

Stanyard, Ron. "Facing the Facts." *Wastes Management* (August 1985): 415.

Statistisches Jahrbuch. Available at http://www.populstat.info/Europe/germanwc .htm (accessed September 29, 2011).

Staudinger, J. J. P. *Disposal of Plastics Waste and Litter*. London: Society of Chemical Industry, 1970.

Steffen, Heinz, and Marc Joachim Prabucki. "Risikoabschätzung bei der Planung neuer Deponien." In Peter A. Wilderer, Die Deponie des 21. Jahrhunderts. Munich: Gesellschaft für Wassergütewirtschaft, 1992.

Stokes, Anne. *A Chink in the Wall: German Writers and Literature in the INF-Debate of the Eighties*. Bern: Peter Lang, 1995.

Stokes, Raymond G. *Constructing Socialism: Technology and Change in East Germany, 1945–1990*. Baltimore, MD: Johns Hopkins University Press, 2000.

Stokes, Ray, and Stephen Sambrook. "Centenary Stories." *Chartered Institute of Wastes Management Journal* (December 2010), p. 16.

Strasser, Susan. *Waste and Want: A Social History of Trash*. New York: Henry Holt and Company, 1999.

Strong, A. Brent. "History of Composite Materials: Opportunities and Necessities." Brigham Young University, n.d. Available at http://strong.groups.et.byu.net/pages/articles/articles/history.pdf (accessed September 14, 2012).

Sumner, J. "Waste Disposal in the United Kingdom." *Waste Disposal* (June 1980): 302.

Tarr, Joel A. *The Search for the Ultimate Sink: Urban Pollution in Historical Perspective*. Akron, OH: University of Akron Press, 1996.

Thoms, Eva Maria. "Köln, wie es stinkt und kracht." *Die Zeit*, May 13, 2004.

Thomson, Andrew. *Modern Public Cleansing Practice*. 3rd ed. London: Technical Publishing Co. Ltd, 1951.

Thywissen, Christian. *Die Abfallwirtschaft in der Bundesrepublik Deutschland*. Frankfurt/M: Peter Lang, 1995.

Tieman, Ross. "A Problem That Comes in Heaps." *Financial Times, Water & Waste Management Special Report*, December 16, 2008.

Tolliday, Steven. *The Rise and Fall of Mass Production*. Cheltenham: E. Elgar, 1998.

Tooze, J. Adam. *The Wages of Destruction: The Making and Breaking of the Nazi Economy*. London: Penguin Books, 2007.

Tope, Otto. *Die Mülltonne: Eine Stiefkind der westdeutschen Städtegestaltung*. Frankfurt: Schön & Wetzel, 1953.

Trend:Research. *Gutachten: Auswirkungen der Auflösung des Umsatzsteuerprivilegs in der Abfallentsorgung* (2010). Available at http://www.bde-berlin.org/wp-content/pdf/2010/umsatzsteuergutachten2010.pdf (accessed November 5, 2012).

Tromans, Stephen. *The Environmental Protection Act 1990: Text and Commentary*. London: Sweet and Maxwell, 1991.

Tushman, Michael, and Charles O'Reilly. "Ambidextrous Organizations: Managing Evolutionary and Revolutionary Change." *California Management Review* 38, No. 4 (1996): 9.

Uekötter, Frank. *Umweltgeschichte im 19. und 20. Jahrhundert*. Munich: Oldenbourg, 2007.

———. *Von der Rauchplage zur ökologischen Revolution: Eine Geschichte der Luftverschmutzung in Deutschland und den USA 1880–1970*. Essen: Klartext, 2003.

Umweltbundesamt (ed.). *Bürger im Umweltschutz: Nichtstaatliche Umweltor-
ganisationen und Bürgerinitiativen.* Berlin: Umweltbundesamt, 1979.
Vince, C. A. *History of the Corporation of Birmingham,* vol. 4. Birmingham:
Corporation of Birmingham, 1923.
Wehler, Hans. *Deutsche Gesellschaftsgeschichte, Bundesrepublik und DDR
1949–1990,* vol. 5. Munich: C. H. Beck, 2009.
Weingart, Peter. "The Moment of Truth for Science: The Consequences of the
'Knowledge Society' for Society and Science." *EMBO Reports* 3 (2002): 703–
706, available at http://www.outreach.psu.edu/programs/rsa/files/Reading_
Weingart_Peter_The_Moment_of_Truth_for_Science_EMBO_reports_3_8_2002
.pdf (accessed July 14, 2009).
Westermann, Andrea. *Plastik und politische Kultur in Westdeutschland.* Zürich:
Chronos, 2007.
"What Britain's Biggest Waste Disposal Authority Does." *Wastes Management*
(July 1986): 376.
Wiegand, Dirk. "Die Entwicklung der deutschen Städtereinigung, der NKT und
die Normung des MGB 240 – eine Erfolgsgeschichte." Conference paper,
Bochum, 2011.
Wiemer, Klaus, and Michael Stern (eds.). *Weniger Abfall: Entwicklungen in
der Abfallwirtschaft nach der Verpackungsverordnung.* Vitzenhausen: M.I.C.
Baeza-Verlag, 1991.
Wildt, Michael. *"Am Beginn der Konsumgesellschaft": Mangelerfahrung, Leben-
shaltung, Wohlstandshoffnung in Westdeutschland in den fünfziger Jahren.*
Hamburg: Ergebnisse, 1994.
Williams, Paul. *Waste Treatment and Disposal.* 2nd ed. London: John Wiley &
Sons, 2005.
Willing, Eckhad. "Ziele und Inhalte der Verpackungsverordnung." In Klaus
Wiemer and Michael Stern (eds.), *Weniger Abfall: Entwicklungen in der Abfall-
wirtschaft nach der Verpackungsverordnung.* Vitzenhausen: M.I.C. Baeza-
Verlag, 1991.
Wilson, Campbell. *"The Ecologist* and the Alternative Technology Movement,
1970–75: New Environmentalism Confronts 'Technocracy.'" *eSharp* 12
(2008): "Technology and Humanity." Available at http://www.gla.ac.uk/
departments/esharp/issues/12winter2008technologyandhumanity/ (accessed
October 20, 2011).
Windmüller, Sonja. *Die Kehrseite der Dinge: Müll, Abfall und Wegwerfen als
kulturwissenschaftliches Phänomen.* Münster: Lit, 2004.
Wines, Richard A. *Fertilizer in America: From Waste Recycling to Resource
Exploitation.* Philadelphia: Temple University Press, 1985.
Wirsching, Andreas. *Abschied vom Provisorium, 1982–1990: Geschichte der
Bundesrepublik Deutschland,* vol. 6. Munich: DVA, 2006.
Wolf, Susan, and Anna White. *Environmental Law.* London: Cavendish, 1995.
Woods, Barrie C. *Municipal Refuse Collection Vehicles.* Appleby in Westmore-
land: Trans Pennine Publishing, 1999.
Wylie, J. C. *The Wastes of Civilisation.* London; Faber and Faber Ltd., 1959.
Zimring, Carl A. *Cash for Your Trash: Scrap Recycling in America.* New Brun-
swick, NJ: London: Rutgers University Press, 2005.

Index

Printed in the United States
by Baker & Taylor Publisher Services